The Curry Trail

Afghanistan
Pakistan
Delhi
Uttar Pradesh
Bangladesh
Bihar
Bengal
India
Mumbai
Hyderabad
Chennai
Kerala
Tamil Nadu
Sri Lanka
Myanmar
Yangon
Hong Kong
Laos
Thailand
Vietnam
Cambodia
Penang
Malaysia
Malacca
Singapore
Sumatra
Indonesia
Java
Japan
INDIAN OCEAN
Mauritius
Fiji

MADHUR JAFFREY'S

ULTIMATE CURRY BIBLE

MADHUR JAFFREY'S
ULTIMATE CURRY BIBLE

INDIA • SINGAPORE • MALAYSIA • INDONESIA
THAILAND • SOUTH AFRICA • KENYA
GREAT BRITAIN • TRINIDAD • GUYANA
JAPAN • USA

EBURY
PRESS

25 27 29 30 28 26

Ebury Press, an imprint of Ebury Publishing,
20 Vauxhall Bridge Road,
London SW1V 2SA

Ebury Publishing is part of the Penguin Random House group of companies whose addresses can be found at global.penguinrandomhouse.com

First published by Ebury Press in 2003
www.eburypublishing.co.uk

A CIP catalogue record for this book is available from the British Library

Editor: Judith Hannam
Photographer: William Lingwood
Props stylist: Penny Markham
Food stylist: Lucy McKelvie
Picure researcher: Anne-Marie Ehrlich

Half-title: *Moghul painting, 18th century*
Frontispiece: *A fighting cock, destined for the pot if he loses, Indian painting c. 1620*

ISBN 9780091874155

Printed and bound in China by C&C Offset Co., Ltd

Penguin Random House is committed to a sustainable future for our business, our readers and our planet. This book is made from Forest Stewardship Council® certified paper.

CONTENTS

This book is dedicated to all the people and institutions that made it possible:

Nodi Murphy, Mark Gevisser, Amina Cachalia, Nelson Mandela, Arvind and Manjula Gokal, Madanjit Ramchod at Kapitan's, Daksha Patel, Xoliswa, Chanchal Ishwarlal, Shanthie Naidoo, Sinda Naidoo, Mariam Vally, Mumtaz Barmania, Hava Barmania, Primrose Sharma, Shahindran Moonieya, Rehana Vally, Pippa Stein, Nadia the fisher-woman, Patel's Restaurant, Hasan at Continental Meats, Monty and Selvarani Moodley at Fenton House, Durban Cultural and Documentation Centre, Sanjeev and Anant Singh, Midi, Yasmeen Murshed, Syed Mushtaque Murshed, Abul Khair, Habib Sattar, Luna Shamsudda, Firdausi Qadri, Nilu Murshed, Mumtaz Khaleq, Alka Mathur, Marina and Shaukat Fareed, Faran Tahir, Iqbal and Saira Ahmed, Tariq Ali, Tahira Mazhar Ali, Sarwat Ahsan, Fazal Hayat, Yousaf Salahuddin, Sameena, Jalal Salahuddin, Jahan Ara Changes, Cheani, Khan Klub, Saika, NW Heritage Hotel, Aziz and Laila Sarfaraz, Shaila Rathore, Amina Ahmed, Zarrin Zardari, Poonam Ayub, Hameed Haroon, Abdullah Hussain Haroun, Parveen Haroun, Bar-B-Q Tonight, Nafisa Bhutto, Rehana Saigol, Khalida Akhund, Dhanpati Harilall, Joan Sharma, Kumari Jaisri, Rani Sookram, Shabiroon Eshak, Shirley Tiwari, Shashi Tripathi, Gulzar Ahamed, Meenakshi Ahamed, Fatima Nathu, Suketu and Sooni Mehta, Usha and Ramesh Mehta, Fatma Zakaria, Kamal Tayebbhoy, Veena Bahadur, Juji and Viru Dayal, Nirula's, Chef Wan, Shahabe Catering, Mallika, Ramanathan Nachiappam, Sala Ramu, Umayal Karuppan, Dr Ghulam Sarwar Yousof, Hajrah Sarwar, the Penang Heritage Trust, Penang Development Corporation, Tourist Authority of Thailand, Bangkok's Oriental Hotel, Chef Sarnsern Gajaseni, Julie Mehta, Bangkok's Grand Hyatt Erawan, Yangon's Strand Hotel, Ma Thanegi, Sally Baughen, Chef Jordon Theodorus, Chetti Inya, Farina Kingsley, Elizabeth Andoh, Meira Chand, Ambassador and Mrs Mahbubanu, Mehreen and Rahul Khosla, Mutthu's, the Singapore Tourism Board, the Indian Womens' Association (Singapore), Bina Batlivala, Renu Bala, Aparna Rao, Devagi Sanmugam, Suhasini Misra, Rawina Bhojwani, Ruchi Bhatia, Sonia Advani, Sangeeta Rajgopal, Samia and Mahboob Mahmood, Singapore's Raffles Hotel, Gretchen Liu, Banana Leaf Apolo, the Museum of Culinary History and Alimentation, Hilary Westwater, Liz Calvert Smith, the British Library, the Victoria and Albert Museum.

INDIAN FOOD AROUND THE WORLD: A BACKGROUND

You think of a curry meal and your mouth lights up in anticipation. Spices, yet to be tasted, begin tickling the palate. There are visions of kebabs to have with your drinks and then, to accompany your curry, mounds of fluffy rice, sweet and sour chutneys and relishes. The effect of such a meal – bliss? Yes. Total satisfaction? Yes. Perhaps more? An English conductor, stopping in New York on his way from London to the Glimmerglass Opera Festival in Cooperstown, once told me a story. He said that there is an alto tenor in the United Kingdom who has to have a very hot curry before each performance as this alone assures him an extra three notes. Once he is allowed his necessary indulgence, his voice just takes off!

As an Indian who has lived for long periods in both Britain and America, and travelled extensively around the globe, I have sampled curries, some familiar and some quite unexpected, on six continents and loved nearly every one. Bangladeshi fish curries, Pakistani meatballs, Gujarati vegetables in Kenya, coconut-enriched curries from Malaysia, South African bean dishes, Trinidadian beef curries – these have now become the treats I cannot live without. As I filled notebook after notebook with recipes collected in private homes, from culinary libraries, restaurants and even the occasional street vendor, I was struck by the ribbon of tradition that runs through them all, traditions that, sometimes, can be traced back to Indian prehistory. This connecting thread and the variations in Indian food around the globe had me gripped with fascination. I had to know more.

A typical, multi-tiered, well-supplied fruit stall in Gujarat offering guavas, custard apples, sweet limes, pomegranates and papayas.

What exactly makes up a curry meal? And when did it all start?

Today, curries are eaten in Singapore, Malaysia, Indonesia, Thailand, South Africa, Kenya, Britain, Trinidad, Guyana and Japan, to list just a few nations. As Indian migrants moved out of India, both east and west, both voluntarily to trade and semi-voluntarily to work as labourers for the British Empire, setting up its

Indian indentured labourers in South Africa, working in one of the many sugar cane plantations of Natal.

sugar or rubber plantations, they took visions of home-cooking with them. The limitations in their new lives, sometimes as very poor field hands, as in Trinidad and Guyana, demanded culinary adjustments. Yet from all this paucity, working its way through layers of repressed memories, a new Indian cuisine would slowly emerge.

Strong, well-established culinary traditions in their new homes, as in Thailand, suggested a merging of 'them and us'. Curries sneaking into Japan became Japanised very quickly. In many African countries, such as Kenya and South Africa, local traditions blended with Indian ones to create very indigenous, completely new curries that nonetheless were identifiably Indian in tone. In Britain and the United States, many, like me, are creating new dishes that meld what we remember with what we can easily buy. A new fish in a new land demands a new technique and perhaps a fresh set of spices. No great culinary tradition dies. It just keeps evolving.

For the purposes of this book, I have designated as a curry any Indian or Indian-style dish with a sauce; just as the British colonialists, who controlled India for centuries before I was born, defined it. It is not exactly my definition. Indians tend to call dishes by their individual names when speaking in their own languages and serve both wet (that is, with a sauce) and dry (those in which the sauce is non-existent or reduced) curries. But the British definition seems to have stuck, so that is the one I use here.

My purpose with this book is two-fold. The first, and most basic, intention is to show how a curry meal may be put together, whether you have a lot of time or a little, access to many ethnic ingredients or very few. The second, which absorbs me intensely, is to compile a history of curries the world over.

I will start in prehistory. With India, you have to. But I will not dwell there long as my story really starts in the 19th century, when Indians started travelling overseas in vast numbers and the British began yearning for their curry lunches in far-flung colonies and in their motherland. (Indian culinary bases were somewhat dispersed when the country was split, first in 1947 to become India and Pakistan, and then again, in 1972, with the creation of Bangladesh – all in my lifetime. Generally, when I refer to India, if it is pre-1947, I will mean the larger sub-continental India in which I was born.)

Excavations in sub-continental India have uncovered four varieties of wheat grain that go back 8,000 years. Grinding stones were found nearby, so we know that the wheat was processed into flour. By 4000 BC, we can already see airy granaries for storing wheat and three-legged pottery *chaklas* or 'boards' for rolling flour dough into flatbreads.

I took a trip recently to Kalibangan, a small, sleepy town on the northern edge of the Rajasthan desert in north-western India. Four and a half thousand years ago it was a thriving metropolis on the banks of a mighty river. The river has dried up and the metropolis has all but vanished, leaving only clues about its glorious past.

The excavated land is littered with pottery shards. You cannot take one step without crushing some underfoot. Food historians will note that pottery was used as storage jars, for cooking pots, even for *tandoor*-like baking ovens. For the wealthy, there were single-handled copper frying pans. Nearby is a field with crisscrossing furrow marks that dates to 2800 BC and is perhaps the oldest such field ever discovered. It is speculated that mustard was cultivated in the long, north-south furrows and horsegram, a legume, in the shorter, east-west furrows that bisected them, a common practice in Rajasthan even today, almost 5,000 years later.

We know both from excavations and from ancient Sanskrit texts that, well before the birth of Christ, all kinds of meats were eaten – cows, deer, pigs, sheep, goats and the native wild fowl, *Galus galus*, from whence all domestic chickens developed. Some of the meat was seasoned, skewered and grilled. Some was marinated in mustard seeds and black pepper and fried in *ghee*, with speculation rife, even then, that oil might be a healthier alternative! Meat, especially venison, was much loved and could be stewed with spice pastes prepared on grinding stones and the juice of sour fruit such as tamarind, mangoes and pomegranates. The 'tarka' or 'baghaar' or 'chownk' technique of throwing whole spices into very hot *ghee* (or oil) and using the combination for seasoning was also known. No meal was considered complete without relishes and chutneys.

Amongst grains, there was not just wheat but millet, barley and rice. One of the Greeks accompanying Alexander to India refers to rice as a 'strange plant, standing in water and sown in beds'. Rice was eaten in most of the country, generally boiled in water, and a coastal meal of white rice, curried crabs and vegetables was not uncommon. Wheat remained the grain of the north-west only, but eventually spread to almost all of north India.

Cooks also had access to sugar cane and its basic products, raw, crystal and refined sugar. There were also honeys, coconuts and dates. Homes had milk, yoghurt (which could be seasoned with ginger, black pepper and cinnamon), butter and *ghee*. There were dozens of legumes that could be stewed or combined with rice. Vegetables such as aubergines, squashes, bitter gourds and mustard greens were cooked in every home.

There were plenty of luscious mangoes and bananas, oranges, pomegranates, grapes and jackfruit. Many of the seasonings that lie at the heart of Indian cuisine

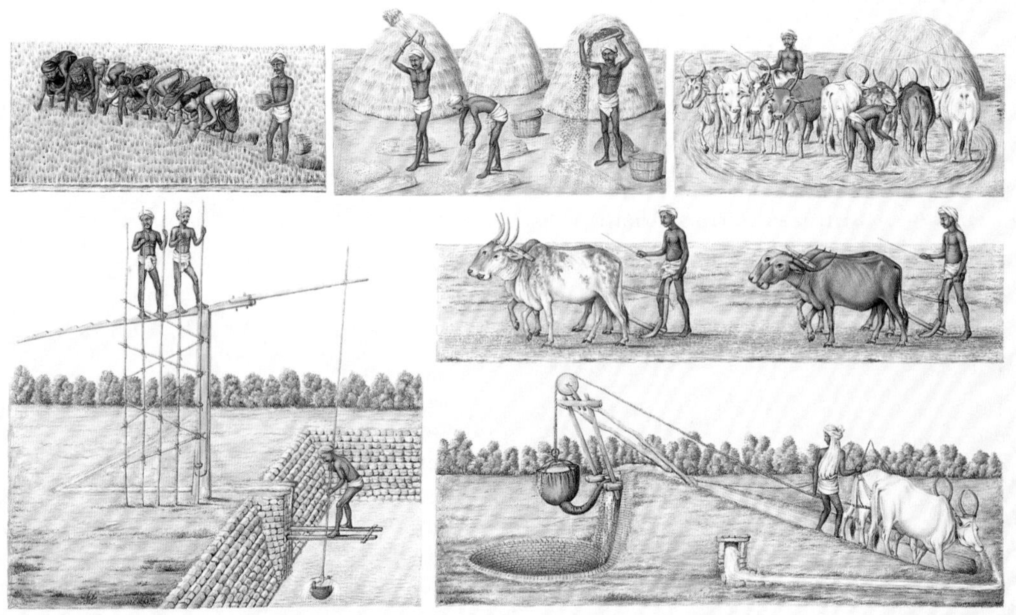

Timeless scenes from Tanjore, South India, *c.* 1828: sowing, threshing, ploughing and drawing water from tanks and wells for irrigation.

A fanciful, 15th century depiction of black pepper being harvested in Quilon, Kerala. The quality of the spice is being examined by the buyer, a European.

today were already part of the cook's magic: tamarind, turmeric, ginger, sesame seeds, mustard seeds, *asafetida*, cumin, curry leaves, coriander, nutmeg, cardamom, cinnamon and black pepper. Black pepper, then the only really hot spice other than mustard, had many names. One was *yavana-priya* or 'loved by the Greeks/Europeans'. Another was *kari*.

Around 500 BC, Vedic India saw the birth of two new religions that frowned on the killing of animals – Buddhism, which claimed many kings and their subjects as adherents, and Jainism, with followers in central and western India. The old-style Vedic religion, which would eventually turn into Hinduism, began to lose some ground. Perhaps to imbue it with fresh energy and to fight off the popularity of competing paths to eternal salvation, Vedic priests began to come up with a vegetarianism of their own. As Hinduism developed, so did vegetarianism. The cow, always revered, would eventually head towards semi-deification, though this happened over time, and as late as AD 800 beef was still being eaten with gusto.

Merriment, with wine and fruit, and the acompaniment of music, in the ladies' quarters: Moghul painting, 18th century.

Arabs had always traded with India. Their graceful *dhows* had skipped along Indian shores since well before the birth of Christ. With the advent of Islam, about AD 800, designs for trade changed to designs for pillage and conquest. By the 12th century, the heart of north India was in Muslim hands and was to stay that way until the 19th century, when overlapping rulers, the Muslims and the British, would tussle for control.

In culinary terms, the coming of a succession of Islamic conquerors was a win-win situation. India has never relinquished any of its traditions, it has only added on, layer upon layer. If meat was beginning to disappear in some circles, it now began to reappear in others. Of all the Muslim styles of cookery presented to it, India fell in love with the delicately nuanced Persian techniques and merged them with its own. This melding would be called Moghlai cuisine, named after the grandest of the Muslim dynasties, the Moghuls. Browned onions became a favoured flavouring for meats, along with garlic and ginger, as did almonds and pistachios and saffron.

For *biryanis*, rice was layered with meats in a combination of ancient Indian and contemporary Persian styles.

When the Europeans began appearing on the horizon in the late 15th century, it was first to trade. Later, lured by the uncountable riches of fabrics, gems and spices, all of them – the Portuguese, Dutch, Spaniards, French and English – chose to conquer and control. They were, initially, more interested in out-manoeuvring each other than in ruling India and, perhaps as a consequence, their culinary legacy is somewhat limited in terms of the styles and techniques they introduced to the nation.

They can certainly be credited with popularising all manner of yeast loaves, buns, rolls and, of course, soups, especially tomato soup, which India has now thoroughly Indianised, and Mulligatawny, where a south Indian soupy *rasam* (pepper-water) was thoroughly Anglicised. *Vindaloos* would become a much-loved marriage of Portuguese and Goan cookery (see Duck Vindaloo, page 108). The European's invaluable contribution consisted of the raw materials that would become a fundamental part of Indian daily meals: chillies, tomatoes, potatoes, corn, kidney beans, coffee and tea. Europeans, especially the British, would eventually be responsible for popularising Indian curries abroad, both in the East and West.

The many servants of Colonel W. R. Gilbert pouring tea to be served with bread and butter, 1825.

We are now at the end of the 18th century and at the start of my story. Indian regional cuisines are well established and much as we know them today. (The British rule India in the guise of the East India Company. On New Year's Eve, 1600, Queen Elizabeth I had signed a charter assigning a trade monopoly to the Honourable East India Company. Ships headed out to the East Indies. It was not until a few decades later that the British discovered that perhaps even greater opportunities for them lay in India. In 1640, after setting up small trading posts in the western costal towns of Surat and Goa, they gained a foothold in Madras, on India's rich south-east coast.) The British in India are eating curries for breakfast, lunch and sometimes dinner, along with their own pies and roasts. Armies of Indian servants tend to their every need.

Rather indirectly, through a study of the registration of last testaments and wills, we have recently learned that one in three Englishmen who came to India in the 17th and 18th centuries left their worldly possessions to Indian wives. Racial lines, it seems, were not clearly drawn in the sand until the 19th century. As more British women sailed into India, as the church grew stronger and as Victorian mores began to prevail, social mingling between the two races started to diminish. By then, however, the British were hooked on Indian food.

India may have been a bright jewel in the royal crown but it was not the only one in Asia. In 1786, Britain acquired Penang Island, off the Malay Peninsula, and designated it part of India. By 1909, British control had extended to the whole of Malaysia, or Malaya as it was then called, and Singapore.

Malaya had had contacts with ancient India, probably starting around the 4th century AD. Indian ruling dynasties, such as the Pallavas and Cholas, had established trading posts, even provinces, there and left an abiding influence on local cultural life well before the 13th century. But by the time the British acquired Penang, most Indians with ancient immigrant forebears had either intermarried or been otherwise absorbed into the culture. There were some newer traders around. Islam was the major religion. Indians and Arabs had, over the centuries, already introduced most of the Indian spices, kebabs (known here as *satays*), *biryanis* and *kormas* to the region.

Tea cartons at a Lipton plantation being loaded on to a pliant elephant.

With heavy investments from shareholders back home, the British began setting up plantations almost as soon as they landed in Malaya. In the 1820s the major cash crop was black pepper, in the 1830s it was sugar and in the 1870s it was coffee. But it was rubber that promised the most profit and vast estates growing 'Raja rubber' began to appear around the beginning of the 20th century.

Unskilled labour, willing to do back-breaking, repetitive work for very little money, was desperately needed to clear the land, build docks and roads and, of course, work in the plantations. It was decided that the Malays were 'unmotivated' (the same was to be said of the Zulus in South Africa somewhat later) and that the Chinese were too sharp to accept the poor conditions willingly. That left the Indians, who could be loaded into ships and brought over with promises of a rosy future. Not just any Indians. South Indian Tamils, generally Hindus of the lowest caste or untouchables, were picked deliberately as they were considered docile, had no particular food taboos and no dread of crossing the caste-destroying 'black waters' of the high seas.

As the estates grew – rubber, tea, oil palms – Indian labour continued to pour in. Migration centres were set up both in India and Malaya to 'facilitate recruitment, shipping and dispersal'. The slave-like labourers lived mostly in wooden shacks and spent their first years paying back their passages from their meagre wages. Schooling for the young was poor and purposely limited to Tamil instruction, as English might have produced 'uppity' children looking for a better life.

Other Indians were brought to Malaya as well. Most policemen and security personnel employed by the British were the tall, turbaned, north Indian Sikhs. There were also traders from Gujarat and Sindh, who set up textile and other businesses, and members of the money-lending Chettiar community from southern Tamil Nadu, who ended up with masses of property by default as loans went unpaid. Prisoners, too, were brought over in their thousands and, once released, many would marry local Muslim Malay women, converting, if needed. But the bulk of the immigrants remained the poor Tamils.

Today, it is the Tamil influence that dominates Malay-Indian food in both Malaysia and Singapore. That, and the influence of the British themselves, who had developed a passion for Indian curry. To understand the curries that the British grew to like, I need to return, briefly, to India, as it was British-Indian eating patterns that were to be repeated in Malaya.

The houses of the British estate managers on tea and coffee plantations in both north and south India were usually built on some high commanding spot, surrounded by flowers that made them feel at home: violets, nasturtiums, agapanthus, arum lilies, fuschias and daisies. Often, the elevation of the tea gardens from the top to the bottom varied by 600–900 metres or 2,000–3,000 feet. The temperature at the foot of the gardens made it possible to establish small fruit orchards containing bananas, oranges, guavas and pineapples. It is thought that the very British curry, in which fruit is either added directly to the stewing meats or served among the great variety of accompanying condiments, developed in these plantations.

The British planters in Malaya lived very similar lives to those in India. Sometimes their cooks were Indian but more often than not they were Hokkien, from southern China. These cooks made curries using excellent spice mixes prepared and sold by the Indians, some Malay seasonings (such as lemon grass) and some Chinese ones, such as soy sauce and star anise. Amongst the condiments were Indonesian *sambals*, Indian chutneys and pickles, and a mix of sliced bananas, pineapples, roasted peanuts, shredded coconut and fried onions.

In 1819, Sir Thomas Stamford Raffles founded Singapore City. It was meant to be part of an interlocking colonial network with its main headquarters in India. As it had grand commercial prospects, it drew Malayans from the hinterlands, as well as Indian labourers who had worked off their passages, Chinese cooks from the plantations and all manner of Europeans. In 1840, a Victorian surgeon recorded dining on 'pork chops, curried fowl, roast duck, ham, cheese and potatoes' washed down with 'good beer, Madeira and claret' at the local London Hotel. A botanist visiting in 1880 admits to a Singapore breakfast of 'beef steaks and mutton chops, one or two well-made curries and rice, eggs and bacon, cold ham, boiled eggs, salads, vegetables and plenty of fresh fruit'.

In 1887, the Armenian Sarkies brothers opened the elegant Raffles Hotel with views of the sea and, in 1892, the Raffles Tiffin Rooms. In both places an elegant meal served on New Year's Day included caviar on toast, fish pie, roast turkey stuffed with truffles and so on, as well as two curries, chicken and dry duck. Curries had just been tacked on to traditional Victorian meals. With the curries, there were always chutneys. Rudyard Kipling, visiting the Raffles Hotel in 1889, so enjoyed his meal that he 'crept back' after a visit to the Botanic Gardens to 'eat six different chutneys with one curry'. It was this mixture of the savoury, hot and sweet that the British relished and continue to enjoy to this day.

So what are Malay curries? *Mamak* food, or the food of the Malay Tamil Muslims, has dishes similar to those eaten in India – with a Malay twist. A *nasi*

Above: Advertising the Raffles hotel in Singapore with a note from Rudyard Kipling, late nineteenth century. Top right: The Raffles Hotel Dining Room where the rich and famous ate their curries. Right: The Raffles Tiffin Rooms set up by the Sarkies brothers for fine dining, serving both curries and continental foods.

Whole Baked Fish, Cooked in the Style of a Fish Head Curry, from Singapore.

biryani and *kurma* (*korma*) are celebratory foods, just as they are in India, but here both generally contain coconut milk. The *biryani* is still layered meat and rice, but here it may contain curry leaves, tomatoes, screw pine leaves and green chillies as well. *Kormas* are still mild and pale in colour, but their seasoning might include white pepper and star anise.

One Malay-Indian fish curry may be enthusiastically seasoned with nearly all the spices used in south India, from mustard and fennel seeds to red chillies and fenugreek (see Whole Baked Fish, Cooked in the Style of a Fish Head Curry, page 148). Another might include a south Indian curry powder on the one hand and the very Chinese oyster sauce, dark soy sauce and rice wine on the other.

South Indian *sambars*, the soupy stews of the Hindu Tamils, are made here with the available Australian split peas and eaten with rice, but *dalcha*, a Muslim version of the dish, is often served with a bread, *roti canai*. All Indian-style breads here are made with white flour, not the wholemeal preferred by most in India.

Curry powders and pastes are sold in most markets. This might suggest standardisation, but they are clearly earmarked for individual dishes – for fish, for *korma*, for chicken, meat and so on. Also, they are nearly always combined with a specific collection of spices, or with very Malay fresh seasonings, such as lemon grass, to produce what I think are the most ebullient curries outside India.

Muslims in Sumatra, northern Indonesia, have a similar history to that of the Malaysians, except that they ended up with the Dutch as their colonial masters. The highly competitive British did not want 'their' labour force going to work for the Dutch, but some labourers, mostly south Indians, did trickle in from Malaysia to work the tin mines and the tobacco and rubber plantations. Indian traders who went as far as Java could even hope for riches. There was already a saying in Gujarat, 'If a man goes to Java, he is presumed to be lost: if he returns, he will bring enough to last seven generations.'

While Javanese kebabs, *satays*, are only minimally influenced by Indian seasonings, the curries of Sumatra are another story. Cumin, coriander, cardamom, cinnamon, curry leaves, all find a place here. The main ingredients in the curry pastes are frequently fresh red chillies, garlic, ginger, turmeric and shallots, but in many dishes the aromatics – kaffir lime leaves, turmeric leaves, galangal and lemon grass – are never far behind.

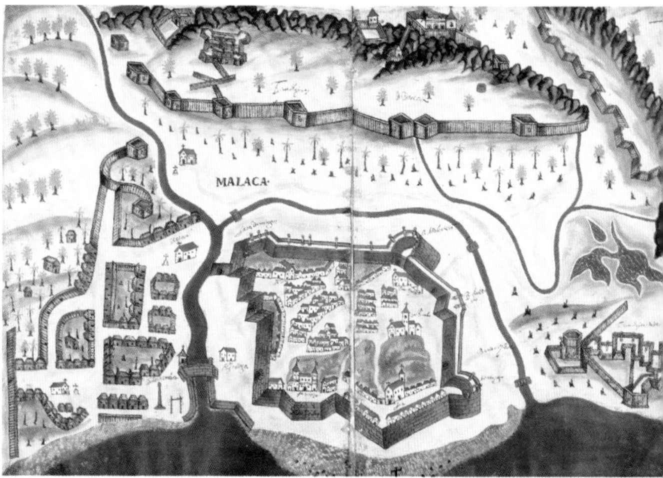

An early 16th-century map showing southern Malaysia and the fortified island of Singapore.

Like Malaysia and Indonesia, Laos, Cambodia and Vietnam had seen a succession of Indian-influenced kingdoms from the 1st century until the 13th, when some of these areas were known as Funan, Champa and Kambuya. Brahmins, Buddhist monks, scholars and craftsmen had all travelled there from India, infusing the local culture with their religion, language, sculpture, dance (just think of Khmer dancing!), literature and, most likely, their food. Not much is known about this period, but when I was in Hanoi, Vietnam, and watched *ban cuan*, the slippery, delicate, ground rice pancakes, being steamed on pieces of muslin, I was sure they were the result of an early Indian connection. South Indian rice flour noodles, *idiappam*, are steamed today in exactly the same way.

Once the French arrived with their colonial dreams, they, too, needed their Indian labourers. Luckily for them, they had their own Indian colonies in south India, Pondicherry and Mahe, to draw from. It is these later immigrants, and the traders and moneylenders who invariably drifted in with them, who probably made the curry powders and pastes that are now put into most Vietnamese curries in the southern areas. These curry powders, often with curry leaves in them, have a decided south Indian flavour.

Sometimes, the curries here are almost like a French stew, with carrots and potatoes (or, rather unusually, sweet potatoes), flavoured only with curry powder or curry paste. Others are very like a Chinese stir-fry, but with the addition of curry powder, fish sauce (*nuoc mam)* and lemon grass. These curries are generally served with rice ('Indian' rice with coconut milk, cashews, raisins, bay leaves, cloves, star anise, onion and ginger is very popular), but noodles or French bread are equally well liked. In Vietnam, curry powder can also be a seasoning for dipping sauces and kebabs.

Thailand too, rather like Indo-China and Java, had ancient cultural ties to India that have stayed in the very fibre of everyday life. But no masses of Indian labour were brought over to this nation. With the later Arabs and Muslim Indian traders did come *biryanis* (*khao moag*), which were made with chicken or lamb, curry powder and coconut milk, and kebabs in the form of *satays*, seasoned here with green coriander roots, curry powder and soy sauce. But it is really the curries, with their rainbow names – green, red, yellow – and the promised richness of coconut milk, that seem to link the Thai love of aromatic herbs such as kaffir lime leaves and lemon grass with both the ancient and more recent arrival of Indians.

I love Thai curries with an unholy passion. They tend to start off with a hand-pounded curry paste containing chillies, shallots, garlic, lemon grass and either galangal or ginger. Dry spices, such as cumin and coriander, are added only in small quantities unless it is a more 'Muslim' curry that demands curry powder. This paste is first sautéed in thick coconut milk until it is fragrant. Then the meat or fish goes in along with fish sauce, palm sugar, tamarind and coconut milk. At the end, torn kaffir lime leaves or holy basil leaves are showered over the top. It is this hot, sweet, sour nature of Thai curries and the way they almost explode with tropical aromas, that make them so addictive.

Next, the spice trail takes us to Myanmar (Burma). Indians had been travelling to Myanmar since ancient times (that is how Buddhism got there in the first place). Most courts had resident Indian astrologers and priests and there had been traders that came and went. When the Europeans started arriving, the Mayanmans dubbed them 'white Indians'. They had the same features, only their colouring was different.

Matters changed dramatically with the British colonisation of Burma in 1852. As Rangoon (now Yangon) became the *de facto* capital of British Burma, Indians poured in, not just to do manual labour and pull rickshaws, but to run both small and large businesses. Because many Indians were already schooled in English, they were chosen to fill the lower echelon jobs in the British civil service. By the start of the Second World War, half of Rangoon was Indian and the Indian languages, Urdu and Hindustani, were acceptable lingua franca in the streets. Indian foods, both authentic and Anglicised, were eaten by the Indians and the British. The only major culinary change so far was that, due to the scarcity of flour, rice was served with most Indian meals.

Nepalese farmers had started fruit, vegetable and dairy farms near Mandalay. In the countryside, the unpopular south Indian Chettiar moneylenders, with their much hated practices, were soon in control of a quarter of the agricultural land. Burmese resentment was high.

The Second World War and the Japanese occupation changed all that. Many Indians left. Some returned but, what with Burmese independence, nationalisation and the rightful insistence on the Burmese language, Indian domination faded away. Most of the Indians in Yangon today are descendents of the poor Tamil labourers whose poverty limited their ability to move on.

Today, there are several styles of Indian food in Myanmar. At a hotel in Yangon, the very colonial Strand, also built by the Sarkies brothers who created the Raffles Hotel in Singapore, I was served a duck *vindaloo* the colonial British-

Burmese way. There was an assortment of four very Burmese relishes on the table to accompany the curry: *balachaung*, a lightly crushed mixture of crisply fried dried prawns, shallots, garlic and dried chillies; a salad of sliced red onion and cucumbers dressed with lime juice and mint; crisply fried shallots; and a radish salad with sesame seeds. On the side was butter rice – rice cooked with *ghee*, cinnamon and cardamom.

The Indian-style food in the streets is another matter. Villagers coming in from the hinterlands generally want their fill of *falooda*, cold dessert noodles served here in a very Burmese variation with ice cream, sago, clear jellies and milk, as well as *biryanis*, made with star anise and cinnamon-flavoured rice, and chicken marinated with yoghurt and ginger juice. Nepalese tea, flavoured with cinnamon and sweetened with jaggery, is also a great favourite. But the bulk of street foods have a south Indian base. Fresh rice flour noodles, the Indian *idiappam*, here called *mon ton san*, are served with sugar and grated coconut, and the fermented rice pancakes, *appams*, called *apon*, are served just with a sprinkling of sugar; in India they are eaten with palm honey or with curries. One of the most unusual Burmese-Indian creations in the market is a '*samosa* salad'. Two very Indian snacks, deep-fried, savoury pastries (*samosas*) and split pea fritters, along with boiled potatoes and tomatoes, are crumbled and dressed with lime juice, as well as a sauce made with *dal*, rather like a thin, south Indian *sambar*.

Burmese curries do use curry powders, but they frequently incorporate lemon grass and fish sauce as well. In Myanmar, where Indians are often referred to in a derogatory way by their colour – the north Indian word for 'black' is *kala* – a dish that is very hot is called *kala aw*, i.e. 'a dish so hot that it would make even an Indian scream'. *Ohn-no khaukswe*, a filling breakfast soup hawked by street vendors, consists of a thin chicken curry poured over noodles. You add a bundle of crisp, hot and sour condiments and eat. It is exquisitely satisfying.

Packaged curry sauces are sold in all Japanese supermarkets. Once the curry is prepared, it is served with Japanese rice.

Not too many Indians travelled to Japan in past centuries, nor do many live there today. Yet a curry *tsunami* seems to have passed over the nation. Most Japanese eat curry at least once a week. Children love '*keema* curry', a curry of minced beef, often with peas, which may be served, *donburi*-style, over a bowl of rice, as well as *danshaku*, a potato croquette filled with curry, and *curray pan*, curry-stuffed buns, which are first steamed and then lightly fried. They are sold, both open and packaged, in the snack section of every department store. At restaurants children are also offered special trays of curried rice topped with curry-dusted, fried prawns.

Adults raiding convenience stores for quick meals may buy tubs of dried curry noodles. Just add boiling water. In the glass-fronted refrigerators of these same stores are stacked chilled dinners of different curries and rice. Beef? Chicken? Vegetable? Just heat and eat.

Then there are the curries you cook yourself. First you go to an ordinary supermarket and get a 'setto', a family-sized (for 2–3 people, the size of a Japanese family these days) packet of *curray-yo* (curry ingredients). Found in the vegetable section, this contains two potatoes, one carrot and two onions, all packaged together. The onions are the round kind, which the Japanese normally do not eat and have come to associate with curry. There is sometimes an illustration of *keema* (minced meat curry), rice and pickles on the top of the packet to indicate, pictorially, what the ingredients are for. Garlic is carefully placed in the shelf just above. You have a choice. If you want it, it is there.

Then you go to the fish/meat section to buy the fish, beef or chicken that will form the base of your curry. Frozen curried rice may be picked up in the frozen rice section. This, the packet says, you may microwave. You still need seasonings.

Today, Japanese supermarkets have an enormous Indian section, often larger than the Chinese, Thai and Korean sections put together. Here you will find some curry powders, mainly for using in mayonnaise or to add to flour for dusting on prawns before frying them. There a few chutneys (*chatsune*, to have with your *curray-ricu*) in bottles or toothpaste-like tubes, and some whole spices. But most of the space is taken up by curry roux.

What is this? It is sold in large, chunky slabs, rather like thick slabs of chocolate with indentations, so you can break off what you need. As it cooks, the roux melts and, along with the pan juices, becomes the sauce. Roux lies at the heart of the curry most Japanese eat. You can buy *amakuchi* (mild), *chukara* (medium) and *karakuchi* (very hot) roux. All are shelf-stablised and can contain any of these things: dried milk, flour, soy sauce, sugar, curry powder, stock, beef fat, soya bean oil, corn oil, pork fat, tomato purée, coconut milk, soy sauce and, sometimes, extra spices such as cumin seeds, cloves or turmeric.

There is one other item to be picked up at the supermarket. You head towards the *tsukemono* ('transformed vegetables' or pickles) department. A section of it is marked *fukujinzuke*, 'pickles for curry'. *Fukujin* are the gods of seven fortunes and these very Japanese pickles contain the produce of seven plants, such as aubergine, *daikon* (mooli), slim cucumbers, mustard leaf, ginger, lotus root and sesame seeds. These are pickled mainly in soy sauce and sugar syrup, but as they are designated specifically for curry, that is what they are used for.

Curries may have come into Japan via Shanghai. The 19th century was a time when the Japanese were examining their diet and trying to introduce red meats to make their people taller and stronger. Beef curries would have fitted the bill perfectly. One of the major commercial companies selling curry roux has done research into the history of Japanese curry and suggests that the first curry may have appeared in 1863 at an International Competition, where cooked Japanese rice was placed next to sliced chillies and a thick sauce. By 1866, a gentleman by the name of Noda had decided that the Japanese preserves, *fukujinzuke*, were the ideal accompaniment to a curry meal. By 1903, the first commercial curry powders were being made in Osaka.

What seemed to have excited the public most, however, was the setting up of an avant-garde tea parlour by Shiseido, the same company that today manufactures and sells cosmetics. It was 1927. The Shiseido Parlour was the first to serve cake with their tea. There was much excitement. On their weekend menus, they added *curray-ricu*, which became outrageously popular with Japanese families. Soon they added the preserves, *fukujinzuke*, and pickled *ramps* to the curry meal.

A curious footnote to curry-eating in Japan: in traditional Japanese restaurants, workers who love curry cannot make it for lunch as it might 'smell up' the pots and the restaurants. If they bring cooked curry from home, which they sometimes do, they must enclose it in airtight containers that may not be mixed with restaurant utensils.

As their network of plantations grew, the British sent Indian labourers as far as Fiji and Australia, and to Sri Lanka, Mauritius, Kenya, Uganda, South Africa and the West Indies, often upsetting the local population balance and sowing the seeds of what were to become deeply unsettling resentments and divisions. It is outside the scope of this book to examine each and every one of these countries in detail, though you will find recipes from many of these regions in this book. To continue my larger culinary story, I now turn west, to South Africa. The lure of money from cash crops such as sugar, mostly, but also arrowroot, bananas, coffee, pineapples and tea persuaded the British to turn west, opening plantations in South Africa's east coast (KwaZulu Natal). Formerly

An Indian woman and her son weeding at her family vegetable plot in South Africa, 1948.

under Boer control, Natal had, in 1843, become a British colony. Zulus, natives of the land, chose to work only minimally before returning home to do their own subsistence farming. Again, docile Indian indentured labour was the solution, especially after the abolition of slavery in British colonies by 1834. This was to be a new system of slavery, protected by a newer set of self-serving laws.

(It should be noted here that, from the 17th century until the 19th century, it had been the Dutch practice to snatch people – men, women and even children – mostly from coastal Indonesia and India, and to take them as slaves to the Cape Town area. Almost 40,000 such slaves were put to work in vineyards and wheat fields and they were much favoured as house servants. Many intermarried with each other and with the local population. They came to be known as Cape Malays and their food – or the European food they influenced – came to be known as Cape Malay food. Today, it includes mild curries and *pilafs*, *sosaties*, curry-flavoured lamb, beef or even ostrich kebabs, and, most famous of all, *babotie*, curried minced meat, studded with rolled lemon leaves and cinnamon sticks, topped with a custard and baked.)

The first ship bearing Indian indentured labourers hit Natal's shores on 16 November 1860. By 1911, a further 383 ships would bring more than 150,000 Indian natives, mostly men, but some women and children as well. All would be put to work in the fields, with the children weeding and cleaning. Recruiters in the Indian regions of Uttar Pradesh and Bihar, as well as both the southern east and west coasts, would get especially active after a famine or pestilence, scooping up hundreds of desperate people who contracted for two lots of five years, after which they could get a free passage home or a piece of land the equivalent of the value of the passage. They were known, generally, as 'coolies', a word that meant 'hired labourers' or 'burden carriers' in India but would become a derogatory term for all Indians. (Decades later, Gandhi, the young, activist South African lawyer, was referred to as 'that coolie lawyer'.)

The heavily packed boats were frequently plagued by storms and disease at sea. Conditions allowed just bare survival. Ships' galleys carried rice, *dal*, *ghee*, mustard and coconut oil, preserved meat, dried fish, flour and a few seasonings – cumin, fenugreek, fresh ginger, tamarind and salt. Daily rations consisted of a little rice, a little flour and a little *dal*. Provisions for labourers working in Natal were not much more generous. This was the monthly ration: 675 g/1½ lb rice or 900 g/2 lb pounded mealies (dried corn), 900 g/2 lb *dal*, 900 g/2 lb dried, salted fish, 450 g/1 lb *ghee* or oil and 450 g/1 lb salt. The great variety of seasonings that are the very soul of Indian food were missing, and the flour seems to have disappeared altogether.

Once their indenture was over, the 'free settlers' used their little plots of land to grow fruit and vegetables, which they either peddled or sold in the market. The male hawkers were known as 'sammies', as their last names sometimes ended in 'sami' or 'swami', and the women hawkers as 'coolie Mary'. Eventually, the Indians were to control the fruit and vegetable market. This was resented to such an extent that the Indians were offered a free passage back 'home' and when they did not take up the offer, they were bundled into 'Indians only' areas where they would not compete with white traders, only with themselves.

Simultaneously, other Indians, who called themselves 'passengers' to distinguish themselves from the 'coolies', were sailing to South Africa – indeed, to other parts of Africa as well – from India's west coast, mostly from Gujarat. Gujaratis can be sharp, persevering businessmen. To service the freed 'coolies', they brought spices, textiles, jewellery and religious objects. The poorer 'free settlers' were from different parts of India, often with different religions. Once freed, most could hardly remember the village they came from. Initially, the culinary know-how and ingredients to recreate Indian fare were just not there. With dim memories of their regional pasts, and with deep bonds forged on the ships that brought them and during their hard work together, they developed a collective 'spicy' cuisine in which regional specifics were replaced by a more general 'Indianness'. The 'Bunny Chow' is a good example of that.

In Durban, the capital of Natal, an Indian merchant, often known by his caste, was called a *bannia*. *Bannias* had been restricted to Gray Street. Here they opened small eateries, mostly for themselves but also for South African blacks who were not allowed to step inside but could be served, hastily and illegally, through the back door. At the start of the 20th century, at landmark Indian restaurants such as Kapitan's and Patel's, if a black wanted a quick curry, a small loaf of bread was hollowed out, the curry ladled inside and garnished with pickles, and the whole sandwich-like meal surreptitiously handed over without benefit of cutlery. The South African blacks named this dish 'Bunny Chow' or 'the food of the Indians'. (For more, see Beans–in-a-Loaf, page 185).

With a lack of flour, especially wholemeal flour, for many decades Indian breads had been lost to the cuisine. But British loaves were available, so it was practical to use them. The most common, cheap dried bean sold in the market was the sugar bean, which, along with corn, must have come from the Americas and most resembles the pinto bean. The curry was made with this. The seasonings, bought off Indian merchants nearby, were seemingly indiscriminate. There were mustard seeds, cumin seeds, curry leaves, fennel seeds, turmeric, cumin, coriander, *asafetida*, cinnamon, mace, cardamom, chillies, garlic, onions and at least two different spice mixes sold by Gujarati mechants. And yet, despite this over-abundance of seasonings, and despite the lack of Indian-style, regional sure-footedness, the final flavour was South African and unbelievably delicious.

Spice stores today specialise in all manner of spice mixtures, some unique to South Africa. Indians buy them, but so do white South Africans, both English and those of German and Dutch extraction. The South African Red Spice Mixture (see page 323) used in every household has roasted cumin, coriander, black pepper, fenugreek and chilli powder in it. There are spice mixes for cooking fish and for chicken curry, and a special curry powder to flavour *potjiekos*, a Boer stew of meat and vegetables cooked in a three-legged, cast-iron pot. There is a curry powder for barbecued *wors* (Boer sausages), one labelled 'Mother-in-law Hot Curry Mix' as it is fiery, and an even fierier one called 'Arson Fire'.

In today's South Africa, many of the richer Indians (most prefer to be called just South Africans) travel back and forth to India, so there is much cross-fertilisation of recipes and ideas. But some tastes, developed over time, are there to stay. First and foremost is the taste for corn or mealies. Many Gujarati fritters and baked savoury cakes, once made with soaked and ground split peas, are now simply made with corn.

Dried fish, offered as part of the ration on the labourer-carrying ships, has also retained its distant appeal, especially for the poor. Many fishermen make a chutney of it, combining soaked, dried fish (they use snoek here) with lightly cooked tomatoes, green chillies and onions. Fresh fish is loved too. Sardine runs on the Natal coast are reported on radios by spotter planes and Indians are known to rush to the scene with plastic bags that have holes punched in them to collect them by the dozen. The sardines are quickly sprinkled with salt, dipped into some of the South African Red Spice Mixture, and fried. Fishermen make crab and fish roe curries. Glorious curries are also made combining fresh fish with vegetables or with sour fruit.

In South Africa, the Indian influence stretches far outside Indian society. Pizzas may be had with a topping of chicken *tikka masala* (see Silken Chicken 'Tikka Masala', page 101), margarita glasses may be rubbed not just with salt but finely chopped green chillies as well, 'parcels', a snack of sausages, comes with chips that are topped with a hot spice *masala*, and many white South Africans talk with delirium about mango pickle sandwiches.

The spread of Indian flavours on this continent does not stop at South Africa. Indian traders or labourers went all over Africa and its surrounding islands, and aspects of Indian food are to be found in most countries. I have had Nigerian stews flavoured with both ground peanuts and curry powder, a mouth-watering combination. In Mauritius, almost half a million indentured workers arrived, starting in 1834. Many were from Uttar Pradesh and Bihar. The local people speak a mixture of Creole, French and Bhojpuri, the 19th-century version of a dialect of the common people of Uttar Pradesh and Bihar. A *samosa* shop proclaims its 'gâteau piment' and bread bought at a store is *boutik ki roti*. *Dalpuris*, breads stuffed with *dal*, have become so universally popular that people queue up for them all day and buy them in pairs to have with curry and perhaps *chatini pomme d'amour grillé* (grilled tomato chutney.)

Many Gujaratis, both Hindu and Muslim, travelled from India's west coast to Kenya and Uganda. There, many not only survived, but flourished, and rags-to-riches stories of those who started off selling *dals* and ended up owning vast amounts of property are legion. Unlike the Indians of South Africa, who learned to speak English, those in Kenya mastered Swahili, giving many of their dishes Swahili names. Chicken with coconut is *kuku paka*, banana fritters are *kitumbia ndizi*, and the much-loved cassava is always *mogo*. Cassava is cooked frequently at home as crisp chips or in curries (with okra or lamb) and, because children relish it, vendors outside schools hawk cassava boiled, mashed and seasoned with salt, red chilli powder and either lemon juice or tamarind chutney.

Hindu and Muslim families here hold on to their traditional foods, but most dishes have been transformed to a degree by Africa and African produce. A Kenyan-Indian family might serve the Portuguese-influenced prawn *peri-peri*, a dish of prawns cooked with bird's eye chillies (the *peri-peri*), garlic, cumin and either lemon juice or vinegar one day, followed by green coriander chicken, maize cooked with mustard seeds and a very Muslim *pilaf* containing rice, meat and cardamom-flavoured stock the next.

In Nairobi, a family could serve a dish of chicken cooked with cumin seeds with an accompaniment of *khichro*, a sweet and sour porridge made in India with wheat and *dals* but here made with wheat and fresh African pigeon peas. They might also have *mogo* chips, and *makkai na vada*, a fritter made of millet in India but, in Kenya and Uganda, prepared with corn meal. Corn meal and semolina are combined with green chillies, green coriander, turmeric and yoghurt, and small soft patties formed on kitchen paper – in India, they would have used muslin – then fried. In every house, there is always a jug of fresh passion fruit juice.

Sugar was also the fuel that propelled a wave of Indian emigration to the West Indies. In 1832, when the evils and advantages of slavery were in their final stages of debate, William Ewart Gladstone, future British Prime Minister, gave his maiden speech in the House of Commons in support of slavery. His bias was hardly surprising as his father was a very active owner of slave-run sugar plantations in British Guyana. When slavery was abolished in 1833, plantation owners in the West Indies were in varying degrees of panic. Until then, heavy labour had been done by African slaves. Some planters, fearing ruin, sold their plantations. Others tried to induce former slaves to work as day labourers, but most had had enough. Cheap labour was desperately needed. John Gladstone, the father of the future Prime Minister, was the most creative of all the plantation owners in the West Indies.

On 4 January 1836, he wrote a letter to a Calcutta firm, Messrs Gillanders, Arbuthnot & Co., describing the prospects for labourers in Guyana and asking if he could get immigrants from India to work his estates. The firm replied saying that it had already supplied Mauritius with several hundred such immigrants and could certainly do so for Guyana. 'We are not aware,' the firm wrote, 'that any greater difficulty would present itself in sending men to the West Indies, the natives being perfectly ignorant of the place they go to or the length of the voyage they are undertaking.'

The voyage lasted anywhere from eleven to eighteen weeks. Initially, the 'natives' were picked up from the streets of Calcutta by recruiters, known as 'coolie-catchers', whose job was to keep their eyes peeled for the desperate. In time, starting around 1848, as recruiting for the neighbouring British colonies of Guyana and Trinidad became more organised, recruiters went further afield, finding a gold mine in the poor, Bhojpuri-speaking villages of Uttar Pradesh and Bihar. This is crucial to my story, as the Indian foods of Trinidad and Guyana are based on fully or half-remembered, 19th-century recipes from these villages, worked out, as best as possible, with the ingredients at hand. In spite of all the hardships endured by their creators, the foods are delicious.

As the poor villagers sailed, quite literally into the sunset (they were going west, after all), swept along by cruel monsoon winds, they sang plaintive songs in Bhojpuri, '*Calcutta say challat jahaaj, Panwariya dheeray chalo*' (The ship is sailing away from Calcutta, O boatman, go slowly). The terms of their service – two five-year contracts for a minimal salary followed by free passage home – were similar to those of the Indians who had journeyed to Malaya, as were the conditions of their passage. Their daily ration consisted of just seven items: 800 g/28 oz rice, 115 g/4 oz *dal*, 30 g/1 oz *ghee* or oil, 15 g/1/2 oz salt, 30 g/1 oz turmeric, 30 g/1 oz onions and 30 g/1 oz tobacco. There were no spices other than turmeric and no vegetables. On the sugar plantations their rations were much the same, with the addition of dried fish, pepper and chillies. Those who were willing to forsake the turmeric could have tamarind instead.

By 1869, Guyana alone had more that 30,000 free labourers who remained after the fulfilment of their contracts in exchange for plots of land offered by planters fearing the loss of cheap labour. More Indian labourers now began to be enticed over from India with the offer of Crown land. Eventually, half the population of Guyana and about a third of Trinidad would be of Indian descent.

As many labourers had acquired the skills to grow rice in their home villages, many chose to specialise in its cultivation. Guyana eventually produced so much rice that some was exported to other West Indian islands. Indian free labourers also grew sugar cane, cacao and vegetables. In Trinidad, the Indians planted cacao under the shade of the taller banana trees and turned it into a healthy cash crop. They also grew some rice, allowing the much loved, scaly cascadura fish to thrive in the paddies, and some vegetables.

Caste differences, so important in India, began to matter less and less. For the orthodox, crossing the high seas had always signified a loss of caste. More importantly, on their passages many had bonded deeply with other shipmates, fellow *jahajis*, all of different castes and religions. Far from real family, they were each other's family now. The colonial government, and the constant exhortations from Christian missionaries, made it difficult for Hindus or Muslims to marry legally, so children were often branded illegitimate. Such pressures convinced many to convert to Christianity or, at a minimum, to drop all caste restrictions amongst themselves. In culinary terms, this meant that meat, sometimes even beef, would now be added to the diets of those who could eventually afford it.

In Guyana, the local chilli most commonly available was the wiri wiri pepper. Though more familiar with the long cayenne variety propagated throughout India, the Indians adopted it with a passion. Hot, round, the size and shape of a cherry, its main characteristic was its powerful, tropical, citrus aroma. It flavours their mango pickle, their spinach *bhaji*, pumpkin, cabbage or potato curry, even their daily *dal* and their celebratory goat curry.

All their cooking terminology is almost understandable to an Indian from India today. When their wedding dish of *bunjay dal*, split peas flavoured with 'bunjayed' or browned onions, garlic and wiri wiri pepper, is cooked, Guyanese first smooth it out using a swizzle stick (*dal ghotni*) then add spinach and a final 'chowkey' ('*chownk*' or '*tarka*') of garlic and cumin seeds. The word *bunjay* came from the north Indian word *bhuna* or 'to brown' and could refer to browning spice mixtures or meats. When a dish has a sauce, it has *soorva*, from the north Indian word for gravy or sauce, *shorva*. Other words for common techniques are newer and heart-warmingly straightforward. For example, anything crushed with a mortar is simply 'ponged'.

Here again, the Indians beloved wholemeal flatbreads were of necessity replaced by a substitute made of locally available ingredients, as wheat was not part of their rations. When they did begin to get flour, it was white flour. Somewhere, sometime, they created a new *roti* (bread) that was half eastern and half western. It was still made on a griddle (*tava*) but was leavened with baking powder. The breads are still in a state of evolution, it seems. To make their *saada roti* puff up today, they have taken to sticking it briefly into a microwave oven!

Trinidad's native chilli is the scotch bonnet (also called congo pepper). Of the habanero family and lantern shaped, its pretty red, yellow and orange colours belie its fierce heat. It is amongst the hottest chillies in the world but it, too, is blessed with a perfume from heaven. It is essential to Trinidadian-Indian cuisine.

When a Trinidadian says, 'Come eat by me,' he may be inviting you to a quick street-side lunch of 'doubles' –

The Great Exhibition of 1851, London. Produce from British colonies in the East and West Indies displayed to great effect.

curried chickpeas, dotted with a hot congo pepper sauce and mango chutney, all rolled up in a pair of fried breads. If he is inviting you home, you may find yourself dining on *dalroti*, flatbreads stuffed with split peas fairly similar to those found in Mauritius but much larger, spinach *bhaji* seasoned with scotch bonnet peppers and garlic, and perhaps a curry chicken.

To make a Trinidadian curry demands seasonings from different corners of the globe, and immigrants from Madeira and Malta have left their influence, too. Fresh 'seasonings' are sold in every market, all tied up in a bundle that includes *saif*, a cross between chives and spring onions, parsley and Spanish thyme. Chop all these up, add chopped garlic, onion, scotch bonnet and chopped *shadow beni*. The last is culantro, a central American herb. (This and the hot pepper are probably amongst the only seasonings left over from the original Arawak tribe that once lived here.) All these chopped fresh ingredients are used as a marinade for the meat, though they may also be put in the sauce. Now you can brown some onions and garlic, add some curry powder and finally the meat and its marinade. Once the meat is tender, a final sprinkling of roasted and ground cumin – sold fully prepared in the market – is almost essential.

Of course, there are many variations of this general recipe and each curry is slightly different. It is the addition of Mediterranean herbs, perfumed scotch bonnet and ground, roasted cumin that makes Trinidadian curries so completely different from all others.

But the evolution of the curry does not stop here. The British, once India's colonial masters, have been the greatest champions of Indian food. While Indians have remained hung up on the details of regional cookery, in a master stroke of unconscious marketing the British have managed to generalise the cuisine, popularise it and sell it to the whole world. They did it because they loved it so much themselves.

Hollywood's version of Eastern dining from *The Drum*, 1938, with Roger Livesey, Raymond Massey and Archibald Batty.

Curry, according to a dictionary of Indo-British words published around 1882, was described this way: 'In the East, the staple food consists of some cereal, either in the form of flour baked into unleavened breads or boiled in the grain as rice is. Such food having little taste, some quantity of a much more savoury preparation is added as a relish. And this, is in fact the proper office of curry in native diet. It consists of meat, fish, fruit, or vegetables, cooked with a quantity of bruised spices and turmeric; and a little of this gives flavour to a large mess of rice.' The dictionary goes on to add that the origin of the word 'curry' could have been the Kannada language word, *karil*, or the Tamil *kari*, meaning 'sauce'.

There are references to curry in British writings as early as the start of the 16th century. We also know that Englishmen frequently dined on Indian meals while travelling through India during the 17th century. What is harder to say for certain is when the British started eating curries in their own homes in Britain.

Curry was popular enough by the early 18th century for the first recipe to appear in London in the fifth edition of Hannah Glasse's *The Art of Cookery Made Plain and Easy*, published in 1747. 'To make Currey the India way', she suggests roasting some coriander seeds over a fire and beating them 'to a powder'. Then she suggests combining the powder with peppercorns, chopped onions, salt, a spoon of rice for thickening, two cut-up fowls or rabbits and some water, and cooking until the meat is tender. As a final fillip, she adds a walnut-sized lump of butter. What we have here is really a mild stew, flavoured by the somewhat exotic, roasted coriander.

William Makepeace Thackeray, who had travelled to India, offers his own recipe in his poem, 'Curry':

> Three pounds of veal my darling girl prepares
> And chops it nicely into little squares
> Five onions next procures the minx
> (The biggest are the best, her Samiwel thinks.)
> And Epping butter nearly half a pound,
> And stews them in a pan until browned.
> What next my dextrous little girl will do
> She pops the meat into the savoury stew,
> With curry powder tablespoons three,
> And milk a pint (the richest that may be),
> And when the dish has stewed for half an hour
> A lemon's ready juice she'll o'er it pour
> Then, bless her! Then she gives the luscious pot
> A very gentle boil – and serves quite hot
> PS – Beef, mutton, rabbit, if you wish,
> Lobsters or prawns, or any kind of fish
> Are fit to make a CURRY. 'Tis, when done,
> A dish for emperors to feed upon.

From what we know, the first Indian restaurant in London opened with fanfare in 1809 at 34 George Street, Portman Square. Its owner, Dean Mahomed, had been

Indians fought on the British side in both World Wars. Here Nepali Gurkha soldiers prepare chapatis in a hospital kitchen, 1915.

a servant to a British officer in India and followed his master to Ireland, then married and moved to London. When the restaurant, Hindustanee Coffee-House, opened, he announced in *The Times*, 'Mahomed, East Indian, informs the Nobility and Gentry, he has fitted up the above house, neatly and elegantly, for the entertainment of Indian gentlemen, where they may enjoy the Hoakah, with real Chilm tobacco, and Indian dishes, in the highest perfection . . . unequalled to any curries ever made in England with choice wines . . .' The restaurant closed in 1812. It was far ahead of its time.

Fast forward to 1999. Gary Younge, writing in the *Guardian*, confirms that Indian food is the most popular cuisine in Britain, and outsells fish and chips two-to-one. He also says that there are now around 8,000 Indian restaurants, up from six in 1950, and that, with about 70,000 employees, more people work in Indian restaurants than in coal mining, shipbuilding and steel combined.

Massive, mechanised factories in the United Kingdom today produce specialised curry pastes to make everything from Goan coconut curry to *tandoori* chicken. Ready-made Indian meals are big business and can be found at popular mass market stores such as Marks & Spencer and Sainsbury, even at Harrods. Food magazines carry Indian recipes almost routinely and curries are standard offering in pubs. What is going on? What happened between the early 19th century and today? An unintended revolution, that's what. I have to add that I consider myself fortunate to have been a very, very small part of this revolution.

Food-loving Britons in India, who had dined on local food in the 19th century, were determined to capture it, like a genie in a bottle, and take it home. They seem to have been at great pains to assemble recipes for curry powder, curry paste and curry sauce (all included here), often with the help of their Indian cooks, thinking that these could stand in for the real thing. Most were simplifications of authentic Indian cuisine but, at a distance, seemed satisfactory enough.

During much of the latter half of the 19th century, most curry sauces were really French white sauces flavoured with curry powder, and sometimes with apples and onions. ('To kill the mutton taste in mutton, add two peeled apples' was common advice then.) Every now and then, mango or coconut or chutney were added as well. Rather like Piccaso painting a woman, this was really an 'impression', in a few strokes, of Indian curry. If a cold dish was desired, these simple curries could also be jelled and chilled (see Cold Veal Curry-in-a-Mould, page 76) or hostesses could make a light, curry-flavoured fish soufflé.

Even Queen Victoria, who herself had Indian servants, served curries at her palace dinners, but under French names such as *cailles aux pommes de terre á l'indienne* (quail and potato curry). If the cookbook written by one of her chefs, Charles Elmé Francatelli, is any guide, these were the usual period curries with curry powder, curry paste, onions and apples. With the coming of the First World War, curries have 'thrift' written all over them. Recipes appear telling housewives how to dress up leftover meats with curry sauces using curry powder, butter, milk, sour apples and lemon juice. Along with an advertisement for National War Bonds, the Savoy Restaurant has two curries on its 1918 dinner menu.

WINDSOR.

HER MAJESTY'S DINNER,

Thursday, 28th June, 1900.

Potages.

Consommé de tortue. Potage des Rois.

Poissons.

Saumon sauce roche. Eperlans frits sauce ravigotte.

Entrées.

Ris de veau à la Senn.

Chaud-froid de volaille à la Reine.

Relevés.

Bœuf braise à la Richelieu.

Selle d'agneau sauce menthe. Petits pois à l'Anglaise.

Rôt.

Cailles aux pommes de terre à l'Indienne.

Entremêts.

Asperges sauce Hollandaise.

Babas au curacao. Eclairs aux fraises.

Croûtes de Chantilly.

Glaces.

Crême au chocolat. Eau de citron.

Buffet.

Hot and Cold Fowls. Tongue. Cold Roast Beef.

Queen Victoria not only had Indian servants, she also served Indian dishes at both her everyday and banquet meals. This is one of her banquet menus, with a quail and potato curry.

The curry world stayed bleak in spite of Veeraswamy's, the first Indian restaurant that opened on Swallow Street, just off Piccadilly Circus, in 1926. Its elegant location and size must have been quite startling. By 1955, according to the *Good Food Guide*, there were only nine Indian restaurants in London and four outside it. I arrived in London in 1957. I must have brought the winds of change with me – not that I could cook worth a farthing in those days. But with the help of airmailed recipes from my mother, I did start teaching myself.

The 1960s and '70s saw a seismic shift. African nationalism had turned militant. Indians en masse were forced to pack their bags and leave Uganda and Kenya in haste. With their British passports, they could seek refuge in Britain. Immigration policies were fairly relaxed so Punjabi villagers from both India and Pakistan arrived with mothers and children in tow, as did thousands of Bangladeshis fleeing lives of poverty. If language was a problem, and it frequently was, a relatively easy business, in which the whole family could toil together, was the restaurant business. Indian restaurants opened by the dozen in Birmingham, Leicester, London, Glasgow, indeed in every British town. With their flocked wallpaper, they all looked similar and, even though their owners came from differing cultural backgrounds, the menus were unbudgeably the same.

I could recite that menu. One could have *vindaloo, madras, bhuna, korma* in a choice of lamb or chicken. There was *tandoori* chicken and chicken *tikka masala*, a creation perhaps devised by combining *tandoori* chicken kebabs with an Indian curry sauce. There was a chickpea curry, a *dal*, an okra dish and the usual assortment of lacklustre *biryani, papadum*, yoghurt relish and *tandoori* breads. Indian restaurants stood for cheap food, something to accompany a glass or many glasses of lager, or indeed, to have after a bout of such at the pub. And so it remained until the early 1980s.

When I got set to do my first cookery programme on television in the autumn of 1982, the BBC thought of it primarily as an educational programme and had no great hopes for it. Much to their surprise, the public seemed eager and ready. The day after I made Lemony Chicken with Green Coriander, I was told that all green coriander in Manchester had sold out. People had more leisure and more money in their pockets. I was cooking real Indian food and the British yearned for it.

Better quality restaurants have opened now, serving authentic Indian regional specialties. Today you may dine on Kenyan Gujarati food in Wembley and Pakistani kebabs in the City. Southhall sells stuffed Punjabi *parathas* (flaky flatbreads) and, in the season, true Indian Alphonso mangoes. If *halal* meat is needed, it is there. If fresh curry leaves are required, there are places to buy them. Even with a small, 2 1/2 per cent South Asian population, Britain has turned into a culinary Little India, an ironic example of reverse colonisation!

The United States, on the other hand, has never had any historical connections with India and no early consciousness of its cuisine other than the little that drifted in with English settlers or English cookbooks. In fact, when an American edition of Hannah Glasse's 1747 cookbook, *The Art of Cookery Made Plain and Easy*, was published in Alexandria, her recipe for curry was left out (though the recipe for Indian pickles was included). Many Sikhs came to work in California as loggers in the early part of the 20th century, but most married Mexican women and have left no culinary trail.

When I came to New York for the first time in 1958, Indian restaurants were poor, often opened by seamen who had jumped ship and married locally. It seemed as if menus from the flock-wallpapered restaurants in England had been xeroxed and sent to proprietors here. They were almost identical, except for authentic *tandoor*-roasted foods, which did not get to the States until a restaurant called Gaylord opened in New York in 1974.

The picture has changed somewhat. There are some noteworthy restaurants scattered around the country, and new ones, with stunning modern design and fine regional dishes, are opening all the time. Regional foods of the highest quality are also cooked in private homes, by India-born women who may be wives of Wall Street entrepreneurs, silicon valley magnates, taxi drivers or small shopkeepers. But younger, American-born Indians, like my daughters, and even non-Indian Americans, like my daughter's friends, think nothing of opening up a good Indian cookbook and wading in. I know that a second generation of young Americans is cooking from my books. Americans love good food and will read cookbooks, take cookery classes, do whatever is needed to produce authentic tasting meals. American supermarket shelves bulge with ever-increasing hot sauces, *salsas*, chutneys and relishes. It is believed that once a love of hot foods takes a hold, there is no going back. It is addictive. The love for Indian food is fitting right in there with the growing national trend.

The bigger cities, such as Chicago and New York, and even some smaller ones, such as Jersey City, have large Indian enclaves with groceries, Gujarati snack shops, south Indian restaurants, sari shops and jewellers. Most ingredients for Indian dishes may be bought easily enough here or from local stores or the proliferating websites. While Indian regional groups tend to love their own regional foods, American ingredients are creeping into the recipes. I've had a wonderful *bhaji* made with purėed spinach and broccoli. I've had fresh California figs stir-fried with curry leaves and mustard seeds and arranged around a roast leg of lamb. American chefs, hungry for new techniques and seasonings, are borrowing from India all the time, adding a little tamarind here, some mustard seeds there and a touch of roasted cumin where you least expect it. In this way the spice trail continues its slow progress across yet another continent, leaving delicious and tangible reminders of Indian influence in its wake.

I just have one more thing to add. As I spun around the world again and again, collecting material for this book, I found myself with a treasure trove of thousands of delicious recipes. Pakistani kebabs by the dozen, corn dishes from Uganda, spicy Indian potato dishes, South African fish offerings, Malaysian *kormas*, haunting Thai curries . . . What was I to include? What must I leave out? I could not possibly fit all of them in. A few have been selected because, historically, they just took my breath away. Most of the recipes I have chosen, however, are the ones that I find I return to again and again, those that continue to thrill me with their tantalising, satisfying flavours.

1

LAMB, PORK, BEEF, VEAL AND GOAT

The meat most commonly eaten throughout India is very fresh goat meat slaughtered that day. As most of the butchers are Muslim, the meat tends to be halal meat, i.e. the animal is butchered according to Muslim dietary laws (which are not all that different from Jewish dietary laws). Lamb is also eaten, as is the fat-tailed sheep (*dumba*), but not on a daily basis.

Most of India's everyday curries are made with cubes of meat that include bone. The sauces have more flavour this way and the tactile enjoyment of working a morsel of food free from the bone with one's fingers and wrapping it in a piece of flat bread or combining it with rice is immeasurable.

When an Indian shops for curry meat, he will ask the butcher for a few marrow bones (goat marrow bones are small), a few cubes of meat that are boneless, some meat from the neck and maybe a few small rib pieces as well. He will definitely have the butcher add some cubed *macchli ka gosht*. This translates as 'fishlike meat'. Whole muscles from the legs and shoulders are removed – it is their shape that gives them their name – and then cut. So what you get in a true Indian curry are meat pieces of varying textures and densities with a sauce whose richness and flavour comes from a combination of spices, oozing marrow, natural bone gelatin and meat juices.

Indians, of course, eat with their hands, and working around bones only adds to the enjoyment. In the West, where goat is hard to find and a knife and fork are the recommended eating implements, boneless lamb comes closest to approximating goat meat. However, if you do have access to a halal butcher of Indian, Pakistani, Bangladeshi or West Indian extraction, it is worth trying any of the lamb dishes with goat meat instead. The cooking time will be a bit longer, about 1½–2 hours. Just ask for good curry meat and make sure the butcher throws in a marrow bone for you to enjoy with the marrow spoon that may be lying unused in some drawer.

I recommend boneless lamb from the shoulder for curries. Most Western butchers balk at this and try to sell you leg meat instead. Resist them. Leg meat has a drier texture. If the butcher does not want to sell you boneless shoulder, buy double the weight of loin lamb chops and ask the butcher to bone those for you. Save the bones for soup. Or buy a whole shoulder and get it boned. About 60 per cent will be meat and 40 per cent bone. Freeze what you do not use immediately.

Beef is eaten by Indian Muslims, Indian Christians and, of course, throughout Pakistan and Bangladesh. Most lamb dishes may also be made with stewing beef, if you like. Just increase the cooking time to 1½ hours. Pakistanis call beef 'big meat' and use it for everything from kebabs to curries.

As curries spread eastward, all the way to Japan, countries began choosing their own meats, their own cuts and their own styles of preparing them. Thais eat with a spoon and a fork, so meats needed to be boned and cut into small pieces. Thais also preferred pork or beef. Malaysia and Indonesia have huge

Muslim, beef-loving populations. Here, too, the meat was generally boneless. Singapore, once it separated from Malaysia, freely imported 'mutton' from Australia but did not like its 'muttony' flavour. I found that today almost everyone in Singapore parboils mutton and then drains it to get rid of the mutton 'smell' before cooking it in curries. (Indeed, one Anglo-American-Indian cookbook with recipes from the 1950s and earlier, suggests 'To kill the mutton taste in mutton, add two peeled apples'.)

There is hardly any lamb in Japan. A meat curry, to be eaten with Japanese rice and chopsticks, is usually made with boneless beef, either cut into manageable pieces or minced.

In the West, the British took to mutton curries in the 19th century. The very popular Mutton Curry at London's Oriental Club (see page 56) called for lean mutton without bone, the head chef declaring that fresh 'leg or chumps will make the best curry'. Today, we find that goat is still relegated to the Asian community, both in the United Kingdom and in the United States. Most curries use lamb or beef. It is, almost always, boneless.

In India, there are hundreds of different ways to cook meat. It may be braised with just browned onions and whole spices such as cardamom and cinnamon. It could be stewed with potatoes and coconut milk. It could be cooked with mustard seeds and curry leaves or with orange juice. Each household, each region, each state, specialises in its own curries.

Further south in Sri Lanka you may be served beef curry flavoured with fennel seeds and pandanus leaves, while in Thailand a coconut-enriched pork curry may be drenched with the aroma of lemon grass and galangal. Indonesians put fresh red chillies and fresh turmeric into their curry pastes and, all the way west, in Trinidad, a beef curry could have both curry powder and a very Mediterranean enchanting mixture of thyme, parsley and garlic.

Sometimes, before a curry is even cooked in north India, the meat is marinated in a mixture of yoghurt, ginger, garlic and perhaps a few spices. These seasonings perform a double function. They tenderise and add flavour. Yoghurt may also be called for during the cooking. It is generally added slowly, a tablespoon at a time, so it is absorbed into the meat juices and does not curdle.

Although flour is never used to thicken an Indian curry sauce, British curry sauces were made rather like French white sauces, with butter, flour, milk or stock and, of course, curry powder. Japanese curries all have flour thickeners. And even in India there are certain sauces that are thickened, not with white flour but with chickpea flour or with ground nuts. The extraordinary Lamb 'Kari' with a Sauce of Ground Nuts (page 50) requires both.

Not all curries have sauces. Sometimes we boil the sauce down until it clings to the meat and almost disappears. At other times, the sauce is very thin and watery. Each dish has its own traditional characteristics. We try and respect that.

THE ORIGINS OF BHUNA

'B*huna*' is the act of browning. Hence the characteristics of a '*bhuna*' dish are that the cooked food has a dryish, browned look. There is no thin sauce. It is all reduced and 'browned' until it clings to the meat.

'*Bhuna*' meats are a world unto themselves and, in terms of how they look and how they are eaten, are first cousins to kebabs. As they are dry, i.e. without a sauce, they may be rolled easily inside breads to become what are now fashionably called 'wraps'. 'Wraps', under different names of course, have been available in India since anyone can remember. They are sold as street snacks under names such as *kaati kebab*. At picnics, we were allowed to roll them ourselves using *pooris*, the puffy, deep-fried breads. At home, my mother made *battas* using our everyday, wholemeal griddle breads, *chapatis*. A sliced onion relish has always been considered the perfect accompaniment to roll in, along with the meat.

Bhuna meats were a fairly common dish in our family. If my mother wanted them to taste a little unusual, she would sprinkle a few drops of aromatic *kewra* (screw pine) water over the top. This made them taste more like bazaar food, which we were never allowed to eat, as it was supposedly unclean, but we certainly drooled over it whenever we drove by. It was hotter, more aromatic and definitely more exciting than the food at home. We knew this because now and then, at a birthday party or when some unexpected guests appeared, my father would send for some. The driver would go with the car to the crowded old city, to the area around the 17th-century mosque, Jama Masjid, and bring back dozens of breads and kebabs all wrapped in starchy, white cloths sent along by my mother. How these cloths made the food any cleaner, I do not know. Even before the cloths got untied, there was that irrepressible aroma of *kewra* emanating from our dinner-to-be. We knew we were in for a treat.

Kerala-style 'Bhuna' Lamb, Pork, Beef or Veal (Kerala Ka Bhuna Gosht)

INDIA

This dish is a great favourite in my sister's Delhi home, where it is prepared by her Malayali cook, who comes from Kerala in south-western India. You may use either stewing lamb or pork – ask your butcher for boneless meat from the shoulder – or boneless stewing veal. All these meats are eaten by the different religious groups in Kerala. Indeed, it is the only state where the sale of beef is perfectly legal.

Serve with rice or flatbreads.

SERVES 4–6

- 2 teaspoons whole cumin seeds
- 4 teaspoons whole coriander seeds
- 2 teaspoons whole mustard seeds
- 2–4 whole, dried, hot red chillies
- 2 teaspoons whole fennel seeds
- 2 teaspoons whole fenugreek seeds
- 5 tablespoons corn or peanut oil
- 3 large shallots, about 140 g/5 oz, peeled and very finely chopped
- 4 cm-/1½ inch piece fresh ginger, peeled and very finely chopped
- 5–6 cloves garlic, peeled and very finely chopped
- 10–15 fresh curry leaves, if available
- 2 medium tomatoes, peeled and chopped
- 900 g/2 lb boneless lamb or pork shoulder or stewing veal or beef, cut into 3 cm/1 1/4 inch pieces
- 1¼–1½ teaspoon salt

Set a small or medium-sized cast-iron frying pan on a medium-high heat. When it is hot, put in the cumin seeds, coriander seeds, mustard seeds, chillies, fennel seeds and fenugreek seeds. Stir them around until they are a shade darker. Quickly empty them out and let them cool slightly. Now put them into a clean coffee grinder or other spice grinder and grind to a powder.

Pour the oil into a wide, preferably non-stick, lidded pan and set over a medium-high heat. When the oil is hot, add the shallots, ginger and garlic. Fry, stirring at the same time, for 4–5 minutes until they turn a golden brown. Add the curry leaves and tomatoes. Cook, again stirring, until the tomatoes are reduced to a thick paste. Add the ground roasted spices. Stir into the paste and cook for a minute. Add the meat and salt. Stir and cook for a further 5 minutes. Add 250 ml/8 fl oz water and bring to a simmer. Cover tightly with the lid, reduce the heat to low, and simmer gently for about 80 minutes or until the meat is tender. (Beef will take about 1½ hours.) Remove the lid, increase the heat to high, and cook, stirring continuously, until the sauce is reduced to the point where it clings to the meat.

My sister Kamal's

Lamb with Cream (Malai Gosht)

INDIA

Here is yet another, much richer version of *bhuna gosht*, this time made with cream. In India, fresh clotted cream or *malai* is used, but whipping cream will do. Normally, water is not used in the cooking at all but if you need a little, sprinkle in a few tablespoons. A heavy non-stick pan makes the cooking much simpler.

The pistachios are sold by all Indian grocers. Blanched, slivered almonds, lightly roasted, may be used as a substitute.

SERVES 4–6

- 350 ml/12 fl oz whipping cream
- 2 tablespoons fresh ginger, peeled and finely grated
- 6 cloves garlic, peeled and mashed to a pulp
- 1¼–1½ teaspoons salt
- 1 teaspoon cayenne pepper
- 900 g/2 lb boneless lamb shoulder, cut into 3-cm/1¼-inch pieces
- 4 tablespoons corn or peanut oil, or *ghee*
- 2 bay leaves
- 2 medium sticks cinnamon
- 10 whole cardamom pods
- 2 whole black cardamom pods, if available
- 1 whole, dried, hot red chilli
- 2 medium onions, about 285 g/10 oz, peeled and sliced into fine half-rings
- ½ teaspoon *garam masala* (see page 327)
- 1 teaspoon ground cumin seeds
- 2 teaspoons ground coriander seeds
- 1 tablespoon chopped peeled, unsalted pistachios, for garnishing

Put the cream in a bowl, add the ginger, garlic, salt (start with the lesser amount) and cayenne pepper, and mix thoroughly. Add the meat, and mix well so that all the meat is covered with the marinade. Cover and refrigerate for at least 4 hours, longer if desired.

When ready to cook the meat, put the oil, or *ghee*, in a large, non-stick, lidded pan and set over a medium-high heat. When hot, add the bay leaves, cinnamon, cardamom and chilli. Within seconds, the chilli should darken. Now stir in the sliced onions, and fry for about 5 minutes or until the onions just start to brown. Add the meat, together with the marinade, stir, and bring to a simmer. Cover the pan, reduce the heat to low, and cook for 40 minutes, stirring occasionally. Remove the lid and increase the heat to medium-high. Add the *garam masala* and extra salt, if needed, as well as the cumin and coriander. Cook, stirring now and then, for a further 15–20 minutes or until all the liquid has been absorbed and the sauce clings to the meat. Sprinkle the pistachios over the top when serving.

Sumatran Lamb Curry (Gulai Pagar Puri) INDONESIA

Indian traders and plantation workers have greatly influenced not just the cuisines of Malaysia and Singapore but those of neighbouring northern Sumatra as well. Muslims around Aceh eat meats with a distinct Indian flavour to them. Just look at this dish. One of the main differences between Indian and Indonesian curries is that the heat here comes from long, hot, fresh red chillies. As I find them hard to get, I have used a combination of red sweet pepper with cayenne pepper and bright red paprika. Sumatrans might add eight small, peeled potatoes about the same time as you add the mixture of coconut milk and water.

SERVES 4–6

140 g/5 oz shallots, peeled and chopped
5 cloves garlic, peeled and chopped
5-cm/2-inch piece fresh ginger, peeled and chopped
1 large red pepper, seeded and chopped
2 teaspoons bright red paprika
1 teaspoon cayenne pepper
4 teaspoons ground coriander
2 teaspoons ground cumin
½ teaspoon ground turmeric
½ teaspoon ground cinnamon
½ teaspoon ground cardamom
400-ml/14-fl oz can coconut milk, left undisturbed for 3 hours or more
6 tablespoons corn, peanut or olive oil
900 g/2 lb boneless lamb shoulder, cut into 2½-cm/1-inch cubes
1¾ teaspoons salt, or to taste
2 tablespoons thick tamarind paste
225 g/8 oz green (French) beans, halved
12 okra pods (small and tender ones are best), topped and tailed
4–5 fresh bird's eye chillies or other fresh green or red chillies, for garnishing

Place the shallots, garlic, ginger, red pepper and 3 tablespoons water in a blender and blend until smooth. Add the paprika, cayenne pepper, coriander, cumin, turmeric, cinnamon and cardamom and blend briefly.

Remove the thick coconut cream from the can and reserve. Pour the remaining, thinner milk into a measuring jug. Add enough water to make 750 ml/1¼ pints.

Pour the oil into a wide, preferably non-stick, lidded pan and set over a medium-high heat. When hot, stir in the paste from the blender and fry for 12 minutes or until the paste is a rich, reddish brown. Put in the meat and stir for a minute. Cover, reduce the heat to medium-low, and cook for 10 minutes, lifting the lid now and then to stir. Add the thinned coconut milk, salt and tamarind paste, stir to mix, and bring to a simmer. Cover and simmer very gently for 45 minutes. Add the green beans and okra. Cover, and simmer for 20 minutes. Slowly stir in the coconut cream as you cook for a further few minutes or until the meat is tender. Garnish with the chillies when serving.

From Sameena at Yousaf Salahuddin's home

Lamb with Potatoes (Aloo Gosht)

PAKISTAN

For me, there is nothing quite as satisfying as this everyday dish of meat and potatoes. It makes me swoon with homesickness. It is served throughout much of Pakistan (as well as many homes in northern India), with rice or flatbreads, as well as pickles and relishes. The meat used is generally goat, with the bone in, but boneless lamb is just as good. I ask the butcher for lamb shoulder chops and have him cut them up into 4-cm/1½-inch pieces. If I am cooking for my family, I leave the bone in; if I have guests, I ask the butcher to remove the bones and give me 900 g/2 lb boneless meat. You will have to buy almost 1.8 kg/4 lb of lamb to get the required amount of boneless meat. This recipe is for 900 g/2 lb of meat, with or without bone.

While this dish is eaten with equal gusto in both Pakistan and India, the technique used for its preparation in Pakistan is somewhat different from that to which I have been accustomed. Much of the cooking is done on a fairly high heat and this changes both the texture and the taste of nearly all the ingredients. Another change is that the all-important browning of the meat and seasonings, what we call the 'bhuno-ing', is done in the middle of the cooking, not at the start. Also, many of the seasonings are coarsely crushed in a mortar instead of being ground to a paste. The differences are subtle. The results are superb!

SERVES 4–6

- 7½-cm/3-inch piece fresh ginger, peeled and chopped
- 5–6 cloves garlic, peeled and chopped
- 2–3 fresh, hot green chillies, chopped
- 1 tablespoon whole coriander seeds
- 4 tablespoons corn or peanut oil, or *ghee*
- 140 g/5 oz shallots,peeled and thinly sliced
- 900 g/2 lb boneless lamb shoulder, cut into 4-cm/1½-inch pieces
- ¼ teaspoon ground turmeric
- ¾–1¼ teaspoons cayenne pepper
- 2 medium tomatoes, 285 g/10 oz, chopped
- 1¾ teaspoons salt
- 2 whole black cardamom pods
- 1 medium stick cinnamon
- 450 g/1 lb small, red waxy potatoes, about 4 cm/1½ inches in diameter, peeled and left whole (larger potatoes may be peeled and cut into similar sized chunks)
- ½ teaspoon *garam masala* (see page 327)
- 4 tablespoons fresh coriander leaves, chopped

Place the ginger, garlic and green chillies in a food processor and chop finely using the pulse or stop and start method. Stop before you have a paste.

Put the coriander seeds in a clean coffee grinder or other spice grinder and grind to a coarse powder.

Put the oil, or *ghee*, in a large, preferably non-stick, lidded pan and set over a medium-high heat. When hot, add the shallots, and fry, stirring, for about 5 minutes, or until the shallots have turned golden brown. Stir in the ginger mixture, and fry for about 2 minutes. Then add the meat, and stir it about for a minute or so. Add the turmeric, cayenne pepper and coarsely ground coriander. Stir a few times. Add 250 ml/8 fl oz water and cook for 5 minutes, stirring from time to time. Add the tomatoes, salt and a further 475 ml/16 fl oz water. Stir, then cover and cook on a medium-high heat for 10 minutes. Add the cardamom and cinnamon. Stir, then replace the lid and continue to cook on a medium-high heat for a further 10 minutes. Add the potatoes, and cook, uncovered, stirring occasionally, until the sauce clings to the meat and you see oil in the bottom of the pan, about 10 minutes. When this point is reached, add another 750 ml/1¼ pints water and bring to the boil. Cover, reduce the heat to low and simmer gently for 10 minutes or until the meat is tender.

For a final melding of flavours, either place the pan over the lowest possible heat, preferably using a heat diffuser, for a further 10 minutes, or put in an oven preheated to 150° C/gas mark 2, again for 10 minutes.

Sprinkle the *garam masala* and fresh coriander over the top before serving.

Lamb with Mustard Seeds (Uppakari)

INDIA

Very popular among the money-lending Chettiar community of Tamil Nadu in southern India, this dish is both easy to prepare and uniquely flavoured. I was actually first served it in a private home in Penang, Malaysia, by a Chettiar family that has had commerce and property there for over a century. The dish had been simplified – the traditional curry leaves, *urad dal,* cinnamon stick and fennel seeds had been left out. What you will find below is the original recipe, without the omissions, as I think its flavour is richer.

SERVES 4

- 4 tablespoons corn or peanut oil
- 2 teaspoons whole brown mustard seeds
- 6–10 whole, dried, hot red chillies, each broken into 3–4 pieces (leave whole if less heat is desired)
- ½ teaspoon *urad dal* or yellow split peas
- 200 g/6½ oz shallots, peeled and thinly slivered
- 10 medium cloves garlic, peeled and cut into fine slivers
- 15–20 fresh curry leaves, if available
- 2 teaspoons fresh ginger, peeled and very finely grated
- 200 g/6½ oz tomatoes, chopped
- 450 g/1 lb boneless lamb shoulder, cut into 2½-cm/1-inch cubes
- ¼ teaspoon ground turmeric
- ¾–1 teaspoon salt

Pour the oil into a wide, preferably non-stick, lidded pan and set over a medium-high heat. When hot, add the mustard seeds, chillies and *urad dal.* As soon as the mustard seeds pop and the *dal* reddens, add the shallots, garlic and curry leaves. Stir and fry for 3 minutes, or until the onions just start to take on some colour. Add the ginger, and stir a few times. Stir in the tomatoes and cook for 2 minutes. Add the lamb and turmeric. Stir and cook for a minute. Add 475 ml/16 fl oz water and the salt. Bring to a boil, cover, reduce the heat to low, and cook gently for an hour or so, until the meat is tender. Remove the lid, increase the heat to high and boil away some of the liquid. You should end up with a thick sauce clinging to the meat.

Rehana Saigol's

Lamb Shanks Braised in a Yoghurt Sauce (Kunna) PAKISTAN

The Chiniot area of Pakistan is known nationally for its fine wood carvers. It should be equally revered for its *kunna*. This uncommonly grand and little known dish consists of large pieces of meat that are braised very slowly in a clay pot buried in hot ashes and earth. The braising liquid consists of aromatic spices, ginger, garlic and yoghurt. The meat gets so tender, it practically falls off the bone. It is luscious.

Since burying clay pots in hot ashes is beyond most of us, I have devised a method that uses lamb shanks and cooks *kunna* slowly in an oven over three, painless hours.

You will need a wide, non-stick pan that can be used both on top of the stove and in the oven. If you do not have one, use a heavy, non-stick roasting pan and, if there is no lid, improvise with a large piece of heavy-duty foil.

I have allowed about half a shank per person. You may take the meat off the bone when serving or else give the bone section to those who love it as much as I do.

The shanks may be served with flatbreads or rice.

SERVES 6

- 3 lamb shanks, about 1.6–1.8 kg/3¾–4 lb
- salt
- freshly ground pepper
- 13-cm/5-inch piece fresh ginger, peeled and coarsely chopped
- 8 cloves garlic, peeled and coarsely chopped
- 4 tablespoons whole coriander seeds
- 8 tablespoons olive or corn oil
- 2 teaspoons whole cumin seeds
- 1 teaspoon whole cloves
- 4 medium sticks of cinnamon
- 2 teaspoons whole black peppercorns
- 475 ml/16 fl oz natural yoghurt, lightly beaten until smooth
- 2–3 teaspoons coarsely ground pure chilli powder or cayenne pepper
- ½ teaspoon ground turmeric

Place the shanks in a single layer and sprinkle all over with ½ teaspoon salt and lots of black pepper. Pat them in.

Put the ginger and garlic in a blender with 4 tablespoons water and blend until smooth. Set aside.

Put the coriander seeds in a clean coffee grinder and grind coarsely. You may use a mortar and pestle for this instead. Set aside.

Preheat the oven to 160°C/gas mark 3.

Pour the oil into a wide, non-stick, lidded pan and set over a high heat. When hot, add the lamb shanks and brown lightly on all sides. Remove. Quickly add the cumin, cloves, cinnamon and peppercorns to the hot oil in the pan. Ten seconds later, add the ginger-garlic paste, stir, and fry for 5–6 minutes or until lightly browned. Take the pan off the heat and add the beaten yoghurt and 475 ml/16 fl oz water. Stir well. Put the pan back on the heat, add the coarsely ground coriander, chilli powder, turmeric and 1½ teaspoons salt, and stir to mix. Put the lamb shanks back into the pan, spoon some sauce over them, and bring to the boil. Cover well, first with foil, crimping the edges, then with the lid, place in the oven and bake slowly for 3 hours, turning the shanks over every 30 minutes.

Remove the pan from the oven and uncover. Set over a high heat and reduce the liquid, basting the shanks as you do so, until you have a thick sauce, about 6–7 minutes.

Afsha Mumtaz's

Lamb Shanks Cooked with Garam Masala (Nahari) INDIA

Amongst Muslim families in both India and Pakistan, this is a much-loved breakfast or brunch dish, to be eaten with *naan*-like breads. Salads, or any vegetables you like, may be served on the side.

The *garam masala* referred to in the title includes the usual nutmeg, mace and cinnamon, but this time fennel and ground ginger are added to the mix to give a special anise-ginger flavour. It is worth noting that fresh and dried ginger, both of which are used here, have entirely different tastes. In India they even have different names.

Crisply Fried Onion Slices (see page 312) are required here. It is best to make them first, as you can use some of the leftover oil to cook this recipe. It will have added flavour.

In India, goat shanks are used. Do use them if you can get them easily. About ten would weigh about the same as the three lamb shanks that I get from my market. But lamb shanks are wonderful too, and they are what I commonly use.

Serves 6

3 lamb shanks, about 1.6–1.8 kg/3¾–4 lb
salt
freshly ground pepper
15-cm/6-inch piece fresh ginger, peeled and coarsely chopped
1 whole nutmeg, crushed into smaller pieces
1 tablespoon mace pieces
2 tablespoons whole fennel seeds
2–3 bay leaves, crumbled
2 medium sticks cinnamon, broken up
1 teaspoon ginger powder
8 tablespoons oil left over from frying the onion slices
2–3 teaspoons cayenne pepper
1 tablespoon bright red paprika
Crisply Fried Onion Slices (see page 312)
2 tablespoons wholemeal flour

TO SERVE
fine julienne of peeled fresh ginger
thinly sliced fresh, hot green chillies
a handful of fresh coriander leaves
lemon wedges

Place the shanks in a single layer and sprinkle all over with ½ teaspoon salt and lots of black pepper. Pat them in.

Put the ginger in a blender with 5 tablespoons water and blend until smooth. Set aside.

Put the nutmeg, mace, fennel, bay leaves and cinnamon in a clean coffee grinder and grind as finely as possible. Put in a bowl. Add the ginger powder and set aside.

Preheat the oven to 160°C/gas mark 3.

Pour the oil into a wide, non-stick, lidded pan and set over a high heat. When hot, add the lamb shanks and brown lightly on all sides. Remove. Quickly add the ginger paste, and stir and fry for 5–6 minutes or until lightly browned. Add the cayenne pepper and paprika. Stir once or twice, then add half the browned onions, well crumbled, the ground spices, 750 ml/1¼ pints water and 1¾ teaspoons salt. Stir well. Put the lamb shanks back into the pan, spoon some sauce over them, and bring to the boil. Cover well, first with foil, crimping the edges, then with the lid, and bake slowly in the oven for 3 hours, turning the shanks over every 30 minutes.

Remove the pan from the oven and uncover. Spoon out as much of the oil floating at the top as possible, and taste for salt. Mix the flour slowly with 4 tablespoons of water and pour this into the pan to thicken the sauce. Stir over a low heat for 5–6 minutes.

The remaining fried onions, ginger shreds, chillies, coriander and lemon should be served on the side for diners to sprinkle on as much as they like.

Masroor Ahmed's

Moghlai Lamb with Spinach (Paalag Gosht)

INDIA

This is the classic Moghul recipe for lamb with spinach. The only new ingredient that has been added over the centuries is probably cayenne pepper. The dish is also known as *saag gosht*. 'Saag' could mean any green, whereas 'paalag' is very specifically spinach.

The spinach needs to be cut fairly small. To do this, hold a handful at a time in a tight wad and slice, crossways, into fine strips.

Serve with Indian breads (as shown opposite), or with rice, and a yoghurt dish.

SERVES *4*

560 g/1¼ lb boneless lamb shoulder, cut into 2.5-cm/1-inch cubes
4 teaspoons ginger, peeled and finely grated
7 cloves garlic, peeled and crushed to a pulp
2 tablespoons ground coriander
5 tablespoons corn or peanut oil
140 g/5 oz onions, peeled and sliced into very fine half-rings
½ teaspoon ground turmeric
¾–1½ teaspoons cayenne pepper
1 teaspoon salt
4 tablespoons natural yoghurt
450 g/1 lb fresh spinach, washed and cut into fine ribbons (see above)

Put the meat in a bowl, add the ginger, garlic and coriander, mix well and set aside for 30 minutes.

Pour the oil into a wide, non-stick, lidded pan and set over a medium heat. When hot, stir in the onions, and fry them, turning the heat down as needed, until they are golden and crisp. Remove the onions with a slotted spoon and spread them out on kitchen paper, leaving as much of the oil behind as possible. Reduce the heat to medium, and put in all the meat, together with its marinade. Add the turmeric, cayenne and salt, and stir for a minute. Cover and cook for 10 minutes, removing the lid occasionally to stir the contents. Remove the lid and add 1 tablespoon of the yoghurt. Stir and cook until the yoghurt is absorbed. Add the remainder of the yoghurt in this way, a tablespoon at a time. Then stir in the spinach. Chop the fried onions and add these as well. Continue to stir until the spinach has wilted. Then cover the pan and cook on a very low heat for about 50 minutes or until the meat is tender, lifting the lid to stir now and then. If the liquid seems to have dried up completely, add a few tablespoons of water at a time and cover again. The spinach should cling to the meat.

Lamb 'Kari' with a Sauce of Ground Nuts — INDIA

The Bohris are an ancient Gujarati community in India that converted to Islam in the 11th century. This dish is one of their specialities. My sister is married to one of the clan, so I come by this recipe in a comforting, familial way.

In Gujarati cities, grocers sell a freshly ground *kari* spice-mix made with watermelon seeds, melon seeds, cashews, peanuts, charoli nuts (rather like hazel nuts), cumin seeds, peppercorns, coriander seeds, chillies and star anise. The last is interesting. Western India always had a flourishing trade with China. The Bohris use star anise freely and, further down the same west coast, Sichuan peppercorns are frequently used when cooking oily fish such as sardines. Spices travel in all directions!

As we cannot get the *kari* spice mix, we must make our own. It can all be done easily in a coffee grinder.

SERVES *4*

FOR THE KARI SPICE MIX

1 teaspoon whole cumin seeds
1 teaspoon whole coriander seeds
2½-cm/1-inch stick of cinnamon, crumbled
6 dried, hot red chillies, crumbled
2 whole star anise, broken up
3 whole cloves
1 teaspoon whole black peppercorns
2 tablespoons raw cashews, broken up
1½ tablespoons roasted peanuts
1½ tablespoons charoli nuts or more peanuts
1½ tablespoons peeled watermelon seeds or more raw cashews
1½ tablespoons roasted chana dal (see page 335) or chickpea flour stirred for a minute in a hot cast-iron frying pan until it is a shade darker

FOR THE LAMB KARI

4 tablespoons corn or peanut oil
1 teaspoon whole cumin seeds
a medium stick of cinnamon
about 20 fresh curry leaves, if available
210 g/7 ½ oz onions, peeled and sliced into fine half-rings
2 teaspoons fresh ginger, peeled and finely grated
6 cloves garlic, peeled and crushed to a pulp
3–4 fresh, hot green chillies, finely chopped
450 g/1 lb boneless lamb shoulder, cut into 2½-cm/1-inch cubes
1 teaspoon salt
340 g/12 oz tomatoes, grated
400-ml/14-fl oz can coconut milk, well-shaken
3 tablespoons lemon juice
2–3 tablespoons fresh coriander, chopped

Grind all the ingredients for the spice mix in a clean coffee grinder or other spice grinder. You will need to do this in stages. Empty the mix into a bowl, and slowly add 600 ml/1 pint water, stirring as you go. Set aside.

Pour the oil into a large, preferably non-stick, lidded pan and set over a medium-high heat. When hot, add the whole cumin seeds, cinnamon stick and, a few seconds later, the curry leaves. Quickly stir in the onions, and fry them for 6–7 minutes or until they turn brown at the edges. Add the ginger and garlic, and stir a few times. Add the chillies, stirring once. Put in the meat and cover. Reduce the heat to medium-low and cook for 10 minutes, lifting the lid now and then to stir. Remove the lid. Stir the spice mixture in the bowl, and pour it in. Add the salt and tomatoes, stir, and bring to a simmer. Cover, reduce the heat to low, and cook for an hour or until the meat is tender. Then add the coconut milk, lemon juice and coriander. Stir to mix, and taste for a balance of seasonings, adding more salt, if needed. If the sauce is too thick, you may thin it with a little water.

Masroor Ahmed's

Hyderabadi Lamb with Tomatoes (Timatar Gosht) INDIA

A light, simple dish that may be eaten with Indian breads or rice, but is also wonderful with all kinds of pasta, Asian or Italian.

SERVES 4

560 g/1¼ lb boneless lamb shoulder, cut into 2½-cm/1-inch cubes
1 tablespoon fresh ginger, peeled and finely grated
6 cloves garlic, peeled and crushed to a pulp
1½ teaspoons ground cumin
½ teaspoon ground turmeric
1¼ teaspoons salt
3 tablespoons corn or peanut oil
210 g/7½ oz onion, peeled and finely chopped
450 g/1 lb fresh tomatoes, peeled, finely chopped and then crushed
3–6 fresh, hot green chillies, chopped
10–15 fresh curry leaves, if available (use fresh basil leaves as an interesting substitute)
2–3 tablespoons chopped fresh coriander

Put the meat in a bowl. Add the ginger, garlic, cumin, turmeric and 1 teaspoon of the salt. Mix well and set aside for 30 minutes. Pour the oil into a wide, non-stick, lidded pan and set over a medium-high heat. When hot, stir in the onions and fry them until the pieces turn brown at the edges.

Add the meat, together with its marinade. Stir and fry for 1 minute. Cover, reduce the heat to medium-low, and cook for 8–10 minutes, removing the lid now and then to stir the contents until the meat is lightly browned. Stir in the tomatoes, the remaining salt, the chillies, curry leaves and coriander, and bring to a simmer. Cover, reduce the heat to very low, and cook gently, stirring occasionally, for about 50 minutes or until the meat is tender.

Lamb in a 'Karhi' Sauce (Karhi Gosht)

INDIA

Karhi is one of the glories of India. It is really a soupy sauce made with chickpea flour and yoghurt. If the yoghurt is old and sour, so much the better. Sometimes *karhi* has dumplings in it (as in the Delhi-style *karhi*), sometimes it has vegetables in it (as in Sindhi *karhi* from western India) and here, in this desert dish from Rajasthan, it has been transformed into a wonderful sauce for meat. I love it with plain rice but you could also serve it with an Indian flatbread.

SERVES 4–6

- 2 tablespoons chickpea flour
- 250 ml/8 fl oz natural yoghurt, the sourer the better
- ¼ teaspoon whole cumin seeds
- ¼ teaspoon whole *kalonji* (nigella)
- ¼ teaspoon whole fenugreek seeds
- ¼ teaspoon whole fennel seeds
- 4 tablespoons corn, peanut or olive oil
- ¼ teaspoon whole brown mustard seeds
- 140 g/5 oz onions, peeled and finely chopped
- 2 teaspoons fresh ginger, peeled and finely chopped
- 4 cloves garlic, peeled and crushed to a pulp
- 675 g/1½ lb boneless lamb, cut into 2½-cm/1-inch cubes
- 1 teaspoon ground cumin
- ½ teaspoon ground turmeric
- ½ teaspoon cayenne pepper
- 1¼–1½ teaspoons salt
- a handful of fresh curry leaves, if available
- 4–5 fresh, hot green chillies, either bird's eye or the cayenne variety

Put the chickpea flour in a bowl. Slowly add 475 ml/16 fl oz water, mixing as you go. Whisk in the yoghurt.

Combine the cumin seeds, *kalonji*, fenugreek and fennel in a small dish.

Pour the oil into a wide, preferably non-stick, lidded pan and set it over a medium-high heat. When hot, add the mustard seeds. As soon as they pop, which will be within a matter of seconds, add the cumin seeds, *kalonji*, fenugreek and fennel seeds. A second later, add the onions, and cook, stirring, for 4–5 minutes, until they turn brown at the edges. Then add the ginger and garlic and stir for a minute. Put in the meat, ground cumin, turmeric, cayenne and salt, and stir for a minute. Cover, reduce the heat to medium-low, and cook for 10 minutes, lifting the lid now and then to stir. Stir the yoghurt mixture and add it to the meat. Stir and bring to the boil, then cover, reduce the heat to low, and cook for about 55 minutes.

Crush the curry leaves lightly with your fingers and throw them into the pot. Throw in the whole chillies as well. Cover and simmer gently for another 5 minutes or until the meat is tender.

THE STORY OF CURRIED PAN ROLLS

This dish, along with Mulligatawny Soup (see page 240), has to take top place amongst the homely, deeply satisfying, soul foods of the mixed-race Anglo-Indian community in India. A pan roll is a crêpe (pancake) that is filled, rolled shut, breaded and shallow-fried. It is served with a simple onion-tomato-garlic sauce. The dish, like its creators, has a mixed ancestry. While the crêpe is European, the filling is a simplified Indian *keema* – spiced, minced lamb.

Over the course of the 20th century, pan rolls quietly became an Indian classic, part of the repertoire of the more versatile cooks hired in upper-middle-class homes. They were certainly served in our home when I was a child. I emailed my older sister a few days ago to ask if she remembered them. She did, with a passion, and said that her cook still makes them. I recalled them being served with tomato ketchup, which my mother always made at home with our over-abundant tomatoes, but my sister is sure that the pan rolls were served with the sauce you will find in this recipe.

There are many versions of the *keema* stuffing. I am offering one overleaf that is partly based on my sister's recipe and partly on my own memory of pan rolls eaten in the homes of childhood Anglo-Indian friends.

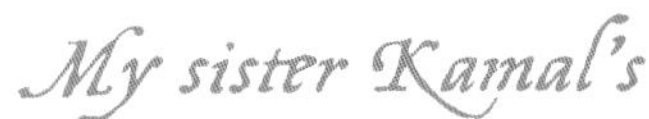

Anglo-Indian Curried Pan Rolls

INDIA

This recipe has several parts to it. You can easily make the *keema* and sauce a day in advance. If you like, even the crêpes may be made days in advance and frozen flat, layered between sheets of greaseproof paper. They need to thaw out completely before you fold them. The pan rolls may be breaded a few hours before eating, covered and refrigerated. The final frying takes just a few minutes.

A confession: try as I might, I could not work out a recipe where the number of crêpes fit the amount of *keema* exactly without going into ridiculous fractions. You will have two crêpes left over. Either freeze them for later use or do as I do: butter them, sprinkle with some sugar and lemon juice, fold them, and just eat them up!

MAKES 8, SERVES 4

FOR THE KEEMA

3 tablespoons corn or peanut oil
5 whole cloves
¼ teaspoon whole peppercorns
¼ teaspoon whole cumin seeds
1 medium stick cinnamon
2 whole, large black cardamom pods
2 bay leaves
2 medium onions, about 285 g/10 oz, peeled and chopped
340 g/12 oz tomatoes, peeled and chopped
2 teaspoons hot curry powder
450 g/1 lb minced lamb
¾ teaspoon salt

FOR THE TOMATO SAUCE

2 tablespoons corn or peanut oil
140 g/5 oz onions, peeled and chopped
3 medium cloves garlic, peeled and finely chopped
340 g/12 oz tomatoes, peeled and chopped
½ teaspoon salt

FOR THE CRÊPE BATTER

2 eggs
250 ml/8 fl oz milk or, for a lighter crèpe, 200 ml/6 fl oz milk mixed with 50 ml/2 fl oz water
½ teaspoon salt
190 g/6 3/4 oz unbleached plain flour
30 g/1 oz unsalted butter, melted

FOR MAKING THE CRÊPES

30 g/1 oz unsalted butter

FOR THE FINAL BREADING AND FRYING

2 eggs
salt and pepper
115 g/4 oz dry, unflavoured breadcrumbs
corn or peanut oil for shallow frying

Make the keema. Pour the oil into a large, preferably non-stick, lidded pan set over a medium-high heat. When the oil is hot, put in the cloves, peppercorns, cumin seeds, cinnamon, cardamom and bay leaves. Allow the bay leaves to darken a shade, then add the onions. Fry, stirring, until the onions have browned slightly. Add the tomatoes, and continue to fry, stirring, until the tomatoes turn to a paste. Put in the curry powder and stir for a minute. Add the lamb and stir it about, breaking up all the lumps with the back of a wooden spoon until it looks evenly grey, then add 250 ml/8 fl oz water and the salt. Stir and bring to the boil. Cover and let the keema cook for 30 minutes. Remove the lid, increase the heat, and boil away all the liquid. Turn off the heat. Put the pan on a counter where you can leave it tilted for 30 minutes. Then spoon out all the extra oil. Pick out the whole spices and discard them.

Make the tomato sauce. Pour the oil into a medium-sized, lidded pan set over a medium-high heat. When the oil is hot, stir in the onion. Allow to cook for a minute, then reduce the heat to medium. Fry the onions until they soften and turn translucent, turning the heat down as needed. Do not let them brown. Add the garlic and fry for a minute on a low heat. Add the tomatoes and salt. Stir and bring to a simmer on a medium-high heat. Cover, reduce the heat to low, and cook gently for about 20 minutes or until the tomatoes have thickened into a sauce.

Make the crêpe batter. Break the eggs into a blender. Add all the remaining ingredients and blend, pushing down with a rubber spatula when needed, until smooth. Set the batter aside for at least 30 minutes.

Make the crêpes. Rub an 20-cm/8-inch non-stick pan generously with butter and set on a medium heat. When hot, pour in a 4 tablespoon-measure of batter. Lift up the pan and quickly tilt it in all directions until the batter flows to the edges. Cook one side until it is lightly browned, and the edges can be lifted, about 1 1/2 minutes or less. Turn the crêpe over with a spatula and cook the second side for 30–40 seconds. Lift the crêpe out and put it on a large plate. Cover with a sheet of greaseproof paper. Repeat until all the batter has been used, rubbing the frying pan very lightly with butter each time. Make sure to put a sheet of greaseproof paper between each crêpe. When all are made, cover the lot with an upturned plate.

Assemble the pan rolls. Spread a crêpe in front of you. Divide the keema into eight portions. Put one portion on the crêpe about 4 cm/1 1/2 inches from the edge nearest you. Spread this keema out to form a 9 x 4 cm/3 1/2 x 1 1/2 inch rectangle. Fold the edge nearest you over the keema. Now fold over the edges to the right and left of you. Fold the crêpe over and over the keema until you have a neat, enclosed, rectangular package. Make all the pan rolls this way.

Bread and fry the pan rolls. Break the eggs into a wide soup plate and beat them. Season lightly with salt and pepper. Put the breadcrumbs in another wide soup plate. Dip the pan rolls first into the eggs, making sure you cover the sides, and then into the crumbs so they are thoroughly coated. Set aside, covered lightly, for several hours, if you like.

Pour oil into a large frying pan to a depth of about 3 mm/1/8 inch and set on a medium heat. When the oil is hot, put in as many pan rolls as the frying pan will hold easily and cook for about 2–3 minutes per side or until golden-red. Lay on a dish lined with kitchen paper. Make all the pan rolls this way and serve hot with some heated tomato sauce on the side.

Adapted from Richard Terry's Indian Cookery, 1861

The Oriental Club's Mid-19th-Century 'Mutton Curry' UK

Chef Terry used butter and did his main cooking in an oven over three hours. Our meat is much more tender today, so I cooked it on top of the stove for about an hour. Also, I used oil, but you could just as easily use butter.

This curry is very good, though nothing that an Indian would recognise.

SERVES 4

4 tablespoons corn, peanut or olive oil, or 60 g/2 oz butter
200 g/7 oz onions, peeled and finely chopped
2 tablespoons 19th-Century British Curry Powder (see page 329)
1 tablespoon 19th-Century British Curry Paste (see page 330)
675 g/1½ lb boned lamb, cut into 2½-cm/1-inch cubes
¾–1 teaspoon salt

Put the oil, or butter, in a heavy, wide, lidded pan and set it over a medium-high heat. When the oil is hot, stir in the onions and fry them until they are lightly browned. Add the curry powder and curry paste. Stir a few times, then add the meat and the smaller quantity of salt. Stir and fry for a minute. Cover and reduce the heat to low. Cook for 10 minutes, lifting the lid now and then to stir. Add 600 ml/1 pint water and increase the heat to bring it to the boil. Cover, reduce the heat to low, and cook very gently for about an hour or until the meat is tender and the sauce is thick. If the sauce remains thin, raise the heat and boil it off. Before serving, taste for salt, adding more if needed.

THE BRITISH 19TH-CENTURY CURRY

I have always wanted to know what a 19th-century British curry tasted like. I knew from books that it was made with curry powder, and that it was served with chutney and rice, but the exact taste was a mystery. I could hardly wrap my tongue around it.

The only way to find out was to unearth a good, authentic recipe. There are many recipes available in libraries. The better ones call for both curry powder and curry paste. But what on earth was curry paste?

Some of the more authentic curries at the time seem to have been prepared at London's Oriental Club in Hanover Square, under the guidance of its *chef de cuisine*, Richard Terry, who claimed to have produced his recipes from 'Native Cooks'. The club catered to officers in the service of the East India Company, retirees and those on furlough, and Mutton Curry was said to be 'highly approved of by members of this club' (for my version of the recipe, see above). Tamarind and other Indian groceries were sold then at Paynes Oriental Warehouse, 328 Regent Street, and the Oriental Depot, 38 Leicester Square.

I had been told by friends at London's MoCHA, the new Museum of Culinary History and Alimentation, which I have supported since its inception, that a slim volume of curry recipes had been written by Richard Terry and published around 1861. This book, called *Indian Cookery*, had been reprinted but the volumes were hard to find. I approached Clarissa Dickson Wright, known to most of us as one of television's Fat Ladies but, more relevantly to me, also as the owner of a superb cookery bookshop in Edinburgh. She did have a copy of the book, which she directly posted to me.

Once I decided that a recipe from chef Richard Terry was the one to pursue, I first made his curry powder (see page 329), then I hunted for a curry paste recipe, which he did not have. He obviously just bought his paste ready-made from the Oriental Depot. (See page 330 for the recipe I found.) Finally, before I embarked on the curry itself, I made what he called his Tomata and Apple Chutnee (see page 302). The meal would thus be complete.

Hyderabadi Minced Lamb with Orange (Narangi Keema)

INDIA

Moghul emperors, with their capitals in northern cities such as Agra and then Delhi, had most of India under control by the 18th century. But they could hardly administer every far-flung region themselves. They appointed governors to do this work but the governors often chafed under their yoke and threatened independence. Such was the case in the southern region of Hyderabad where the court, with much time and leisure on its hands, also developed a unique cuisine. Its base was Moghul and Muslim, not unlike the 'parent' court in Delhi. To it were added south Indian ingredients used by local Hindus, such as curry leaves, mustard seeds and tamarind. It was also the custom of Hyderabadi rulers to take Turkish and Persian wives, who were considered great beauties, partly because of their light skin. In their bridal palaquins came their own culinary preferences, like sesame seed paste and the use of oranges and orange rind.

This is a most unusual dish. I had never eaten anything like it before. And I came upon it most serendipitously. I was filming in Bombay with the wonderful Danish actor Stellan Skarsgard, the Indian actor Naseeruddin Shah (who appears in *Monsoon Wedding*) and my daughter Sakina. The director of the film came from Hyderabad, and one evening we were at his apartment when a lady, I think it was his sister, began talking about a dish called *Narangi Keema*. I was entranced by the name, Minced Lamb with Orange. What could it be? Why had I never heard of it before? I asked for the recipe. She hastily scribbled a few lines on a scrap of beige paper.

Fifteen years later, I still have that scrap of paper (I file everything) and here is the recipe. It is amazingly good.

SERVES *4–6*

FOR PREPARING THE ORANGE RIND

1 large orange

1 teaspoon ground turmeric

1 teaspoon salt

FOR PREPARING THE MINCED LAMB

3 tablespoons corn or peanut oil

2 medium onions, peeled and sliced into fine half-rings

2 teaspoons ground cumin

1 tablespoon ground coriander

4 cloves garlic, peeled and crushed to a pulp

FOR PREPARING THE MINCED LAMB (cont.)

2 tablespoons fresh ginger, peeled and finely grated
4 tablespoons natural yoghurt
900 g/2 lb minced lamb
½ teaspoon ground turmeric
½ teaspoon ground cayenne pepper
250 ml/8 fl oz fresh orange juice
1½ teaspoons salt

TO SERVE

1–3 fresh, hot green chillies, sliced into very fine rounds
30 g/1 oz fresh coriander leaves, coarsely chopped
30 g/1 oz fresh mint leaves, finely chopped
1 teaspoon garam masala (see page 327)

Peel off the orange rind, making sure to leave the white pith behind. Cut the rind into very fine, 2½-cm/1-inch long julienne strips. Combine the turmeric and salt with 1½ litres/2½ pints water in a pan and bring to the boil. Pour half into a measuring jug and reserve. Add the rind to the boiling liquid in the pan and boil rapidly for 1 minute. Empty the pan through a sieve set over a sink. Pour the reserved turmeric water back into the pan and bring back to the boil. Put the rind back into the pan and boil again for a minute, then again strain through the sieve set over the sink. Rinse the rind under cold running water and set aside.

Pour the oil into a large, non-stick, lidded pan set over a medium-high heat. When the oil is hot, stir in the onions and fry for 6–7 minutes or until reddish-brown. Add the cumin and coriander and stir for 30 seconds. Add the ginger and garlic. Stir and fry for a minute. Add the yoghurt, a tablespoon at a time, and stir it in, making sure it is absorbed before adding more. Put in the meat, turmeric and cayenne pepper. Stir and cook for about 5 minutes, breaking up all the lumps in the meat. Add the orange juice, orange rind and salt. Stir and bring to a simmer. Cover, reduce the heat to low, and simmer gently for 40 minutes. Add the chillies, coriander, mint and *garam masala*. Stir to mix. Cover and continue to cook gently for a further 10 minutes.

Marina Fareed's

Meatballs in a Curry Sauce (Kofta Curry)

PAKISTAN

There are hundreds of recipes for meatballs in South Asia. Here is a delicious Pakistani version. You may make it with minced beef or lamb. The secret to its success lies in spicing the meat and letting it marinate overnight in the refrigerator. Also, I like to add beef stock to the sauce for added richness. You may, of course, use water instead. If your beef stock is salted, taste the sauce before adding any salt at all.

It is easier to form meatballs with wet hands. I make two balls at a time, one in each hand. The work goes faster and the balls are more evenly sized.

SERVES 6

FOR THE MEATBALLS

- 675 g/1½ lb minced beef or lamb
- 1 medium onion, very finely chopped
- 2 tablespoons ground coriander
- 1 tablespoon ground cumin
- 3 cloves garlic, peeled and crushed to a pulp
- 7½-cm/3-inch piece fresh ginger, peeled and finely grated
- 1 teaspoon cayenne pepper
- 4 tablespoons finely chopped coriander leaves
- 1 teaspoon salt
- 1 egg, lightly beaten
- freshly ground black pepper

FOR THE SAUCE

- 7½-cm/3-inch piece fresh ginger, peeled and chopped
- 5 cloves garlic, peeled and coarsely chopped
- 2 fresh, hot green chillies, coarsely sliced
- 4 tablespoons olive or rapeseed oil
- 2 medium onions, peeled and finely chopped
- 2 medium tomatoes, chopped
- 1 tablespoon tomato purée
- 1½ tablespoons ground coriander
- ¼ teaspoon ground turmeric
- ½–1 teaspoon cayenne pepper
- 1¼ teaspoons salt
- 1.2 litres/2 pints beef stock or water
- 2 sticks cinnamon, about 7½ cm/3 inches long
- 4 whole big, black cardamom pods
- 2 bay leaves
- 5 whole cloves
- 4 whole cardamom pods
- 10 black peppercorns

Put the meat in a bowl, add all the remaining ingredients for the meatballs, mix well and form 4-cm/1½-inch meatballs. Return the meatballs to the bowl or place on a large plate. Cover with cling film and refrigerate overnight.

Put the ginger, garlic, green chillies and 4 tablespoons water in a blender. Blend until you have a smooth paste.

Pour the oil into a wide, preferably non-stick, lidded pan. Set over a medium-high heat. When the oil is hot, put in the onions. Stir and fry them for about 5 minutes or until they turn brown at the edges. Add the paste from the blender. Stir and fry it for a minute. Put 2 tablespoons of water in the blender, swish it around and pour this, too, into the pan. Also put in the tomatoes, and fry them, stirring at the same time, until they begin to give up their liquid and the sauce starts to thicken. Add the tomato purée and stir for a minute. The tomatoes should begin to brown. Add the coriander, turmeric, cayenne and salt. Stir for a minute. Add the stock or water and bring to the boil.

Meanwhile, tie up the cinnamon, black cardamom, bay leaves, cloves, cardamom and peppercorns in a piece of muslin and drop it into the sauce. Once the sauce is boiling, cover it, reduce the heat and let it simmer gently for 20 minutes. Taste for salt at this stage. Remove the lid and gently drop in all the meatballs. Shake the pan, spoon the sauce over the meatballs, and bring to a simmer. Cover and simmer gently for 40 minutes, turning the meatballs gently now and then. If the sauce thickens too much and starts to catch, thin it slightly with either stock or water. Discard the muslin bag, squeezing all the juices back into the pan, before serving.

From the Grand Hyatt Erawan, Bangkok

Pork or Beef in Penang Chilli Sauce (Penang Moo) THAILAND

With its Muslim Malay influence this wonderful curry is still very hot. It is best enjoyed with plain rice.

SERVES 4

400-ml/14-fl oz can coconut milk, left undisturbed for 3 hours
2 tablespoons corn or peanut oil
½ quantity Thai-Style Penang Chilli paste (see page 319)
8 fresh kaffir lime leaves
450 g/1 lb boneless loin of pork, or well-marbled beef sirloin cut into 5 cm x 2½ cm x 3 mm/2 x 1 x ⅛ inch slices
2 tablespoons fish sauce (*nam pla*)
1 teaspoon palm sugar, or light brown sugar
1 fresh red chilli, cut, crossways, into fine rounds, for garnish

After 3 hours, the coconut cream will have risen to the top of the can. Open it carefully, take out 4 tablespoons of the cream, and put them into a wide, non-stick pan or non-stick wok set over a medium-high heat. Add the oil, the chilli paste and six of the lime leaves. Stir and fry until the chilli paste is golden. The paste should emit a pleasing 'fried' aroma and the oil should separate from it. Now add the meat. Stir and cook for a minute. Add the fish sauce, palm sugar, the remaining coconut milk (stir the can first) and 120 ml/4 fl oz water. Stir to mix and bring to a simmer. Cook on a low heat for 15–20 minutes or until the sauce is thick and the meat is cooked.

Cut the remaining lime leaves in half lengthways, removing the central rib. Now cut these, crossways, into very fine strips. Ladle the curry into a warm serving dish and garnish with the sliced red chilli and the lime-leaf strips.

Chinese Red-Cooked Pork with Curry — HONG KONG

'Red-cooked' dishes are really stews made with meats such as pork, duck or goose, soy sauce, rice wine, sugar, ginger, spring onions and spices such as star anise and cinnamon. By the time the meat is tender, the sauces are glazed and shiny. Curry powder is used in many Hong Kong dishes, from baked savoury pies and turnip cakes to stuffed buns and stir-fries. Here, it is used in a traditional red-cooked dish to great effect.

If you wish to make this dish ahead of time, do not reduce the sauce. The reduction process takes only a few minutes and is best done just before you eat. Meanwhile, it helps to keep the meat moist. This is best served with plain rice.

SERVES 4

3 tablespoons corn or peanut oil
560 g/1¼ lb boneless pork shoulder, cut into 2½-cm/1-inch cubes
3 slices of fresh ginger
3 cloves garlic, peeled and very lightly mashed but left whole
4–5 spring onions, sliced thinly crossways
2 tablespoons finely chopped Chinese celery or the leafy tops of ordinary celery
2 teaspoons curry powder
2 tablespoons *tamari*
1 tablespoon sugar
3 tablespoons Chinese rice wine

Pour the oil into a large, non-stick, lidded pan and set on a medium heat. When the oil is hot, add the pork, ginger and garlic and stir a few times. Cover and cook for 10 minutes, lifting the lid now and then to stir the contents. The pork pieces should brown lightly. Remove the lid. Add the spring onions, celery and curry powder. Stir for a minute. Add the *tamari*, 250 ml/8 fl oz water, the sugar and the rice wine. Stir and bring to the boil. Cover again with the lid, reduce the heat to low, and cook for 50–60 minutes or until the meat is tender. Just before serving, uncover, increase the heat to medium-high, and reduce the sauce until it is thick and glazed. Stir as you do this.

Goan Pork with Potatoes

INDIA

You may well call this a simple *vindaloo*. (For more on *vindaloos*, see Duck Vindaloo, page 108.) It has the pork, the garlic, the chillies and the vinegar, but all in gentle proportions. It is a superb dish that is best enjoyed with plain rice.

I like to use small red potatoes here, the larger of which may be halved, though any waxy potato will do.

SERVES 4

2 teaspoons whole brown mustard seeds
1 teaspoon whole cumin seeds
2 teaspoons whole coriander seeds
3 whole cloves
140 g/5 oz onions, peeled and chopped
5 cloves garlic, peeled and chopped
2½-cm/1-inch piece fresh ginger, peeled and chopped
2 tablespoons cider vinegar
¾–1 teaspoon cayenne pepper
2 teaspoons bright red paprika
salt
½ teaspoon ground turmeric
½ teaspoon freshly ground black pepper
560 g/1¼ lb boneless pork shoulder, cut into 2½ cm/1-inch cubes
3 tablespoons corn or peanut oil
340 g/12 oz waxy red potatoes, peeled and cut into 2½-cm/1-inch chunks
½ teaspoon sugar

Put half the mustard seeds and all the cumin seeds, coriander seeds and cloves in a clean coffee grinder or other spice grinder and grind as finely as possible.

Put this spice mixture, as well as the onion, garlic, ginger, vinegar, cayenne pepper, paprika and 3 tablespoons water into a blender. Blend until smooth.

Rub 1 1/4 teaspoons of salt, plus all the turmeric, black pepper and 2 tablespoons of the spice paste from the blender all over the pork pieces. Put in a plastic bag and refrigerate for at least 30 minutes, longer if desired.

Pour the oil into a large, heavy, non-stick, lidded pan and set over a medium-high heat. When the oil is hot, add the remaining mustard seeds. As soon as they pop, which will be in a matter of seconds, put in the remaining spice paste. Stir and fry for 5–6 minutes or until the paste is lightly browned. Put in the pork, together with its marinade. Stir for a minute. Cover and reduce the heat to medium. Let the meat cook for about 10 minutes, lifting the lid now and then to stir. The meat should get lightly browned. Add 750 ml/1 1/4 pints water, the potatoes, 1/2 teaspoon salt and the sugar. Stir and bring to the boil. Cover, reduce the heat to low, and cook very gently for 50–60 minutes or until the meat is tender.

Pork in a Mustard Spice Mix

INDIA

The flavour in this curry sauce comes from both the ground mustard in the spice mix and the whole mustard seeds that have been popped in hot oil. I love to serve this with dark, leafy greens and rice.

SERVES 4

560 g/1¼ lb boneless pork shoulder, cut into 2½-cm/1-inch cubes
1 tablespoon fresh ginger, peeled and finely grated
6 cloves garlic, peeled and crushed to a pulp
1¼ teaspoons salt
¼ teaspoon ground turmeric
3 tablespoons corn or peanut oil
½ teaspoon whole mustard seeds
15–20 fresh curry leaves, if available
5 teaspoons My Mustard Spice Mix (see page 326)
255 g/9 oz tomatoes, peeled and finely chopped

Rub the pork cubes well with the ginger, garlic, salt and turmeric. Cover and set aside for 30 minutes, or up to 8 hours if desired, refrigerating if necessary.

Pour the oil into a large, preferably non-stick, lidded pan and set over a medium-high heat. When the oil is hot, put in the whole mustard seeds. As soon as they pop, which will be in a matter of seconds, add the curry leaves and, a second later, the pork, together with its marinade. Stir for a minute. Cover, reduce the heat to medium, and let the meat cook for the next 5 minutes, stirring now and then and replacing the cover each time. The meat should brown lightly. Add the mustard spice mix and stir for a minute. Add the tomatoes and cook, stirring, until the tomatoes turn pulpy, about 2 minutes. Now add 250 ml/8 fl oz water, stir, and bring to the boil. Cover, reduce the heat, and cook very gently, lifting the lid occasionally to stir the contents, for 50–60 minutes or until the meat is tender. Check for salt before serving.

Stir-Fried Pork in a Chinese Curry Sauce

HONG KONG

British-style curry sauces spread as far east as Shanghai and Hong Kong but the Chinese, instead of using cream and butter, which were not part of their diet, turned to a new, 20th-century staple in East Asia, canned evaporated milk. The Thais in Bangkok had begun to pour it into their coffee. The Indians in Bengal, instead of stirring milk for hours, used it to make quick, thickened yoghurts. In the Philippines, it was added to all manner of desserts, including *leche flan*. In Shanghai and Hong Kong, however, it went into curry sauces, which became equally popular with the British and with the Chinese. Serve with rice.

SERVES 4

FOR MARINATING THE PORK

- 450 g/1 lb boneless pork loin, cut into thin rectangles about 2½ cm x 5 cm x 3 mm/ 1 x 2 x ⅛ inches
- ½ teaspoon salt
- 1 tablespoon Chinese rice wine or dry sherry
- 1 egg white, lightly beaten
- 2 teaspoons cornflour
- 2 teaspoons oriental sesame oil

FOR COOKING THE PORK

- 3 tablespoons corn or peanut oil
- 1 tablespoon peeled and very finely chopped shallots
- 5 cloves garlic, peeled and very finely chopped
- 1 whole, dried, hot red chilli, crumbled
- 2 tablespoons curry powder mixed with 4 teaspoons oriental sesame oil
- 120 ml/4 fl oz chicken stock
- 4 tablespoons canned evaporated milk
- 1 teaspoon sugar
- 1 teaspoon salt
- 1 teaspoon cornflour mixed with 4 tablespoons chicken stock

Mix the pork with all the marinade ingredients. Cover and refrigerate for 30 minutes, or up to 8 hours if desired.

Just before you want to eat, pour the oil into a wok or large frying pan set over a medium-high heat. When the oil is hot, add the shallots, garlic and chilli. Stir vigorously a few times. Put in the pork. Stir for 2 minutes. Put in the curry paste. Stir once or twice. Pour in the stock and stir once. Add the evaporated milk, sugar and salt. Stir a few times. Reduce the heat to low, add the cornflour mixture, and continue to stir on a low heat until the sauce thickens. Serve immediately.

Vietnamese Pork with Lemon Grass

VIETNAM

I had this dish at a restaurant in Ho Chi Minh City. As I watched its preparation, I was surprised when the chef pulled out a box of curry powder for part of the seasoning. It was not the curry powder itself that drew my curiosity. I had already known that the Indian traders who came for business as early as the 1st century AD had left an impression on southern Vietnamese cuisine. It was the aroma of the curry powder . . . I could smell the curry leaves. When I looked inside the box, I saw them, dozens of dried leaves, lending their heady aroma to the ground spices. I had not previously seen curry leaves anywhere north of Malaysia.

Not much curry powder was used in the cooking, just enough to suggest the ancient mingling of peoples.

SERVES 4

- 450 g/1 lb boneless pork loin, cut into slices about 2½ cm/1 inch wide, 3 mm/⅛ inch thick and 5 cm/2 inches long
- 1 tablespoon Chinese light soy sauce
- 2 teaspoons fish sauce (*nuoc mam*)
- 1 teaspoon cornflour
- 1 stick fresh lemon grass, bottom knot removed, then sliced finely for about 15 cm/6 inches and these slices then chopped finely
- 3 tablespoons peeled and very finely chopped shallots or onions
- 2–3 fresh, hot green chillies, such as bird's eye, finely chopped
- freshly ground black pepper
- 1 teaspoon sugar
- 1 tablespoon corn, peanut or olive oil
- ½ teaspoon hot curry powder

FOR THE STIR-FRYING

- 3 tablespoon corn, peanut or olive oil
- 90 g/3 oz shallots or onions, peeled and thinly sliced
- 5 tablespoons coriander leaves

Put the meat slices in a bowl with the marinade ingredients, mix well, cover, and refrigerate for an hour, and up to 2 hours if desired.

Pour the oil into a large wok or frying pan and set over a medium-high heat. When the oil is hot, put in the shallots or onions. Stir and fry until the onions are slightly browned, about 2 minutes. Put in all the meat, together with its marinade, increase the heat to high, and fry, stirring continuously, until the meat is just cooked through. Garnish with the coriander leaves.

From the Grand Hyatt Erawan, Bangkok

Beef and Potato 'Mussaman' Curry (Mussaman Nua)

THAILAND

Use a dense, waxy variety of potatoes, not the crumbly kind. Boil them ahead of time and leave them to cool. Then peel and dice them before you start your cooking.

For the beef you may use well-marbled steak instead of beef skirt.

SERVES 4

- 400-ml/14-fl oz can of coconut milk, left undisturbed for 3 hours or more
- 4 tablespoons corn or peanut oil
- 85 g/2½ oz shallots, peeled and very thinly sliced
- 1 bay leaf
- 5 tablespoons Mussaman Curry Paste (see page 322)
- 450 g/1 lb beef skirt, first cut against the grain into long slices, about 2½ cm/1 inch wide and 3 mm/⅛ inch thick, and then into shorter 5-cm/2-inch long segments
- 1½ tablespoons fish sauce (*nam pla*), or to taste (if extra saltiness is required, you may add salt)
- 1 teaspoon thick tamarind paste (see page 345), or lemon juice
- 1 teaspoon palm sugar or brown sugar
- 2 smallish red potatoes, about 180 g/6 oz, boiled, cooled, peeled and cut into 2-cm/¾-inch dice and sprinkled lightly with salt

Carefully open the can of coconut milk and remove 4 tablespoons of the thick cream that will have risen to the top. Stir the remaining contents of the can well and set aside.

Pour the oil into a large, non-stick, lidded pan and set over a medium heat. When the oil is hot, add the shallots and stir them about. When they just start to turn brown at the edges, reduce the heat to medium-low. Continue to fry, stirring at the same time, and turning the heat down as needed, until the shallots are golden brown and crisp. Remove them with a slotted spoon and spread them out on a double layer of kitchen paper to crisp up further.

Add the thick coconut cream, the bay leaf and the Mussaman Curry Paste to the oil in the pan. Stir and fry until the oil separates and the paste is lightly browned. Add the beef and stir for a minute. Reduce the heat to low and add the fish sauce, tamarind, palm sugar, potatoes and 175 ml/6 fl oz water. Stir and bring to a simmer. Cover and simmer on a very low heat for 5 minutes or until the meat is just cooked. Add the reserved coconut milk and stir it in. Taste for a balance of flavours, adding anything you think is needed. Bring back to a simmer.

Sprinkle the fried shallots over the top before serving.

Red Beef Curry

SRI LANKA

The lovely red colour of this curry comes from rather a lot of chilli powder. I use a mix of cayenne pepper and paprika but you can change the proportions to suit yourself. Serve this either with plain rice or Jasmine Rice (see page 254). If you cannot find ground fennel, you can grind the seeds yourself in a clean coffee grinder or other spice grinder.

SERVES 4

- **450 g/1 lb stewing beef, cut into 2½-cm/1-inch pieces**
- **1 teaspoon ground coriander**
- **1 teaspoon ground cumin**
- **1 teaspoon ground fennel**
- **½–1 teaspoon cayenne pepper**
- **2 teaspoons bright red paprika**
- **freshly ground black pepper**
- **3 tablespoons corn or peanut oil**
- **1 medium stick cinnamon**
- **4 whole cardamom pods**
- **½ teaspoon fenugreek seeds**
- **4 tablespoons peeled and finely sliced shallots**
- **2 cloves garlic, peeled and cut into fine slivers**
- **2 thin slices of fresh ginger**
- **5-cm/2-inch piece of fresh or frozen pandanus leaf (*rampe, bai toey, daun paandaan*)**
- **10–15 fresh curry leaves, if available**
- **¾ teaspoon salt**
- **2 teaspoons lemon juice**
- **175 ml/6 fl oz canned coconut milk, from a well-shaken can**

Put the meat in a bowl. Add the ground coriander, cumin, fennel, cayenne pepper, paprika and lots of black pepper. Mix well to coat the beef and set aside for 15–20 minutes.

Pour the oil into a large, non-stick, lidded pan and set on a medium-high heat. When the oil is hot, add the cinnamon, cardamom, fenugreek, shallots, garlic, ginger, pandanus leaf and curry leaves. Stir for 2 minutes or until the onions have become translucent. Add the meat, and continue to stir for a further 2–3 minutes or until the meat is lightly browned. Add the salt, 350 ml/12 fl oz water and the lemon juice, and bring to the boil. Cover, reduce the heat to very low, and simmer gently for 1 hour and 20 minutes or until the meat is tender. If the water dries out, just add a little bit more. Lift the lid to stir once or twice during this period. Stir in the coconut milk and bring to a simmer. Taste for salt.

Beef, Pork or Lamb Curry with Fresh and Dried Coriander

SRI LANKA

Many Sri Lankan curries are gloriously aromatic. This one gets its mélange of heady aromas not only from the inclusion of fresh and dried coriander, but also from the use of pandanus leaves (known as *rampe* in Sri Lanka), which link the island's cuisine to South-East Asia, curry leaves, which link it to south India, cinnamon, which Sri Lanka produces in vast quantities, and cardamom. Pandanus leaves may be bought in frozen packets from Indian and South-East Asian grocers. In Thailand, they are known as *bai toey*.

SERVES 4

2 teaspoons whole brown mustard seeds
½ teaspoon whole peppercorns
3 tablespoons whole coriander seeds
2 cloves
60 g/2 oz chopped shallots
1-cm/½-inch piece of fresh ginger, peeled and chopped
3 medium cloves garlic, peeled and chopped
30 g/1 oz chopped fresh coriander
1–2 fresh, hot green chillies, sliced
3 tablespoons corn or peanut oil
1 medium stick cinnamon
2 whole cardamom pods
10–15 fresh curry leaves, if available
5-cm/2-inch length of fresh or frozen pandanus leaf (*rampe, bai toey, daun paandaan*)
450 g/1 lb stewing beef, pork or lamb, cut into 2½-cm/1-inch pieces
¼ teaspoon ground turmeric
1 teaspoon fresh lemon juice
¾–1 teaspoon salt
250 ml/8 fl oz coconut milk, from a well-shaken can

Put the mustard seeds, peppercorns, coriander seeds and cloves into a clean coffee grinder or other spice grinder. Grind as finely as possible.

Put the shallots, ginger, garlic, coriander and chillies into a blender along with 5 tablespoons of water. Blend, pushing down as many times as needed with a rubber spatula, until you have a smooth purée.

Pour the oil into a large, non-stick, lidded pan and set over a medium-high heat. When the oil is hot, add the cinnamon, cardamom, curry leaves and pandanus leaf. Stir for 5 seconds, then add the meat. Stir and fry until the meat is browned on all sides. Reduce the heat to medium and add the spice mixture from the coffee grinder. Stir for a minute. Now add the mixture from the blender. Stir and fry for 5 minutes. Add 600 ml/1 pint water, the turmeric, lemon juice and salt. Stir to mix and bring to a simmer. Cover and cook on a very low heat for about 1 hour 20 minutes for beef, 60–80 minutes for lamb and pork. Stir once or twice during this period. Add the coconut milk and heat through. Check for salt, adding a bit more if needed.

From the Tiffin Restaurant, Port of Spain

Curry Beef

TRINIDAD

As with other Trinidadian curries, this one has a little bit of India, a little bit of the Mediterranean, plus a little from the original Amerindians of the island.

You may make your own roasted and ground cumin seeds, *amchar masala* and curry powder, but you should know that West Indian shops sell all of them ready-made in packets and that they are generally very good.

SERVES 4

FOR THE MARINADE

6 tablespoons peeled and finely chopped onion
2 large cloves garlic, peeled and chopped
2 spring onions, with just the white and light green parts sliced into rings
2 tablespoons finely chopped parsley
2–3 tablespoons finely chopped culantro or fresh coriander
1 loosely packed tablespoon fresh thyme leaves, or ½ teaspoon dried
¼ congo pepper (scotch bonnet or habanero), chopped (handle with care), or 3 bird's eye chillies, chopped
½ teaspoon ground ginger
½ teaspoon salt
freshly ground black pepper
450 g/1 lb stewing beef, cut into 2 1/2-cm/1-inch pieces

FOR COOKING THE MEAT

3 tablespoons corn, peanut or olive oil
2–3 cloves garlic, peeled and crushed to a pulp
1 tablespoon hot curry powder
½ teaspoon salt
900 ml/1½ pints beef stock or water
½ teaspoon ground, roasted cumin seeds (see page 339)
1 teaspoon *amchar masala* (see page 324)

To make the marinade, put the onion, garlic, spring onions, parsley, culantro, thyme, congo pepper, ginger, salt, pepper and 2 tablespoons water into a blender. Blend to a smooth paste, pushing down with a rubber spatula when necessary. In a bowl, mix the meat well with the marinade. Cover and refrigerate for 30 minutes, or up to 3 hours.

Pour the oil and garlic into a wide, non-stick, lidded pan and set over a medium-high heat. As soon as the garlic starts to sizzle and brown, add the curry powder. Stir it for 10 seconds. Reduce the heat to medium, add the beef, together with its marinade, and stir for a minute. Cover, reduce the heat still further to medium-low, and cook for 10 minutes, lifting the lid to stir now and then. Now add the stock or water, the salt, cumin and amchar masala. Stir and bring to a simmer. Reduce the heat to low and cook, covered, for about 1 hour and 20 minutes or until the meat is tender. If the sauce is too thin, reduce it by uncovering and cooking over a medium-high heat, stirring frequently.

With great help from Elizabeth Andoh

Japanese-Style Beef Curry

JAPAN

Having spent a day in a Tokyo kitchen with every possible brand of roux and with different meats, I think I can make a Japanese-style curry without a trip to a Japanese supermarket. Here is my recipe.

SERVES 4

FOR MARINATING THE BEEF

450 g/1 lb beef skirt or well-marbled steak, cut crossways, with a knife held at a slight angle, into 3-mm/⅛-inch thick slices that can be cut further into slices about 2½ cm x 2 cm x 3 mm/1 x ¾ x ⅛ inch

4 tablespoons *tamari*

2 teaspoons sugar

1 tablespoon sake

1 tablespoon hot curry powder

2 teaspoons cornflour

1 teaspoon corn, peanut or olive oil

2 cloves garlic, peeled and crushed

1 teaspoon fresh ginger, peeled and very finely grated

FOR THE SAUCE

2 teaspoons cornflour

175 ml/6 fl oz beef stock

2 teaspoons *tamari*

1 teaspoon sugar

1 teaspoon sake

4 tablespoons whipping cream

FOR THE FINAL COOKING

3 tablespoons corn, peanut or olive oil

1 medium onion, about 140 g/5 oz, sliced into 3-mm/⅛-inch thick half-rings

2 medium carrots, each about 90 g/3 oz, peeled and cut at a diagonal into 3-mm/⅛-inch thick slices

To marinate the meat, place it in a bowl, add all the other ingredients, and mix well. Cover and set aside for 15 minutes, or up to 2 hours, refrigerating if necessary.

To make the sauce, mix together all the ingredients in the order listed. Set aside.

When ready to cook the curry, pour the oil into a large, non-stick, lidded pan and set over a medium-high heat. Add the onion and carrots. Stir and fry for about 4 minutes or until the onions are slightly translucent. Then add the meat, together with its marinade, and fry, continuing to stir, for a minute. Cover, reduce the heat to medium low, and cook for about 5 minutes, lifting the lid to stir the contents now and then. Take the pan off the heat. Stir the sauce and pour it into the pan. Stir and put the pan back on a medium-low heat. Cook for a minute, continuing to stir. Serve immediately.

THE JAPANESE LOVE OF CURRY

The rest of the world hardly knows this, but one of the most popular foods in Japan today is curry, or *curray* as they say here.

On my previous trips to this country, I had seen plastic models of curry-over-rice displayed in the windows of simple, homely restaurants, along with the sushi, sashimi, noodle dishes and grilled foods we associate with Japan. One year, a male guide-cum-translator in Kyoto had casually said that he loved to cook and that his favourite food was curry. He made his own, he proudly added. All this information had been deposited in my head but to no great effect until I started working on this book.

A fresh visit to Japan revealed the extent to which curry has permeated Japanese eating habits. Curry is as popular in Japan as hamburgers are in the United States, and is eaten by families, including children, at least once a week. It can be a flavouring in a noodle soup or it could be used to stuff steamed buns, but, mostly, it is eaten over Japanese rice with the accompaniment of special Japanese pickles designated for curries, known as *fukujinzuke*.

Curries may also be made at home and frequently are. All supermarkets sell the fixings. From the vegetable section you pick up a special packet containing onions, carrots and potatoes. It is marked 'for the purpose of making curry'. You then pick up the already-diced meat for the curry, and a packet of roux, which will provide the sauce, and finally some pickles.

It is the roux that makes Japanese curries different from all others in the world. Some believe that Indian curries came here via Shanghai, where there was a huge Indian population, and that the flour-thickened and slightly sweet sauce has links to Chinese cuisine. Others think that it is the beef stews (*nikujaga*) containing round onions, carrots and potatoes, introduced to Japan in the 19th century in order to make the population taller and more Western-sized, that are the true progenitors.

The roux, which comes in chocolate-like slabs, contains stocks, thickeners, fats and curry powder. It can also have coconut milk or evaporated milk to provide creaminess.

Shabiroon Eshak's

Goat Curry

GUYANA

Goat meat is sold by most halal butchers and all West Indian and Guyanese butchers. If you ask for curry goat meat, it will be an assortment from the legs, the ribs, the neck, plus some marrow bones, etc. The meat cubes always come with bone and have most flavour if cooked this way.

The wiri-wiri pepper is sold by West Indian grocers. It is small and looks like an orange-red cherry. If you cannot get it, use about an eighth of a fiery scotch bonnet/habanero pepper (without seeds).

You may use this recipe for chicken, lamb or beef, adjusting the cooking times as necessary. Beef will take about the same time, lamb about 60–70 minutes and chicken about 25–30 minutes in all.

SERVES 4

- 900 g/2 lb goat meat (bone-in), cut into cubes
- ½ lemon
- 6 cloves garlic, peeled and chopped
- 3 wiri-wiri peppers, stalks removed and chopped (see above for alternatives)
- 1½ tablespoons cumin seeds, roasted and ground (see page 339)
- 1½ tablespoons Guyanese *garam masala* (see page 328)
- 1½ tablespoons curry powder
- 1 small onion, about 90 g/3 oz, peeled and sliced into fine half-rings
- 1 spring onion, cut crossways into thin slices
- 3 tablespoons finely chopped celery tops (the delicate leaves)
- 3 tablespoons corn or peanut oil
- 1½ teaspoons salt
- 4 smallish potatoes, about 140 g/5 oz, peeled and halved

Wash the goat meat and put in a bowl. Add the juice of half a lemon plus the lemon shell and water to cover. Wash well and drain thoroughly.

Put the garlic, the peppers and 3 tablespoons water into a blender and make a purée. Empty into a bowl. Stir in the cumin seeds, *garam masala*, curry powder and enough water to make a thick paste. Put the onion, spring onion and celery tops into a separate bowl.

Pour the oil into a wide, lidded pan and set over a medium-low heat. Put in the spice paste and cover. Cook for 2–3 minutes, removing the lid now and then to stir. Add the meat cubes and increase the heat to medium. Stir and cook the meat for a minute. Add the salt and cook, covered, for 20 minutes, removing the lid occasionally to stir. The water must almost dry out. Now add 600 ml/1 pint water, stir, and bring to a simmer. Cover and cook on a medium-low heat for 50 minutes. Add the potatoes. Cover and cook for 5 minutes, removing the lid now and then to stir the contents. Add another 475 ml/16 fl oz water. Cover and simmer on a medium-low heat for 30 minutes.

THE STORY OF GOAT CURRY

Goat curries are much loved throughout Jamaica, Trinidad, Barbados and Guyana. They are cooked in a fairly similar manner, but do have slight variations. This recipe is Guyanese.

For those Guyanese whose ancestors worked the sugar plantations, meat was a luxury. Most days they made do with vegetables, grains and beans, supplemented with fish. Goat curries were celebratory and have retained that association. Whenever friends gather for a party, it is expected that the host will cook up a large pot of goat curry. It could be chicken curry, or beef liver curry for Muslim families, but goat remains an emotional favourite for all creeds.

As the indentured labourers here came mainly from the north Indian states of Uttar Pradesh and Bihar, their spice mixes hint at, but are not exactly the same as, what is used in those Indian states today. For the Guyanese *garam masala*, spicing concepts from both states have been combined to produce a dark, generic mix that is, for me, unexpected – but utterly delicious. As all the spices are roasted before being ground, meat curries here have a dark look, unlike the green, red and yellows of Thailand or the reds and browns of India. This particular curry requires not only the dark *garam masala* but some roasted and ground cumin seeds (also dark and sold ready-roasted and ground by West Indian grocers) and a leavening of a more common, yellowish, Guyanese curry powder ('Try and get "Lala's"', I was advised.) The combination is very Guyanese and quite wonderful. Meats are always browned in the spice mixture, a step known in Guyana as '*boonjay*', probably from the '*bhuna*' ('to brown') of India.

Guyana uses its own very special chilli, the wiri-wiri pepper, to give a heavenly tropical-citrus aroma to its foods. The wiri-wiri shares this aroma with the fiery-hot scotch bonnets/habaneros/congo peppers of Trinidad and the almost-sweet ajicitos dulces or cuchacha of Cuba and the Dominican Republic. Its heat lies somewhere in the middle but its aroma is equally intense. The other seasonings which give a recognisably Guyanese flavour to this country's foods are celery tops, spring onions, garlic and onions.

Sir Ranald Martin's

Cold Veal Curry-in-a-Mould

UK

Sir Ranald was a British doctor. His hobby, it seems, was collecting recipes from the courts of maharajahs and from regiment messes. When he returned to London in 1840, he acquired a huge practice and enjoyed his well-earned salary entertaining 'mostly men and women of distinction'. His dinners were famous for the Indian dishes prepared from the host's recipes, which were eventually published in the 1930s, in a book entited *Curry Recipes, Selected from the Unpublished Collection of Sir Ranald Martin*.

This recipe has been adapted from that collection. It is very mild, very British-Indian and very 19th century. I find it utterly intriguing.

SERVES 6–8

3 thick slices of veal shank with bone, cut as for osso bucco, about 1.15 kg/2½ lb
salt
freshly ground black pepper
3 tablespoons corn or peanut oil
1 medium sour apple, such as a Granny Smith, peeled and chopped
1 medium onion, finely chopped
4 teaspoons hot curry powder
1 tablespoon mango chutney
2 packets (4 teaspoons) unflavoured gelatin powder

Season the veal on all sides with salt and pepper. Pour the oil into a large, wide, lidded pan and set over a medium-high heat. When the oil is hot, put in the veal pieces in a single layer and brown on both sides. Throw the apple and onion into the pan, in between the veal pieces. Stir everything around as best you can until the onions are lightly browned. Add the curry powder and continue to brown for a further 30 seconds. Now add 1.2 litres/2 pints water, 1½ teaspoons salt and the mango chutney, and bring to the boil. Cover, reduce the heat to low, and cook for 2½ hours. Remove the veal pieces. Take all the meat off the bone in big chunks, place in a bowl and set aside. Also remove all the marrow. Now put the bones back in the pan and continue to simmer the stock gently, uncovered, for another hour. Turn off the heat and remove the bones.

Pour off 120 ml/4 fl oz of the stock and allow it to cool, leaving the rest in the pan. When it has cooled completely, sprinkle over the gelatin and stir it in. Meanwhile, bring the stock in the pan to a simmer, then take off the heat. Pour the gelatin stock into the hot stock and stir. Cut the meat into 5-mm/¼-inch thick slices. Rinse out a large glass or metal bowl or loaf-shaped mould and lay the meat in it as evenly as you can. Stir in the gelatin stock. Cover and refrigerate overnight.

Remove the fat congealed on the top, unmould by upturning on a plate, and serve.

2

POULTRY AND EGGS

As all domestic chickens the world over are descendants of *Gallus gallus*, a wild fowl native to northern India, Myanmar (Burma) and surrounding areas, India has been cooking chickens and their ancestors since antiquity. Over time, certain traditions have become quite set. The most important one is that for almost every chicken dish, whether the bird is roasted in a *tandoor* oven or cut into pieces and curried with a sauce, the skin is always removed. Indians have taken this tradition with them wherever they have travelled.

I remember walking into a very up-market butcher's shop in Durban, South Africa. Many South Africans of Indian descent live here. In one refrigerated display case, arranged like Tiffany jewellery, are a dozen whole chickens. Not a sign of flabby yellow skin or globules of fat to be seen. From wingtip to drumstick, all you see is clear, pale pink flesh, glowing in translucent splendour.

In India, the chicken is sold with the skin on. It needs to be yanked off. I find this fairly easy to do with the help of kitchen paper, which stops the skin from slipping away from my fingers. Generally, families buy whole chickens and cut them up with bone, into smaller parts for curries. Breasts are cut into four to six pieces, legs into two to three, wings into two, and necks and gizzards are generally thrown in, too, as most people love them. You may, of course, buy chicken parts if you are partial to just light or dark meat.

Chicken may be cooked with a Moghlai sauce full of browned onions and cardamom or it may be cooked in a south-Indian manner with coconut milk or roasted black pepper. A Thai chicken curry might be perfumed with kaffir lime leaves and lemon grass, whereas a Malaysian *korma* might have white pepper and white poppy seeds. Chicken is often cooked with vegetables such as potatoes – the chicken adds flavour to the potato and the potato adds a bit of texture to the curry sauce.

This chapter has some duck recipes as well. Besides the hunted ducks that fly annually from northern climes to more southern shores, much of south India and South-East Asia has great flocks of ducks that are raised in flooded paddy fields. From Indonesia to India, they are made into the most wonderful curries. Again, most, if not all, of the skin is removed first. They may be braised slowly with a sauce of green chillies and tamarind or with cinnamon, cardamom and tomatoes. It is the slow cooking that makes the flesh buttery soft.

The variety of duck I have used here is sold as Peking duck. It has a long, oval body. I not only remove as much skin as I can easily, but also a lot of the fat that lies just underneath. It is always a good idea to cook duck curries a day in advance, as you can skim off the fat before reheating it.

Egg curries are a convenience food. Make a quick sauce, hard boil some eggs and put the two together. These may be eaten with breads, toasted or otherwise, or rice. The British, while they were colonial masters in India, made curry sauces with curry powder and used them over their breakfast eggs. The sauce is on page 331. You can make your breakfast eggs the 19th-century way.

Gulzar Ahamed's

Green Coriander Chicken (Dhania Chicken) KENYA

This is a favourite amongst the Ismaili Muslims of Kenya, and with good reason. It has an exquisite flavour and may well be one of the best chicken dishes I have ever eaten. Serve it with Indian breads, with wholemeal pitta bread or with any rice dish.

You may use a whole chicken, cut into serving pieces, or else use just four chicken legs, as I do. All the chicken pieces must be skinned.

SERVES 4

7½-cm/3-inch piece fresh ginger, peeled and coarsely chopped
5 good-sized cloves garlic, peeled and coarsely chopped
salt
2 teaspoons lemon juice
4 chicken legs, skinned and separated into drumsticks and thighs
1 medium tomato, about 140 g/5 oz, chopped
90 g/3 oz fresh coriander leaves and small stems
2–3 fresh, hot green chillies, coarsely chopped
1 teaspoon tomato purée
3 tablespoons olive or corn oil
250 ml/8 fl oz natural yoghurt, lightly beaten with a fork

Put the ginger, garlic, ¼ teaspoon salt and the lemon juice into a blender. Add about 2 tablespoons water and blend, pushing down with a rubber spatula if necessary, until smooth. Place the chicken pieces in a stainless steel or non-metallic bowl. Pour the ginger mixture over the top and rub it in. Cover the bowl with cling film and refrigerate for 30 minutes or for up to 24 hours.

Without bothering to clean out the blender goblet, put the tomato, coriander, chillies, tomato purée, ¾ teaspoon salt and 2 tablespoons water into it. Blend until smooth.

Pour the oil into a large, non-stick, lidded pan and set over a high heat. When very hot, put in the chicken pieces, together with the marinade. Fry, stirring, until the chicken pieces are light brown on all sides, about 10 minutes. Add the tomato mixture from the blender. Continue to cook, stirring, until the sauce is thick and clings to the chicken and the oil separates from it, another 10 minutes. Add the yoghurt. Stir and cook until the yoghurt disappears and leaves a thick sauce edged with oil, 4–5 minutes. Cover, reduce the heat as low as possible, and cook for 5–10 minutes or until the chicken is tender. If you think that the pan is drying out too much, stir in a tablespoon or two of water.

Hava Barmania's

Curried Whole Chicken, Durban-Style (Roast Chicken)

SOUTH AFRICA

The Barmanias, a Muslim family whose roots are in Surat, Gujarat, make a mean, Indian-style chicken. The entire bird is skinned (all butchers sell fully skinned, whole chickens in this town), then marinated and then roasted in a covered dish until it is meltingly tender. The spicing pays homage to India in general, but is not recognisably Gujarati. It is, however, irresistibly delicious and quite easy to prepare.

You can ask your butcher to skin the whole bird for you. If you wish to do it yourself, start at the breast and work your way to the legs. You can use kitchen paper to help you yank the skin off the legs. The wings are a bit harder, so I just leave the skin on their tips.

SERVES 3–4

- 1 chicken, about 1¾ kg/3¼ lb, skinned whole
- 4 tablespoons lemon juice
- 5-cm/2-inch piece fresh ginger, peeled and chopped
- 3 cloves garlic, peeled and chopped
- 3 fresh, hot, green chillies, chopped
- 1 teaspoon salt
- 2 tablespoons olive oil
- 1 teaspoon ground cumin
- 1 teaspoon ground coriander
- ½ teaspoon pure chilli powder, the coarser the better
- freshly ground black pepper

Using a sharp knife, make two deep, diagonal slits in each breast, going all the way to the bone. Make two deep slashes in the thighs and drumsticks as well. Place the chicken, breast up, in a roasting tin (or round or square cake tin) lined with a very large sheet of heavy foil that can enclose the bird eventually .

Put the lemon juice, ginger, garlic, fresh chillies, salt, olive oil, cumin and coriander in a blender and blend until you have a paste. Rub this paste all over the chicken, inside and out, making sure you go into all the slits. Set aside for 30 minutes.

Meanwhile, preheat the oven to 200°C/gas mark 6.

Dust the top of the chicken with the chilli powder and black pepper. Bring the foil over the top of the chicken and crimp it so the bird is completely enclosed. Place in the middle of the oven and bake for 1 hour. Open up the foil and baste the chicken with the accumulated juices. Continue to bake, uncovered, for a further 15 minutes, basting the bird two or three times during this period.

Chicken with Spinach (Saag Murgh)

INDIA

This is the classic north Indian recipe for chicken cooked with spinach. I like to chop my spinach very, very finely but you could also put it into the blender and make a paste of it. Serve with Indian breads or rice.

SERVES 4

285 g/10 oz spinach, well washed and chopped coarsely
Crisply Fried Onion Slices, made according to the recipe on page 312, using 3 small onions, each about 90 g/3 oz
2 small onions, about 180 g/6 oz, chopped
5-cm/2-inch piece fresh ginger, peeled and chopped
4 cloves garlic, peeled and chopped
5 tablespoons oil saved from frying the onions
5 whole cardamom pods
1 medium stick cinnamon
2 teaspoons ground coriander
1 teaspoon ground cumin
½–1 teaspoon cayenne pepper
1 chicken, about 1¾ kg/3¼ lb, skinned and cut into small serving pieces
6 tablespoons natural yoghurt
85 g/2½ oz tomatoes, peeled and chopped
1¾ teaspoons salt

Place the spinach, together with 120 ml/4 fl oz water, in a large, non-stick, lidded pan and bring to the boil on a medium heat. Cover and cook for 3–5 minutes or until the spinach is tender and most of the water has evaporated. Chop the spinach very finely or blend it. Set aside. Wipe out the pan.

Crumble the fried onions and set aside.

Put the chopped onions, ginger, garlic and 3–4 tablespoons water into a blender and blend, pushing down with a rubber spatula when necessary, until you have a smooth paste.

Pour the oil into the same large pan and set over a medium-high heat. When the oil is hot, put in the cardamom and cinnamon. Let them sizzle for a few seconds, then pour in the paste from the blender. Stir and fry for about 5 minutes or until the paste is lightly browned. Add the coriander, cumin and cayenne pepper. Stir for a minute. Add the chicken pieces, and continue to stir for another minute. Over the next 5 minutes add a tablespoon of yoghurt at a time and keep browning the chicken. Add the tomatoes and stir for 2 minutes. Add the spinach and stir for a further minute. Now add 300 ml/10 fl oz water, the crumbled onions and salt. Stir to mix and bring to a simmer. Cover, reduce the heat to very low, and simmer gently for 25 minutes, stirring now and then.

Yasmeen Murshed's

Sweet-and-Sour Chicken 'Rizala' (Bogra Rizala) BANGLADESH

There is more than one style of *rizala*. The Dhaka *rizala*, for example, is neither sweet nor sour and is often served at the end of the Ramadan festival of Id. The Calcutta *rizala* requires that the meat be cooked entirely in milk/yoghurt. This north Bengali Bogra *rizala* recipe comes from my friend Yasmeen's mother. It is a classic. Gently sweet and sour (combining sugar and aromatic lime juice), it has a scrumptious dark sauce made entirely without spices that is rich with browned onions and cooked-down yoghurt. The style of the dish may be best described as 'Moghul-Bengali'.

Note that the green chillies do not give much heat to the dish. They may, however, be bitten into whenever the diner desires.

SERVES 4

- Crisply Fried Onion Slices, made according to the recipe on page 312, using 3 small onions, each about 90 g/3 oz
- 2 small onions, about 180 g/6 oz, chopped
- 5-cm/2-inch piece fresh ginger, peeled and chopped
- 4 cloves garlic, peeled and chopped
- 4 tablespoons oil saved from frying the onions, plus 1 tablespoon *ghee*, or more oil
- 1 chicken, about 1¾ kg/3¼ lb, skinned and cut into small serving pieces
- 6 tablespoons natural yoghurt
- 1½ teaspoons salt
- 6–10 whole bird's eye chillies, with small slits cut in them
- 1¾ teaspoons sugar
- 2 tablespoons lemon or lime juice (if you can get meyer lemons or small aromatic Asian limes, do use their juice)

Crumble the fried onions and set aside.

Put the chopped onions, ginger, garlic and 3–4 tablespoons water into a blender and blend, pushing down with a rubber spatula when necessary, until you have a smooth paste.

Put the oil and ghee in a large, non-stick, lidded pan and set over a medium-high heat. When hot, pour in the paste from the blender. Stir and fry for about 5 minutes or until the paste is lightly browned. Add the chicken pieces. Continue to stir for a further minute. Over the next 5 minutes add 1 tablespoon of yoghurt at a time and keep browning the chicken. Now add 175 ml/6 fl oz water, the crumbled onions and salt.
Stir to mix and bring to a simmer. Cover, reduce the heat to very low and simmer gently for 20 minutes, turning the chicken pieces over now and then. Add the chillies, sugar and lemon or lime juice. Stir to mix. Cover and continue to cook on a very low heat for another 10 minutes.

Royal Chicken Korma (Shani Murgh Korma) INDIA

My dish here is a real Indian *korma*, rich and ideal for entertaining. I have made enough for six to eight people as this is very much a party dish.

The whole spices may be fished out before serving.

SERVES 6–8

1 teaspoon saffron threads
4 tablespoons whipping cream, heated until hot
5–6 tablespoons corn or peanut oil
12 whole cardamom pods
4 medium sticks cinnamon
6 bay leaves
2.3 kg/5 lb boneless, skinless chicken thighs
2 medium onions, about 285 g/10 oz, sliced into fine half-rings
2 tablespoons fresh ginger, peeled and finely grated
8 cloves garlic, peeled and crushed to a pulp
4 tablespoons whole, peeled almonds
4 tablespoons sultanas
2 tablespoons ground coriander
1 tablespoon ground cumin
250 ml/8 fl oz natural yoghurt, lightly whisked until smooth
2½–3 teaspoons salt
2 teaspoons cayenne pepper
½ teaspoon *garam masala* (see page 327)

Use a small cup to soak the saffron threads in the hot cream. Set aside for 2–3 hours.

Pour the oil into a large, wide, lidded pan and set over a medium-high heat. When the oil is hot, add the cardamom, cinnamon and bay leaves. Stir once and put in as many chicken pieces as the pan will hold easily in a single layer. Brown the chicken on both sides, then remove to a bowl, leaving behind as many of the whole spices as you can. Brown all the chicken this way, then set aside in the bowl. Add the onions to the pan. Stir and fry them until they are reddish-brown. Add the ginger and garlic and stir for a minute. Add the almonds, sultanas, coriander and cumin. Stir once, then return the chicken to the pan, along with any accumulated juices. Also add the yoghurt, salt and cayenne pepper. Stir to mix and bring to a simmer. Partially cover with the lid and cook on a medium heat for 10 minutes. Increase the heat to high and cook, stirring, until most of the liquid has boiled away and a thick sauce clings to the meat. Stir in the saffron cream, *garam masala* and 120 ml/4 fl oz water. Cover tightly and leave on the lowest possible heat for 5 minutes.

THE ORIGINS OF THE KORMA

All *korma*-style meat dishes probably originated in the Islamic courts of the Moghuls (16th–19th centuries) and of the Muslim rulers of the Indian subcontinent that preceded them (10th–16th centuries). I say '*korma*-style', as I cannot find the word itself in any Moghul or earlier reference. Today, the word *korma* has developed two distinct meanings. In India, Pakistan and Bangladesh, the lands of its evolution, it generally suggests a rich banquet/party dish, using a lot of yoghurt in the cooking as well as expensive spices and flavourings such as cardamom, nutmeg, saffron and nuts. Turmeric is almost never used and the sauce tends to be pale, thick and creamy.

In Malaysia, *kormas* or *kurmas*, in a slight variation of the Indian ones, are enriched not with nuts, cream and saffron but with yoghurt and coconut milk. The 'heat' comes from white pepper and, sometimes, fresh green chillies. *Kormas* here always have the faint sweetness of fennel seeds and sometimes of star anise as well.

In the world of Indian restaurants in the West, especially in the United Kingdom, *korma* has come to mean something entirely different. Here it is a mild, creamy dish of lamb, chicken or beef, designed, it seems, for those who do not like their food too hot. I do not know how this particular version evolved. Indian restaurants in the West had limited menus with standardised dishes. There were 'hot' dishes, such as the *vindaloo* (which were never true Goan *vindaloos* but just super-hot meat dishes) and, as a contrast, there were the 'mild' *kormas* that were pale in colour and spicing.

Yasmeen Murshed's

Nawab of Dhaka's Family Korma

BANGLADESH

A dish in the true Moghul tradition, this recipe comes from a royal Bangladeshi family of Kashmiri origins. Here the chicken is cooked entirely in milk, so do use a heavy, non-stick pan. Serve with a rice dish or with flatbreads.

Serves 4

- ½ teaspoon saffron threads
- 1 tablespoon rose water
- 1 teaspoon *kewra* (screw pine) water
- 2 onions, each about 180 g/6 oz, chopped
- 5-cm/2-inch piece fresh ginger, peeled and chopped
- 4 cloves garlic, peeled and chopped
- Crisply Fried Onion Slices, made according to the recipe on page 312, using 3 small onions, each about 90 g/3 oz
- all the oil saved from frying the onions, strained
- 4 small potatoes, each about 50 g/2oz, peeled and halved
- 1 tablespoon *ghee*
- 5 whole cardamom pods
- 1 medium stick cinnamon
- 1 chicken, about 1.45 kg/3 1/4 lb, skinned and cut into small serving pieces
- ½ teaspoon grated nutmeg
- ¼ teaspoon ground mace
- 6 tablespoons natural yoghurt
- 175 ml/6 fl oz milk, warmed
- 1½ teaspoons salt, or to taste

Soak the saffron threads in the rose water and *kewra* water and set aside for 2–3 hours.

Put the chopped onions, ginger, garlic and 3–4 tablespoons water into a blender and blend, pushing down with a rubber spatula when necessary, until you have a smooth paste. Crumble the fried onions and set aside.

Pour the oil reserved from frying the onions into a large, non-stick, lidded pan and set on a medium heat. When hot, put in the potatoes and fry them until they are lightly browned on all sides. Remove them with a slotted spoon and set aside.

Pour away all but 4 tablespoons of the oil. Add the *ghee* (or another tablespoon of the oil) and set on a medium-high heat. When hot, put in the cardamom and cinnamon. Let them sizzle for a few seconds, then pour in the paste from the blender. Stir and fry for about 5 minutes until lightly browned. Add the chicken, nutmeg and mace. Continue to stir for a further minute. Over the next 5 minutes, add the yoghurt, a tablespoon at a time, and keep browning the chicken. Now stir in the milk, the crumbled onions and salt, and bring to a simmer. Cover, reduce the heat as low as possible, and simmer gently for 25 minutes, turning the chicken pieces over now and then. Add the saffron mixture, stir well, and continue to cook, covered, on a very low heat for a further 5 minutes.

Chef Wan's

Malay Chicken Korma

MALAYSIA

As shoppers wander through Malaysia's open markets, they inevitably come across someone selling spices for curries. Some of the spices are whole, some powdered and some ground into a wet paste. All are as fresh as they can be. What the shopper has to do then is say what he or she wants to cook and the salesperson immediately starts pushing the requisite spices into little plastic bags, in a variety of combinations.

For a Malay-style *korma*, the most important ingredient is what is called the 'white curry base'. This consists of ground coriander, cumin, white pepper, fennel and white poppy seeds, often in a paste form. The whole spices, which go into a separate bag, include star anise, cinnamon and cardamom. A third bag holds a paste of shallots, garlic and ginger.

Armed with these, our shopper could prepare a *korma* with great ease. Malaysia's *kormas*, like those of India and Pakistan, are considered delicacies reserved for ceremonious occasions such as weddings and thanksgivings. All Indian grocers sell white poppy seeds. If you cannot get them, use slivered almonds.

For the final garnishing, you may also use Crisply Fried Onion or Shallot Slices (see page 312).

SERVES 4

2 teaspoons white poppy seeds
5-cm/2-inch piece fresh ginger, peeled and chopped
4 cloves garlic, peeled and chopped
85 g/2½ oz shallots, peeled and chopped
1 tablespoon whole coriander seeds
2 teaspoons whole cumin seeds
½ teaspoon whole fennel seeds
1 teaspoon whole white peppercorns
4 tablespoons corn or peanut oil
1 whole star anise pod
1 medium stick cinnamon
5 whole cardamom pods
1 medium onion, peeled and sliced into fine half-rings
1½ kg/3½ lb chicken, cut into bite-sized pieces
450 g/1 lb potatoes, peeled and cut into 4-cm/1½-inch chunks
3 medium carrots, about 225 g/8 oz, peeled and cut into 4-cm/1½-inch pieces
1 medium tomato, chopped
2 teaspoons salt
¼ teaspoon cayenne pepper
3 tablespoons natural yoghurt
250 ml/8 fl oz well-stirred coconut milk (from a can will do)
1½–2 tablespoons lemon juice
fresh mint or coriander, for garnishing

Check through the poppy seeds for stones, then soak them in 2 tablespoons boiling water for 2 hours.

Put the soaked poppy seeds, together with their soaking liquid, plus the ginger, garlic and shallots in a food processor and process until you have a paste.

Place the coriander, cumin, fennel and white peppercorns in a clean coffee grinder or other spice grinder and grind them until you have a coarse powder.

Pour the oil into a wide, preferably non-stick, lidded pan and set over a medium-high heat. When the oil is hot, add the star anise, cinnamon and cardamom. Stir once, then add the onion. Stir and fry until the onion turns reddish-brown. Add the ginger paste, and fry, stirring at the same time, for 2–3 minutes. Reduce the heat to medium and add the ground spices. Stir them for a minute. Add the chicken and stir vigorously for 6–7 minutes or until the chicken releases its liquid. Now put in the potato, carrots, tomato, salt and cayenne pepper. Stir a few times, add 350 ml/12 fl oz water, and bring to the boil. Cover, and cook on a medium-high heat for 15 minutes. Reduce the heat to low, and cook for a further 10 minutes.

Meanwhile, beat the yoghurt in a bowl. Add the coconut milk and lemon juice, then stir gently into the chicken. Cook, uncovered, on a low heat for 5 minutes, stirring now and then.

Garnish with the coriander or mint before serving.

Gulzar Ahamed's

Chicken with Coconut (Kuku Paka) KENYA

In Kenya, *kuku* is chicken and *paka* is coconut, and this dish, which combines the two, may well be the most popular Kenyan-Indian creation. I love it. The family who provided me with the recipe were owners of what was once Nairobi's premier department store, Ahameds. The dynasty began with a man named Ahamed – he only had the one name – who sold fruit and vegetables in Bombay's Crawford Market. He got into trouble with the police and fled, signing up with labourers bound for East Africa. To work off his passage, he took on a job with a tailor, earning enough in a few years to buy his own sewing machine. But not only that. The First World War was about to break out and this four foot eleven man managed to find the relevant British colonel in the middle of a game reserve and wrest from him a contract to be the chief supplier to the army. He made a fortune and went on to invest it wisely in real estate.

I have heard many stories of Indians in Kenya and Uganda that are similar. Of course, later political upheavals that followed independence caused many Indians to leave. But some, like Mrs Gulzar Ahamed, who is a mean cook, have hung on, feeling very much that Kenya is her country too.

Kuku Paka is served with rice. It could be plain rice or another from the selection in this book.

I use a whole chicken cut up into serving pieces. You could certainly use chicken parts, if you prefer.

SERVES 4

FOR MARINATING THE CHICKEN

a 1.45–1.5-kg/3¼–3½-lb chicken, skinned and cut into serving pieces
1 tablespoon peeled and finely grated fresh ginger
4 cloves garlic, peeled and crushed to a pulp
1 teaspoon salt
½ teaspoon cayenne pepper
1 tablespoon lemon juice

FOR THE SAUCE

180 g/6 oz tomatoes, chopped
140 g/5 oz onions, peeled and chopped
2 bird's eye chillies, chopped
2 tablespoons freshly grated coconut, or grated frozen, or desiccated
¾ teaspoon salt
1 tablespoon ground cumin
3 tablespoons corn or peanut oil
400-ml/14-fl oz can of coconut milk, well shaken
4 tablespoons fresh coriander leaves, finely chopped
1 teaspoon lemon juice

Marinate the chicken. Put the chicken in a bowl, mix in the marinade ingredients, and rub them all over the chicken pieces. Cover and set aside for 1½–3 hours, refrigerating the chicken if necessary.

Make the sauce. Put the tomatoes, onions, chillies, coconut, salt and cumin into a blender. Blend until you have a paste.

Pour the oil into a wide, non-stick, lidded pan and set over a medium-high heat. Add the paste from the blender almost immediately. Stir, occasionally at first, then more frequently later, when it thickens, for about 7–8 minutes or until the paste is lightly fried and no longer watery. Add the chicken and reduce the heat to medium-low. Stir for a minute. Cover loosely with a lid and allow to cook for 12–15 minutes, removing the lid now and then to stir. At the end of this period, the chicken should be lightly browned on all sides. Add the coconut milk and 50 ml water. Stir and bring to a simmer. Cover and simmer very gently on a low heat for a further 15 minutes. Turn off the heat and add the coriander and lemon juice. Stir to mix.

Anne Markey Mahbubani and Gretchen Liu's

Singapore-Style South-Indian Chicken Curry SINGAPORE

Singapore's 'curries' are like no other. This south Indian-style one is a blend of mostly Indian seasonings put together with simplified Malay ease. Made with curry powder, this curry is surely one of the best, the kind I imagine was enjoyed for tiffin by the British at the Raffles Hotel on a lazy Sunday afternoon, eaten with a mound of rice and a host of chutneys and pickles. The Raffles Hotel itself has modernised and changed since my early visits there. The old Hokkien chefs who cooked these hybrid curries have been replaced with Indian ones from India, with different sensibilities. But these curries can still be found in small restaurants and in most homes. This particular recipe comes from a Filipino maid who cooked it at the home of the curator of the Raffles Hotel Museum, Gretchen Liu.

For this recipe, my instructions were to get south Indian curry powder from a spice stall at the Farrer Road wet market in Singapore. If you are travelling there, do pick it up. Otherwise, use any of the south Indian curry powders, which are generally sold as Madras Curry Powder.

I have used chicken legs here but you may use any chicken cut of your choice. You could also use a whole, 1.35-kg/3-lb chicken, cut into serving pieces and skinned. You will only need to increase the amount of salt slightly.

Most Malaysian curries are eaten with rice.

SERVES 4

- 2½ tablespoons curry powder (see note above)
- 4 chicken legs, about 1.15/2½ lb, skinned and divided into drumsticks and thighs
- 3 tablespoons corn or peanut oil
- 6 medium shallots, about 325 g/11 oz, very finely chopped (this may be done in a food processor, using the pulse/stop and start method)
- 5-cm/2-inch piece fresh ginger, peeled and very finely chopped
- 6 cloves garlic, peeled and very finely chopped
- 15–20 fresh curry leaves, if available
- 1 medium cinnamon stick
- 4–5 dried, hot red chillies
- 4 small, waxy red potatoes, each about 90 g/3 oz, peeled and halved
- 1¾ teaspoons salt
- 350 ml/12 fl oz coconut milk, from a well-shaken can
- 2 tablespoons thick tamarind paste (see page 345), or 1½ tablespoons lemon juice mixed with ½ teaspoon sugar
- 2 medium tomatoes, each cut into 8 pieces

Rub 1½ tablespoons of the curry powder all over the chicken pieces and set aside. Mix the remaining curry powder with 250 ml/8 fl oz water and set aside.

Pour the oil into a large, preferably non-stick, lidded pan and set over a medium-high heat. When the oil is hot, put in the shallots, half the ginger, half the garlic, the curry leaves, cinnamon stick and red chillies. Stir and fry for 5 minutes or until golden. Add the curry powder-water mixture and continue to stir and cook for about 4 minutes. Now add the chicken, potatoes, salt and 250 ml/8 fl oz water. Stir and bring to the boil. Cover, reduce the heat to low and simmer gently for 25 minutes. Add the coconut milk and tamarind. Stir and cook, uncovered, for a further 3–4 minutes. The dish can be prepared up to this point several hours in advance.

Just before serving, reheat the curry if needed and add the tomatoes and the remaining ginger and garlic. Stir and cook, uncovered, for 3–4 minutes.

Anne Markey Mahbubani and Gretchen Liu's

Peranakan (Nonya) Chicken Curry — SINGAPORE

This curry is similar to the previous one but its flavours are different: a mixture of Nonya (which itself is a melding of Chinese and Malay) and Indian. It uses curry powder, a Nonya-style one, but adds fresh local seasonings such as lemon grass and fresh kaffir lime leaves. It is highly aromatic.

For this recipe, my instructions were to get a Peranakan (Nonya) curry powder from a spice stall at the Farrer Road wet market in Singapore. If you are travelling there, do pick it up. Otherwise, use any curry powder of your choice, such as My Curry Powder (see page 324), or Bolst's Hot Curry Powder, which is sold by most Indian grocers.

I have used chicken legs here but you may use any chicken cut of your choice. You could also use a whole, 1.35-kg/3-lb chicken, cut into serving pieces and skinned. You will only need to increase the amount of salt slightly.

If the lemon grass stalks are slim use four. If they are fat and large, two would be sufficient.

Use any smallish waxy potatoes. I use red ones.

Most Malaysian curries are eaten with rice.

SERVES 4

- 2½ tablespoons curry powder (see above)
- 4 chicken legs, about 1.15kg/2½ lb, skinned and divided into drumsticks and thighs
- 2–4 sticks lemon grass
- 3 tablespoons corn or peanut oil
- 5 slices of fresh ginger, each the size of a 10-pence piece
- 4 small, waxy potatoes, each about 90 g/3 oz, peeled and halved
- 3 medium shallots, about 180 g/6 oz , very finely chopped (this may be done in a food processor, using the pulse/stop and start method)
- 8 fresh kaffir lime leaves, very finely chopped
- 10 fresh curry leaves, very finely chopped
- 2–3 fresh, hot green chillies, very finely chopped
- 1¾ teaspoons salt
- 350 ml/12 fl oz coconut milk, from a well-shaken can
- 2 tablespoons thick tamarind paste (see page 345), or 1½ tablespoons lemon juice mixed with ½ teaspoon sugar
- 2 medium tomatoes, each cut into 8 pieces
- 1 teaspoon sugar

Rub 1½ tablespoons of the curry powder all over the chicken pieces and set aside.

Cut off the tops of the lemon grass so you have 15–18-cm/6–7-inch lengths. Put the pieces on a chopping board and split them in half, lengthways, using a sharp knife. Fold each piece into thirds, lengthways, and tie up these pieces with kitchen twine. Set aside.

Pour the oil into a large, preferably non-stick, lidded pan or wok and set over a medium-high heat. When the oil is hot, put in the ginger slices. Stir and fry until they are brown, pressing on them now and then. Remove the ginger slices and discard. Add the potatoes to the oil and brown them on all sides. Remove with a slotted spoon and set aside. Put the shallots into the pan. Stir and fry for 3–4 minutes or until golden. Add the remaining curry powder, the lemon grass, lime leaves, curry leaves and green chillies. Continue to stir and cook for about 4 minutes. Now put in the chicken, the potatoes, salt and 475 ml/16 fl oz water. Stir and bring to the boil. Cover, reduce the heat to low, and simmer gently for 20 minutes. Add the coconut milk and tamarind. Cook, uncovered, for a further 5 minutes, spooning the sauce over the chicken. The dish can be prepared up to this point several hours in advance.

Just before serving, reheat the curry if needed and add the tomatoes and sugar. Stir and cook, uncovered, for 3–4 minutes.

Remove the lemon grass before serving.

Vietnamese Chicken Curry (Cari Ga) VIETNAM

Many stew-like curries from South Vietnam traditionally require both a curry powder and a curry paste. I find I can do without the paste. They also require thickening with cornflour, although I find that canned coconut milk is thick enough.

SERVES 4

- 2½ tablespoons hot curry powder
- 4 chicken legs, about 1.15 kg/2½ lb, skinned and divided into drumsticks and thighs
- 140 g/5 oz shallots, peeled and chopped
- 1 stick lemon grass, the knot at the end removed and the bottom half cut crossways into fine slices, or 1 teaspoon ground lemon grass
- 5-cm/2-inch piece fresh ginger, peeled and chopped
- 6 cloves garlic, peeled and chopped
- 4 dried, hot red chillies, crumbled
- 4 tablespoons corn or peanut oil
- 1 stick cinnamon
- 1 bay leaf
- 1 large onion, about 225 g/8 oz, peeled and cut into 8 pieces
- 2 medium tomatoes, chopped
- 4 small, waxy potatoes, each about 90 g/3 oz, peeled and halved
- 2 medium carrots, peeled and cut into 4-cm/1½-inch chunks
- 1 tablespoon fish sauce (*nuoc mam*)
- 1 teaspoon sugar
- about ¾ teaspoon salt
- 350 ml/12 fl oz coconut milk, from a well-shaken can

Rub 1½ tablespoons of the curry powder all over the chicken pieces and set aside.

Put the remaining curry powder, shallots, lemon grass, ginger, garlic and chillies in a blender along with 4–5 tablespoons water. Blend until smooth, pushing down with a rubber spatula when necessary.

Pour the oil into a large, preferably non-stick, lidded pan and set over a medium-high heat. When the oil is hot, put in the cinnamon and bay leaf. Stir once, then add the onion. Stir and fry until the pieces turn brown at the edges. Put in the paste from the blender. Fry, stirring at the same time, for 2–3 minutes or until lightly browned. Add the tomatoes. Stir and fry until they have turned to a paste. Add the chicken pieces. Stir for a minute. Cover, reduce the heat to medium-low, and cook for a further 7–8 minutes, lifting the lid now and then to stir.

Now put in the potatoes, carrots, fish sauce, sugar and 250 ml/8 fl oz water. Stir and bring to the boil. Cover, reduce the heat to low, and simmer gently for 25 minutes. Taste for salt and add as much as you need. Stir. Add the coconut milk. Stir and cook, uncovered, for a further 3–4 minutes.

From the Grand Hyatt Erawan, Bangkok

Chicken in a Yellow Curry Sauce (Gaeng Kari Gai) THAILAND

Yellow curries are well loved all over Thailand, but, most especially, amongst the Muslim communities in Bangkok and the south, nearer the Malaysian border. The garnish, instead of being kaffir lime leaves and basil leaves, is generally crisply fried shallots, very similar to the crisply fried onions of India and the Arab world. Thai curries are generally served with rice but, if the sauce is thinned down enough, rice noodles are not inappropriate.

SERVES 4

400-ml/14-fl oz can of coconut milk, left undisturbed for 3 hours or more
4 tablespoons corn or peanut oil
85 g/2½ oz shallots, peeled and very thinly sliced into slivers
5 tablespoons Yellow Curry Paste (see page 321)
1 teaspoon hot curry powder
450 g/1 lb boned and skinned chicken thighs, cut into 2-cm/¾-inch pieces
1½ tablespoons fish sauce (*nam pla*), or to taste
1 teaspoon thick tamarind paste (see page 345), or lemon juice
1 teaspoon palm sugar or brown sugar

Carefully open the can of coconut milk and remove 4 tablespoons of the thick cream at the top. Stir the remaining contents of the can well and set aside.

Pour the oil into a large, non-stick, lidded pan and set over a medium heat. When the oil is hot, put in the shallots and stir them about. When they start to turn brown at the edges, reduce the heat to medium-low. Continue to stir and fry, turning the heat down as needed, until the shallots are golden brown and crisp. Remove them with a slotted spoon and spread out on a double layer of kitchen paper to crisp up further.

Add the thick coconut cream and the curry paste to the oil in the pan. Stir and fry until the oil separates and the paste is lightly browned. Add the curry powder and stir a few times. Add the chicken and stir for a minute. Reduce the heat to low and add the fish sauce, tamarind, palm sugar and 175 ml/6 fl oz water. Stir and bring to a simmer. Cover, reduce the heat as low as possible, and simmer for 15 minutes or until the chicken is cooked through. Stir in the reserved coconut milk. Taste for a balance of flavours, adding more fish sauce, sugar or tamarind if needed. Bring to a simmer. Cover and simmer very gently for 2–3 minutes.

Sprinkle the fried shallots over the top before serving.

Chicken Curry with a Cashew-Coconut Sauce SRI LANKA

Two home-grown Sri Lankan products, cashews and coconuts, are combined here to make a rich, heavenly curry. The thickening for the sauce is provided not only by the cashews, but also by the rice, which is first roasted and ground. The only other place I have seen rice used in this way is in north-eastern Thailand.

As there is a lot of delicious sauce to soak up, this is best served with rice.

SERVES 4

- a 1.35-kg/3-lb chicken, skinned and cut into serving pieces
- 2 tablespoons ground coriander
- 2 teaspoons ground cumin
- 2 teaspoons ground fennel
- ½ teaspoon cayenne pepper
- salt
- 1 tablespoon any raw, milled rice
- 2 tablespoons desiccated, unsweetened coconut
- 3 cardamom pods
- 2 whole cloves
- 2 tablespoons chopped, raw cashews
- 4 tablespoons corn or peanut oil
- 1 medium stick cinnamon
- ½ teaspoon whole fenugreek seeds
- 5 tablespoons finely slivered shallots
- 2 medium cloves garlic, peeled and slivered
- 1 fresh, hot green chilli, chopped
- 5-cm/2-inch piece fresh or frozen pandanus leaf (*rampe*, *bai toey*, *daun paandaan*)
- 140 g/5 oz tomatoes, peeled and chopped
- 120 ml/4 fl oz coconut milk, from a well-shaken can

Put the chicken pieces in a large bowl. Add the coriander, cumin, fennel, cayenne pepper and 1 teaspoon salt. Rub the spices all over the chicken and set aside for 15–20 minutes.

Put the rice in a small cast-iron frying pan, set over a medium-high heat, and stir until it just turns golden. Add the coconut and stir it until it is golden too. Remove to a plate and allow the mix to cool. Now put this mixture, as well as the cardamom and cloves, in a clean coffee grinder or other spice grinder and grind finely. Add the cashews and grind them with the spices. You might need to stir the seasonings if they jam up a bit. Empty into a medium bowl and slowly add 120 ml/4 fl oz water, mixing as you go. Set this paste aside.

Pour the oil into a large, lidded pan and set over a medium-high heat. When the oil is hot, put in the cinnamon, fenugreek, shallots, garlic, chilli and pandanus leaf. Stir for 2 minutes or until the shallots start to turn translucent. Add the chicken and brown lightly, stirring as you do so. Add the tomatoes, 600 ml/1 pint water and another 1½ teaspoons salt. Stir in the spice and nut paste. Bring to the boil, cover, reduce the heat to low, and cook gently for 30 minutes. Stir in the coconut milk and heat through.

Burmese Chicken Curry (See-Pyan)

MYANMAR

As Burmese curry powder seems to have elements of both Indian-style curry powders and *garam masala*, I have used a combination of the two for this recipe. You will notice that lemon grass and fish sauce are used here as well, showing clearly, in culinary terms, how Myanmar is geographically placed – between India and Thailand.

SERVES 4–6

- a 1.15-kg/2½-lb chicken, skinned and cut into small serving pieces
- 2 teaspoons hot curry powder
- ½ teaspoon *garam masala* (see page 327)
- 1¼ teaspoons salt
- 2 medium onions, about 285 g/10 oz, chopped
- 3 cloves garlic, peeled and chopped
- 2½-cm/1-inch piece fresh ginger, peeled and chopped
- ½ teaspoon cayenne pepper
- 2 teaspoons bright red paprika
- 6 tablespoons corn or peanut oil
- 2 medium tomatoes, peeled and chopped
- 1 tablespoon fish sauce (*nam pla*)
- 1 stick lemon grass (use the bottom 15 cm/6 inches, lightly mashing the bulbous end), or 1 teaspoon ground, dried lemon grass

Place the chicken in a single layer in a wide dish. Sprinkle the curry powder, *garam masala* and salt over it and rub them into the chicken. Set aside for 20 minutes or longer, covering and refrigerating if necessary.

Put the onions, garlic, ginger, cayenne pepper and paprika into a blender and blend, adding a few tablespoons of water if needed, until smooth.

Pour the oil into a large, wide, non-stick, lidded pan and set on a medium-high heat. When the oil is hot, pour in the paste from the blender. Stir and fry for 6–7 minutes or until the paste has darkened and reduced. Add the chicken, and continue to fry, stirring, for a further 3–4 minutes or until the chicken is lightly browned. Add the tomatoes, fish sauce and lemon grass. Toss the chicken for another 2 minutes. Add 250 ml/8 fl oz water, stir, and bring to the boil. Cover, reduce the heat to low, and cook gently for 25 minutes. Remove the lid, increase the heat a little and let the sauce thicken a bit more for 2–3 minutes. The oil should have risen to the top.

Saira Ahmed's

'Kadhai' Chicken (Karhai Murgh)

PAKISTAN

When I left India almost forty years ago, my mother gave me three essential kitchen utensils, a grinding stone (*sil batta*), a brass platter for making dough (*paraat*) and a cast-iron *kadhai*. I still have all three, each glistening with years of wear, each inscribed with my name.

Kadhais are used, just like the wok, for deep-frying, stir-frying, steaming and – only in South Asia – for reducing milk to make sweets. In this particular recipe, it is used for stir-frying chicken very quickly and easily to produce an uncommonly delicious dish.

This recipe may be made with skinless and boneless breast meat or thigh meat. You could mix the two but, as breasts cook faster than thighs, I tend to use one or the other.

The onion, garlic and ginger need to be very, very finely chopped. I do this in a food processor, using the pulse/stop and start method.

SERVES 4

1 kg/2¼ lb boneless, skinless chicken thighs or breasts, cut into 2½-cm/1-inch pieces
3 tablespoons corn, peanut or olive oil
1 medium onion, about 140 g/5 oz, very finely chopped
4 cloves garlic, peeled and very finely chopped
4-cm/1½-inch piece fresh ginger, peeled and very finely chopped
1¼ teaspoons salt
¾–1 teaspoon cayenne pepper
½ teaspoon ground turmeric
6 tablespoons natural yoghurt
8 tablespoons tomatoes, peeled and finely chopped

FOR THE FINAL FLAVOURING

1 tablespoon fresh, peeled ginger, cut into very fine shreds
7–8 tablespoons fresh coriander leaves, finely chopped
2–3 fresh, hot, green chillies, finely chopped
1 teaspoon *garam masala* (see page 327)
7–8 tablespoons tomatoes, peeled and finely chopped

Pour the oil into a well-seasoned wok, *kadhai* or large, non-stick, lidded pan and set over a medium-high heat. When the oil is hot, put in the onion, garlic and ginger. Stir-fry for about 4–5 minutes or until golden-brown. Add the salt, cayenne pepper and turmeric. Stir once or twice, then put in the chicken. Stir and fry until the chicken pieces turn opaque on the outside. Add the yoghurt and tomato. Stir and cook for 4–5 minutes or until the yoghurt disappears. Cover and cook on a mediumheat for about 10 minutes for dark meat and about 6 minutes for light meat, stirring now and then. Stir in all the final flavouring ingredients, cover, reduce the heat to low, and cook for a further 3 minutes.

From Sarwar Bibi at Tahira Mazhar Ali's home

Mung Dal with Chicken (Dal Gosht)

PAKISTAN

A meal-in-one. All you need with this dish is a salad and either rice or a South-Asian bread. Even a store-bought wholemeal pitta bread will do. Some pickle would be very nice too.

SERVES 4–6

- 275 g/9½ oz mung dal (hulled and split mung beans), washed in several changes of water and drained
- 5 good-sized cloves garlic, peeled and chopped
- 7½-cm/3-inch piece fresh ginger, peeled and chopped
- 1 teaspoon ground turmeric
- 2 teaspoons salt
- 1½ teaspoons cayenne pepper
- 4 tablespoons corn, peanut or olive oil
- 1 large shallot, about 45 g/1 1/2 oz, sliced into fine half-rings
- 1 medium tomato, peeled and finely chopped
- 1 fresh, hot, green, cayenne-type chilli, split in half (if using jalapeños, use 2 thin slivers from a chilli and just a few of the seeds)
- 1 teaspoon garam masala (see page 327)
- ½ teaspoon whole cumin seeds
- 1.15 kg/2½ lb chicken pieces, skinned and cut small (each thigh into 2 pieces, each breast segment into 3 pieces, etc.)

Put a kettle on to boil. You will need hot water as you cook.

Combine the *mung dal* and 900 ml/32 fl oz water in a medium, lidded pan and bring to the boil. Skim away the froth as it rises to the top. Partially cover with the lid, reduce the heat to low, and cook for 20 minutes. Turn off the heat and set aside. Meanwhile, put the garlic, ginger and 4 tablespoons water in a blender. Blend until smooth.

Put the turmeric, salt and cayenne pepper in a small cup. Add 2 tablespoons water to make a paste.

Pour the oil into a large, wide, heavy, lidded pan and set over a medium-high heat. Put in the shallot slices and stir and fry until medium brown. Add the garlic-ginger paste. Stir and fry for 2 minutes. Now add 250 ml/8 fl oz boiling water. Continue to cook on a medium-high heat, stirring now and then, until the sauce appears very thick and golden. Add the turmeric mixture. Stir and fry for a minute. Add 50 ml/2 fl oz hot water. Stir until you have a thick paste again. Add the tomato and stir for a minute. Now add another 50 ml/2 fl oz hot water and stir until the tomato softens into a paste. Add the split green chilli, *garam masala* and cumin seeds, as well as a further 50 ml/2 fl oz hot water. Stir and cook until the sauce thickens again. Add the chicken pieces. Stir and cook them for 5 minutes. Cover, reduce the heat to low and cook for 5 minutes. The chicken will release its juices. Remove the lid, increase the heat to medium-high, and cook, stirring, for 5 minutes. Add the cooked *dal*, 475 ml/16 fl oz water, and bring to the boil. Cover, reduce the heat to low, and cook gently for 25 minutes.

Saira Ahmed's

Minced Chicken Curry (Murgh Keema)

PAKISTAN

All dishes made with minced meat are as close to comfort food as you can get. I do not know why. Maybe it is because they give us an 'I do not have to chew hard, I do not have to think' feeling. Whether the minced meat comes in the form of meat loaves, meatballs or hamburger-like patties, they tend to go down easily.

Pakistanis are great meat eaters but many, including the hosts on my last trip, are conscientiously following health guidelines and cutting down on red meat. For an everyday meal, they might well have this curry, some *dal* (a dried bean/split pea dish) and a vegetable with some flatbreads.

When I was in Myanmar, I had the national dish from Mandalay called *Mon Ti*. It was a simple minced chicken curry served with rice noodles. Try this curry the same way, on top of Rice Noodles, the recipe for which is given on page 271. Sprinkle thinly sliced raw onions and coriander leaves over the top before serving.

SERVES 4

3 tablespoons corn or peanut oil
1 medium onion, chopped
3 cloves garlic, peeled and chopped
450 g/1 lb minced chicken, or turkey
¼ teaspoon ground turmeric
¼ teaspoon cayenne pepper
5 tablespoons natural yoghurt
2 medium tomatoes, peeled and chopped
¾–1 teaspoon salt
225 g/8 oz red or waxy potatoes, peeled and cut into 2-cm/¾-inch dice, or 1 red or green pepper, seeded and cut into 2-cm/¾-inch dice

Pour the oil into a large, wide, lidded pan and set over a medium-high heat. When the oil is hot, put in the onion. Stir and fry until the onion begins to turn brown at the edges. Add the garlic and stir for a minute. Add the chicken, turmeric and cayenne pepper. Stir, breaking up all lumps until chicken is no longer pink. Add the yoghurt and stir and cook until the yoghurt is absorbed. Add the tomatoes, salt and potatoes (or pepper). Stir and cook for a minute. Cover, reduce the heat to low, and cook gently for 15 minutes or until the potatoes are tender. Taste for salt and serve.

Silken Chicken 'Tikka Masala' UK

Here is an Indian dish with an unusual pedigree. It was, most likely, developed by Indian restauranteurs in the United Kingdom. Its closest relative in India is 'Tandoori Chicken in a Butter-Tomato Sauce', where the chicken pieces are marinated, grilled in a *tandoor* oven and then folded into a spicy, buttery, tomato sauce. For the 'Chicken Tikka Masala', carried on the menu of every single British-Indian restaurant, it is boneless chicken cubes, already marinated and grilled, that are folded into a more conventional curry sauce. It is easily one of the most popular dishes in the United Kingdom and I am forever being asked for its recipe.

To make it, you must first prepare the sauce, then the Silken Chicken 'Tikka' Kebabs on page 219, and then combine the two. What was once a delightfully creative hybrid dish, is now a *fait accompli*.

This may be served with Indian flatbreads or rice.

SERVES 4

- 4 tablespoons corn, peanut or olive oil
- 140 g/5 oz onions, sliced into fine half-rings
- 1 tablespoon fresh ginger, peeled and finely grated
- 5–6 cloves garlic, peeled and crushed to a pulp
- 1 tablespoon ground coriander
- ½ teaspoon ground turmeric
- ¾ teaspoon cayenne pepper
- 2 teaspoons bright red paprika
- 4 tablespoons natural yoghurt
- 2 medium tomatoes, about 285 g/10 oz, peeled and very finely chopped
- 350 ml/12 fl oz chicken stock
- ¼ teaspoon salt, more if the stock is unsalted
- ¼ teaspoon *garam masala* (see page 327)
- 4 tablespoons chopped fresh coriander leaves
- freshly made Silken Chicken 'Tikka' Kebabs (see page 219)

Pour the oil into a large, preferably non-stick, lidded pan and set over a medium-high heat. When the oil is hot, put in the onions. Stir and fry until they turn reddish-brown, about 6–7 minutes. Add the ginger and garlic, and continue to fry, stirring, for a minute. Add the coriander, turmeric, cayenne pepper and paprika. Stir for 10 seconds. Add a tablespoon of the yoghurt. Stir and fry until it is absorbed. Add the remaining yoghurt this way, a tablespoon at a time. Put in the tomatoes. Fry them for 3–4 minutes or until they turn pulpy. Keep mashing them with the back of a wooden spoon to help the process along. Add the stock and salt, and bring to a simmer. Cover, reduce the heat to low, and simmer gently for 15–20 minutes. The sauce should turn thick. Stir in the *garam masala* and coriander, taste for balance of flavours, and add more salt if you need it.

Whenever the kebabs are cooked, reheat the sauce and fold in the meat pieces. Serve immediately.

From the Tiffin Restaurant, Port of Spain

Curry Boneless Chicken

TRINIDAD

As orders for 'curry boneless chicken' come in, Lola, the chef at the Tiffin restaurant in Port of Spain, as always, wants to know, 'Any pepper any ting?'

This curry is made with slices of boneless breast meat that sit marinating in a very Trinidadian mixture of 'seasonings'. These include a kind of spring onion, known locally as *saif* (possibly from chives), onions, lantern-shaped, hot congo peppers, and garlic and thyme (there is a strong Mediterranean influence here as well.) There is also parsley and *culantro* (also known as *shadow-beni*), a New-World herb that tastes so much like coriander that the Indians who landed here began to call it *bandhania* or green-coriander-of-the-woods.

To fill the order, Lola heats some oil in a frying pan, throws in some crushed garlic and curry powder, followed by the chicken, which is quickly stir-fried. She adds a little water, a little roasted cumin and some of Trinidad's famous *amchar masala* and the dish is done. It is either served between two slices of bread as a sandwich with lavish sprinklings of hot, hot, hot pepper sauce ('any pepper any ting?') or else rolled in a flatbread called *roti* (see Guyanese Flaky Bread, page 282), along with some chickpeas and potatoes.

I absolutely love it in a sandwich. Because it is just as good cold, I often take it on picnics or eat it straight out of the refrigerator, with a salad, for lunch.

To slice the chicken breasts evenly, it is best if you freeze them in a single layer for 35–45 minutes first. When they are half-frozen and firm, it is easy to cut them uniformly.

I find it somewhat curious that Trinidadians do not use fresh ginger in their curries. They do, however, use ground ginger, as you will notice in this recipe.

You may make your own roasted and ground cumin seeds, *amchar masala* and curry powder according to recipes on pages 339 and 324, but you should know that West-Indian shops sell all of them ready-made in packets and that they are generally very good.

SERVES 4

FOR THE MARINADE

6 tablespoons peeled and finely chopped onion

2 large cloves garlic, peeled and chopped

2 spring onions, white and light green parts only, sliced into rings

2 tablespoons finely chopped parsley

2–3 tablespoons finely chopped culantro or fresh coriander

1 loosely packed tablespoon fresh thyme leaves, or ½ teaspoon dried

⅛ of a congo pepper (scotch bonnet or habanero), chopped (handle with care and remove seeds), or 3 bird's eye chillies, chopped

½ teaspoon ground ginger

½ teaspoon salt

freshly ground black pepper

450 g/1 lb boned and skinned chicken breasts, cut crossways into 3-mm/1/8 inch thick slices

FOR COOKING THE CHICKEN

3 tablespoons corn, peanut or olive oil

2–3 cloves garlic, peeled and crushed to a pulp

1 tablespoon hot curry powder

½ teaspoon salt

½ teaspoon ground, roasted cumin seeds (see page 339)

1 teaspoon *amchar masala* (see page 324)

Make the marinade. Put the onion, garlic, spring onion, parsley, culantro, thyme, congo pepper, ginger, salt, black pepper and 2 tablespoons water into a blender. Blend to a smooth paste, pushing down with a rubber spatula when needed.

Put the sliced chicken in a bowl. Add the marinade and mix well. Cover and refrigerate for 30 minutes or for up to 3 hours.

Pour the oil into a wide, non-stick pan, add the garlic, and set over a medium-high heat. As soon as the garlic starts to sizzle and brown, add the curry powder. Stir it for 10 seconds. Reduce the heat to medium, add the chicken, together with its marinade, and stir for 3–4 minutes or until all the pieces turn white. Add 120 ml/4 fl oz water, the salt, cumin and *amchar masala*. Stir and bring to a simmer. Reduce the heat to low and cook, uncovered, for 2–3 minutes, stirring now and then.

Chicken and Bamboo Shoots in Red Curry

THAILAND

This is the curry that I lived on for a good three months as I travelled through Thailand. It was available in most small and big town cafeterias. It was always good: a reliable standby for all occasions. I always ate it with rice.

Thais always have lots of raw vegetables on the side to nibble on: long beans cut into 7½-cm/3-inch lengths, crisp bean sprouts that have been 'topped and tailed', herbs such as holy basil, and all manner of lettuces. You could make such a plate, substituting French or green beans if long beans are unavailable, and leave it on the table.

In Thailand, freshly boiled, tender bamboo shoots are sold in most markets. Look for good quality, canned, winter bamboo shoots (see page 334 for more details). You could either buy them already sliced or else slice them the same size as the chicken pieces. All canned bamboo shoots should be drained and rinsed before use.

SERVES 4–6

- 400-ml/14-fl oz can of coconut milk, left undisturbed for 3 hours or more
- 2 tablespoons corn or peanut oil
- 5 tablespoons Red Curry Paste (see page 318)
- 450 g/1 lb boned and skinned chicken breasts, cut crossways into 3-mm/⅛-inch thick slices
- 140 g/5 oz drained and washed, sliced bamboo shoots
- 2 tablespoons fish sauce (*nam pla*), or to taste
- 1 teaspoon thick tamarind paste (see page 345), or lemon juice
- 1 teaspoon palm sugar or brown sugar
- 4 fresh kaffir lime leaves or a teaspoon of julienned lemon rind
- 15–20 fresh sweet basil (*bai horappa*) leaves or ordinary basil leaves

Carefully open the can of coconut milk without disturbing it too much and remove 4 tablespoons of the thick cream that will have settled at the top. Stir the remaining contents of the can well and set aside.

Pour the oil into a wide, preferably non-stick, pan and set over a medium-high heat. When the oil is hot, add the coconut cream and the curry paste. Stir and fry for 3–4 minutes or until the oil separates and the paste is lightly browned. Reduce the heat to low and add the chicken, bamboo shoots, fish sauce, tamarind (or lemon juice), sugar and the reserved coconut milk. Stir and bring to a simmer. The chicken should turn white and cook through by the time the first bubbles begin to appear. Simmer on a low heat for a minute.

Either tear up the lime leaves or else remove the central vein and cut them into fine strips. These and the basil leaves should be scattered over the top when serving.

Cardamom and Black Pepper Chicken

UK

There are many versions of this recipe floating around London's Indian restaurants, and it was probably created by a British-Indian chef. It is a quick and really delicious dish, perfectly geared to restaurant cooking where boneless chicken breasts are convenient to buy and prepare. The marination can be done ahead of time and individual orders take just minutes to cook. All this just happens to be very convenient for the home cook as well.

To slice the chicken breasts evenly, it is best if you freeze them in a single layer for 35–45 minutes first. When they are half-frozen and firm, it is easy to cut them uniformly.

SERVES 4

FOR MARINATING THE CHICKEN

6 tablespoons onion, peeled and finely chopped
5-cm/2-inch piece fresh ginger, peeled and finely chopped
2 large cloves garlic, peeled and chopped
½ teaspoon salt
½ teaspoon cayenne pepper
½ teaspoon freshly ground black pepper
450 g/1 lb boned and skinned chicken breasts, cut crossways into 3-mm/⅛-inch thick slices

FOR COOKING THE CHICKEN

3 tablespoons corn, peanut or olive oil
1 medium stick cinnamon
8 whole cardamom pods
140 g/5 oz onions, peeled and sliced into fine half-rings
½ teaspoon ground cumin
½ teaspoon ground coriander
4 tablespoons natural yoghurt
5 tablespoons tomato, grated
1 teaspoon salt
¼ teaspoon *garam masala* (see page 327)
2–3 teaspoons lemon juice

Make the marinade. Put the onion, ginger, garlic, salt, cayenne pepper, black pepper and 3 tablespoons water into a blender. Blend to a smooth paste, pushing down with a rubber spatula when needed. Put the sliced chicken in a bowl. Add the marinade and mix well. Cover and refrigerate for 30 minutes, or up to 3 hours if desired.

Pour the oil into a wide, non-stick pan set over a medium-high heat. When the oil is hot hot, add the cinnamon and cardamom. Stir for 10 seconds. Put in the onion and fry, stirring at the same time, for 6–7 minutes or until the onion turns a reddish-brown colour. Add the cumin and coriander. Stir once. Add the yoghurt, a tablespoon at a time, and stir until it is absorbed. Add the tomato and stir for a minute. Reduce the heat to medium, add the chicken, together with its marinade, and cook, stirring, for 3–4 minutes or until all the chicken pieces turn white. Add 175 ml/6 fl oz water, the salt and *garam masala*. Stir and bring to a simmer. Reduce the heat to low and cook, uncovered, for 2–3 minutes, stirring now and then.

From Sameena at Yousaf Salahuddin's home

Braised Quail (Bater)

PAKISTAN

This quail is often part of winter lunches served on sunny verandahs and courtyards of grand homes in Lahore. All the guests come bedecked in their winter finery, which for most of them (as with most north Indians), means exquisite Kashmiri shawls.

The quail used here were wild and quite small.

SERVES 4 AS A MAIN COURSE, 8 AS A STARTER

7½-cm/3-inch piece fresh ginger, peeled and finely chopped
5 cloves garlic, peeled and chopped
2 fresh, hot, green, cayenne-type chillies, chopped (if using a jalapeño, use one, with its seeds)
3 tablespoons corn, peanut or olive oil
30 g/1 oz unsalted butter
2 medium onions, sliced into very fine half-rings
1 teaspoon cayenne pepper
2 teaspoons whole coriander seeds, ground to a coarse powder
1¼ teaspoons salt
¼ teaspoon ground turmeric
2½ medium tomatoes, peeled and very finely chopped
120 ml/4 fl oz natural yoghurt, lightly beaten
8 quail
½ teaspoon *garam masala* (see page 327)

Put the ginger, garlic and chillies in a blender along with 4 tablespoons water and blend until smooth.

Put the oil and butter in a large, wide, heavy, lidded pan and set over a medium-high heat. When hot, add the onions. Stir and fry, turning the heat down to medium as needed, until the onions are a medium brown. Add the ginger-garlic mixture. Stir and fry on a medium-heat for 3–4 minutes. Add 250 ml/8 fl oz water, as well as the cayenne pepper, coriander, salt, turmeric, tomatoes and yoghurt. Bring to the boil on a medium-high heat. Cook, stirring frequently, until the sauce is thick and the oil separates from it. Add the quail. Stir and fry for 3–4 minutes. Cover tightly, reduce the heat to low, and braise gently for 1 hour and 15 minutes or until the quail are tender. They should cook in their own juices. If they dry out, add a few tablespoons of water. Turn the birds around and stir gently every 6–7 minutes. Sprinkle over the garam masala 5 minutes before the cooking ends and stir it in.

THE VINDALOO CURRY

Vindaloos, created in the Portuguese-Indian colony of Goa, were generally made with pork and seem to have got their name from their most important seasonings, the Portuguese word for wine, *vinho* (in this case, wine vinegar), and for garlic, *alhos*. We have always assumed that the wine in the name stood for wine vinegar. But lately, I have begun to wonder if the early, 400-year-old Portuguese recipe did indeed use wine, albeit wine that had turned somewhat vinegary over its long passage in a rocking and rolling ship. The vinegar used these days is made from what Goans have the most of, rice or coconut palms.

A *vindaloo* that may have started off as a simple stew, acquired more and more Indian flavourings over time, and today even the name *vindaloo* stands for 'hot, hot, hot' the world over. In Goa, however, the heat is hardly its chief characteristic. It is the combination of spices – you can buy a mixed *vindaloo masala* in the bazaars – and the use of vinegar, which acts as a preservative, is what makes *vindaloos* different from other Goan foods. Because of the preserving qualities of vinegar, *vindaloos* are considered a perfect wedding dish that, once made, may be served again and again over several days.

All along the tropical south-western coast of India I have found wedding and other banquet dishes that use souring agents – tamarinds, the kokum fruit and, of course, vinegar. These wedding foods (which can also be made with fish) are heated up daily to control the bacteria but never see the inside of a refrigerator.

While most *vindaloos* are made with pork, which Catholic Goans eat readily, they are also made with the ducks that paddle freely in the thousands of flooded rice fields. The dish then becomes accessible to the many Muslims and Hindus of the area.

The ducks that I get in our markets are the Peking variety, usually weighing anywhere between 2–3.2 kg/4½–7 lb and, unlike chickens, are long-breasted. I used a 2.7-kg/6-lb duck here. It is best to ask the butcher to joint it for you, cutting the bird into serving pieces. The legs should be detached and divided into two pieces each and the breast area cut neatly into four sections, once across and once lengthways. The wings should be separated as well. They have very little meat but I tend to cook them along with the rest of the duck as they add flavour to the sauce. In India, the bird is usually skinned. What I do – and this I do myself – is to cut off all the hanging flaps of fat and skin but leave some skin on each piece. I always cook the duck a day in advance. It not only tastes better but also allows me to remove most of the fat that congeals at the top. Yes, I do refrigerate it!

Duck Vindaloo (Duck Vindalho)

INDIA

Vindaloos are invariably served with rice in India but I often enjoy serving them with boiled, browned potatoes and any strong, slightly bitter green such as sautéed endive.

SERVES 6

- ½ teaspoon ground turmeric
- 1 tablespoon ground cumin
- 1 tablespoon bright red paprika
- 1 tablespoon ground coriander
- 1 teaspoon cayenne pepper
- 1½ teaspoons *garam masala* (see page 327)
- 4 tablespoons corn or peanut oil
- a 2.7-kg/6-lb duck, jointed and partially skinned, as suggested above
- ½ teaspoon whole brown mustard seeds
- ¼ teaspoon whole fenugreek seeds
- 15 fresh curry leaves, if available
- 2 medium onions, about 285 g/10 oz, peeled and sliced into fine half-rings
- 2 tablespoons peeled and finely grated fresh ginger
- 10 medium cloves garlic, peeled and crushed to a pulp
- 2 medium tomatoes, peeled and chopped
- 120 ml/4 fl oz cider vinegar
- 2 ¾ teaspoons salt
- 1 tablespoon sugar

Mix together the turmeric, cumin, paprika, coriander, cayenne pepper and *garam masala* in a small bowl and set aside.

Pour the oil into a large, wide, lidded pan and set over a medium-high heat. When the oil is hot, put in as many duck pieces, skin side down, as the pan will hold easily in a single layer. Lightly brown the duck, about 3–4 minutes per side, and remove to a bowl. Brown all the duck pieces this way and remove.

Add the mustard and fenugreek seeds to the hot fat and, as soon as the mustard seeds start to pop, which will happen in a matter of seconds, put in the curry leaves and onions. Stir and fry them until the onions begin to turn brown at the edges. Now put in the ginger and garlic. Stir and fry for a minute. Add the mixed spices from the small bowl and stir for 30 seconds. Add the tomatoes and cook, stirring, until they have softened, about 2–3 minutes. Scrape the bottom of the pan as you do this. Now add the browned duck pieces, the vinegar, salt, sugar and 475 ml/16 fl oz water. Stir and bring to the boil. Cover, reduce the heat to low, and cook gently for 45 minutes, lifting the lid occassionally to stir. Increase the heat to medium-low and simmer, partially covered, a bit more vigorously, stirring more frequently, for a further 30 minutes or until the duck is tender and the sauce has thickened slightly. Remove as much fat as possible before serving.

Duck Cooked in the Delhi Hunter's Style (Shikar Ki Buttuck)

INDIA

During the winter months when my father and brothers went hunting, they usually came back with a lot of duck and venison. The duck were often mallards, which were then cooked in our kitchens with cinnamon and nutmeg. Sometimes hunters cooked their ducks in the fields where they hunted them. In one Bombay cookbook, that began compiling its recipes in 1934 and has updated them many times since, a Zarene S. Kothavala gives this recipe for a Tired Hunter's Duck:

Clean the bird but do not remove the feathers. Mix mud and water to make a thick paste. Cover the whole bird with this to make a crust about half an inch thick. Make a wood fire and allow the embers to get red hot. Bury the mud-covered bird under the embers and forget all about it for an hour or so – except for fanning the embers from time to time. When ready, the feathers should come away easily with the baked mud; the bird and all the juices are retained intact.

I have used the more readily-available Peking duck here, rather than mallard. See notes on *vindaloo* curry (page 107) on how to cut it into serving pieces.

I like to cook the duck a day before I serve it. This way I can remove all the fat that congeals at the top.

SERVES *4*

4 tablespoons corn or peanut oil
a 2.7-kg/6-lb duck, jointed and partially skinned, as suggested on page 107
1 medium stick cinnamon
7 whole cardamom pods
2 bay leaves
2 medium onions, about 285 g/10 oz, sliced into fine half-rings
2 tablespoons fresh ginger, peeled and finely grated
6 medium cloves garlic, peeled and crushed to a pulp
½ teaspoon ground turmeric
1 tablespoon ground cumin
1 tablespoon bright red paprika
1 tablespoon ground coriander
1 teaspoon cayenne pepper
1½ teaspoons *garam masala* (see page 327)
2 medium tomatoes, peeled and chopped
2 teaspoons salt
½ teaspoon ground cinnamon
¼ teaspoon freshly grated nutmeg

Pour the oil into a large, wide, lidded pan and set over a medium-high heat. When the oil is hot, put in as many duck pieces, skin side down, as the pan will hold easily in a single layer. Lightly brown the duck, about 3–4 minutes per side, and remove to a bowl. Brown all the duck pieces this way and remove.

Add the cinnamon stick, cardamom and bay leaves to the hot fat and, 10 seconds later, add the onions. Stir and fry until the onions begin to turn brown at the edges. Now put in the ginger and garlic. Stir and fry for a minute. Add the turmeric, cumin, paprika, coriander, cayenne pepper and *garam masala*. Stir for 30 seconds. Add the tomatoes, and cook until they have softened, about 2–3 minutes, stirring and scraping the bottom of the pan as you do this. Now add the browned duck pieces, the salt and 475 ml/16 fl oz water. Stir and bring to the boil. Cover, reduce the heat to low, and cook gently for 1 hour and 15 minutes or until the duck is tender, lifting the lid to stir now and then. Check for salt, adding more if needed. Add the cinnamon and nutmeg and continue to cook, stirring now and then, for a further 10 minutes. Remove as much fat as possible before serving.

Duck and Green Beans in a Green Curry Sauce THAILAND

Thais often put vegetables into their curries at the very end of the cooking time so that they stay almost raw. Small aubergines are a favourite but long beans are popular as well. You will need about seven long beans, cut into 5-cm/2-inch pieces. If you cannot get them, use twenty-five French or green beans halved.

SERVES 4

450–675 g/1-1¼ lb boneless duck breasts
400-ml/14-fl oz can coconut milk, left undisturbed for 3 hours or more
5 tablespoons Green Curry Paste (see page 320)
1½–2 tablespoons fish sauce (nam pla), or to taste
2 teaspoons thick tamarind paste (see page 345), or lemon juice
1 teaspoon palm sugar or brown sugar
7 long beans, cut into 5-cm/2-inch pieces, or French beans, prepared as described above
4 fresh kaffir lime leaves or a teaspoon of julienned lemon rind
15–20 fresh sweet basil (*bai horappa*) leaves or ordinary basil leaves
a handful of fresh bean sprouts, if available, topped and tailed
2–3 fresh hot, red and green bird's eye chillies, cut into fine rounds, optional

Put a non-stick, lidded frying pan on a low heat. Place the duck breasts, skin side down, in the pan and let them render their fat slowly. now and then, turn the breasts on their side, holding them down with tongs, to draw out the protruding fat. This process may take 25 minutes. The fatty side of the breasts will have browned. Brown the opposite side for a minute. Remove the breasts and set aside on a plate until they have cooled. Now, cut them crossways, into 3-mm/⅛-inch thick slices. Remove all but 2 tablespoons of the duck fat and save for other uses.

Carefully open the can of coconut milk and remove 4 tablespoons of the thick cream that will have settled at the top. Stir the remaining contents of the can well and set aside.

Place the pan containing the 2 tablespoons of duck fat over a medium heat. When the fat is hot, add the thick coconut cream and the green curry paste. Stir and fry until the oil separates and the paste is lightly browned. Reduce the heat to low and stir in the fish sauce, tamarind (or lemon juice), sugar, the well-stirred coconut milk, the duck slices and 475 ml/16 fl oz water. Cover and simmer on a very low heat for about 1¼ hours or until the duck is tender. Taste for a balance of flavours, adding more fish sauce, sugar or tamarind if needed. Stir in the green beans, and simmer very gently for 2 minutes.

Just before serving, either tear up the lime leaves or else remove the central vein and cut them into fine strips, and stir, together with the basil leaves, into the curry. Garnish with the bean sprouts and chilli slices, if desired.

Hard-Boiled Eggs in an Anglo-Indian Red Lentil Curry Sauce

INDIA

Those of us who have Anglo-Indian friends know how wonderful and distinct their cooking is. Here is one of their recipes. It is generally served with rice, chutneys and relishes.

SERVES 4–6

- **6 dried, hot red chillies**
- **200 g/6½ oz red lentils**
- **90 g/3¼ oz *chana dal* or yellow split peas**
- **½ teaspoon ground turmeric**
- **1½ teaspoons salt**
- **4 cloves garlic, peeled and coarsely chopped**
- **7½-cm/3-inch piece fresh ginger, peeled and chopped**
- **4 tablespoons corn, peanut or safflower oil**
- **1 medium onion, about 140 g/5 oz, sliced into very fine half-rings**
- **2 medium tomatoes, grated on a coarse grater (discard the skin that remains in your hand)**
- **8–12 hard-boiled eggs (depending on number of people eating), peeled and halved**
- **a little cayenne pepper or bright red paprika for garnishing**
- **lemon wedges for serving**

Soak the chillies in 5 tablespoons of boiling water for 1 hour or until slightly softened.

Combine the red lentils and *chana dal* and wash in several changes of water. Drain. Put in a good sized pan, add the turmeric and 900 ml/32 fl oz water, and bring to the boil. Reduce the heat to low, cover partially with a lid, and cook for about 1¼ hours or until softened. Add the salt and stir to mix. The sauce will be fairly salty at this stage.

Put the chillies, their soaking liquid, the garlic and ginger into a blender. Blend until smooth.

Pour the oil into a medium, preferably non-stick, frying pan and set over a medium-high heat. When the oil is hot, put in the onion. Stir and fry until the onion slices are a rich reddish colour and slightly crisp. Add the garlic-ginger-chilli paste. Stir and fry for 2–3 minutes or until the oil begins to separate from the seasonings. Add the tomatoes. Stir and fry for 3–4 minutes or until thickened. Now empty the contents of the frying pan into the pan with the lentils. Add 600 ml/1 pint water and stir to mix. Bring to a simmer and simmer on a low heat for a minute.

To serve, place the halved eggs, cut side up, in a single layer in a warmed, large, shallow dish. Heat the sauce through and, if it has thickened too much while sitting, thin it with water. It should have the consistency of flowing double cream. Pour it over the the eggs but leave them visible. Garnish with a light sprinkling of cayenne pepper or paprika and serve with wedges of lemon. Extra sauce may be served on the side.

THE ANGLO-INDIAN INFLUENCE

Curried hard-boiled eggs came into their own during British rule in India. Colonial Britons loved their curries and their eggs in the morning and often the two were combined into one dish that was eaten with rice for both breakfast and lunch.

Indians, of course, had their own traditional sauced egg dishes. There was the Tomato Kut of Hyderabad in which halved hard-boiled eggs were imbedded in a spicy tomato purée lightly thickened with chickpea flour and flavoured with tamarind, or, my father's favourite, a spicy stew of innards with hard-boiled eggs in it.

British-Indian egg curries tended to be much simpler and ranged from eggs added to cooked lentils, the lentils acting as the sauce, to eggs in a sauce made with onions, flour, curry powder, stock, apples, lime juice and chutney – very popular in Britain in the19th and early 20th centuries. Also popular were eggs smothered with semi-French white sauces made with curry powder (see page 331 for Curry Sauce.)

The recipe on page 113 has been adapted from a turn-of-the-century Anglo-Indian cookbook. By Anglo-Indian, I do not mean a Briton living in India, or one with a history in India, though that, confusingly, was often the British usage. By Anglo-Indian, I mean a person of mixed race. India has had a whole community of mixed race people for almost 400 years. Anglo-Indians in India define themselves as having a male ancestor of English, Scottish, Welsh or Irish origin who was married to an Indian.

In the 17th and 18th centuries when British men came to India alone, they often took Indian wives, the rich amongst them living a life of Riley as 'white nabobs'. Amongst the poorer British sailors and tailors, some married, some did not, but most had liaisons, produced children and thus added to the growing Anglo-Indian community. Great numbers of this community were in Calcutta, which was the British seat of government until 1911 when the capital moved to New Delhi, though cities such as Madras had a fair share as well.

By the time Queen Victoria's reign was in full swing, Britain's grasp on India had tightened, it was a full colony, more women were joining their men and the church was discouraging contact between the races.

But the Anglo-Indians, who were used by the British as buffers between themselves and the native population, were there to stay. They were encouraged by the British to run the railways and post offices and hence they spread throughout the nation. They had European names, wore European clothes and were Christians, though their looks, foods and language hinted broadly at their dual heritage.

Hard-Boiled Eggs in a Delhi-Style Sauce

INDIA

Ideal for a Sunday brunch or late supper, this is the kind of curried, hard-boiled egg curry that I had in my Delhi home. We ate it with flatbreads or rice, sometimes even with slices of bread. There were always pickles and chutneys on the side.

SERVES 4

- 4 tablespoons corn, peanut oil or olive oil
- 140 g/5 oz onion, sliced into fine half-rings
- 1 tablespoon fresh ginger, peeled and finely grated
- 5–6 cloves garlic, peeled and crushed to a pulp
- 1 tablespoon ground coriander
- 1 teaspoon ground cumin
- ½ teaspoon ground turmeric
- ¾ teaspoon cayenne pepper
- 1 teaspoons bright red paprika
- 4 tablespoons natural yoghurt
- 2 medium tomatoes, about 285 g/10 oz, peeled and very finely chopped
- 350 ml/12 fl oz chicken stock
- ¼ teaspoon salt, more if the stock is unsalted
- 120 ml/4 fl oz whipping cream
- ¼ teaspoon *garam masala* (see page 327)
- 1–3 fresh, hot green bird's eye chillies, either left whole or finely chopped (the latter will make the dish hotter)
- 4 tablespoons fresh coriander leaves, chopped
- 8 hard-boiled eggs, peeled and halved lengthways

Pour the oil into a large, preferably non-stick, lidded pan and set over a medium-high heat. When the oil is hot, add the onions. Stir and fry until they turn reddish-brown, about 6–7 minutes. Put in the ginger and garlic, and stir and fry for a minute. Add the coriander, cumin, turmeric, cayenne pepper and paprika. Stir for 10 seconds. Add the yoghurt, a tablespoon at a time, stirring until it is absorbed. Stir in the tomatoes and cook for 3–4 minutes or until they turn pulpy. Keep mashing them with the back of a wooden spoon to help the process along. Add the stock and salt, and bring to a simmer. Cover, reduce the heat to low, and simmer gently for 15–20 minutes. The sauce should turn thick. Stir in the cream, *garam masala,* chillies and chopped coriander. Taste for a balance of flavours, and add more salt if you need it. Lay the hard-boiled eggs in the sauce in a single layer, cut side up, and spoon some sauce over them.

Hard-Boiled Eggs with a British Curry Sauce UK

SERVES 2 Hard boil four eggs, peel them and then cut them in half, lengthways. Pour some of the Curry Sauce over the top (see page 331) and serve with toast or rice.

Chef Wan's

Poached Eggs in a Creamy Malay Curry Sauce (Gulai Lemak Telor) MALAYSIA

In this Malaysian dish, eggs are broken into a split pea and coconut sauce and allowed to poach in the hot liquid. I prefer to let my eggs poach separately. Then I serve them this way: I mound about four tablespoons of freshly cooked plain rice in the centre of an old-fashioned soup plate. I place an egg on top of the rice. Then I ladle some hot sauce over and around the egg.

A word about the sauce. The fact that it is made with *toovar dal* (hulled and split pigeon peas) makes it clear that that its origins are very likely the *sambars* of south India, which use this *dal* as a base. *Sambars* and rice were part of the daily diet of most migrating Tamil labourers. The use of ginger, shallots, chillies and tamarind also pulls this dish in India's direction. But two ingredients – lemon grass and dried anchovies – give it a quintessentially Malay flavour, especially when combined with coconut milk.

Instead of using dried anchovies, which are hard to find, I use canned ones.

SERVES 4

200 g/7 oz *toovar dal*, picked over, washed in several changes of water and drained
3–4 canned anchovies, chopped
85 g/2½ oz shallots, chopped
2-cm/¾-inch piece fresh ginger, peeled and chopped
10–20 bird's eye chillies, chopped
¼ teaspoon ground turmeric
2 stalks fresh lemon grass (use the bottom 18 cm/7 inches)
400-ml/14-fl oz can of coconut milk, well shaken
2 tablespoons thick tamarind paste (see page 345), or 1½ tablespoons lemon juice
2 teaspoons salt, or to taste
4 eggs

Combine the *dal* and 850 ml/1¼ pints water in a medium, lidded pan. Bring to the boil, cover partially, reduce the heat to low and cook very gently for 1¼ hours or until tender.

Meanwhile, put the anchovies, shallots, ginger, chillies, turmeric and 2–3 tablespoons water into a blender and blend until smooth.

When the *dal* is tender, stir in the seasonings from the blender. Bruise the bulbous ends of the lemon grass stalks and, if necessary, fold them into thirds and tie them up. Drop these into the *dal*. Stir in the coconut milk, tamarind paste (or lemon juice) and salt. Bring to a simmer again and simmer gently, uncovered, for 10 minutes, stirring occasionally.

Remove the lemon grass and push the sauce through a coarse strainer. It should be as thin as single cream. If it is too thick, add some water. Taste for a balance of salt and sour and make any necessary adjustments. This sauce can be prepared ahead of time, covered and refrigerated. Heat through before serving.

Just before serving, poach the eggs. Pour water to a depth of 5 mm/¼ inch into a large, non-stick, lidded pan and set over a medium heat. When the water just begins to simmer, gently break the eggs into the pan, side by side. They will fill the pan. Reduce the heat to low, cover partially, and cook until the eggs are done to your liking. Remove the lid and take the pan off the heat. Remove the eggs with a slotted spatula. Serve as suggested above or, if you prefer, put all the eggs in a shallow serving dish and pour some of the heated sauce around them. The rest of the sauce should be passed on the side. The rice may also be passed on the side.

Indian-Style Curried Omelette Pie

USA

Lately, I have started making the traditional Indian *masala* omelette in a large pie shape as it is easier to serve. One pie will serve several people at once and wedges are so easy to cut. I have added some ingredients that may be considered 'new American', such as fresh shiitake mushrooms, cherry tomatoes and also cream, which gives a certain richness and is not commonly used in Indian egg dishes.

You need a large, non-stick frying pan for this pie, preferably one with a metal handle as it needs to sit under the grill briefly. A 25–28-cm/10–11-inch pan is ideal, though you could make do with something slightly smaller.

I often serve this for Sunday brunch with Potatoes with Ginger (see page 176), which is like an Indian hash brown, and a green salad.

SERVES 4–6

- 12 large eggs
- salt
- 50 ml/4 tablespoons double cream
- 3 tablespoons olive oil
- ½ teaspoon whole cumin seeds
- 4 button mushrooms, cut into small dice
- 6 fresh shiitake mushrooms, stalks removed, cut into small dice
- 6 spring onions, halved lengthways and then cut, crossways, into fine slices, including most of the crisp green parts
- 2 fresh, hot green chillies, finely chopped
- 4 tablespoons fresh green coriander leaves, finely chopped
- 10 cherry tomatoes, cut into 8
- 2 teapoons hot curry powder

Break the eggs into a bowl and beat them lightly. Stir in ¼ teaspoon salt and the cream.

Set the grill to heat.

Pour the oil into a large, non-stick pan (see note above) and set it over a medium-high heat. When the oil is hot, put in the cumin seeds. Let them sizzle for 10 seconds. Now put in the button mushrooms, shiitake mushrooms, spring onions, chillies, coriander, cherry tomatoes and curry powder. Stir for 2–3 minutes. Stir in ½ teaspoon salt. Add the egg mixture. Stir slowly from the bottom of the pan with a flat spatula until you have some thick curds but the bottom and top of the pan are still covered with a somewhat thickened liquid, about 2 minutes. The eggs should be very lightly set. Place the pan under the grill until the top browns and the eggs are fully set, about 2 minutes.

Remove the pan. Go around the edges with a thin spatula to release the pie. Slide the spatula under the pie to make sure it is not caught at the bottom. Now reverse a large plate on top of the pan and then flip the pan so the pie is in the plate. But it is the wrong side of the pie that is uppermost, so get a large, round serving platter and reverse it over the pie. Flip one more time and you are in business.

3

FISH AND SEAFOOD

It is almost impossible for anyone who knows Indian food only from Indian restaurants to even imagine India's great wealth of fish and seafood dishes. All of India's east, south and west is neatly outlined by a vast 'V' where salty seas lick palms heavy with fattened coconuts. Village kitchens along estuaries and meandering backwaters produce oyster fritters, coconut-enriched prawn curry, fish baked between banana leaves, fish steamed with crushed mustard seeds and crabs poached in spicy tamarind broth.

I remember walking into a 16th-century Portuguese church in the south-western Indian state of Kerala where Vasco da Gama had once been buried. The sun had been blistering but just one step inside the stone church and I was in a dark, cool haven. A church worker had, similarly, taken shelter and was sitting on a corridor bench. He had opened up his three-tiered tiffin-carrier and was deeply immersed in his lunch. I watched discreetly. One container had the rice. It was the partially milled parboiled rice that is much loved here. Its fat, puffy grains were meant to absorb the curry in the second container. Fresh sardines, about 13 cm/5 inches long, had been cleaned and poached in a very red sauce of chillies, shallots and sour, smoked tamarind. If further tastes were needed, the third container held pickles. I so wanted to share his lunch but had to make do instead with a prawn curry freshly prepared for me on the beach by a fisherman. I could hardly complain.

Even though the day was hot, the sardine curry was in no danger of spoiling. The tamarind, a preservative, saw to that. Sour tamarind is used with fish and seafood the length of India's southern coast for many reasons. First of all, it is a coolant. In hot climates, this is important. Then, it is a preservative. Fish dishes at weddings are often cooked in tamarind broth and then stored in rows of narrow-necked earthenware pots. If they are brought to the boil once every day, they can last for a week without refrigeration. There is also the matter of taste. If slightly sweet coconut milk in used in the cooking, tamarind acts as a souring, balancing foil.

The Indo-Persian Parsi community smothers fish in a coconut-coriander chutney and then steams it wrapped in a banana-leaf-package. North Indians and Pakistanis marinate whole river fish in yoghurt and *ajowan* seeds (which are a bit like thyme) and then bake them whole in clay *tandoor* ovens. In Bengal, lobsters may be put into a mustard seed, mustard oil and chilli sauce and then steamed. In Kerala, fish might be poached in roasted spices, such as black pepper, coriander and fenugreek.

In Bengal, fish is eaten with rice, in north India and Pakistan it is eaten with wheat bread, and in Kerala, the coconut-infused curries may be eaten with fresh, home-made rice noodles, *idiappam*. Over much of coastal India, fish is rubbed with turmeric and salt and set aside before being cooked. Salt firms up the fish and turmeric is an antiseptic. There are always good reasons, other than flavour, for most traditional Indian culinary decisions.

Traders began leaving India well before the start of the Christian era. Most sailed east with the prevailing monsoon winds, heading towards Vietnam, Thailand, Malaysia and Indonesia. Most were from fish-eating, coastal families. With them they took their fish recipes and the required seasonings, such as mustard seeds, turmeric and curry leaves. Even today, evidence of this can be seen all over South-East Asia.

When indentured labourers were taken by the British in the first half of the 19th century to build railroads in Uganda or run sugar and coffee plantations in South Africa, many also came from coastal villages in what is now Tamil Nadu. They were allowed very limited rations on the boats that ferried them, but dried fish and tamarind were included. They could roast or fry the fish with a few spices, put it in a tamarind sauce and eat with it rice. By the end of the century, as more Indian traders set up spice shops in South Africa, and as indentured labourers were freed, fish cookery began to take new forms. Regional culinary traditions had been lost and new ones were created as spices became available. Anything went. Spice shops began mixing their own standardised 'fish *masala*'. Fish was cooked with baby aubergines or with okra. Tomatoes and/or tamarind were added. Coconut milk, which had been forgotten, slowly began to make a comeback. Crabs were steamed with lemon grass, as it was available, and then put into a curry sauce.

In Malaysia, Singapore and northern Indonesia, there was excellent fish to be had. If whole fish was expensive, fish heads were not. Singapore's famous fish head curry was born this way. Chinese noodle soups were combined with coconut curry bases to make dozens of curried fish soups. In Thailand, curry pastes, made with a mixture of fresh kaffir lime skin, lemon grass and galangal and some dry curry spices, were used to cook everything from lobsters to crabs.

Not all fish or seafood is available everywhere so, in this chapter, I have offered many alternative suggestions. You will have to experiment with your local fish. It is better to get very fresh fish, whatever it be, than to hunt all day for a specific fish preferred in a recipe. Good old salmon can replace many of the fish. Lobsters and crabs are always used live as that is the Asian tradition.

Here are some general directions for buying and preparing fish and seafood. If there is a local fish market, head in that direction. It will always be better than your supermarket. Learn about your local Chinese or Vietnamese fish markets. They will have good fish. Any fish you buy should look glossy, bright-eyed and have pleasingly red gills. If it is at all slimy or dull-eyed, leave it alone.

Remember that some seafood does freeze well. This includes prawns and squid.

For methods on preparing prawns, squid, clams, mussels, crabs and lobsters, see Special Ingredients and Techniques at the back of this book.

Mutthu's

Singapore-Style Prawn Curry

SINGAPORE

Prawn curries may be made with or without coconut milk. Here is an unctuous one that is adapted from the curry served at the famous Mutthu's restaurant in Little India, Singapore. Its origins are very south Indian. It should be eaten with rice.

Directions for peeling, deveining and cleaning prawns are on page 343.

SERVES 6

- 4 tablespoons corn or peanut oil
- 1 teaspoon whole cumin seeds
- ½ teaspoon whole fennel seeds
- ¼ teaspoon whole fenugreek seeds
- 10–15 fresh curry leaves, if available
- 3 good-sized shallots, about 90 g/3 oz, finely sliced into slivers
- 4 cloves garlic, peeled and sliced into fine slivers
- 1 medium tomato, about 180 g/6 oz, peeled and finely chopped
- 1 teaspoon fresh ginger, peeled and very finely grated
- 1 tablespoon ground coriander
- 1 teaspoon ground cumin
- ¼ teaspoon ground turmeric
- 1 teaspoon cayenne pepper
- 1 tablespoon bright red paprika
- 1 tablespoon thick tamarind paste (see page 345), or 2 teaspoons lemon juice
- 1 teaspoon salt
- 900 g/2 lb raw, headless, shell-on prawns, peeled and deveined (if buying prawns with heads, you will need an additional 450 g/1 lb)
- 400-ml/14-fl oz can of coconut milk, well shaken
- a handful of fresh coriander, chopped

Pour the oil into a wide pan and set over a medium-high heat. When the oil is hot, put in the cumin, fennel and fenugreek seeds. Five seconds later, put in the curry leaves. Stir once, then add the shallots and garlic. Reduce the heat to medium and fry, stirring, until the shallots have softened and are golden. Stir in the tomatoes and ginger, and cook until the tomatoes have softened, mashing them with the back of a wooden spoon to help the process along. Add the ground coriander, cumin, turmeric, cayenne pepper and paprika. Stir once, then add 250 ml/8 fl oz water, the tamarind paste (or lemon juice) and the salt. Stir and bring to a simmer. Reduce the heat to low, and simmer very gently for 10–15 minutes. This sauce may be prepared several hours in advance, if desired.

Just before serving, heat the sauce through, then add the prawns and the well-stirred coconut milk. Bring to a simmer, stirring as you do so. As soon as the prawns turn opaque, turn off the heat. Stir in the chopped coriander and serve.

Prawn Curry with Roasted Spices

SRI LANKA

Sri Lanka has south India to its north and South-East Asia to its east. Its food has aspects of both, as this recipe shows. The pandanus leaves and lemon grass hint at Thailand, Malaysia and Indonesia, while the cumin and coriander show the influence of India. The sauce for these prawns is both rich and aromatic. It is best served with rice.

Directions for peeling, deveining and cleaning prawns are on page 343.

SERVES 4–5

4 whole, dried, hot red chillies
1 tablespoon whole coriander seeds
1 teaspoon whole cumin seeds
½ teaspoon whole fenugreek seeds
1 small stick cinnamon
2 cardamom pods
2 whole cloves
3 tablespoons corn or peanut oil
60 g/2 oz shallots, finely slivered
1 small, fresh, hot green chilli, cut into slivers (including the seeds)
2 teaspoons fresh ginger, peeled and grated to a pulp
3 cloves garlic, crushed to a pulp
7½-cm/3-inch piece pandanus leaf (*bai toey, rampe, daun paandan*)
1 stick fresh lemon grass (use the lower 15 cm/6 inches and lightly crush the bulbous bottom), or 1 teaspoon dried, ground lemon grass
½–¾ teaspoon salt
1 teaspoon bright red paprika
450 g/1 lb raw, headless, shell-on prawns, peeled and deveined (if buying prawns with heads, you will need an additional 225 g/8 oz)
175 ml/6 fl oz coconut milk, from a well-shaken can

Put the red chillies, coriander, cumin, fenugreek, cinnamon, cardamom and cloves in a small, cast-iron frying pan and set over a medium heat. Stir until the spices turn a shade darker and emit a roasted aroma. Remove from the pan and allow to cool. Then grind them in a clean coffee grinder or other spice grinder.

Pour the oil into a wide, lidded pan and set over a medium-high heat. When the oil is hot, put in the shallots and green chilli. Stir and fry for about 2 minutes. Add the ginger and garlic. Stir for about 15 seconds. Now pour in 350 ml/12 fl oz water and add the reserved roasted spices, pandanus leaf, lemon grass, salt and paprika. Stir and bring to a simmer. Cover, reduce the heat to low, and simmer gently for 15 minutes. Stir in the prawns and coconut milk. Stir and bring to a simmer on a low heat. As soon as the prawns are opaque all the way through, they are done. Check for salt, adding more if needed.

Goan Prawn Curry (Samar Codi)

INDIA

This dish may well be the pride of what was once Portuguese Goa. The sauce is quite thin, which makes it all the better to savour with plain rice.

Directions for peeling, deveining and cleaning prawns are on page 343.

SERVES 4

- 2 teaspoons whole coriander seeds
- 1 teaspoon whole cumin seeds
- 8 whole peppercorns
- 1 teaspoon cayenne pepper
- 1 tablespoon bright red paprika
- ½ teaspoon ground turmeric
- 2 teaspoons peeled and finely grated fresh ginger
- 4 cloves garlic, peeled and crushed to a pulp
- 2 tablespoons corn or peanut oil
- 1 medium onion, very finely chopped
- 400-ml/14-fl oz can of coconut milk, well shaken
- ¾ teaspoon salt, or to taste
- 1 tablespoon thick tamarind paste (see page 345), or lemon juice
- 675 g/1½ lb raw, headless, shell-on prawns, peeled and deveined (if buying prawns with heads, you will need an additional 340 g/12 oz)

Put the coriander seeds, cumin seeds, peppercorns, cayenne pepper, paprika and turmeric in a clean coffee grinder or other spice grinder. Grind as finely as possible, then empty into a bowl. Add the ginger, garlic and about 4 tablespoons water, or enough to make a thick paste. Stir to mix and set aside.

Pour the oil into a large, non-stick, lidded pan or well-seasoned wok and set over a medium-high heat. When the oil is hot, add the onion. Stir and fry until the onion is translucent. Add the spice paste. Stir and fry for 2 minutes. Now add 300 ml/10 fl oz water and bring to a simmer. Cover, reduce the heat to medium-low, and simmer, vigorously, for 10 minutes. Add the coconut milk, salt and tamarind. Mix well and bring to a simmer again. Add the prawns and simmer gently, stirring frequently, until they turn opaque.

Southern Malaysian Prawns

MALAYSIA

This little masterpiece from the southern tip of the country has bits of China, bits of India and bits of Malaysia in it. It is a stir-fried curry made in a wok, though a large frying pan will do equally well. Have all the ingredients ready before you start cooking as they go in in rapid succession.

The yellow bean sauce comes both in a paste and whole-bean form. If it contains whole soya beans, just chop them up first.

Directions for peeling, deveining and cleaning prawns are on page 343.

SERVES 4

1 teaspoon oyster sauce
1 teaspoon Chinese dark soy sauce
½ teaspoon sugar
2 teaspoons Chinese rice wine (such as Shao Hsing) or dry sherry
3 tablespoons corn or peanut oil
85 g/2½ oz shallots, sliced
1½ teaspoons fresh ginger, peeled and finely chopped
5 cloves garlic, peeled and finely chopped
4–8 bird's eye chillies
1 tablespoon yellow bean sauce
1 teaspoon curry powder
10–15 fresh curry leaves, if available
450 g/1 lb raw, headless, shell-on prawns, peeled and deveined (if buying prawns with heads, you will need an additional 225 g/8 oz)
salt, if needed

Combine the oyster sauce, soy sauce, sugar, rice wine and 4 tablespoons water in a small bowl. Stir and set aside.

Pour the oil into a wok or heavy, non-stick, lidded frying pan and set over a medium-high heat. When the oil is hot, add the shallots, ginger, garlic and chillies. Stir rapidly for a minute. Add the bean sauce and stir once. Add the curry powder and stir once. Add the curry leaves and prawns, and stir rapidly once or twice. Add the oyster sauce mixture and stir once. Cover, reduce the heat to low, and cook for about 2 minutes or until the prawns are just cooked through. Remove the lid, increase the heat to medium-high, stir once or twice, taste for salt, and serve.

Prawns in a Green Curry Sauce

THAILAND

The green curries at the Oriental Hotel in Bangkok are often served with fresh rice noodles, a salted duck's egg and a piece of fried fish. Of course, you may have plain jasmine rice instead of the noodles. There are many possibilities for dessert afterwards, but nothing beats seasonal mangoes served with a small mound of coconut-flavoured glutinous rice!

Directions for peeling, deveining and cleaning prawns are on page 343.

SERVES 4

- 400-ml/14-fl oz can of coconut milk, left undisturbed for 3 hours or more
- 2 tablespoons corn or peanut oil
- 5 tablespoons Green Curry Paste (see page 320)
- 1½ tablespoons fish sauce (*nam pla*), or to taste
- 1 teaspoon thick tamarind paste (see page 345), or lemon juice
- 1 teaspoon palm sugar or brown sugar
- 560 g/1½ lb raw, headless, shell-on prawns, peeled and deveined (if buying prawns with heads, you will need an additional 60 g/2 oz)
- 4 fresh kaffir lime leaves, or 1 teaspoon of lemon rind, julienned
- 15–20 fresh sweet basil (*bai horappa*) leaves or ordinary basil leaves

Carefully open the can of coconut milk without disturbing it too much and remove 4 tablespoons of the thick cream that has accumulated at the top. Stir the remaining contents of the can well and set aside.

Pour the oil into a large, non-stick, lidded frying pan or sauté pan and set over a medium heat. When the oil is hot, add the thick coconut cream and the green curry paste. Stir and fry until the oil separates and the paste is lightly browned. Reduce the heat to low and add the fish sauce, tamarind, sugar and 120 ml/4 fl oz water. Stir and bring to a simmer. Cover and simmer on a very low heat for 5 minutes. Stir in the reserved coconut milk. Taste for a balance of flavours, adding more fish sauce, sugar or tamarind if needed. Stir in the prawns, bring to a simmer, cover, and cook very gently for 3–5 minutes or until the prawns have turned opaque.

Either tear up the lime leaves or else remove the central vein and cut them into fine strips. Just before serving, scatter these, and the basil leaves, over the top of the prawns.

Kerala Squid Curry

INDIA

As with many stew-like fish dishes from Kerala, you can make the basic sauce, full of the aromas of roasted coriander and peppercorns, ahead of time, adding the coconut milk and squid whenever you are ready to eat.

If you buy frozen squid (which is usually excellent), it will come already cleaned. If you wish to clean the squid yourself, directions are given on page 345. Look for small, young squid as they are very tender and cook fast. Make sure you pat the squid dry before adding them to the sauce.

This dish is traditionally eaten with rice but may be served over any Asian noodles. I love it that way.

SERVES 6

2 tablespoons whole coriander seeds
1 teaspoon whole black peppercorns
¼ teaspoon whole fenugreek seeds
3 tablespoons corn, peanut or olive oil
1 teaspoon whole brown mustard seeds
140 g/5 oz onions, sliced into fine half-rings
4 large cloves garlic, peeled and sliced into fine slivers
2 teaspoons fresh ginger, peeled and finely grated
10–15 fresh curry leaves, if available
¾ teaspoon cayenne pepper
2 tablespoons bright red paprika
¾–1 teaspoon salt
2–3 teaspoons thick tamarind paste (see page 345), or lemon juice
400-ml/14-fl oz can coconut milk, well-stirred
450 g/1 lb cleaned squid, the body cut, crossways, into 5-mm/¾-inch rings and the heads, with eyes and sac removed, halved
4–5 bird's eye chillies

Put the coriander seeds, peppercorns and fenugreek seeds into a small, cast-iron frying pan and set over a medium heat. Stir and roast until the coriander seeds turn a shade or so darker. They will emit a roasted aroma. Remove to a bowl to cool slightly, then grind in a clean coffee grinder or other spice grinder.

Pour the oil into a wide, lidded pan and set over a medium-high heat. When the oil is hot, put in the mustard seeds. As soon as they start to pop, a matter of seconds, add the onions and garlic. Stir and cook until golden. Add the ginger and stir once or twice. Reduce the heat to low. Now add 300 ml/10 fl oz water, the roasted and ground spices, the curry leaves (crush them lightly with your fingers first), the cayenne pepper, paprika, salt and tamarind. Bring to a simmer, cover, and cook very gently on a low heat for 5 minutes.

Just before serving, bring the sauce to a simmer again. Add the coconut milk, squid and chillies. Simmer, uncovered, stirring gently, until the squid turn opaque all the way through.

Squid in a Tomato-Chilli Sauce

INDIA

This simple dish, with its refreshing tomato sauce, may be served with rice, breads (even crusty loaves) or any kind of pasta/noodles, either Asian or Italian. You may use fresh summer tomatoes, if they are available. Just peel and chop them finely. I used a can of whole tomatoes, crushing the tomatoes well with my hands. I do not know why, but whole tomatoes that I crush myself make a better sauce than a can of ready-chopped tomatoes.

As squid freezes well, I often buy blocks of it that way. It comes already cleaned. If you wish to clean the squid yourself, directions are given on page 345. Look for small, young squid as they are very tender and cook fast. After washing them, pat them dry.

SERVES 4

800-g/1 ¾-lb can of whole tomatoes
3 tablespoons corn, peanut or olive oil
1 teaspoon whole brown mustard seeds
3 whole, hot, dried red chillies
10–15 fresh curry leaves, if available
4 cloves garlic, peeled and crushed to a pulp
1 tablespoon fresh ginger, peeled and finely grated
1 teaspoon ground cumin
1 teaspoon ground coriander
½ teaspoon ground turmeric
1¼ teaspoons salt
½ teaspoon sugar, if needed
450 g/1 lb cleaned squid, the body cut, crossways, into 5-mm/¼-inch rings and the heads, with eyes and sac removed, halved
3 tablespoons fresh coriander, chopped

Empty the can of tomatoes into a bowl. Crush all the whole tomatoes with your hands.

Pour the oil into a wide pan and set on a medium-high heat. When the oil is hot, put in the mustard seeds. As soon as they start to pop, a matter of seconds, put in the chillies. They will darken immediately. Put in the curry leaves and take the pan off the heat. Put in the garlic and ginger and stir off the heat for a minute. Add the cumin, ground coriander and turmeric, and stir for a second. Now add the tomatoes with their juice. Put the pan back on a medium-high heat, add the salt, stir, and bring to a simmer. Simmer gently, uncovered, for 20 minutes, stirring now and then. Taste and add the sugar if the tomatoes are too sour. Add the squid and chopped coriander. Bring to a simmer over a medium heat, stirring as you go. The squid should turn opaque very quickly. Simmer for a minute and turn off the heat.

Scallops in a Green Curry Sauce

THAILAND

This is very similar to the recipe on page 126 but there are slight differences. For example, the scallops need to be browned before being put in the sauce.

SERVES 4

- 400-ml/14-fl oz can of coconut milk, left undisturbed for 3 hours or more
- 3 tablespoons corn or peanut oil
- 5 tablespoons Green Curry Paste (see page 320)
- 1½ tablespoons fish sauce (*nam pla*), or to taste
- 1 teaspoon thick tamarind paste (see page 345), or lemon juice
- 1 teaspoon palm sugar or brown sugar
- 450 g/1 lb scallops (without coral)
- 4 fresh kaffir lime leaves, or a teaspoon of julienned lemon rind
- 15–20 fresh sweet basil (*bai horappa*) leaves or ordinary basil leaves

Make the sauce. Carefully open the can of coconut milk without disturbing it too much and remove 4 tablespoons of the thick cream that has accumulated at the top. Stir the remaining contents of the can well and set aside.

Pour 2 tablespoons of the oil into a large, non-stick frying pan and set over a medium heat. When the oil is hot, add the coconut cream and the green curry paste. Stir and fry until the oil separates and the paste is lightly browned. Reduce the heat to low. Add the fish sauce, tamarind, sugar, the reserved coconut milk and 2 tablespoons water. Stir and bring to a gentle simmer. Taste for balance of flavours, adding more fish sauce, sugar or tamarind if needed.

Just before serving, pour the remaining oil into a separate, large, non-stick pan and set on a medium-high heat. When the oil is very hot, add half the scallops in a single layer. Let them brown lightly on one side. Turn them over and brown the other side. Remove to a bowl and brown the remaining scallops the same way.

Heat the sauce and put in all the scallops. Stir the scallops around gently for 2–3 minutes or until they are just cooked through.

Either tear up the lime leaves or else remove the central vein and cut them into fine strips. These and the basil leaves should be scattered over the top of the scallops when serving.

Small Clams, Mussels or Cockles in a Red Goan Sauce (Thisri)

INDIA

This Goan speciality is generally eaten with rice. I use a delicious small clam known as a Manila clam. It is about 2½ cm/1 inch in length. Use whatever is small, good and fresh in your area.

SERVES 4

- **800–90 g/1¾–2 lb small clams, mussels or cockles**
- **3 tablespoons corn or peanut oil**
- **210 g/7½ oz onions, peeled and finely chopped**
- **1 tablespoon very finely grated, peeled fresh ginger**
- **7 cloves garlic, peeled and crushed to a pulp**
- **1 teaspoon cayenne pepper**
- **1 tablespoon bright red paprika**
- **½ teaspoon ground turmeric**
- **1 tablespoon ground cumin**
- **1 teaspoon ground coriander**
- **2 teaspoons thick tamarind paste (see page 345) or lemon juice**
- **½ teaspoon salt**
- **400-ml/14-fl oz can of coconut milk, well shaken**

Scrub the shellfish with a brush and leave to soak in a bowl of cold water for 1 hour. Some people like to add a tablespoon of cornmeal to the water to help the molluscs get rid of the sand in their shells.

Make the sauce. Pour the oil into a large, wide, lidded pan and set over a medium heat. When the oil is hot, put in the onions. Stir and fry for about 5 minutes or until the onions are translucent, turning down the heat as needed. Add the ginger and garlic. Stir for a minute. Now put in the cayenne pepper, paprika, turmeric, cumin and coriander. Stir for 10 seconds. Add 500 ml/16 fl oz water, the tamarind, salt and coconut milk. Stir and bring to a simmer. Cover, reduce the heat to low, and simmer gently for 20 minutes. Add the molluscs and return to a simmer. Cover and simmer vigorously for about 5 minutes or until the molluscs open up. Remove the lid and turn off the heat.

Kerala Crab Curry

INDIA

This recipe will feed four people, assuming there are other foods on the table as well. If you just want a crab-fest, you may easily double or triple the recipe. All cooking times will remain the same, only the pan will need to get larger. I prefer pans that are wider than they are high as it is much easier to stir the crabs.

What I use when making this recipe is the live, Maryland blue crab. It is, on average, about 13 cm/5 inches in diameter, at first bluish but turning to a lovely reddish-orange during cooking. I know that such crabs are available all over South-East Asia. You can use uncooked frozen crab claws or lobster tails for this recipe as well. Just make sure that you defrost them and crack them first. Find out what your best local crab is and then try and adapt it to the recipe.

As eating crabs is a fun but messy business, give all your guests some kitchen paper and keep it informal.

SERVES *4*

3 tablespoons corn or peanut oil
1 teaspoon whole mustard seeds
3–4 whole, dried, hot red chillies
140 g/5 oz onions, finely chopped
2 teaspoons fresh ginger, peeled and finely grated
7 cloves garlic, peeled and crushed to a pulp
½ teaspoon cayenne pepper
2 teaspoons bright red paprika
1 teaspoon ground cumin
1 teaspoon ground coriander
½ teaspoon ground turmeric
255 g/9 oz tomatoes, peeled and chopped
1½ teaspoons salt
15–20 fresh curry leaves, if available
6 live crabs, preferably female blue, each about 140 g/5 oz (female crabs have a wider apron), or your local crab

Make the sauce. Pour the oil into a large, wide, lidded pan and set over a medium-high heat. When the oil is hot, put in the mustard seeds. As soon as they start to pop, a matter of seconds, add the chillies. They will swell and darken in seconds. Quickly add the onions. Stir and fry for about 5 minutes, or until the onions begin to turn brown at the edges. Add the ginger and garlic and stir for a minute. Add the cayenne pepper, paprika, cumin, coriander and turmeric. Stir for 10 seconds. Add the tomatoes, 475 ml/16 fl oz water, the salt and curry leaves. Stir and bring to a simmer. Cover and simmer on a low heat for about 25 minutes or until the tomatoes have softened.

Bring a large pot of water to a rolling boil. Drop in the live crabs and cover. Let the water return to the boil, and boil for 1 minute. Drain and wash each crab carefully under cold running water.

Place a crab on a chopping board and remove the meat according to the instructions given on page 338. Repeat with the other crabs.

Bring the sauce to the boil and put in all the crab parts. Stir and bring to a simmer. Cover and simmer for about 6–10 minutes or until the crabs are just cooked through. Stir a few times as the crabs cook.

Lobster in a Yellow Curry Sauce

THAILAND

This dish tastes best when prepared with a live lobster. However, if you find that hard to handle, use frozen lobster tails. Just defrost them and cut them crossways with a cleaver into 2.5-cm/1-inch sections. Snip the softer shell on the underbelly with a pair of kitchen scissors so you will be able to get at the flesh later.

This recipe may be doubled. The cooking times will remain the same. Just use a larger pan.

SERVES 2–4

- 400-ml/14-fl oz can of coconut milk, left undisturbed for 3 hours or more
- 4 tablespoons corn or peanut oil
- 5 tablespoons Yellow Curry Paste (see page 321)
- 1 teaspoon hot curry powder
- 1 teaspoon salt
- 1 live lobster, about 675 g/1½ lb
- 3–4 fresh kaffir lime leaves, if available, or 6 curry leaves or basil leaves

Make the sauce. Carefully open the can of coconut milk without disturbing it too much and remove 4 tablespoons of the thick cream that will have accumulated at the top. Stir the remaining contents of the can well and set aside.

Pour the oil into a large, non-stick, lidded pan and set over a medium heat. When the oil is hot, add the coconut cream and the curry paste. Stir and fry until the oil separates and the paste is lightly browned. Add the curry powder and stir a few times. Add the coconut milk, 120 ml/4 fl oz water and the salt. Stir and bring to a simmer. Cover and continue to simmer on a very low heat for 5 minutes. This sauce may be prepared 2 hours in advance and kept covered.

Lay the live lobster on a chopping board and cut up as described on page 341.

Bring the curry sauce to a simmer. Put in all the lobster pieces and stir. Bring to a simmer, cover, and continue to simmer gently for about 10 minutes, stirring and spooning the sauce over the lobster pieces now and then, until they are just cooked through. Lightly crush the kaffir lime leaves (or curry or basil leaves) and add them to the lobster pan. Stir once and serve immediately.

Selvarani and Monty Moodley's

Fish Curry with Aubergines

SOUTH AFRICA

This recipe comes from Fenton House, a Durban 'pub' that specialises in music, as well as tripe and bean curry, fish roe curry, trotters curry and this – fish curry with aubergines.

Selvarani's grandfather came to South Africa as an indentured worker to till the sugar plantations. The day I was at the restaurant, the Moodleys' daughter had just qualified to be a doctor in London. The parents were beside themselves with pride and joy and were cooking in celebration.

The fish they used is known locally as white salmon. You may use ordinary salmon here, but fillets of sea bass are also very good and are what I prefer to use.

In South Africa, small purple, white and green aubergines are as easily available as they are in East and South Asia. They are generally a little bigger than eggs, and weigh about 60 g/2 oz each. If you cannot get them, use the same total weight of long aubergines, of either the Italian or Japanese variety. Cut them into 5-cm/2-inch lengths and then cut shallow crosses at both ends. Some varieties will cook faster than others, so keep an eye on them.

Serve with Plain Jasmine Rice (see page 254).

SERVES *4*

- 3 tablespoons corn or peanut oil
- 6 small aubergines, about 340 g/12 oz, with deep crosses cut on the ends farthest from the stems
- ¼ teaspoon whole fenugreek seeds
- 140 g/5 oz onions, very finely chopped
- 5 cloves garlic, peeled and very finely chopped
- 1 large or two small tomatoes, about 225 g/8 oz, grated
- 1½ teaspoons South-African Red Spice Mixture (see page 323)
- ¼ teaspoon ground turmeric
- ¼ teaspoon ground cumin
- 1 teaspoon ground coriander
- salt
- 1 tablespoon thick tamarind paste (see page 345), or lemon juice
- 450 g/1 lb sea bass fillets (unskinned), cut into 5-cm/2-inch pieces, or see above
- freshly ground black pepper
- 8–10 fresh curry leaves, if available
- 3–4 fresh, hot green and red bird's eye chillies
- 2 tablespoons fresh coriander, chopped

Pour the oil into a large, lidded pan and set over a medium-high heat. When the oil is hot, put in the aubergines and stir them until they are lightly browned on all sides.

Remove with a slotted spoon. Reduce the heat to medium and put in the fenugreek seeds. A second later, add the onions. Stir and fry until they are golden brown. Add the garlic and stir for a few seconds. Put in the tomato, 250 ml/8 fl oz water, the Red Spice Mixture, turmeric, cumin, ground coriander and ½ teaspoon salt. Stir and bring to a simmer. Cover and continue to simmer on a very low heat for 10 minutes. Add the aubergines, tamarind, another 250 ml/8 fl oz water and ¼ teaspoon salt. Stir and return to a simmer. Cover and cook on a very low heat for 20 minutes or until the aubergines are soft.

Meanwhile, dust the fish fillets lightly with salt and pepper on both sides. Slip them into the pan in a single layer and baste them with the sauce. Cover the pan and cook on a very low heat for 5–10 minutes or until the fish is just cooked through. Crush the curry leaves and throw them in. Add the chillies and fresh coriander just before serving.

Kapitan's

Fish Curry with Half-Ripe Mango

SOUTH AFRICA

The Kapitan restaurant in Johannesburg comes with a reputation. A sign behind my table reads, 'This is the restaurant where Mandela dined'. The red flock wallpaper and the dozens of Chinese lanterns hanging from the ceiling give the place the timeless air of a mythic bordello. The first branch was opened in Durban in 1887 by the present owner's great-grandfather. He had worked on a P&O Liner named *Kapitan* that ferried indentured labourers to Natal province. His son opened the Johannesburg branch in 1914. Officially meant only for Indians, it soon had black and coloured clients as well.

As we sit down to dine, chutneys and pickles appear – ginger slices in lemon juice, mango pickle, shredded ginger and mango chutney . . .

The curries, which are served with saffron rice and South African cake flour *chapatis*, are variously seasoned with lemon grass (there is a strong Malay influence in the nation as well), tamarind and half-ripe mango.

For the fish, you may use unskinned sea bass fillets, unskinned catfish fillets, skinless salmon fillets, skinless haddock fillets or pomfret fillets, all cut, crossways, into smaller pieces. In South Africa, the fish of choice is king klip.

SERVES 4–6

- 675 g/1¼ lb fish fillets (see above), cut crossways into 2½-cm/1-inch wide pieces
- salt
- freshly ground black pepper
- 140 g/5 oz onions, peeled and chopped
- 7.5-cm/3-inch piece fresh ginger, peeled and chopped
- 5 cloves garlic
- 4 tablespoons corn or peanut oil
- ½ teaspoon whole brown mustard seeds
- 10–12 fresh curry leaves, if available
- 2 teaspoons ground coriander
- 1 teaspoon ground cumin
- ½ teaspoon ground turmeric
- 1¼ teaspoons South-African Red Spice Mixture (see page 323)
- 3 smallish tomatoes, about 340 g/12 oz, grated or blended
- 8–10 pieces of peeled, half-ripe, hard mango, about 2½-cm/1-inch square
- 50 ml/2 fl oz coconut milk, from a well-shaken can

Spread the fish out on a plate and lightly season both sides with salt and pepper.

Put the onions, ginger and garlic in a blender with 4 tablespoons water and blend until you have a smooth paste.

Pour 3 tablespoons of the oil into a large, non-stick, lidded pan and set over a medium-high heat. When the oil is hot, put in the fish pieces in a single layer and brown lightly on all sides. Remove to a plate. Add the remaining tablespoon of oil and put in the mustard seeds. As soon as they begin to pop, a matter of seconds, add the curry leaves and, a second later, the paste from the blender. Stir and fry for about 5 minutes or until the paste is lightly browned. Add the coriander, cumin, turmeric and Red Spice Mixture. Stir for 30 seconds. Now add the tomatoes, 475 ml/16 fl oz water and 1 ¾ teaspoons salt. Bring to a simmer. Cover and continue to simmer on a low heat for 5 minutes. Remove the lid and add the mango. Return to a simmer and cook gently for 5 minutes. Now put in the fish pieces in a single layer and spoon the sauce over them. Cover and cook very gently for 5 minutes.

Nadia's

Fish Curry with Okra

SOUTH AFRICA

I got this simple recipe from a fisherwoman in a Durban fish market. Nadia also passed along a nugget of information that I did not know. She said that for most South-African Indians, cooking with coconut milk is a relatively recent phenomenon. For their fish sauces, they traditionally used spices, tamarind and sometimes tomatoes.

Use any fish, such as unskinned king fish fillets, skinless salmon fillets, catfish fillets, pomfret fillets with skin or without, unskinned mackerel or sea bass fillets or filleted haddock. The fish should be cut, crossways, into 2½–5-cm/1–2 inch pieces.

The okra may be omitted from this recipe if you like.

SERVES 4–6

2 teaspoons whole brown mustard seeds
3 smallish tomatoes, about 340 g/12 oz, chopped
4 cloves garlic
3 tablespoons corn or peanut oil
12 small okra pods, topped and tailed
1/2 teaspoon whole cumin seeds
140 g/5 oz onions, peeled and finely chopped
10–15 fresh curry leaves, if available
3–4 fresh, hot green chillies, left whole
4–5 tablespoons fresh coriander, finely chopped
1½ teaspoons South-African Red Spice Mixture (see page 323)
½ teaspoon ground cumin
1 tablespoon thick tamarind paste (see page 345), or lemon juice
salt
560 g/1¼ lb filleted fish (see above) with skin, cut crossways into 2½-cm/1-inch pieces
freshly ground black pepper

Put 1½ teaspoons of the mustard seeds into a clean coffee grinder or other spice grinder and grind as finely as possible. Save in the grinder container.

Put the tomatoes and garlic in a blender and blend until smooth.

Pour the oil into a large, lidded pan and set over a medium-high heat. When the oil is hot, put in the okra. Stir and fry until lightly browned on all sides. Remove with a slotted spoon and set aside.

Quickly add the remaining mustard seeds, plus the cumin seeds, to the hot oil. As soon as the mustard seeds begin to pop, a matter of seconds, put in the onions. Stir and fry the onions for about 5 minutes or until they begin to brown. Now add the blended tomatoes and garlic, the curry leaves (lightly crushed in your fingers first), chillies, coriander, Red Spice Mixture, cumin, ground mustard, tamarind, 1½ teaspoons salt, the okra and 250 ml/8 fl oz water. Stir and bring to the boil. Cover, reduce the heat to low and simmer gently for 10 minutes.

Meanwhile, lightly season the fish pieces with salt and pepper. Once the sauce has cooked for 10 minutes, slide in the fish pieces in a single layer. Spoon some sauce over them. Cover and cook on a very low heat for about 10 minutes or until the fish is just done. Check for salt before serving.

Chef Wan's

Pomfret Curry (Tumis)

MALAYSIA

When I had this dish in Penang, it was made with fresh pomfret steaks. Pomfret is a flat, firm-fleshed fish much loved throughout much of South and South-East Asia. It has no real equivalent elsewhere, though the Florida pampano, and plaice and sole come close. You may use unskinned fillets or steaks. This sauce is enough for about 675 g/1½ lb of cleaned fish.

SERVES 2–4

- 7 hot, dried red chillies
- 140 g/5 oz chopped shallots
- 3 large cloves garlic, peeled and chopped
- 2.5 x 1 cm/1 x ½ inch piece fresh galangal, peeled and chopped, or 1/2 teaspoon ground galangal, or 2½-cm/1-inch piece of fresh peeled ginger, chopped
- 4-cm/1 ½-inch piece fresh turmeric, if available, peeled and chopped, or ½ teaspoon ground turmeric
- 1 teaspoon bright red paprika
- ¼ teaspoon shrimp paste, or 2 anchovies from a can
- 2 pomfrets, each about 450 g/1 lb, cleaned and then each cut, crossways, into 4 pieces, or see above
- salt
- 4 tablespoons corn or peanut oil
- 4 teaspoons thick tamarind paste (see page 345)
- 120 ml/4 fl oz coconut milk, from a well-shaken can

Either soak the chillies in hot water for an hour or put them in a bowl with 4 tablespoons of water and microwave them for a few minutes and then drain them when they have softened.

Put the chillies, shallots, garlic, galangal, turmeric, paprika, shrimp paste and 4 tablespoons of water into a blender and blend, pushing down with a rubber spatula if necessary, until you have a smooth paste.

Lightly season the fish pieces with salt and set aside.

Pour the oil into a large, non-stick, lidded pan and set over a medium-high heat. When the oil is hot, put in the fish pieces. Brown them lightly on all sides, remove and set aside on a plate. Remove the pan from the heat and add the paste from the blender. Return the pan to the heat and fry the paste, stirring at the same time, for about 6 minutes or until the paste has browned lightly. Add 475 ml/16 fl oz water, 1 1/4 teaspoons salt and the tamarind. Stir and bring to a simmer. Cover and simmer gently for 5 minutes. Now stir in the coconut milk, then slide in the fish pieces in a single layer. Spoon the sauce over the fish and return to a simmer. Cover and simmer on a low heat for 5 minutes or until the fish is just cooked through.

From Zaffar Hai's family

Hyderabadi Fish with a Sesame Sauce (Macchi Ka Salan)

INDIA

Here is a south-Indian Muslim classic, a Hyderabadi fish dish with a spicy, sesame sauce. It combines Hindu and Muslim culinary styles with true Hyderabadi panache. For example, the use of browned onions to thicken a sauce is very Muslim. The use of tamarind, mustard seeds and curry leaves, however, is very Hindu.

Serve it either in a traditional manner with rice, or do what I sometimes do and serve it with boiled potatoes with parsley and lightly sautéed broccoli. I love it this way as the ample sauce seems to lend itself so well to these simply-cooked vegetables.

SERVES 4–6

- 2 teaspoons cayenne pepper
- ½ teaspoon ground turmeric
- 2 tablespoons desiccated, unsweetened coconut
- 4 teaspoons ground coriander
- 115 g/4 oz sesame seeds (the beige kind)
- corn or peanut oil for shallow frying
- 2 medium onions, about 285 g/10 oz, sliced into fine half-rings
- 2 tablespoons peanut butter
- 5-cm/2-inch piece fresh ginger, peeled and chopped
- 2 cloves garlic, peeled and chopped
- 2–3 tablespoons thick tamarind paste (see page 345)
- 1½ teaspoons salt
- 1 teaspoon whole brown mustard seeds
- 1 teaspoon whole cumin seeds
- 10–15 fresh curry leaves, if available (or use Thai basil or ordinary basil leaves as a very different substitute)
- 900 g/2 lb fish fillets, such as unskinned sea bass or king fish, skinless salmon, or unskinned pomfret or catfish, cut into 5-cm/2-inch pieces
- salt
- freshly ground black pepper

Make the fish sauce. Combine the cayenne pepper, turmeric, coconut and coriander in a large bowl.

Put the sesame seeds in a medium, cast-iron pan and set over a medium-high heat. Stir and roast the seeds until they start 'jumping' and emit a roasted aroma. Remove the pan from the heat and put in all the spices from the bowl. Continue to roast and stir off the heat for a further minute (the pan will still be very hot). Empty the spices back into the bowl and allow them to cool. Now grind them as finely as possible in a clean coffee grinder or other spice grinder (you will probably need to do this in several batches). Do not worry if you see some whole sesame seeds in the mixture.

Pour the oil to a depth of 3 mm/1/8 inch into a large frying pan and set over a medium-high heat. When the oil is hot, put in the onions and stir and fry them, turning the heat down as needed, until the slices are reddish-brown and crisp. This will take 10–12 minutes. Remove the slices with a slotted spoon, saving all the oil left behind in the pan, and spread out on a double thickness of kitchen paper. Strain the oil and reserve.

Put the fried onions, peanut butter, ginger, garlic, tamarind (start with 2½ tablespoons), salt and 250 ml/8 fl oz hot water into a blender and blend until smooth. Add the already-ground spices and another 250 ml/8 fl oz hot water. Stir to mix with a rubber spatula and blend again. Taste for a balance of flavours, adding more salt or sour as you see fit.

Pour 3 tablespoons of the reserved oil into a large, non-stick pan and set over a medium-high heat. When the oil is hot, put in the mustard and cumin seeds. As soon as the mustard seeds begin to pop, a matter of seconds, take the pan off the heat and put in the curry leaves and the sauce from the blender. Add another 250 ml/8 fl oz hot water to the blender, swish it around and pour it into the sauce in the pan.

The fish sauce is now ready. It may be refrigerated or frozen until needed. All you have left to do is to lightly season the fish on both sides with salt and pepper and then slip them, in a single layer, into the sauce in a large, wide pan. Poach on a low heat, spooning the sauce over the fish until it is cooked through. If the sauce seems too thick, thin with a little water.

Grilled Fish in a Sri Lankan Tomato-Coriander Curry Sauce

SRI LANKA

In Sri Lanka, fish pieces are fried and then put into the prepared sauce. I have chosen to grill the fish instead. Also, Sri Lankans sometimes grind their brown mustard seeds for curry sauces and at other times they just use English mustard powder. I have deviated slightly and used Dijon mustard.

Varieties of fish vary so much from country to country. For this recipe you may use filleted haddock, halibut, cod, sea bass, salmon or sole. Thick fillets will hold up better than small thin ones.

The sauce may be prepared ahead of time, though the fish should be grilled and finished off just before eating.

SERVES 2–4

- 450 g/1 lb filleted fish (see note above)
- salt
- ½ teaspoon ground turmeric
- 5 tablespoons corn, peanut or olive oil
- 1 small stick cinnamon
- 2 cardamom pods
- 1 medium onion, sliced into very fine half-rings
- 2 cloves garlic, peeled and crushed to a pulp
- 1 teaspoon ground fennel
- 1 teaspoon ground coriander
- ¾ teaspoon cayenne pepper
- 3 medium tomatoes, about 350–425g/12–15 oz, peeled and very finely chopped
- 30 g/1 oz fresh coriander, very finely chopped
- 1 tablespoon Dijon mustard
- 4 tablespoons double cream (optional)

Lightly dust the fish on both sides with ¼ teaspoon salt and ¼ teaspoon ground turmeric. Cover and refrigerate until needed.

Pour 3 tablespoons of the oil into a large, preferably non-stick, lidded pan and set over a medium-high heat. When the oil is hot, put in the cinnamon and cardamom and, 5 seconds later, the onion and garlic. Stir and fry for about 4 minutes or until the onion just starts to brown. Add the fennel, ground coriander, cayenne pepper and the remaining turmeric. Stir once. Now add the tomatoes, chopped coriander, ½ teaspoon salt and 250 ml/8 fl oz water. Bring to the boil, cover, reduce the heat to low, and simmer gently for 15–20 minutes or until the tomatoes have softened. Stir in the mustard, turn off the heat and leave the sauce in the pan. If using cream add it now.

Just before serving, preheat the grill. Bring the sauce in the pan to a gentle simmer.

Arrange the fish on a baking sheet in a single layer. Thin tail ends may be tucked under. Pour the oil over the fish. Grill just until the top is lightly browned. Carefully place the fish pieces in the sauce in a single layer, browned side up. Spoon over some sauce and poach gently for 5 minutes.

Fish in Red Curry Sauce

THAILAND

I use fillets of unskinned sea bass in this curry, but you could use king fish steaks, peeled prawns or squid just as easily. If the fillets are very large, you should cut them, crossways, into 7½-cm/3-inch pieces. Serve with plain jasmine rice or aromatic jasmine rice.

SERVES 4

- 400-ml/14-fl oz can of coconut milk, left undisturbed for 3 hours or more
- 3 tablespoons corn or peanut oil
- 5 tablespoons Red Curry Paste (see page 318)
- 1½ tablespoons fish sauce (*nam pla*), or to taste
- 1 teaspoon thick tamarind paste (see page 345), or lemon juice
- 1 teaspoon palm sugar or brown sugar
- 450 g/1 lb fish (see note above)
- salt
- 4 fresh kaffir lime leaves, or a teaspoon of lemon rind, julienned
- 15–20 fresh sweet basil (*bai horappa*) leaves

Carefully open the can of coconut milk without disturbing it too much and remove 4 tablespoons of the thick cream that will have accumulated at the top. Stir the remaining contents of the can well and set aside.

Pour the oil and the coconut cream into a large, non-stick, lidded pan or well-seasoned wok and set on a medium-high heat. When the oil is hot, put in the curry paste. Stir and fry until the oil separates and the paste is lightly browned. Reduce the heat to low and add the fish sauce, tamarind, sugar and 175 ml/6 fl oz water. Stir and taste for a balance of seasonings. Cover and simmer on a very low heat for 5 minutes. Stir in the reserved coconut milk. Lightly dust the fish pieces with salt and then slide them into the sauce in a single layer. Bring to a simmer. Spoon the sauce over the fish pieces, cover, and simmer very gently until they just cook through.

Just before serving, either tear up the lime leaves or else remove the central vein and cut them into fine strips. Scatter these (or the lemon rind) and the basil leaves over the top of the fish when serving.

Salmon Curry

USA

This is one of my favourite party dishes. I have combined techniques from Bengal and Goa for a dish that tastes marvellous but keeps me in the kitchen for a minimum length of time. I have made this curry for six people but also, at a benefit for my husband's chamber music group, for sixty. All I did was increase the ingredients proportionately, but not the cooking times. The final poaching of the fish has to be done with the fish pieces in a single layer. So if you double the recipe use two pans.

SERVES 6

FOR MARINATING THE FISH

900 g/2 lb skinless salmon fillet, preferably centre-cut
⅓ teaspoon salt
⅓ teaspoon cayenne pepper
⅓ teaspoon ground turmeric

FOR THE POACHING SAUCE

2½ teaspoons whole brown mustard seeds, plus another ½ teaspoon
1½ tablespoons ground coriander
1 teaspoon ground cumin
¼ teaspoon ground turmeric
1 teaspoon curry powder (I use Bolst's Hot Curry Powder, but use any)
½ teaspoon cayenne pepper
¾ teaspoon salt
180 g/6 oz tomatoes, grated
2 tablespoons extra virgin olive oil
1 tablespoon mustard oil (or substitute more of the olive oil if you like)
½ teaspoon whole fennel seeds
15–20 fresh curry leaves

Cut the salmon fillet into manageable serving pieces, about 5 x 7½ cm/2 x 3 inches. Dust both sides with the salt, cayenne pepper and turmeric and rub into the fish. Place the fish in a plastic bag and refrigerate for 1–6 hours.

Grind 2½ teaspoons of the mustard seeds in a clean coffee grinder or other spice grinder. Put in a bowl. Add the ground coriander, cumin, turmeric, curry powder, cayenne pepper, salt, tomatoes and 120 ml/4 fl oz water. Mix well and set aside.

Pour the two oils into a large pan and set over a medium-high heat. When the oil is hot, put in the remaining mustard seeds. As soon as they begin to pop, a matter of seconds, add the fennel seeds. Stir once and put in the curry paste, as well as another 250 ml/8 fl oz water and the curry leaves. Bring to a simmer. Reduce the heat to low and simmer gently for 10 minutes. (The sauce can be refrigerated several hours.)

To poach the fish, reheat the sauce in the pan and lay the fish pieces in it in a single layer. Simmer on a low heat until the bottom of the fish pieces appear to be done, about 5 minutes. Carefully turn the fish pieces over and cook for a further 4–5 minutes or until the fish is just cooked through.

Birdie's

Curried Stew Fish

TRINIDAD

You may make this with a whole, 900-g/2-lb red snapper or with a similar-sized fish cut crossways into 2½-cm/1-inch thick steaks. Do not throw away the head and tail. They will add flavour to the sauce and someone may enjoy getting at the bits of flesh they contain. If you wish to cook the fish whole – I have conveniently baked it – make sure you have a long, ovenproof dish that can hold it easily. I use a glass Pyrex dish that I bought originally for baking lasagne.

In Trinidad, half of a large Maggi cube plus water are used instead of the chicken stock in this recipe. You may do the same if you wish.

Many Caribbean islanders wash all meat and fish in water that has salt and lime juice added to it.

SERVES 2–4

FOR WASHING THE FISH

900-g/2-lb red snapper
2 teaspoons salt
about 1 tablespoon lemon juice

FOR MARINATING THE FISH

salt
6 tablespoons onions, peeled and diced
2 spring onions, the white and light green parts only, sliced crossways
3 cloves garlic, peeled and chopped
freshly ground black pepper
½ teaspoon ground turmeric
1 tablespoon lemon juice

FOR THE CURRY SAUCE

3 tablespoons corn, peanut or olive oil
140 g/5 oz peeled and finely chopped onion
2 cloves garlic, peeled and chopped
⅛ congo pepper (scotch bonnet, habanero), chopped (remove seeds and be extra careful), or 3 bird's eye chillies, chopped
4 teaspoons hot curry powder
300 ml/10 fl oz grated tomatoes
400 ml/14 fl oz chicken stock
1/2 teaspoon salt (more if the stock is unsalted)

Wash the fish. Using a sharp knife, make deep, slightly diagonal slits across the fish on both sides at 2½-cm/1-inch intervals. Rub with the salt and lemon juice, going well into the stomach and cavities. Wash off with cold water and pat dry with kitchen paper. Put into a baking dish.

Marinate the fish. Rub the fish all over with ½ teaspoon salt and set aside as you prepare the rest of the marinade. Put the onions, spring onions, garlic, pepper, turmeric, lemon juice, ½ teaspoon salt and 2 tablespoons water into a blender. Blend, pushing down with a rubber spatula when needed, until you have a smooth paste. Rub this paste all over the fish, going deep into the slits and cavities. Set aside for about 30 minutes.

Make the curry sauce. Pour the oil into a wide, lidded pan and set over a medium-high heat. When the oil is hot, put in the onions, garlic and hot pepper. Stir and fry for 4–5 minutes or until the onions begin to brown. Add the curry powder and stir for 10 seconds. Put in the tomatoes, chicken stock and salt. Stir and bring to the boil. Cover, reduce the heat to low, and cook gently for 30 minutes.

Meanwhile, preheat the oven to 180°C/gas mark 4. Pour the sauce over the marinated fish, cover the dish with foil, and bake for 30 minutes.

Afsha Mumtaz's

Dry Masala Fish (Sookhi Macchi) — INDIA

This is perhaps the most-loved fish dish in our family. What is more, it is very easy to prepare.

SERVES 2–4

- 900-g/2-lb red snapper
- salt
- 6 tablespoons natural yoghurt
- 1 tablespoon lemon juice
- 2 teaspoons home-made *garam masala* (see page 327)
- 1 teaspoon cayenne pepper
- 1 tablespoon peeled and finely grated fresh ginger
- 5 cloves garlic, peeled and crushed to a pulp
- 2 tablespoons corn, peanut or olive oil

Wash the fish well, then pat dry with kitchen paper. Using a sharp knife, make deep, slightly diagonal slits across the fish on both sides at 2½-cm/1-inch intervals. Rub with ½ teaspoon salt, going well into the slits, stomach and cavities. Set aside for 10 minutes.

Combine the yoghurt, lemon juice, *garam masala*, cayenne pepper, ginger, garlic and ¼ teaspoon salt in a bowl and mix well. Rub most of this paste all over the fish, again going into all the slits on both sides and into the cavities. Retain about 2 tablespoons.

Place the fish on a rack set on a baking sheet (to catch the drippings) and set aside for 10 minutes.

Preheat the grill, arranging a shelf so that the top of the fish will be a distance of about 13–15 cm/5–6 inches from the source of heat.

Dribble half the oil over the top of the fish and grill for 9–10 minutes or until browned. Turn the sheet around halfway through this period to ensure even colouring. Now carefully turn over the fish. Spread the remaining spice paste on the second side (it will have lost some of its original marinade) and dribble the remaining oil over the top. Grill this side for about 8 minutes or until it, too, is browned. Turn off the grill and heat the oven to 180°C/gas mark 4. Let the fish bake for 10 minutes. Serve immediately.

Whole Baked Fish, Cooked in the Style of a Fish Head Curry

SINGAPORE

I tested this dish with fish heads. Not once, but twice. My China Town fish market did not have a red snapper head, so I chose the head of a pretty fish with yellow spots labelled 'mero'. I cooked it, and the sauce was good but the meat in the head was most unsatisfactory. I decided to compromise with a whole fish, a red snapper. It was perfect. You may also use striped bass or sea bass.

Serves 2–4

FOR MARINATING THE FISH

900-g/2-lb fish, such as a red snapper, sea bass or striped bass
⅓ teaspoon salt
⅓ teaspoon cayenne pepper
⅓ teaspoon ground turmeric

FOR THE BAKING SAUCE

3 tablespoons corn or peanut oil
1 teaspoon whole brown mustard seeds
1 teaspoon whole cumin seeds
½ teaspoon whole fenugreek seeds
½ teaspoon whole fennel seeds
15–20 fresh curry leaves
200 g/7 oz onions, peeled and finely chopped
6 cloves garlic, peeled and cut into fine slivers
6 fresh green or red bird's eye chillies, cut crossways into thin rounds
2 teaspoons fresh ginger, peeled and finely grated
180 g/6 oz tomatoes, peeled and finely chopped
2 tablespoons ground coriander
1 tablespoon ground cumin
4 teaspoons ground fennel
½ teaspoon ground turmeric
1 teaspoon cayenne pepper
4 teaspoons bright red paprika
3 tablespoons thick tamarind paste (see page 345)
1¾ teaspoons salt
400-ml/14-fl oz can of coconut milk, well shaken
12 fresh okra pods, topped and tailed

Marinate the fish. Using a sharp knife, cutting crossways and starting near the gills, make three or four deep, slightly diagonal slits on both sides of the fish. Dust, inside and out, with the salt, cayenne pepper and turmeric and rub into the fish. Slip the fish into a plastic bag and refrigerate for 1 hour or longer.

Make the baking sauce. Pour the oil into a wide, lidded pan and set over a medium-high heat. When the oil is hot, put in the mustard and cumin seeds. As soon as the mustard seeds begin to pop, a matter of seconds, put in the fenugreek and fennel seeds. Two seconds later, put in the curry leaves, onions, garlic and chillies. Stir and fry for 2 minutes. Now add 4 tablespoons water, cover, reduce the heat to low, and cook for a further 5 minutes or until the onions soften. Add the ginger and tomatoes. Stir for

2 minutes. Add the ground coriander, cumin, fennel, turmeric, cayenne pepper and paprika. Stir for 10 seconds. Add 475 ml/16 fl oz water, the tamarind and salt. Mix well, cover and simmer gently for 15 minutes. Stir in the coconut milk.

Preheat the oven to 180°C/gas mark 4.

Place the fish in a large baking dish and pour the sauce over the top. Drop the okra into the sauce wherever you can find the space. Cover with foil and bake for about 25 minutes, spooning the sauce over the fish now and then.

A Note on Fish Head Curry

I have been trying to get this recipe for twenty-five years since a trip to Singapore for *Gourmet* magazine, when I discovered that one of the best dishes in Singapore was the Fish Head Curry served in just two of Little India's restaurants. When I went to try for myself, I was served an enormous, meaty fish head, large enough to feed four hungry mouths, floating in a sea of sauce. My plate was a banana leaf. It was heaven. When I asked the restaurant owners how the curry was prepared, I got a mixture of blank stare and run-around. The only way to learn how to make the curry was to watch the entire process, from beginning to end, hence the desperate appeal to my niece. I so wanted that recipe for this book.

Knowing I wanted to include the recipe in this book, I sent an urgent appeal to a dear niece who lives in Singapore. With her help it was arranged that we be at Mutthu's restaurant at 6 am, which is when the preparations for the Fish Head Curry started.

It all begins with the sauce, which is prepared in an enormous stainless steel pot. In goes a ton of oil. Then a hail of fennel seeds, cumin seeds and fenugreek seeds. They are stirred with a paddle that you could row a boat with. Great handfuls of fresh curry leaves are thrown in. They hiss and splutter. Showers of sliced onions and garlic follow. The paddle moves them about. Ginger and tomatoes are added. What next? Twenty-six giant ladles of chilli powder, five of ground cumin, five of ground coriander., nine of ground fennel and five of turmeric . . . and so it went until there was a sludge. Tamarind juice and coconut milk thinned all this out into a proper sauce.

Meanwhile, enormous red snapper heads, each weighing 1–2 kg/ 2¼–4½ lb, already washed and scaled, were being rubbed with salt and turmeric before being lightly steamed. When an order came in, a few ladles of sauce, a fish head and some okra pods were deposited in a wok and cooked through. Diners tucked in as if there were no tomorrow.

4

VEGETABLES

Vegetables are essential to all Indian meals. They may be on the table in the form of a salad, they may be immersed in a yoghurt raita or they may appear in a pickled form. They may just consist of green chillies and coriander leaves ground into a fresh chutney. However humbly presented, they will be there.

They may also be sitting in splendour as the main dish, perhaps stuffed with spices (see Stuffed Vegetable Curry, page 154) or with different sauces poured over them (see The Best Aubergines Ever, page 166). Even the humblest of families will try and put one vegetable on the table. It might just be potatoes or mustard greens or Cold, Spiced Aubergine (see page 168), where the aubergine is roasted, peeled, mashed and then lightly seasoned with a dressing of hot oil and spices.

Some vegetable dishes cook quickly and easily. The Pakistani cabbage dish, Green Cabbage 'Sabzi' (see page 160), requires that you throw slivered cabbage, tomatoes, onions, garlic, ginger, turmeric, cayenne pepper and salt all together into a wok and allow them to steam for 10 minutes. Then you add a little oil and stir-fry quickly. What could be simpler? The taste of the dish depends entirely upon the freshness of the cabbage.

Most South Asian nations have superb produce. Vegetables are picked in the early hours and come to local markets in bullock-drawn carts, trucks, vans, on the backs of camels or elephants, and even loaded on to bicycles. Freshness is never in doubt. Tomatoes may not have the best shape but their flavour is unbeatable. Shoppers can buy large pumpkins and gourds whole or in family-sized portions. Most vegetables are seasonal. Peas and cauliflower are available in the winter, pencil-sized cucumbers only in the summer, and monsoon mushrooms, well, in the monsoon season.

Many vegetables may be cooked together. Winter carrots may be combined with winter fenugreek greens. Cauliflower is adored with potatoes and peas. Spinach and mustard greens may be slow-cooked with green chillies and tomatoes. The permutations allowed by this mixing and matching are endless.

In south India, vegetables are often diced and just boiled or steamed, after which they are covered with a simple coconut-yoghurt-cashew sauce, which can be made entirely in a blender (see South-Indian Mixed Vegetable Curry, page 156). In the Western state of Gujarat, vegetables are often very lightly stir-fried with just mustard seeds and slivered chillies, and in Delhi, cumin seeds and *asafetida* are the spices used frequently in the daily cooking of potatoes and beetroots.

As curries spread both east and west out of India, much of the variety and delicacy of the vegetable dishes was lost. Many of the 19th-century migrants were from south India or from the north Indian states of Uttar Pradesh and Bihar. In Trinidad and Guyana, it was the Uttar Pradesh traditions that seem to have prevailed, with many substitutions and simplifications. Cumin, both roasted and plain, remained a beloved seasoning. In Singapore and Malaysia, it was the south Indian Tamil traditions that seem to dominate. Australian yellow split peas were now cooked with chunky vegetables, just like the sambars of the old country. Split peas were also used as a seasoning. All very Tamil.

Thai curries may consist mostly of meat and aromatic sauces, but with them are served a plate-load of raw vegetables such as long beans, bean sprouts and green herbs. Hindu Gujarati traders who travelled to Africa from India's west coast in the 20th century remained vegetarian and re-energised the older Gujarati community that was already there with fresher, more authentic recipes. The Potato and Pea Curry (see page 172), flavoured with cumin and mustard seeds, from a Johannesburg, Gujarati Hindu family, is an excellent example of that community's cooking today.

Eleven dishes in this chapter fall into the 'curry' category. The remaining ten may be classified as accompaniments to a curry meal.

A great many of my recipes call for grated tomatoes. I discovered this technique of puréeing tomatoes about fifteen years ago in India and have been seeing it more and more ever since. It certainly seems to have spread all over India and to South Africa as well. You'll find notes on preparing tomatoes, ginger, garlic and chillies, all much needed in Indian cooking, in the section on special ingredients at the back of this book.

Manjula Gokal's

Stuffed Vegetable Curry (Aku Shaak) SOUTH AFRICA

This Gujarati speciality from South Africa is definitely a party dish. Aubergines, onions and tomatoes are stuffed with a heady mixture of peanuts, coconut, ginger and spices and cooked slowly in what becomes a sweet, hot and sour sauce. It is, in some respects, rather like a spicy ratatouille, which may be served alone or with meats.

It does require a wide, heavy pan. I have one that is 28 cm/ 11 inches wide and 10 cm/4 inches deep, which is just perfect.

The ideal aubergines to use here are the small, egg-sized ones found in Asian markets. Sometimes they are purple, sometimes green, sometimes white and sometimes striated. However, if you cannot find them, long, purple ones, sold as Italian or Dutch aubergines, work just as well. You will need to cut them into chunky pieces that are, roughly, about 5 cm/2 inches square. You should have about six such pieces. Even the very large aubergines may be cut into similar-sized chunks. Just make sure that each piece has skin on at least one side or it will fall apart in the cooking.

SERVES 8

4 tablespoons chickpea flour
2 tablespoons roasted peanuts, ground in a clean coffee grinder or other spice grinder
2 tablespoons desiccated, unsweetened coconut
1 tablespoon fresh ginger, peeled and finely grated
4–5 cloves garlic, peeled and crushed to a pulp
1½ teaspoons hot, fresh green chillies, finely chopped
2 teaspoons salt
1½ teaspoons cayenne pepper
1½ teaspoons ground turmeric
2 tablespoons jaggery, well-crumbled, or soft brown sugar
15 g/½ oz fresh coriander, chopped
2 tablespoons ground coriander
2 tablespoons ground cumin
corn, peanut or olive oil, a little for the stuffing and more to line the cooking pan generously
1 teaspoon lemon juice
6 small, round aubergines or larger ones as described above
4 onions, each about 75–85 g/2½–3 oz
4 tomatoes, each about 90 g/3 oz
1½ teaspoons whole brown mustard seeds
¼ teaspoon ground *asafetida*
4 whole, dried, hot red chillies
3 medium boiling potatoes, about 340 g/ 12 oz, peeled and quartered lengthways
1 green pepper, seeds removed and cut into 2-cm/¾-inch squares
255 g/9 oz tomatoes, grated

Put the chickpea flour, peanuts, coconut, ginger, garlic, green chillies, salt, cayenne pepper, turmeric, jaggery (or sugar), chopped coriander leaves, ground coriander and cumin into a bowl. Mix. Add 1 tablespoon oil and rub it in. Add the lemon juice and 1–2 tablespoons of water to get a crumbly paste.

Cut deep crosses in the bottom of the aubergines if they are round, and into any of the cut ends if they are chunks. Stuff some paste into them. Cut deep crosses in the tops of the tomatoes and onions. Stuff them in the same way. A fair amount of stuffing will be left over. Leave it in the bowl.

Pour enough oil into the bottom of the pan to line it generously to a depth of about 1½ mm/1⁄16 inch and set on a medium-high heat. When the oil is hot, put in the mustard seeds, *asafetida* and red chillies. As soon as the mustard seeds begin to pop, a matter of seconds, put in the potatoes. Stir for 30 seconds. Cover and cook for 3–4 minutes, removing the lid now and then to stir. Carefully put the onions and aubergines into the pan, cut side up. Cover and continue to cook on a medium-high heat for 7–8 minutes. Uncover and add about 4 tablespoons water. Jiggle and move the vegetables around gently. Put back the lid, reduce the heat to low, and cook for 15 minutes. Move the vegetables gently again. Put in the tomatoes, cut side up. Scatter the pepper pieces over the top. Add the grated tomatoes to the stuffing left in the bowl, mix well, and then pour this mixture over the peppers. Cover again with a lid and continue to cook on a low heat for a further 20–25 minutes or until the tomatoes are just done.

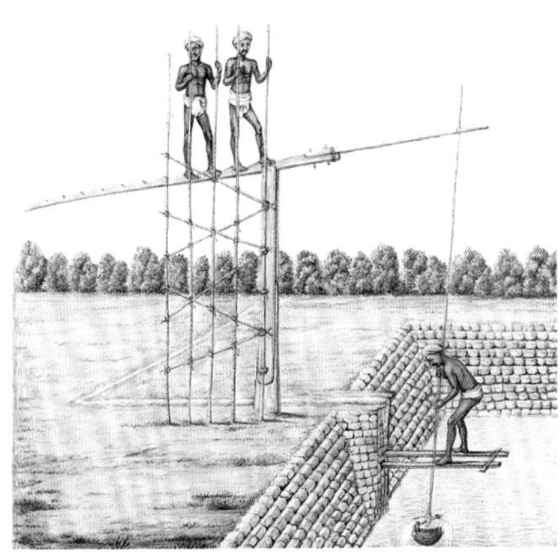

South-Indian Mixed Vegetable Curry (Kurma) INDIA

This is one of the easiest vegetable curries to make. You boil any diced vegetables you like in flavoured water and then cook them briefly in a coconut-cashew sauce made entirely in a blender. This is usually eaten with rice or rice noodles.

Grated, frozen coconut is now sold by most Indian and South-East Asian grocers. It comes in flat packets so you can conveniently break off what you need. You may also substitute desiccated, unsweetened coconut. Just soak it first in the same volume of hot water for 30 minutes and then add it, with its soaking liquid, to the blender.

SERVES 4

- 2 tablespoons raw cashews, chopped
- 3 medium tomatoes, about 340 g/12 oz, chopped
- 60 g/2 oz fresh coconut, grated
- 1 teaspoon salt
- 3–4 bird's eye or other green chillies, chopped
- ½ teaspoon *garam masala* (see page 327)
- 4 tablespoons chopped coriander leaves
- 1 tablespoon corn, peanut or olive oil
- ½ teaspoon whole brown mustard seeds
- 1 teaspoon *chana dal* or yellow split peas
- 10 fresh curry leaves, if available
- 125 g/4½ oz carrots, cut into 2-cm/¾-inch dice
- 115 g/4 oz peas (defrosted frozen peas may be used)
- 115 g/4 oz 2-cm/¾-inch cauliflower florets
- 115 g/4 oz French beans, cut into 2-cm/¾-inch lengths
- 1 tablespoon natural yoghurt

Cover the cashews in hot water and soak for 1 hour. Drain.

Put the tomatoes, coconut, salt, chillies, *garam masala* and cashews into a blender. Blend until you have a smooth paste. Add the chopped coriander and blend for a second only. You should still see flecks of green.

Pour the oil into a medium, lidded pan and set over a medium heat. When the oil is hot, put in the mustard seeds and *chana dal*. As soon as the mustard seeds begin to pop and the dal reddens, a matter of seconds, put in the curry leaves, carrots, peas, cauliflower and beans. Stir once and add 250 ml/8 fl oz water. Bring to the boil, cover, reduce the heat to low, and simmer for 3 minutes or until the vegetables are crisp-tender. Stir in the paste from the blender and return to a simmer. Simmer gently, uncovered, for 2 minutes, stirring now and then. Fold in the yoghurt and turn off the heat.

Stir-Fried South-Indian Green Beans

INDIA

The seasonings here are very typical of India's south-eastern coast.

SERVES 4

salt
340 g/12 oz French beans, cut into 2½-cm/ 1-inch pieces
1 tablespoon corn, peanut or olive oil
⅛ teaspoon ground *asafetida*
1 teaspoon whole mustard seeds
½ teaspoon *urad dal*
2 dried, hot red chillies
8–10 fresh curry leaves, if available
1½ teaspoons lemon juice
¼–½ teaspoon cayenne pepper

Bring 2.2 litres/3½ pints water to a rolling boil. Add 1 tablespoon salt and the beans. Boil rapidly for about 4 minutes or until the beans are just cooked through. Drain and, if not serving straight away, rinse under cold running water and drain. Set aside.

Just before serving, pour the oil into a frying pan and set over a medium-high heat. When the oil is hot, put in the *asafetida*, mustard seeds, *urad dal* and chillies. As soon as the mustard seeds pop and the *dal* turns reddish, put in the curry leaves and then the beans. Turn off the heat. Toss the beans and mix well. Add the lemon juice, cayenne pepper and about ½–¾ teaspoon salt. Mix again. If the beans are not at the right temperature, put them on a very low heat until warmed through.

Courgette and Green Pepper 'Sabzi' (Tori Aur Hari Mirch Ki Sabzi)

INDIA

When your garden is overflowing with courgettes and green peppers, as mine is now, this is a perfect dish to make with them. Last year, when I was in France, I got seeds for a round courgette that is flourishing here in upstate New York. Both the round and long ones will do.

You can make your own *chaat masala* or buy it ready-made from a store.

SERVES 3–4

- 3 tablespoons olive or corn oil
- a generous pinch of ground *asafetida*
- ½ teaspoon cumin seeds
- ¼ teaspoon whole brown mustard seeds
- 560 g/1¼ lb courgettes, peeled and cut into 4-cm/1½-inch long and 1-cm/½-inch thick fingers (if using round courgettes, cut into quarters, lengthways, and then crossways into 1-cm/½-inch thick wedges)
- 1 large green pepper, about 200 g/7 oz, quartered lengthways, seeds removed and cut crossways into 1-cm/½-inch wide slices
- 2 tablespoons natural yoghurt
- 1 tablespoon ground coriander
- ½ teaspoon salt or a bit more
- ½ teaspoon *chaat masala* (see page 325) or a generous pinch of cayenne pepper and a squeeze of lemon juice

Pour the oil into a large pan or wok and set over a medium-high heat. When the oil is hot, put in first the *asafetida* and then, in quick succession, the cumin and mustard seeds. As soon as the mustard seeds begin to pop, a matter of seconds, add the courgette and the green pepper. Stir and fry for 5 minutes. Add the yoghurt, and cook, stirring, until it has been absorbed. Reduce the heat to low and add the coriander and salt. Stir for a minute. Add the *chaat masala* and toss. Taste for balance of flavours.

From Saira Ahmed's home

Green Cabbage 'Sabzi' (Band Gobi Ki Sabzi) PAKISTAN

In many Pakistani homes the emphasis is generally on meat dishes, so vegetables tend to be very simply cooked. Here is one such excellent version of cabbage. Use the youngest, greenest cabbage you can find. Then quarter it, lengthways, core it and cut it into very thin, long shreds. If you prefer, you may shred the cabbage quarters in a food processor, using the grating blade, rather as you would for coleslaw.

About that word *sabzi*. Along with conquerors, it came into northern India from Iran, *sabz* meaning 'green' in Persian and *sabzi* going on to mean 'vegetable' in all of northern India. (Hence a vegetable seller is still a *sabziwallah*.) In what is probably a total misuse of the word, inhabitants of both Pakistan and northern India, including myself, say that we are preparing a cabbage or cauliflower or turnip *sabzi*, perhaps to suggest that we are preparing them as vegetables, not with meat or lentils.

Serves 6

1.15-kg/2½-lb green cabbage, trimmed, cored and either cut into very fine, long slivers or shredded (about 900 g/2 lb after trimming)
1 medium tomato, about 140 g/5 oz, cored, halved and cut into slices
1 medium onion, about 140 g/5 oz, halved lengthways and cut into thin slices
1 tablespoon garlic, peeled and crushed
1 tablespoon fresh ginger, peeled and finely grated
¾ teaspoon ground turmeric
1¼ teaspoons cayenne pepper
1½ teaspoons salt
4 tablespoons corn, peanut or olive oil

Put all the ingredients except the oil into a large *karhai*, wok or large, wide pan. Add 120 ml/4 fl oz water, stir or shake to mix and cover well. Turn the heat to medium-high. When steam starts to come out from under the lid, lower the heat to a simmer and cook gently for about 10 minutes or until the cabbage is completely wilted and almost cooked. Remove the lid, add the oil and increase the heat to high. Stir and cook for 5–6 minutes or until all the liquid has evaporated and you are able to stir and fry the cabbage briefly.

Carrot Curry with Shallots and Chilli

SRI LANKA

Ground fennel is a common ingredient in the curries of Tamil Nadu (India) and the island nation of Sri Lanka just south of Tamil Nadu. You can buy ground fennel seeds from Indian grocers. They can also be easily ground in a clean coffee grinder or other spice grinder.

SERVES *4*

- 2 tablespoons corn or peanut oil
- 60 g/2 oz shallots, peeled and chopped
- 1 fresh, hot green chilli, finely chopped
- 450 g/1 lb medium carrots, peeled and cut either into 2½ cm x 5 mm x 5mm/1 x ¼ x ¼ inch sticks or 5-mm/¼-inch thick rounds
- 1 teaspoon ground cumin
- 1 teaspoon ground coriander
- ½ teaspoon ground fennel
- ⅛ teaspoon cayenne pepper
- ¼ teaspoon ground turmeric
- 10–15 fresh curry leaves, if available
- ½ teaspoon salt
- 175 ml/6 fl oz coconut milk, from a well-shaken can

Pour the oil into a heavy, medium-sized pan and set over a medium heat. When the oil is hot, put in the shallots and green chilli. Stir and fry for about 2 minutes or until the shallots have softened a bit. Add the carrots, cumin, coriander, fennel, cayenne pepper, turmeric, curry leaves and salt, and continue to fry, stirring at the same time, on a medium heat for about 2–3 minutes. Add the coconut milk and bring to a simmer. Cover, reduce the heat to low, and simmer very gently for 5 minutes.

Cauliflower in a Mustard Seed Sauce — USA

Here is another dish I created for our parties.

SERVES 4

FOR THE SAUCE

1 tablespoon whole brown mustard seeds
1 tablespoon ground coriander
1½ teaspoon ground cumin
¼ teaspoon ground turmeric
½ teaspoon cayenne pepper
1 teaspoon salt
1 medium tomato, grated

FOR BROWNING THE CAULIFLOWER

5 tablespoons olive oil, or an equal combination of olive and mustard oil
1 head cauliflower, about 2 kg/2¼ lb, broken into large florets
½ teaspoon whole brown mustard seeds
2½-cm/1-inch piece fresh ginger, peeled and cut into very fine shreds
15 fresh curry leaves, if available

Put the mustard seeds into a clean coffee grinder or other spice grinder and grind coarsely. Pour into a bowl. Add all the other ingredients for the sauce, as well as 250 ml/8 fl oz water. Mix and set aside.

Pour the oil into a large pan and set over a medium-high heat. When the oil is hot, put in all the cauliflower florets and stir and fry until they are a rich brown in spots. Remove with a slotted spoon and put in a bowl as they get done. Add the mustard seeds to the same oil. As soon as they begin to pop, a matter of seconds, put in the ginger shreds, and stir and fry them until they start to brown. Now put in the spice paste, another 350 ml/12 fl oz water, the curry leaves and the cauliflower. Bring to a simmer over a medium-low heat, and cook, turning the cauliflower over several times, until just tender. You should end up with a very thick sauce clinging to the cauliflower. Adjust the heat as necessary to achieve this.

Quick Cauliflower 'Bhaji' (Gobi Ki Bhaji) USA

Here is a quickly cooked dish that I created for our everyday meals. It is 'dry'. Whatever sauce there is, clings to the florets. Just make sure that you do not make these florets too big. They should be medium sized, about 5 cm/2 inches in length and no wider than 4 cm/1½ inches. Each flower 'head' should have an attached 'stem' so it does not look too squat.

SERVES 3–4

1 teaspoon ground coriander
1 teaspoon ground cumin
¼ teaspoon ground turmeric
½ teaspoon cayenne pepper
¾ teaspoon salt
3 tablespoons corn, peanut or olive oil
½ teaspoon whole mustard seeds
½ teaspoon whole cumin seeds
2 whole, dried, hot red chillies
2½-cm/1-inch piece fresh ginger, peeled and first cut into thin slices and the slices then stacked and cut into thin slivers
225 g/8 oz cauliflower florets
90 g/3 oz tomatoes, peeled and chopped

Put the coriander, cumin, turmeric, cayenne pepper and salt into a small bowl. Add 4 tablespoons water and mix. Set aside.

Pour the oil into a large, lidded pan and set on a medium-high heat. When the oil is hot, put in the mustard seeds, cumin seeds and chillies. As soon as the mustard seeds begin to pop, a matter of seconds, put in first the ginger and then the cauliflower. Stir and fry the cauliflower for about 2 minutes or until it picks up some brown spots. Reduce the heat to low. Stir in the spice paste, cover, and continue to cook on a low heat for about 6 minutes. Stir in the tomatoes. Replace the lid, and cook for a further 6 minutes or until the cauliflower is just tender.

Sweetcorn with Fresh Herbs

USA

I devised this dish for a benefit party to aid my husband's chamber music group, Clarion Concerts. Keeping up the tradition of Indian migrants the world over, I find myself adapting Indian spices and techniques to the best of American ingredients. Here, I used the pale, whitish, Silver Queen sweetcorn that grows abundantly in upstate New York, taking it off the cob with a sharp knife in wide ribbons and separating the kernels before I stir-fried them.

SERVES 6

- 3 tablespoons extra virgin olive oil
- 1 teaspoon whole brown mustard seeds
- ½ teaspoon whole cumin seeds
- ¼ teaspoon *kalonji* seeds (nigella)
- 2 teaspoons peeled fresh ginger grated to a pulp
- 1–2 fresh, hot green chillies, finely chopped
- 6 sweetcorn
- 4 tablespoons chopped fresh coriander
- 2 tablespoons finely chopped fresh mint
- 3 spring onions, finely chopped, using all the white and some of the green sections
- 2 tablespoons finely chopped fresh dill
- 2 tablespoons lemon juice
- ¾–1 teaspoon salt
- freshly ground black pepper
- 30 g/1 oz unsalted butter, optional

Pour the oil into a large, preferably non-stick, lidded pan or wok and set over a medium-high heat. When the oil is hot, put in the mustard and cumin seeds. As soon as the mustard seeds begin to pop, a matter of seconds, put in the *kalonji*. Stir once, then add the ginger and chillies. Stir for 30 seconds, put in all the sweetcorn, coriander, mint, spring onions and dill, and toss well to mix. Add 4 tablespoons water, the lemon juice, salt and black pepper. Toss again to mix and cover. When steam begins to escape from under the lid, reduce the heat to low and cook for about 2–3 minutes. Toss again and taste for a balance of seasonings, making any adjustments you think necessary. If you like, stir in the butter just before serving.

Jahan Ara Changez's

Aubergine Slices on a Yoghurt Bed (Boorani) PAKISTAN

An Afghani dish much admired along Pakistan's border with Afghanistan and by those of Afghani descent living in Pakistan. Of the many versions of the dish, you will find two here, this one and the following recipe, a variation made with the addition of tomato sauce. Both are superb. I suspect that all *booranis* are of Persian origin. The use of turmeric, however, is very South Asian.

SERVES 4–6

2 Italian aubergines, each about 225 g/8 oz
salt
ground turmeric
corn, peanut or olive oil for shallow frying, enough to have a depth of 6 mm/¼ inch in a frying pan
1 medium onion, peeled and finely chopped
¼ teaspoon cayenne pepper
475 ml/16 fl oz natural yoghurt, the creamier the better
freshly ground black pepper
mint sprigs for garnishing

Peel the aubergine and cut them crossways at a slight diagonal into oval slices that are about 1 cm/½ inch thick. Spread out in a plate in a single layer. Dust both sides with about ½ teaspoon salt and ¼ teaspoon turmeric. Rub the seasonings in and set aside for an hour.

Pour the oil into a large, lidded pan and set over a medium-high heat. When the oil is hot, dry off the aubergine slices with kitchen paper and put in as many as the pan will hold in a single layer. Fry, turning, until both sides are a reddish-brown, about 3 minutes on one side and 2 minutes on the other. Remove the slices with a slotted spoon and leave to drain on a plate lined with kitchen paper.

Remove all but 2 tablespoons of the oil from the frying pan and set it on a medium heat. Put in the onion, and fry, stirring, until the onion pieces turn a medium brown. Add the cayenne pepper, a pinch of turmeric and ¼ teaspoon salt. Stir once. Add 6 tablespoons water and stir. Lay the aubergine slices in slightly overlapping rows on top of the onions. Bring to a simmer, cover, reduce the heat to low, and simmer gently for 5 minutes. Turn the aubergine slices over, replace the lid, and cook gently for a further 5 minutes. Turn off the heat.

Just before serving, empty the yoghurt into a bowl and add ½ teaspoon salt and some black pepper. Whisk lightly until smooth. Pour the yoghurt into a large platter. Lay the aubergine slices over the top, preferably in a single layer. Spoon any remaining onion sauce in the pan over the top, garnish with the mint, and serve.

The Best Aubergines Ever

USA/AFGHANISTAN

Here is a rather grand dish I created by combining the *boorani* of Afghanistan, with its layers of satiny aubergine, yoghurt and tomato, and the street snacks that I grew up with in Delhi, laden with chickpeas and tamarind chutney. It is entirely vegetarian and can be served either as a main course or as a side dish with other Indian meat dishes or, indeed, with a roast leg of lamb.

Three sauces are required here, all of which may be made a day in advance. Only one of them, the tomato-chickpea sauce, will need reheating just before you serve. The others can be cold or at room temperature.

I use three large aubergine and cut each of them, crossways, into five thick slices. The slices are generally 3 cm/1¼ inches or so thick, depending upon the size of the vegetable. They flatten a lot as they cook.

SERVES 6

3 tablespoons salt
3 large aubergines, each about 500 g/ 1 lb 2 oz
peanut or corn oil for deep-frying

FOR THE TOMATO-CHICKPEA SAUCE

3 tablespoons peanut or corn oil
2 whole, dried, hot red chillies
1 teaspoon whole brown mustard seeds
3 cloves garlic, peeled and finely chopped
800-g/28-oz can good quality whole tomatoes, finely chopped, with their liquid
10 fresh curry leaves, if available (use basil as an alternative with a different flavour)
410-g/15-oz can chickpeas, drained and rinsed, or 350 g/12 oz cooked and drained chickpeas
¾ teaspoon salt
1 teaspoon ground cumin
1 teaspoon ground coriander
¼ teaspoon ground turmeric

FOR THE YOGHURT SAUCE

10 tablespoons natural yoghurt
¼ teaspoon salt
¼ teaspoon ground roasted cumin seeds (see page 339)

FOR THE TAMARIND CHUTNEY

2 tablespoons thick tamarind paste (see page 345)
2 tablespoons sugar
¼ teaspoon salt
¼ teaspoon ground, roasted cumin seeds (see page 339)

FOR THE FINAL SERVING

a little extra salt and freshly ground pepper
fresh mint or coriander leaves for garnishing

Pour 3 litres/4¾ pints water into a very large bowl or large pan. Add the 3 tablespoons salt and stir well.

Trim the aubergine, slicing off the very top and bottom, and then peel them. Cut them, crossways, into about five slices each. Each slice should be about 3–5 cm/ 1¼–1½ inches thick. Put the slices into the salty water as you cut them. The slices will float. Upturn a plate on top of the slices and balance a weight (such as a clean glass jar filled with water) on top of the plate. Set aside for 3–10 hours.

Remove the slices from the water and pat them dry.

Pour about enough oil into a large pan to come to a depth of 2 cm/¾ inches, and set over a medium heat. Allow time for it to get very hot, then put in as many aubergine slices as the pan will hold in a single layer and fry for 3–4 minutes on each side or until reddish-gold. Remove to a large plate or tray lined with a double thickness of kitchen paper. Fry all the aubergines this way, adding more oil, if needed, and using as many plates or trays as you see fit. I like to change the kitchen paper at least once. I also pat the tops of the slices with more kitchen paper. The aubergines may now be set aside for 3–4 hours, if desired.

Make the tomato-chickpea sauce. Either use 3 tablespoons from the frying oil or, if you prefer, fresh oil and pour it into a large, lidded pan. Set the pan over a medium-high heat and, when the oil is very hot, put in the chillies and mustards seeds. As soon as the mustard seeds begin to pop, a matter of seconds, add the garlic. Stir quickly once, then put in the tomatoes, curry leaves, chickpeas, salt, cumin, coriander and turmeric. Stir and bring to a simmer. Cover, reduce the heat to low, and simmer gently for 20 minutes. Remove the two chillies before serving.

Make the yoghurt sauce. Put the yoghurt in a small bowl and beat lightly with a fork or small whisk until smooth. Stir in the salt and roasted cumin. Cover and refrigerate if not using within 2 hours.

Make the tamarind chutney. Combine the tamarind paste, sugar, salt and roasted cumin in a small cup. Mix well. Cover and refrigerate if not using within 2 hours.

When ready to serve, preheat the oven to 160°C/gas mark 3. Spread out the aubergine slices in a single layer on a baking sheet and dust very lightly with salt and black pepper. Place in the oven and heat through, about 15 minutes. If oil accumulates at the bottom of the sheet, pour it out.

Heat the tomato-chickpea sauce.

Arrange the aubergine slices on a very large platter in a single layer. Pour a small ladleful of the tomato chickpea sauce on top of each slice. Centre 2 teaspoons of the yoghurt sauce on top of the tomato-chickpea sauce and then put a generous dot of the tamarind chutney on top of the yoghurt. Garnish with the mint or coriander leaf.

Cold, Spiced Aubergine (Bharta) — INDIA

This may be served at room temperature or cold at all Indian meals. It also goes well with cold meats such as chicken and lamb.

The last step, of pouring the seasoned oil over the top, should be done just as you get ready to serve.

SERVES 4

- 1 large aubergine, about 600 g/1 lb 5½ oz
- 2 tablespoons shallots, peeled and finely chopped
- 2 tablespoons fresh mint, finely chopped
- 3 tablespoons fresh coriander, chopped
- 3 tablespoons tomato, peeled, seeded and chopped
- 2–3 bird's eye chillies, finely chopped
- 1 tablespoon lemon juice
- ¾–1 teaspoon salt
- 3 tablespoons corn, peanut or olive oil
- ½ teaspoon whole brown mustard seeds
- 2 whole, dried, hot red chillies

Preheat the grill, setting a shelf so the top of the aubergine will be at a distance of 15 cm/6 inches from the source of the heat.

Prick the aubergine, put it on a foil-lined baking sheet and place under the grill. Let one side get completely charred before turning it slightly. Allow the aubergine to char slowly and completely on all sides. It should also turn flabby and soft. Remove and peel. Mash the insides and put them in a bowl. Add the shallots, mint, coriander, tomato, chillies, lemon juice and salt. Mix, and check for a balance of flavours. Cover and set aside, refrigerating if necessary.

Just before serving, put the aubergine mixture in a serving dish.

Pour the oil into a small pan and set over a medium-high heat. When the oil is hot, put in the mustard seeds and chillies. As soon as the mustard seeds begin to pop, a matter of seconds, pour the oil and spices evenly over the aubergine mixture.

Mushroom and Green Coriander Curry

PAKISTAN

This is a very refreshing way to cook ordinary button mushrooms. I like to add a little cream at the end but the original recipe does not call for it so you could easily leave it out.

SERVES 6

5 tablespoons corn or peanut oil
2 medium sticks of cinnamon
2 smallish onions, about 180 g/6 oz, very finely chopped (this can be done in a food processor using the pulse/start and stop method)
3 fresh, hot green chillies, finely chopped
250 ml/8 fl oz natural yoghurt
salt
900 g/2 lb button mushrooms
¼ teaspoon ground cloves
¼ teaspoon ground cardamom seeds
60 g/2 oz fresh coriander leaves and small stems, well chopped
3 tablespoons double cream, optional

Pour the oil into a wide, heavy, lidded pan or wok, and set over a medium-high heat. When the oil is hot, put in the cinnamon. Stir once, then quickly add the onions and green chillies. Stir and fry for 5–7 minutes or until the onions are a golden-brown. Take the pan off the heat and add the yoghurt and ½ teaspoon salt. Return the pan to the heat and cook, stirring, until all the yoghurt is absorbed and you can see the oil at the edges. Put in the mushrooms, another ¾–1 teaspoon salt, the cloves and cardamom and all the coriander. Stir, reduce the heat to low, cover, and cook gently for 10–15 minutes, stirring now and then. Remove the lid, increase the heat to medium-high, and boil off some off the liquid, stirring as you do so. Add the cream, if desired, and stir it in.

Zarrin Zardari's

Okra with Onions (Sel Bhindi)

PAKISTAN

This is a simple but delicious way of cooking okra. It comes from the Sindh region of Pakistan. You may pound the coriander seeds and red chilli in a mortar, as they do in Pakistan, or else whir them quickly in a clean coffee or spice grinder.

SERVES 3–4

2 teaspoons whole coriander seeds
1 whole, dried, hot red chilli, seeds removed, broken up coarsely
3 tablespoons corn or peanut oil
340 g/12 oz fresh okra, topped and tailed, then sliced in half, lengthways
1 smallish onion, about 90 g/3 oz,sliced into fine half-rings
¾–1 teaspoon salt
¼ teaspoon ground turmeric
2 tablespoons fresh coriander, finely chopped

Either put the coriander seeds and chilli in a mortar and pound with a pestle until you have a coarse powder or else put both in a clean coffee grinder or other spice grinder and run the machine briefly to achieve the same result. Set aside.

Pour the oil into a large, preferably non-stick, pan and set over a medium heat. When the oil is hot, put in the okra, ideally in a single layer. Stir and fry for about 10 minutes or until the okra is very lightly browned on all sides. Add the onions. Stir and cook for a further 5 minutes or until the onions, too, begin to brown. Add the coriander-chilli mixture, the salt and turmeric. Reduce the heat to low, and cook, stirring, for another 5 minutes. Taste for a balance of seasonings. Add the coriander and serve.

Potatoes with Browned Onions (Bihari Bhujia) PAKISTAN

These potatoes are generally eaten with Pakistani breads and pickles but they also taste quite wonderful with roast lamb! The round chillies used in this recipe are labelled as such and are about 2 cm/¾ inch in length. Dried cayenne-type chillies may be substituted. Normally, this dish is cooked in a well-seasoned *karhai* (wok) but a wide, non-stick pan will do.

SERVES 8

- **1.15 kg/2½ lb medium russet or red new potatoes**
- **120 ml/4 fl oz corn or other vegetable oil**
- **4 medium onions, sliced into very fine half-rings**
- **15 dried, hot, round red chillies, or 8 of the dried, long cayenne type**
- **2 teaspoons whole cumin seeds**
- **1 teaspoon cayenne pepper**
- **2 teaspoons ground turmeric**
- **2 teaspoons salt**

Peel the potatoes and cut them in halves, lengthways. Keep them covered in a bowl of water as you work. Cut each potato piece in half, crossways, into 3-mm/⅛-inch thick slices. Leave in the water.

Pour the oil into a large *karhai* or a large, wide, preferably non-stick, lidded pan and set over a medium-high heat. Put in all the sliced onions, and fry, stirring, for 5 minutes. Now add the whole chillies. (At this point, drain the potatoes and leave them in a colander.) Continue to fry and stir, turning the heat down as needed, until the chillies are dark and crisp. Lift the chillies out with a slotted spoon and set aside. Keep frying the onions until they are reddish-brown and crisp. Remove the onions with a slotted spoon and spread them out on a baking sheet lined with kitchen paper.

Put the cumin seeds into the remaining hot oil and then, 5 seconds later, add the drained potatoes. Also add the cayenne pepper, turmeric and salt. Stir well and cover. Cook on a medium-high heat for 5 minutes, stirring now and then. Reduce the heat to very low, stir again, and cover. Cook gently for 10 minutes or until potatoes are almost done, lifting the lid now and then to stir.

Meanwhile, remove the oily kitchen paper from under the onions and spread the onions out over fresh kitchen paper so they dry out and crisp further. Crumble up the onions and spread them over the potatoes during the last minutes of cooking. The chillies may be crumbled along with the onions, or, for a milder taste, use them whole as a garnish when serving.

Manjula Gokal's

Potato and Pea Curry (Mattar Batata)

SOUTH AFRICA

Manjula and her husband Arvind live in the fashionable and gated Sandton community of northern Johannesburg. This is not the sort of area they could even have aspired to during the years of apartheid. She is tall and stately and a superb cook. As they are of Gujarati origin, their food is as Gujarati as they can manage – but, of course, they do make use of conveniences, such as frozen peas.

I used eight, smallish red potatoes, which were exactly 450 g/1 lb in total weight. After peeling them, I just cut them into halves.

SERVES 4–6

3 tablespoons corn or peanut oil
½ teaspoon whole brown mustard seeds
½ teaspoon whole cumin seeds
½ teaspoon whole, dried, hot red chillies
a generous pinch of ground *asafetida*
450 g/1 lb boiling potatoes, peeled and cut into chunky pieces (see note above)
¼ teaspoon cayenne pepper
1 teaspoon ground cumin
1 teaspoon ground coriander
¼ teaspoon ground turmeric
1 teaspoon sugar
285 g/10 oz frozen peas, defrosted
1½ teaspoons salt
3 medium tomatoes, about 450 g/1 lb, grated on the coarsest side of a grater

Pour the oil into a medium, lidded pan and set over a medium-high heat. When the oil is hot, throw in the mustard seeds, cumin seeds, red chillies and *asafetida*. As soon as the mustard seeds begin to pop, a matter of seconds, add the potatoes. Stir and fry until the potatoes brown a little. Now add the cayenne pepper, cumin, coriander, turmeric and sugar. Stir once or twice and put in the peas. Stir a few times, then add 250 ml/8 fl oz water and 1 teaspoon salt. Bring to the boil, cover, reduce the heat to low, and cook gently for 15 minutes. Stir in the grated tomatoes and remaining salt. Simmer gently, uncovered, for a further 10 minutes.

Potato and Tomato Curry with Green Coriander (Aloo Timatar)

INDIA

One of the most popular curries from the streets of Hindu north India, this is generally eaten with Deep-Fried Puffed Breads (see page 280), pickles and yoghurt relishes. Food shops near most temples sell versions of this dish, along with curried pumpkins and squashes. No garlic or onions are used in the cooking. They are meant to arouse base passions and are frowned upon, especially on holy days. In our family, this was offered as the occasional Sunday breakfast treat, just as New Yorkers might sit down to bagels, cream cheese and smoked salmon or Londoners might indulge in scrambled eggs and smoked salmon. Not everyday foods, for sure, but foods that go to the heart of the matter.

SERVES 4–6

675 g/1½ lb waxy, red potatoes, ideally around 8 weighing 90 g/3 oz each
1½ teaspoons salt
1 teaspoon ground coriander
1 teaspoon ground cumin
½–1 teaspoon cayenne pepper
¼ teaspoon ground turmeric
3 tablespoons corn, peanut or olive oil
⅛ teaspoon ground *asafetida*
½ teaspoon whole cumin seeds
½ teaspoon whole brown mustard seeds
2 whole, dried, hot red chillies
1 teaspoon fresh ginger, peeled and grated
180 g/6 oz fresh tomatoes, grated
2 tablespoons natural yoghurt
4 tablespoons fresh coriander, finely chopped

Boil the potatoes, drain them, and allow to cool. (Do not refrigerate.) When they are cool enough to handle, peel the potatoes and, if they are about the size suggested above, break them coarsely by hand into about eight pieces each. Put them in a bowl. Add the salt, coriander, cumin, cayenne pepper and turmeric. Toss to mix and set aside.

Pour the oil into a large, wide, non-stick, lidded pan and set over a medium-high heat. When the oil is hot, put in the *asafetida*, cumin seeds, mustard seeds and chillies. As soon as the mustard seeds begin to pop, a matter of seconds, put in the ginger. Stir for a few seconds, then add the grated tomatoes. Stir and cook for 5–6 minutes or until the oil separates from the tomato purée. Add the potatoes and stir to mix. Now add 350 ml/ 12 fl oz water, stir, and bring to a simmer. Cover, reduce the heat to low, and simmer gently for 20 minutes.

Put the yoghurt into a small bowl and beat lightly. Add about 4 tablespoons of the sauce from the potatoes and mix it in. Stir in the chopped coriander and mix again. Now pour this mixture into the pan with the potatoes. Stir once to blend and turn off the heat. Check for salt, adding more, if needed.

Potato and Cauliflower Curry

INDIA

This is a typical, festive, Punjabi-style curry. It is generally eaten with breads, yoghurt *raitas* and pickles but may be served with almost any meal.

SERVES 4–6

- 140 g/5 oz onions, peeled and chopped
- 5-cm/2-inch piece fresh ginger, peeled and chopped
- 4 cloves garlic, peeled and chopped
- 8 tablespoons corn, peanut or olive oil
- 2 good-sized boiling potatoes, about 340 g/12 oz, boiled, cooled, peeled and cut into 4 x 2½ x 2½ cm/1½ x 1 x 1 inch pieces
- 450 g/1 lb cauliflower florets, cut so they are just slightly bigger all round than the potato pieces
- a generous pinch of ground *asafetida*
- ½ teaspoon whole cumin seeds
- 1 teaspoon ground coriander
- ½ teaspoon ground cumin
- ½ teaspoon ground turmeric
- ½ teaspoon cayenne pepper
- 180 g/6 oz tomatoes, grated
- 1½ teaspoons salt
- 3–4 fresh, hot green chillies (such as bird's eye or the cayenne variety), whole, but with small slits cut in each

Put the onions, ginger, garlic and 4 tablespoons water in a blender and blend until smooth.

Pour the oil into a large, preferably non-stick, lidded pan and set over a medium-high heat. When the oil is hot, put in the potatoes and cauliflower. Fry, stirring, until they are lightly browned. Remove with a slotted spoon and set aside.

Off the heat, remove all but 3 tablespoons of oil from the pan (you may reuse it in another dish), then return the pan to the heat. Put in the *asafetida* and then, a second later, the cumin seeds. A few seconds after that, put in the onion mixture from the blender. Stir and fry it for 3–4 minutes. Put in the ground coriander, cumin, turmeric and cayenne pepper. Stir for a minute, then add the tomatoes and cook, continuing to stir, for a further 2 minutes. Now add the cauliflower and potatoes, 600 ml/1 pint water, the salt and the chillies. Stir to mix, bring to a simmer, cover, and cook on a very low heat for 2–3 minutes. Taste for salt before serving.

Potatoes with Ginger

USA

One of my favourite late Sunday breakfasts, and one we often serve our house guests, consists of Indian-Style Curried Omelette Pie (see page 118), these potatoes and a large green salad. I like to make this with waxy potatoes, such as smallish red ones or new potatoes.

SERVES 6

- 675 g/1½ lb small red potatoes or new potatoes
- 3 tablespoons olive oil
- ½ teaspoon whole cumin seeds
- ½ teaspoon whole brown mustard seeds
- 2 medium shallots, peeled and chopped
- ¾–1 teaspoon salt
- freshly ground black pepper
- ¼ teaspoon cayenne pepper
- 2 teaspoons fresh ginger, peeled and finely grated

Put the potatoes in a pan with water to cover and boil until tender. Drain, allow to cool completely, then peel and cut into 5-mm/¼-inch dice.

Pour the oil into a large, non-stick pan and set over a medium-high heat. When the oil is hot, put in the cumin and mustard seeds. As soon as the mustard seeds begin to pop, a matter of seconds, put in the potatoes, shallots, salt, black pepper and cayenne pepper. Stir and fry until the potatoes are nicely browned in spots. Add the ginger, and cook, stirring, for another minute or so.

Veena Bahadur's

Spinach with Radish Greens (Saag)

INDIA

In India, we often combine different greens to make what is generically referred to as *saag*. Here, in my youngest sister's recipe, one of winter's most popular greens, those taken off the tops of white radishes, are combined with spinach. Radish tops are bristly to the touch but that roughness vanishes as they cook. The tops retain some pungency, though. As I eat a lot of red radishes, I use their tops instead. They are just as good when they are nice and fresh.

If you like, you can add a dollop of butter before serving.

SERVES 4–6

4 tablespoons corn or peanut oil
1 teaspoon whole cumin seeds
3 hot, dried red chillies
2 medium onions, about 285 g/10 oz, peeled and sliced into fine half-rings
900 g/2 lb spinach, washed, drained and chopped into 5-mm/¼-inch pieces
225 g/8 oz radish greens, chopped like the spinach (remove coarse stems first)
1¼ teaspoons salt, or to taste

Pour the oil into a wide, lidded pan and set over a medium-high heat. When the oil is hot, put in the cumin seeds and chillies. As soon as the chillies darken a shade, a matter of seconds, add the onions. Stir and fry for 6–7 minutes or until onions turn a reddish colour. Add the spinach, radish greens and salt. Cook, stirring, on a medium-high heat, until all the liquid disappears, about 15 minutes. Cover and cook on a very low heat for a further 5 minutes. You may remove the whole chillies before serving.

Spinach Bhaji

GUYANA

Here is a delicious way that the Guyanese cook spinach. The spinach needs to be cut into very fine ribbons. The best way to do this is to hold a good bunch of leaves together and then slice them, crossways, into fine shreds.

SERVES 4–6

3 tablespoons corn or peanut oil

2 cloves garlic, peeled and crushed to a pulp

1 small onion, about 45 g/1½ oz,sliced into fine half-rings

1 spring onion cut, crossways, into thin slices

1 wiri-wiri pepper (see page 336), finely chopped, or any fresh, hot green chilli, finely chopped

560 g/1¼ lb fresh spinach, cut into fine ribbons or shreds

1 teaspoon salt, or to taste

Pour the oil and garlic into a wide, lidded pan and set on a medium-low heat. Stir around briefly until the garlic is light brown. Add the onion, spring onion and chilli pepper. Stir until they soften. Stir in the spinach and salt. Cover and cook for about 20 minutes, stirring now and then. Remove the lid and cook for a further 3–5 minutes or until the spinach is almost but not completely dry.

5

DALS, BEANS AND SPLIT PEAS

You can take meats and fish and vegetables away from an Indian but you cannot take away his *dal* and his bread or, if he is a rice-eater, his rice. That is the core of his meal.

Technically, a *dal* is a dried pea that has been split. But, for some reason, all dried beans and peas, and all legumes, are now generally classified in India as *dal*.

Most are of ancient lineage. *Urad*, *mung*, *masoor* (red lentils), chick peas and *toovar dal* have been either mentioned in ancient Sanskrit texts or found in archaeological digs that go back to 2500 BC. So the acts of growing, cooking and eating them have been continuous for over 4,000 years. Somehow, our ancestors knew that eating a meal that consisted of rice or wheat, legumes and perhaps some yoghurt made healthy nutritional sense, providing protein and roughage as well as deep satisfaction. *Mung* has always been considered the most digestible of *dals* and so is given to the very young and the very old without fear. *Toovar dal*, in the form of *sambar* (see page 190), is eaten on a daily basis by many south Indians, along with rice. It is their meat and potatoes. We combine *dals* with rice, with meat, with vegetables and, in my home town, use them to stuff deep-fried puffed breads. They can be soaked and ground, then made into fritters and pancakes. They may even be made into desserts.

For everyday cooking, one *dal* amongst the dozens in a home larder is chosen (or it could be a mixture) and just boiled with a little turmeric and salt. Turmeric is the spice that acts as an antiseptic, both inside and outside the body. As each *dal* has its own texture and flavour, the daily choice provides instant variety. When it is fully cooked, salt is stirred in. Many people believe that a *dal* will not become tender if it is salted at the beginning. Since I was given this advice at my mother's knee, I follow it instinctively, though I must add that I have seen it proved wrong time and again. Finally, a little oil or *ghee* is heated, some spices or seasoning are thrown in, and this combination is poured over the *dal* in a step known variously as *tarka*, *baghaar* or *chownk*. It perfumes and spices up the *dal* immediately. The last of these words, *chownk*, is interesting. Hold on to it. I will return to it shortly.

The early indentured labourers, packed into ships by the British for journeys east and west that they hardly understood, were mostly men – women came much later. They were either from the two southern coasts, mostly Tamil Nadu and some from Kerala, or they were from the poorer northern states of Uttar Pradesh and Bihar. The were allowed some rations of *dal* but these soon dwindled after they landed and, for most, there was hardly any time left for cooking once they started working in the fields. The *dals* they had grown up with and which they wished to duplicate were *mung* from the north and *toovar* from the south. Initially, these might have been brought in by Indian traders, but for most were either too expensive or not available at all. What we do know is that, today, nearly all the Malaysians and Singaporeans of Indian descent have turned to the easily found yellow split peas that are imported from Australia. The same has happened in Trinidad and Guyana, though the split peas are probably from closer by in the Americas. The *dals* are still cooked in the same manner and, in Trinidad and Guyana, the final seasoning step is simply called 'choka', in memory of a half-forgotten word.

Perhaps because southern Indian migrants could not duplicate the exact taste of their *sambars*, or for some other reason, the *sambars* in both Malaysia, South Africa and Myanmar have grown more and more multi-purpose or elaborate. My Malaysian Split Pea Curry with Vegetables (see page 192), a glorified *sambar*, is enriched with a purée of nuts. In Myanmar, the word *kala*, or 'black', is often added in front of Indian dishes. (*Kala aw* is a dish so hot that it would even make the Indians scream!) *Kala hin*, at a cafeteria run by Chettiars, a trading community from south India, was described as a vegetable soup and turned out to be a thin *sambar*-like dish made with yellow split peas, tomatoes and okra. At a market in Yangon, I had something even more curious – a *samosa* salad. (A *samosa* is a stuffed, savoury pastry.) Fritters, made with soaked yellow split peas, as well as crushed *samosas* and boiled potatoes, were sprinkled with lime juice, showered with mint and shredded cabbage, and then doused with a very elaborate *sambar* that had both yellow split peas and chickpea flour in it. Here the *sambar* was happily serving as a sauce! In South Africa, I was offered what was suspiciously like a *sambar* by a wonderful cook, a young South African of south Indian descent. He had enriched what he called a *dal* with a butter and yoghurt sauce.

The *dal* recipes that you will find in this chapter are either for *dals* that can stand by themselves as curries, such as the Beans-in-a-Loaf (see page 185), the Natal Red Kidney Bean Curry (see page 182) or for *dals* that can serve as accompaniments to curry meals. The last seven recipes fall into the latter category.

Manjula Gokal's

Natal Red Kidney Bean Curry

SOUTH AFRICA

The red kidney bean, despite its distant, Central and South American origins, is considered very much a South-African bean today. Manjula Gokal, of Gujarati ancestry, uses them as much as her fellow countrymen, only she transforms them into a slightly sweet, slightly sour, Gujarati feast food.

SERVES 6

- 255 g/9 oz dried red kidney beans
- 3 tablespoons vegetable oil
- 3 whole, dried, hot red chillies
- ½ teaspoon whole brown mustard seeds
- ½ teaspoon whole cumin seeds
- a generous pinch of ground *asafetida*
- 10–15 fresh curry leaves, if available
- 3 medium tomatoes, about 450 g/1 lb, grated on the coarsest part of the grater
- ¼ teaspoon ground turmeric
- 1 teaspoon ground coriander
- 1 teaspoon ground cumin
- 1–2 fresh, hot green chillies, finely chopped
- 1 clove garlic, peeled and crushed
- 1 teaspoon peeled fresh ginger grated to a pulp
- 1 teaspoon sugar
- 1½ teaspoons salt

Cover the beans generously in water and leave to soak overnight. Drain the next day, put in a medium-large pan, add 1½ litres/2½ pints water, and bring to the boil. Partially cover with a lid, reduce the heat to low, and cook gently for 2–2½ hours or until the beans are tender.

Meanwhile, pour the oil into a medium pan and set over a medium-high heat. When the oil is hot, put in the red chillies, mustard seeds, cumin seeds and *asafetida*. As soon as the mustard seeds begin to pop, add the curry leaves and tomatoes. Stir once, then add the turmeric, coriander, cumin, green chillies, garlic, ginger, sugar and salt. Stir and bring to the boil. Reduce the heat to low and simmer gently for 5 minutes.

When the beans are tender, pour the spiced tomato mixture into the pan with the beans. Bring to a simmer, and cook, uncovered, on a very low heat, for 20 minutes.

THE STORY OF BUNNY CHOW

According to legend, 'bunny chows' started in Durban, where there was a large concentration of Indians, in the early 1900s. In the Indian hierarchy that was developing in South Africa, 'passengers' – those who paid their own way to the New Country – were a cut above the 'coolies', who arrived as indentured labour. However, they were frequently economic refugees themselves, small-time entrepreneurs who were hoping to set up in a trade. The trader caste, in India, is known as *bannias* and the word 'bunny' is thought to be a distortion of that name. '*Bannia* food' – which soon stood for all Indian food – was served then by Indians to Indians in small, crude restaurants.

According to the laws of the time, whites, of course, could not associate with Indians, but Indians could not allow African blacks into their restaurants either. Wily Indians soon worked out a way to serve any blacks who came to their back doors, or to holes in their walls, needing food quickly and quietly. They could not give them plates and cutlery, which would need to be returned and therefore slow down the transaction. So they created a quick 'take-away' dish that was to become famous as 'bunny chow'.

They took a small loaf of white bread and sliced off the top crust. Then they hollowed out the loaf, removing its inside in one neat piece. The shell, serving as a trencher-cum-plate, was now ready to be filled with whatever curry was asked for, the stuffing, once torn up, serving as the spoon.

The outside is Western, the inside is completely Indian. But here, all regional Indian distinctions have been obliterated. Initially, during years of poverty, very few spices could be had or afforded. Now, when most spices are readily available, memory of regional 'home foods' has dulled and been replaced by a general 'Indianness' which shows itself in the 'the more the merrier' approach to seasonings. Yet the final taste is unforgettably wonderful.

From Patel's, Gray Street, Durban

Beans-in-a-Loaf (Vegetarian Bunny Chow) SOUTH AFRICA

To attempt a 'bunny', get large, hamburger bun-sized, round, crusty rolls. Cut off the top crusts, laterally. Remove the insides from the bottom halves, preferably in one piece, fill them with the beans, and top with some pickles. Now put the 'lid' back on – and bite. I often serve the beans in a soup plate and offer crusty bread, pickles, chutneys and relishes on the side.

SERVES 4–6

255 g/9 oz dried pinto or cannellini beans, picked over, washed and drained
½ teaspoon ground cumin
1 teaspoon ground coriander
¼ teaspoon ground turmeric
1 teaspoon hot curry powder
¼ teaspoon cayenne pepper
4 tablespoons peanut or corn oil
a generous pinch of ground *asafetida*
½ teaspoon whole brown mustard seeds
½ teaspoon whole cumin seeds
¼ teaspoon whole fennel seeds
1 medium onion, peeled and quartered, lengthways, and then cut crossways into thin slices
10–15 fresh curry leaves, if available
3 cloves garlic, peeled and crushed to a pulp
2 teaspoons fresh ginger, peeled and grated
180 g/6 oz tomato, peeled and finely chopped
1¼ teaspoons salt
1 teaspoon ground *amchoor*, or 2 teaspoons lemon juice
¼ teaspoon *garam masala* (see page 327)

Cover the beans generously in water and leave to soak overnight. Drain the next day, and put in a heavy, lidded pan, along with 1½ litres/2½ pints water and bring to the boil. Partially cover with the lid, reduce the heat to low, and simmer gently for 2 hours or until the beans are tender. Add a little additional boiling water if the beans run dry.

Mix together the cumin, coriander, turmeric, curry powder and cayenne pepper in a small bowl.

Pour the oil into a large, preferably non-stick, lidded pan and set over a medium-high heat. When the oil is hot, put in the *asafetida*, then, a second later, the mustard and cumin seeds and, a second after that, the fennel seeds. Follow them quickly with the onion and curry leaves, so the fennel does not burn. Stir and fry until the onions are lightly browned. Add the garlic and ginger and stir for a minute. Add the ground spices from the bowl and stir for 10 seconds. Add the tomatoes and stir them around until they soften. Add 500 ml/16 fl oz water, the salt, *amchoor* and *garam masala*. Bring to a simmer. Cover, reduce the heat to low, and simmer gently for 15 minutes.

Add this seasoning mixture to the cooked beans. Stir, bring to a simmer and cook, uncovered, on a low heat, stirring from the bottom now and then, for 20 minutes.

Shirley Tiwari's

Chickpea, Potato and Cabbage Curry

GUYANA

This is a great favourite at wedding banquets in Guyana. In India, although chickpeas and potatoes are cooked together all the time, cabbage is rarely added.

Use young, green cabbage here. The outer, very green leaves will provide lots of flavour, so do not discard them. Halve the cabbage, put it flat side down, and then cut it, lengthways, into 1-cm/½-inch wide strips. Then cut the strips, crossways, into 1-cm/½-inch squares.

SERVES 4–6

200 g/6½ oz dried chickpeas (see page 310 for using canned chickpeas or using a pressure cooker)
140 g/5 oz onions, peeled and chopped
4 cloves garlic, peeled and chopped
2 wiri-wiri peppers, or ⅛ of a congo pepper (scotch bonnet, habanero), without seeds, or 3 bird's eye chillies, chopped
4 tablespoons corn, peanut or olive oil
1 tablespoon hot curry powder
1 teaspoon roasted and ground cumin seeds (see page 339)
3 medium potatoes, about 450 g/1 lb, peeled and cut into 2-cm/¾-inch dice
1½ teaspoons salt, or to taste
340 g/12 oz green cabbage, its leaves cut into 1-cm/½-inch squares, as suggested above

Soak the chickpeas overnight in 1.2 litres/2 pints water. Drain the next day and put in a pan. Add 1.2 litres/2 pints fresh water and bring to the boil. Cover, reduce the heat to low, and cook very gently for 1–3 hours or until the chickpeas are very tender. If the water in the pan threatens to dry out, add more boiling water. Drain the chickpeas, reserving the cooking liquid. Pour the liquid into a measuring jug and add enough water to make 600 ml/1 pint.

Put the onions, garlic, wiri-wiri peppers (or chillies) and 4 tablespoons water into a blender and blend until smooth.

Pour the oil into a heavy, preferably non-stick, lidded pan and set over a medium-high heat. Put in the paste from the blender. Stir and fry for 2–3 minutes, then reduce the heat to medium low. Cover and cook for a further 2–3 minutes, removing the lid to stir frequently. Add the curry powder and roasted cumin. Stir once and put in the chickpeas, potatoes, salt and the mixture of chickpea-cooking liquid and water. Bring to the boil, cover, reduce the heat; and cook gently, stirring now and then, for 20–25 minutes, or until the potatoes are tender. Add the cabbage and a further 250 ml/8 fl oz water. Stir and bring to a simmer. Cover and simmer gently for 10–15 minutes or until the cabbage has just softened. Taste for salt before serving.

Easy Chickpea Curry

INDIA

I make this spicy, north India-style curry – a modern version of the chickpeas I ate in the streets of Delhi – very frequently, as it cooks both easily and quickly. I use canned chickpeas and, although it looks like a long list of seasonings, they actually all grind together in one go in the blender.

SERVES 4–6

340 g/12 oz drained weight canned chickpeas (from a 540-g can)
2 smallish tomatoes, about 225 g/8 oz, chopped
5-cm/2-inch piece fresh ginger, peeled and chopped
4 cloves garlic, peeled and chopped
3–6 fresh, hot green chillies, chopped
30 g/1 oz fresh coriander leaves, chopped
1 tablespoon ground coriander
2 teaspoons ground cumin
½ teaspoon ground turmeric
½ teaspoon cayenne pepper
salt
3 tablespoons corn, peanut or olive oil
1 medium stick cinnamon
5 whole cardamom pods
2 bay leaves
2 medium potatoes, about 255 g/9 oz, peeled and cut into 2-cm/¾-inch dice
140 g/5 oz onions, finely chopped

Leave the chickpeas to drain in a colander.

Put the tomatoes, ginger, garlic, chillies, coriander leaves, ground coriander, cumin, turmeric, cayenne pepper, 1 teaspoon salt and 5–6 tablespoons water in a blender and blend until smooth, pushing down with a rubber spatula when necessary.

Pour the oil into a wide, medium, lidded pan and set over a medium-high heat. When the oil is hot, put in the cinnamon, cardamom and bay leaves. Ten seconds later, add the onions and potatoes. Stir and fry for about 6 minutes or until the onions are lightly browned. Add the paste from the blender. Stir for a minute. Cover, reduce the heat to medium-low, and cook 6–7 minutes, lifting the lid now and then to stir. Add the chickpeas, ¼ teaspoon salt and 250 ml/8 fl oz water. Stir and bring to a simmer. Cover, and cook gently on a low heat for 20 minutes, stirring occasionally.

Xoliswa and Amina Cachalia's

Corn and Beans for Nelson Mandela (Umngqusho)

SOUTH AFRICA

As I was not able to get samp, I used the only other large kerneled white corn that is available, posole or hominy. This has already been cooked with an alkali and had its hull removed. It is sold by some ethnic grocers. Even after an overnight soak, it still takes about five hours to cook. But these five hours are quite painless. You may also use canned posole. After draining, you will require 425 g/15 oz. As this corn is fully cooked, just add it to the cooked beans when the recipe suggests it.

SERVES 6

- 140 g/5 oz white, giant posole
- 180 g/6 oz dried pinto beans
- 3 tablespoons corn, peanut or olive oil
- 1 medium onion, peeled and chopped
- 2–3 cloves garlic, peeled and chopped
- 3–4 small, fresh, hot, red and green chillies, chopped
- 340 g/12 oz peeled and chopped tomatoes
- 2 teaspoons salt

Cover the posole generously with water and leave to soak overnight.

Cover the beans generously with water and leave to soak overnight.

Drain the posole and put in a pan with 1.66 litres/2¾ pints water. Bring to the boil, cover, reduce the heat to low, and cook gently for 5 hours or until tender. Drain, reserving the liquid.

Drain the beans and put in a pan with 1.2 litres/2 pints fresh water. Bring to the boil, partially cover with a lid, reduce the heat to low, and cook gently for 2 hours or until tender. Drain, reserving the liquid.

Pour the oil into a pan and set over a medium-high heat. When the oil is hot, put in the onions. Stir and fry until the pieces turn slightly brown at the edges. Add the garlic and chillies and stir for a minute. Add the tomatoes. Stir and fry for about 3 minutes or until the tomatoes turn to a paste.

Combine the cooked, drained posole, the cooked, drained beans and the tomato mixture in one pan. Add the salt and 700 ml/25 fl oz liquid from cooking the posole and beans, plus water, if needed. Bring to a simmer, stirring as you do so. Simmer very gently, stirring now and then, for an hour.

DINNER WITH MANDELA

Sometimes, a single human being can transform a dish, inject elements of one culture into another, and make the new creation a part of the national consciousness. When Nelson Mandela was a child growing up in Qunu, a small village in south-eastern South Africa, he frequently ate what many others of his Xhosa nation could afford – maize and beans, both of which grew locally, boiled together into a kind of stew, *umngqusho*.

As an adult Mandela often yearned for the *umngqusho* of his childhood. Amongst his African National Congress colleagues were a South-African couple of Indian descent, Yusuf and Amina Cachalia. Madiba, as Mandela is respectfully referred to after the name of his clan, loved South-African *biryani* (see page 266). Amina could certainly make him that. But the *umngqusho* he hungered for was far too boring. So she slowly began to Indianise it, adding some onion, garlic, chillies and tomatoes. Now this Xhosa-Indian dish is a staple in Mandela's home.

When I was getting set to travel to South Africa for this book, I contacted Amina in Johannesburg and this very beautiful, highly knowledgeable woman, graciously arranged for me to meet about a dozen ladies of Indian origin, all, like her, connected in various ways to the African National Congress. We were all to gather at the residence of the Indian Consul General where these same ladies would cook their favourite South-African-Indian foods.

When I arrived there, Amina took me aside, saying, 'Madiba is sending his cook, Xoliswa, to make his special Xhosa-Indian *umngqusho*.' Before I could leap with excitement, she added, 'Of course, this is not certain, but Madiba is planning on being here himself. He cannot resist all these ladies. And he loves Indian food.'

Halfway through the cooking, as I was running from crab curry to *biryani* with my notebook, there was a flashing of light bulbs, a trail of photographers running backwards and in walked the tall and handsome Mandela.

For me, it was the best of days. He sat at the head of the table and I sat to his right for the entire three-hour lunch. I have to say that Nelson Mandela certainly tucked into his *biryani* and did not do so badly with the Xhosa-Indian *umngqusho* either.

Toovar Dal with Courgette

INDIA

This is the traditional *sambar* of south India, the dish that is eaten daily with rice or rice pancakes, *dosas*, or with the steamed rice discs known as *idlis*. It is always made with *toovar dal*, hulled and split pigeon peas, which are darker, and duskier, in flavour than *mung dal* or red lentils. Every day, *sambar* is varied slightly as different vegetables are added to the basic *dal*. It could be white radish one day, kohlrabi the next, aubergines the third and squash the following day. The vegetable, if it is firm, may be poached or boiled first in tamarind water and then added to the cooked split peas. The texture of a *sambar* is generally thin and soupy.

The spice mix that gives this dish its flavour, *sambar* powder, may be bought, ready-prepared, from Indian grocers or you could make it yourself. My recipe is on page 326. Rather like a curry powder, it may be used to cook meats and other dishes as well.

SERVES 4

- 140 g/5 oz *toovar dal*, washed in several changes of water and drained
- ½ teaspoon ground turmeric
- 2 tablespoons thick tamarind paste (see page 345)
- 2 tablespoons *sambar* powder (see page 326)
- 1½ teaspoons salt
- 4 tablespoons vegetable oil
- ½ medium courgette, cut into 2½-cm/1-inch long and 1-cm/½-inch thick fingers
- 1 teaspoon fresh, hot green chilli, finely chopped
- a generous pinch of ground *asafetida*
- ¾ teaspoon whole brown mustard seeds
- ½ teaspoon whole *urad dal*
- 3 whole, dried, hot red chillies
- 10–15 fresh curry leaves, if available

Combine the *dal*, turmeric and 600 ml/1 pint water in a pan, stir and bring to a simmer. Partially cover with a lid, reduce the heat to low, and simmer gently for about an hour or until tender. Mash the *dal* with a wooden spoon and add the tamarind, *sambar* powder, salt and 475 ml/16 fl oz water. Stir to mix.

Pour 3 tablespoons of the oil into a large pan and set over a medium-high heat. When the oil is hot, put in the courgette and chilli. Stir for about 5 minutes or until the courgette is slightly browned. Pour the contents of the frying pan into the pan containing the *dal*. Stir to mix. Bring to a simmer and cook gently for 5 minutes.

Pour the remaining oil into a small frying pan and set over a medium-high heat. When the oil is hot, put in the *asafetida*, mustard seeds, *urad dal* and red chillies. As soon as the mustard seeds begin to pop, crush the curry leaves lightly in your hand and throw them in. Now quickly pour the contents of this small pan over the *sambar*.

THE ORIGINS OF DALCHA

In Malaysia's restaurants, if you order Roti Canai (see page 285), the very large, paper-thin flatbreads of the region, *dalcha*, a wonderful stew of split peas, vegetables and ground nuts, is often served on the side, almost as a dipping sauce. Here the *dalcha* is often quite thin, full of chunkily cut vegetables such as aubergines and potatoes. In Malaysian homes, the *dalcha* can be thicker. Indeed, if I were to define the Malaysian *dalcha*, I would call it a grand, vegetarian, curried stew.

The *dalchas* of Malaysia, are, quite obviously, directly descended from the *dalchas* of Indian Muslims who migrated there from south India in the 19th and early 20th centuries. These were themselves adapted from the *sambar*s of south Indian Hindus. Let me try and trace this through and see how it probably happened.

The Hindus of south India have, for a thousand years or more, cooked an ancient legume, *toovar dal* (hulled and split pigeon peas) with vegetables, adding tamarind as both a souring and cooling agent. This is generally known today as *sambar*. (See the preceding recipe.)

When Muslims started coming into south India in medieval times, they showed a preference for legumes they were familiar with, such as red lentils (*masoor dal*) and small, split chickpeas (*chana dal*). They began to cook them very much in the *sambar* manner, adding vegetables and tamarind and many of the same spices, but sometimes, instead of vegetables, they put in meat. This became known as *dalcha*. Today, Hyderabad's *dalcha* is the most famous of all and I have had it cooked both with vegetables and with meat.

It is this *dalcha* that Muslim immigrants from the south took with them to the 'new' country, Malaysia. They rarely used meat, but did add some of the spices that meat might have demanded, such as cinnamon, cardamom and cloves. They enriched the legumes further by adding puréed nuts, which also helped prevent the split pea stew from separating.

Shahabe Catering's

Malaysian Split Pea Curry with Vegetables (Dalcha)

MALAYSIA

In Malaysia, a split pea imported from Australia and known as the Australian yellow split pea is used for this dish today. It is much mellower than the yellow split pea I am used to in the West. What I do is combine *toovar dal* and *chana dal* for a similar flavour but, if you like, you can use just yellow split peas.

You may use all almonds or all cashews instead of a combination of the two.

SERVES 6–8

2 tablespoons chopped raw cashews
2 tablespoons chopped blanched almonds
4–5 cloves garlic, peeled and chopped
7½-cm/3-inch piece fresh ginger, peeled and chopped
1 tablespoon whole coriander seeds
1 teaspoon whole cumin seeds
¼ teaspoon whole fennel seeds
1 tablespoon whole white peppercorns
200 g/6½ oz *toovar dal*
200 g/6½ oz *chana dal*
½ teaspoon ground turmeric
4 tablespoons peanut oil or *ghee*, plus 1–2 tablespoons ghee, or 15–30 g/½–1 oz unsalted butter for optional garnish
1 medium stick cinnamon
6 whole cardamom pods
6 whole cloves
140 g/5 oz red onion, peeled and thinly sliced
30 g/1 oz fresh mint chopped
1 large aubergine, peeled and cut into 4 x 5 cm/1½ x 2 inch chunks
285 g/10 oz potatoes, peeled and cut into 4-cm/1½-inch chunks
250 ml/8 fl oz coconut milk, from a well-shaken can
1 tablespoon plus ½ teaspoon salt
1 medium tomato, coarsely chopped
2–3 tablespoons thick tamarind paste **(see page 345)**
3 fresh, hot green chillies, cut into diagonal slices, for garnish

Soak the cashews and almonds in 120 ml/4 fl oz water overnight or for at least 4 hours. Put the nuts and liquid into a blender and blend until smooth. Remove to a bowl.

Put the garlic and ginger into the blender (no need to wash it first) with a tablespoon or two of water and blend until smooth.

Put the coriander, cumin, fennel and peppercorns into a clean coffee grinder or other spice grinder and grind as finely as you can.

Combine the *toovar dal* and *chana dal* in a bowl. Wash in several changes of water and drain. Put in a medium, lidded pan, add 1.7 litres/2¾ pints water, and bring to the boil. Skim off the scum that rises to the top with a slotted spoon. Add the turmeric and stir.

Partially cover with the lid and reduce the heat to low. Simmer gently for 1¼ hours or until the split peas are tender. Turn off the heat.

Pour the oil (or *ghee*) into a large, preferably non-stick, lidded pan and set over a medium heat. When the oil is hot, put in the cinnamon, cardamom and cloves. Stir once and add the onion. Stir and cook for 4–5 minutes or until the onion softens and just begins to brown. Add the mint and stir once. Add the aubergine and potato. Stir for 2 minutes. Add the garlic-ginger paste and stir for a minute. Add the cooked *dal*, the coconut milk, 475 ml/16 fl oz water, the ground spices and salt and bring to a simmer. Partially cover with the lid, and simmer very gently for 30 minutes. Stir in the nut paste, tomato, tamarind paste and chillies, and bring to a simmer. Simmer gently, uncovered, for 10 minutes. Taste for a balance of flavours. If the consistency is too thick, add a little water. Extra *ghee* or melted butter may be poured over the top before serving.

Parveen Haroon's

Black-Eyed Beans with Spinach and Dill — PAKISTAN

This dish, from the Sindh region of Pakistan, has decided Persian overtones. It is eaten with Tomato-Garlic Rice (see page 255), and any pickles of your choice.

The souring ingredient here is the dried Persian lime. You have to crack it and remove its black insides. Discard all seeds and lightly crush the dried pulp. These limes are sold by Middle-Eastern grocers. If you cannot get dried limes, use 1–2 tablespoons fresh lemon juice.

Coarsely ground pure chilli powders are sold in Korean markets (they are used to make *Kimchee*). Middle-Eastern grocers sell an aleppo pepper that is equally good. If you cannot find either of these, use ¾–1½ teaspoons cayenne pepper.

SERVES 6

- **200 g/6½ oz dried black-eyed beans**
- **salt**
- **3 tablespoons corn or peanut oil**
- **1 teaspoon whole cumin seeds**
- **1 teaspoon whole brown mustard seeds**
- **4 cloves garlic, peeled and chopped**
- **15–20 fresh curry leaves, if available**
- **450 g/1 lb spinach, washed, finely chopped, and left to drain in a colander**
- **7–8 tablespoons very finely chopped fresh dill**
- **6 tablespoons natural yoghurt**
- **1½–2 teaspoons coarsely ground, pure chilli powder**
- **1 dried lime or 1–2 tablespoons fresh lemon juice**

Cover the dried beans generously with water and leave to soak overnight. Drain them the next day, put in a pan with 1 litre/1¾ pints fresh water and bring to a simmer. Partially cover with a lid and cook for 50–60 minutes or until tender. Stir in 1½ teaspoons salt.

Pour the oil into a large pan or wok and set over a medium-high heat. When the oil is hot, put in the cumin and mustard seeds. As soon as the mustard seeds begin to pop, a matter of seconds, put in the garlic and curry leaves. Stir once, then add the spinach and dill. Stir and cook until most of the liquid in the spinach is absorbed. Add the yoghurt, and continue to cook, stirring, until the yoghurt is absorbed. Reduce the heat to low and add 350 ml/12 fl oz water, the chilli powder and ¼ teaspoon salt. Stir. Crack the lime and take out the dried black pulp. Remove any seeds and crush the pulp. Add it to the spinach. Now pour all the contents of the spinach pan into the pan containing the beans. Stir and bring to a simmer. Cover, and simmer gently for 10 minutes.

Sonia Advani's

Bean Curd Cooked in the Pickling Style (Achari Bean Curd)

SINGAPORE

When meats or vegetables are prepared in the 'pickling' style, it means that whole fennel, *kalonji* (nigella) and mustard seeds are added in the initial stages of cooking. It is a very Indian technique and does, indeed, owe its inspiration to the spices that are used in making Indian pickles. Here, in an interesting twist, the pickling spices are used with a very non-Indian food – bean curd. This dish was created by modern Indians living in Singapore who had all their Indian spices in their spice boxes and easy access to the ubiquitous, nutritious bean curd.

I used two large cakes of firm bean curd, each weighing 425 g/15 oz. You can approximate that weight by using smaller or larger cakes.

SERVES 6

850 g/1 lb 14 oz firm bean curd
3 tablespoons corn, peanut or olive oil
¼ teaspoon whole brown mustard seeds
¼ teaspoon whole fennel seeds
¼ teaspoon whole *kalonji* (nigella seeds)
2 teaspoons fresh ginger, peeled and grated to a pulp
4 cloves garlic, peeled and crushed to a pulp
285 g/10 oz fresh tomatoes, peeled and finely chopped
1 teaspoon ground coriander
½ teaspoon cayenne pepper
¼ teaspoon ground turmeric
1½ teaspoons red wine vinegar
1 teaspoon salt
½ teaspoon sugar, if needed

Spread one end of a tea towel on a large plate. Lay the bean curd cakes on it in a single layer. Fold the remaining tea towel over the top. Invert another large plate on the top and put a weight, such as a large can, on the top. Set aside for 45 minutes. Uncover, then cut the bean curd into 2-cm/¾-inch cubes and set aside.

Pour the oil into a large, preferably non-stick, lidded pan and set over a medium-high heat. When the oil is hot, put in the mustard seeds. As soon as they begin to pop, a matter of seconds, put in the fennel and *kalonji*. A second later, put in the ginger and garlic, turning down the heat to medium. Stir for a minute, then add the tomatoes, coriander, cayenne, turmeric, vinegar and salt. Stir and cook on a medium heat for 3–4 minutes or until the tomatoes turn to a paste.

Add 500 ml/16 fl oz water and bring to a simmer. Cover and simmer gently for 5 minutes. Add the bean curd and the sugar, if needed. Stir gently and return to a simmer. Cover and simmer on a low heat for 10 minutes, turning the bean curd pieces in the sauce now and then.

Manjula Gokal's

Chickpea Flour 'Kadhi' with Whole Urad Peas (Arad Karhi)

SOUTH AFRICA

Kadhis are soupy dishes made with chickpea flour and buttermilk or, as here, with yoghurt. The more sour the yoghurt, the better the flavour. If your yoghurt is very fresh, try leaving it unrefrigerated and in a warmish place overnight.

SERVES 4

- 90 g/3 oz *sabut urad* (whole *urad*), picked over, washed and drained
- 175 ml/6 fl oz natural yoghurt
- 2 tablespoons chickpea flour
- 1 teaspoon ground coriander
- 1 teaspoon ground cumin
- ½ teaspoon ground turmeric
- 2 teaspoons fresh ginger, peeled and finely grated
- 1 large clove garlic, peeled and crushed
- 1¼ teaspoons salt
- 1 teaspoon sugar
- 3 small, fresh, hot green chillies, slit in half
- 2 tablespoon corn or peanut oil, or *ghee*
- ¼ teaspoon ground *asafetida*
- 1 teaspoon whole brown mustard seeds
- 3 dried, hot red chillies
- ½ teaspoon whole cumin seeds
- ¼ teaspoon whole fenugreek seeds
- 10–15 fresh curry leaves, if available

Put the *urad* in a lidded pan. Cover generously with water and bring to the boil. Boil for 2 minutes, then cover, remove from the heat, and set aside for 1 hour. Drain. Put the *urad* back in the pan, add 750 ml/1¼ pints water and bring to the boil. Partially cover with the lid, reduce the heat to low, and boil for 10 minutes. Drain. Put in a bowl and cover with fresh cold water. Using both hands, rub the peas lightly between your palms to remove as many of the black skins as possible. The skins will float to the top. Pour off the water at the top of the bowl; the skins will flow out with it. Do this several times. Now drain, put the *urad* back in the pan with another 700 ml/1¼ pints water and bring to the boil. Partially cover with the lid, reduce the heat to low and boil for 10 minutes or until just tender. Drain. Wash once more in cold water to get rid of more skins.

Put the yoghurt in a bowl and mix well with a wooden spoon. Add the chickpea flour and mix until smooth. Stir in the coriander, cumin, turmeric, ginger, garlic, salt and sugar. Now slowly mix in 475 ml/16 fl oz water. Add the green chillies and the *urad*.

Pour the oil into a small, lidded pan and set it over a medium-high heat. When the oil is hot, put in the *asafetida*, the mustard seeds, red chillies and cumin seeds. As soon as the mustard seeds begin to pop, take the pan off the heat and put in the fenugreek seeds, the curry leaves and, a second later, the yoghurt mixture. Stir, put the pan back on the heat, and bring to a simmer. Partially cover with the lid, reduce the heat to low, and simmer gently for 10–15 minutes, stirring now and then.

Yasmeen Murshed's

Red Lentils with Lime and Cheese (Limbu Dal)

BANGLADESH

Bangladeshis use the skin and leaves of a lime that is very similar to the kaffir lime of Thailand to flavour this simple *dal*. A very unusual addition is a grated Bangladeshi cheese similar to Greek haloumi. Jarlsberg cheese or a mild cheddar may be substituted here.

If any bits and pieces of leftover kebabs are lying around, they may be crumbled in as well, though they are not essential.

Serve with rice and other fish or meat curries.

SERVES 4

- 180 g/6 oz red lentils
- 1 small onion, about 60 g/2 oz, peeled and chopped
- ¼ teaspoon ground turmeric
- salt
- 2 tablespoons *ghee* or corn oil
- 4 fresh, hot green chillies, such as bird's eye chillies, 3 slit slightly but left whole and the last chopped finely
- 1 tablespoon lime juice
- 2½ cm x 5 mm/1 inch x ¼ inch piece fresh kaffir lime rind
- 2 fresh kaffir lime leaves
- 2–3 tablespoons grated cheese (haloumi, Jarlsberg or mild cheddar)
- 2–3 tablespoons of crumbled, leftover kebabs, optional

Put the lentils in a lidded pan with 1 litre/32 fl oz water, the onion and turmeric, and bring to the boil. Do not let the pot boil over. Skim off the scum that rises to the surface with a slotted spoon. Partially cover with the lid, reduce the heat to low, and cook for 40–50 minutes or until tender. Stir in about 1 teaspoon salt, adding more if needed. Push the *dal* through a coarse sieve.

In a small pan, heat the *ghee* or oil until very hot. Put in the slit chillies. Let them sizzle for 3–4 seconds, then pour the contents of the frying pan over the lentils. Cover the pan quickly to trap the aromas.

Just before serving, set the lentils over a low heat.

Put the lime juice and lime rind into a large, warmed, serving bowl. Tear up the lime leaves and add them to the bowl. Add the cheese, chopped chilli and any kebab bits. Once the lentils are very hot, pour them into the bowl, stirring as you do so. Serve immediately.

Shamim Fatima's

Whole Red Lentils with Garlic and Mint (Geeli Sabut Masoor)

INDIA

Whole red lentils, sold by South-Asian grocers as *sabut masoor,* look rather like brown lentils and cook like them too. The flavour is similar, though not exactly the same. Here is a simple, and totally addictive way to prepare them.

I got this recipe from a salesperson at a grocery. It is where I shop regularly in New York for my Indian spices. We always chat. Shamim tells me how my cookbooks are selling (she has a variety of Middle-Eastern and South-Asian cookbooks displayed behind her), and what is new and worth trying. One day, as I was paying for a packet of *sabut masoor,* she said, 'I just cooked these yesterday. They were really delicious. I made them the usual way, with garlic and mint.'

In India, one person's 'usual way' is not another's, so I asked her to explain what she did with them. It was so good – and easy – that I had to include an adaptation of it here.

SERVES 4

- 3 tablespoons corn, peanut or olive oil, or ghee
- 2 cloves garlic, peeled and crushed to a pulp, plus 2 cloves garlic, each peeled and sliced, lengthways, into 3 wide slivers
- ½ teaspoon cayenne pepper
- 185 g/6¾ oz *sabut masoor* (whole red lentils), or brown or green lentils
- ½ teaspoon ground turmeric
- 1 teaspoon salt
- 3–4 tablespoons finely chopped fresh mint
- 3–4 fresh, hot green chillies (such as bird's eye or the cayenne variety), chopped

Put 1 tablespoon of the oil, the crushed garlic and the cayenne pepper into a medium, lidded pan and set on a medium-high heat. When the pan begins to sizzle, stir once or twice. Now put in 750 ml/27 fl oz water, the *sabut masoor,* the turmeric and ¾ teaspoon salt. Stir and bring to the boil. Partially cover with the lid, reduce the heat to low, and cook for about 55 minutes or until the lentils are tender. Add the mint and green chillies. Stir and simmer for a further 5 minutes. Taste for salt, adding another 1/4 teaspoon or so if necessary.

Pour the remaining oil into a small pan, along with the garlic slivers. Put the pan on a medium-low heat. Stir. As soon as the garlic turns golden-red, empty the contents of the pan, oil and garlic, into the pan with the lentils.

Saika's

Red Lentils from the Khyber Pass (Khyber Pass Ki Masoor Dal)

PAKISTAN

In the brown hills of the Khyber Pass, Saika, the woman of the house, cooked red lentils, round squash and wholemeal breads for lunch. It was the once-a-week 'no-meat' day, declared so by the Pakistani government worried by the nation's excessive meat-eating habits. While butchers are not allowed to sell meat that day, most families get around the restriction by buying their meat a day in advance and freezing it. Not so Saika. She was an observer.

SERVES 4

180 g/6 oz red lentils
¼–1 teaspoon cayenne pepper
salt
2 tablespoons *ghee* or corn oil
1–2 whole, dried hot red chillies
2 cloves garlic, peeled and lightly crushed

Put the lentils in a lidded pan with 1 litre/32 fl oz water and bring to the boil. Do not let the pot boil over. Skim off the scum that comes to the surface with a slotted spoon. Partially cover with the lid, reduce the heat to low, and cook for 40–50 minutes or until tender. Stir in the cayenne pepper and about 1 teaspoon salt. Taste, adding more salt as needed.

In a small pan, heat the *ghee* or oil until very hot. Put in the red chillies. As soon as they darken, put in the garlic. When the garlic pieces turn golden-brown on both sides, pour the oil and seasonings into the pan of lentils. Cover the pan quickly to trap the aromas.

Yasmeen Murshed's

Red Lentils with Five Spices

BANGLADESH

Most lentils and beans are boiled in the same way all over the world. It is the seasonings that make the difference. Here is the Bangladeshi version of red lentils, cooked with a final *tarka* of the five-spice mixture containing equal portions of whole cumin, fennel, mustard, fenugreek and nigella seeds. The spices may be mixed at home or bought ready-prepared as a mixture known by its Bengali name, *panchphoran*.

SERVES 4

180 g/6 oz red lentils
¼ teaspoon ground turmeric
1 medium onion, sliced into very fine half-rings
1–1¼ teaspoons salt
2 tablespoons corn oil
1–2 whole, dried, hot red chillies
1 teaspoon *panchphoran* (see page 343)

Put the lentils, turmeric and half the sliced onion in a lidded pan with 1 litre/32 fl oz water and bring to the boil. Do not let the pot boil over. Skim off the scum that rises to the surface with a slotted spoon. Partially cover with the lid, reduce the heat to low and cook for 40–50 minutes or until tender. Add the salt and mash the *dal* and onion well with a potato masher.

In a small pan, heat the oil until very hot. Put in the red chillies. As soon as they darken, put in the *panchphoran*. Stir once and put in the remaining onion. Stir and fry until the onion turns reddish-brown. Pour the oil and seasonings into the pan of lentils. Cover the pan quickly to trap the aromas.

Saira Ahmed's

Mung Dal with Green Chillies (Mung Dal) PAKISTAN

A simple, everyday Pakistani *dal* which may be served with rice or breads.

SERVES 4

180 g/6 oz hulled and split *mung dal*
¼ teaspoon ground turmeric
1–1¼ teaspoons salt
2–3 tablespoons olive oil or *ghee*
½ medium onion, sliced into fine half-rings
2 whole cloves garlic, lightly crushed
1–3 fresh, hot green chillies, cut into 2½-cm/1-inch lengths
3 tablespoons fresh coriander leaves, coarsely chopped

Wash the *dal* in several changes of water and drain.

Combine the *dal* with 900 ml/32 fl oz water in a lidded pan and bring to the boil. Do not let it boil over, turning the heat down as necessary. Skim off the scum that rises to the surface with a slotted spoon, and add the turmeric. Reduce the heat to low, partially cover with the lid, and simmer gently for 40–50 minutes or until the *dal* is tender. Stir in the salt and turn off the heat.

Pour the oil or *ghee* into a small frying pan and set over a medium-high heat. When the oil is hot, put in the onion. Stir and fry until the onion is medium-brown. Add the garlic and continue to stir and fry until the onion turns reddish and the garlic is golden. Add the chillies. Fry for another 30 seconds, then pour the contents of the frying pan, oil and spices, into the pan containing the *dal*. Cover immediately with the lid to trap the aromas. Stir gently before serving. Scatter the coriander leaves over the top when you do so.

Mung and Toovar Dal Cooked in a South-Indian Manner

INDIA

A simple mixture of two *dals*, finished off with south-Indian seasonings. This is usually eaten with rice.

SERVES 4

- **90 g/3 oz hulled and split *mung dal***
- **90 g/3 oz hulled and split *toovar dal***
- **a generous pinch of ground *asafetida***
- **½ teaspoon cayenne pepper**
- **¼ teaspoon ground turmeric**
- **2 teaspoons fresh ginger, peeled and finely grated**
- **3 cloves garlic, peeled and crushed to a pulp**
- **1 medium shallot, peeled and cut into fine slivers**
- **3 fresh, hot green chillies, finely chopped**
- **1–1¼ teaspoons salt**
- **2–3 tablespoons olive oil or *ghee***
- **½ teaspoon whole brown mustard seeds**
- **2 dried, hot red chillies**
- **8–10 fresh curry leaves, if available**
- **3 tablespoons fresh coriander leaves, coarsely chopped**

Wash the two *dals* in several changes of water and drain.

Combine the *dals* with 1 litre/32 fl oz water in a lidded pan and bring to the boil. Do not let them boil over, turning the heat down as necessary. Skim off the scum that rises to the surface with a slotted spoon and add the *asafetida*, cayenne pepper, turmeric, ginger, garlic, shallots, green chillies and salt. Stir. Reduce the heat to low, partially cover with the lid, and simmer gently for 50–60 minutes or until the *dals* are tender.

Pour the oil or *ghee* into a small frying pan and set over a medium-high heat. When the oil is hot, put in the mustard seeds and red chillies. As soon as the mustard seeds begin to pop, a matter of seconds, crush the curry leaves lightly in your hand and throw them in. Quickly empty the contents of the frying pan, oil and spices, into the pan containing the *dals*. Cover immediately with the lid to trap the aromas. Stir gently before serving. Scatter the coriander leaves over the top when you do so.

6

KEBABS AND SOUPS

I've grouped kebabs and soups together as they are generally served at the start of a meal. Kebabs probably originated in the Arab world and were once (and still can be), very simple: little cubes of meat, marinated in olive oil and garlic and then skewered and grilled over wood or charcoal.

Arabs carried the dream of these morsels to far-off lands where they have traded since antiquity – India, Indonesia, Malaysia, Thailand, Vietnam and even as far as Japan. This dream made the gentlest of landings in dozens of ports. As soon as it hit land, a process of transformation began. Local influences enveloped the little kebabs. In India, where a tradition of skewered and grilled meats already existed, they picked up ginger, black pepper, cumin, ground coriander and yoghurt as marinades, and spicy chutneys as dipping sauces. In Indonesia they turned into the slightly sweet satays around Java, but elsewhere the Indian spiciness remained. In Thailand, pork often became the meat of choice, with curry powder being used both in the marinade and in the basting sauce; Vietnam added lemon grass to the marinating ingredients and served its kebabs with a dipping sauce that included fish sauce (*nuoc mam*), lime juice and sugar. The Japanese decided to brush their kebabs, chicken *yakitori*, with a salty, winey syrup of soy sauce, sake and sugar.

It is important to note that kebabs took root in India (a country that was to split into India, Pakistan and Bangladesh), probably because there was already an established tradition of similar foods, going back to the time of the Hindu epic, the Mahabharata, 400 BC–AD 1. It is in India that we see the largest variety. Kebabs here are grilled, roasted, baked, shallow-fried, deep-fried, cooked in a pot, in eggshells or on heated stones. They may be made with minced meat, cubed meat, ribbons of meat or cooked meat. There are chicken drumstick kebabs, fish kebabs, kebabs stuffed with hard-boiled eggs and kebabs in a yoghurt sauce. It is an infinite range.

Of course, there is a good reason for it. Kebabs may have originated in the Muslim world. But this world held Hindu India in varying degrees of control from the 10th until the 19th centuries, a very long period. Muslim potentates did not rule from a distance. Unlike the British who were to follow them, they conquered the land and lived in India as Indians, their food melding into Hindu Indian food, each borrowing from the other until distinctions no longer mattered. It was a unique situation, not repeated elsewhere.

Perhaps because India was such a large nation to manage, imperial power in the capital, Delhi, had to be delegated to governors in the north, south, east and west. These governors often asserted their independence and set up their own feudal kingdoms. In culinary terms, this only had an upside. With time on their hands, feudal Muslim rulers, like those in Awadh (now Uttar Pradesh) and Hyderabad could concentrate on their kitchens.

Now we come to one of the greatest contradictions in Islam. Drinking is forbidden. Yet, most of the greatest Muslim potentates in India drank and kebabs were the favourite accompaniment (in the 16th and 17th centuries it was supposedly fruit and fruit juices.) This remains true to this day.

I have my own story to tell here. I come from an ancient Hindu family with roots in the capital city, Delhi. With the coming of Muslim rule, our community, which consisted of professionals – lawyers, writers, etc. – took to working in the Muslim courts as lawyers, historians, translators and even ministers. In the Moghul period (16th–19th centuries), the men mastered the court language, Persian, and all the Moghul court manners. (My mother's wedding dress can only be described as Moghul-Edwardian. Of course, by this time we were being ruled by the British and my grandfather was a judge in the British-Indian high court! We moved with the times.)

Among the things we picked up was Moghul food, which we ate along with what could be called our own Delhi Hindu food. Our community was known as *sharabi-kebabis*, or those who liked to drink and eat. Sweets, traditionally, were considered a waste of time and an aunt, when offered a sweetmeat at a wedding banquet looked askance and is reputed to have said, 'Good heavens, if I had room left in my stomach I would have eaten another kebab!'

The evolution of the kebab has not ended. While one can get a whole range of Moghlai-style kebabs using ground, fried onions (*berista*) and ground nuts in their marinades, some of the newer kebabs I had in Karachi, Pakistan, were smothered with, among other ingredients, tomato ketchup, before being grilled.

In Durban, South Africa, where a large Indian population likes its margarita glasses encrusted with salt and chillies, there is a trendy, high-end butcher who sells raw meat patties, seasoned with garlic, ground coriander, ginger, cumin and nutmeg, that he calls '*masala* hamburgers' or 'Hollywood chops'. They are big sellers.

In north Indian restaurants and in Indian restaurants abroad, it has become quite the custom to sprinkle the ubiquitous, packaged, *chaat masala* on all kebabs, especially those emerging from *tandoor* ovens. *Chaat* is a special category of Indian snack food. Kebabs have never been included, as *chaat* is always vegetarian. *Chaats* are meant to titillate the palate with their very hot and sour seasonings. When I was a child, my mother seasoned all our *chaat* foods herself – boiled potatoes, dumplings and fruit. (See the recipe for Fruit Chaat, page 310.) Today, you can buy a generalised, packaged *chaat* seasoning in every market. Somebody, probably in the 1960s, decided that these seasonings could be used for roasted and grilled meats and we were off and away on another 'trend' that combined a very Muslim kebab with a very Hindu spice combination. A *chaat masala* always contains sour, dried mango powder (*amchoor*), ground roasted cumin, chilli powder and pungent black salt. (My recipe is on page 325.) Whether you need it or not is another matter. I will suggest when I think it could lend a helping hand.

Chutneys, however, are always served with kebabs. Not the sweet, preserve type of chutney – though you may certainly serve it if you wish – but fresh chutneys made with herbs or tomatoes or a mixture of nuts and herbs. (See pages 296–311.).

When I was growing up in India and we sent our driver off to the area around Jama Masjid, Delhi's 17th-century mosque, to get us some kebabs, the kebabs always came smothered with paper-thin onion rings. They were meant to be eaten with the kebabs but also served a double function. They kept the kebabs moist. Directions on how to make these Raw Onion Rings are on page 313.

Kebabs may be eaten with drinks and as part of a main meal. In many Muslim families, leftover kebabs are a much loved breakfast food, to be eaten with flatbreads. If some are still left by lunchtime, they are crumbled into dishes of dried beans and split peas.

Indians do not really drink soups. Having said that, as with everything else in India, there are dozens of exceptions to the rule. Many Muslim communities drink *aab gosht*, or meat broths, in cups at the start of a meal. The Bohris, another Muslim community from the Gujarat, drink almond soup and soups made with split peas. In south India, pepper water and other thin distillations from spices and split peas and tomatoes or tamarind are often served as digestives at the start of a meal and, of course, while the British were in India, they created their own soups, out of which Mulligatawny and tomato soup, served with fried croutons or crisped slices of bread, remain embedded in the Indian culinary repertoire.

What I have done here is to choose the soups that I like most from India, as well as from the regions that India influenced, mostly those in South-East Asia. These South-East Asian curried soups, whether they be from Burma, Malaysia, Thailand or Vietnam, are very different from each other in flavour but are prepared and served in a fairly similar manner. The broth itself contains coconut milk, noodles and either curry paste or powder or both. This base is always added to with fresh, crisp, salty or hot ingredients such as bean sprouts, crisply fried onions, fresh herbs, chillies, lime juice and peanuts. These soups are filling and often eaten as quick meals. In smaller quantities, they may be served as first courses. They are highly aromatic and addictive.

Grilled Lamb Kebabs (Mutton Tikka) INDIA

These simple kebabs may also be cooked on an outdoor grill.

SERVES 4

6 tablespoons natural yoghurt
3 tablespoons corn, peanut or olive oil, plus more for brushing on the meat while grilling
1 tablespoon fresh ginger, peeled and finely grated
2 cloves garlic, peeled and crushed to a pulp
¾ teaspoon cayenne pepper
1 teaspoon bright red paprika
½ teaspoon *garam masala* (see page 327)
1 teaspoon salt
560 g/1¼ lb boneless lamb, cut into 2½-cm/1-inch cubes
about ½ teaspoon *chaat masala* (see page 325)
sprigs of fresh mint
lime or lemon wedges

Put the yoghurt in a sieve lined with a piece of muslin. Set the sieve over a bowl and leave for 2 hours to drip. Scrape the drained yoghurt into a bowl. Add the 3 tablespoons oil, ginger, garlic, cayenne pepper, paprika, *garam masala* and salt. Mix well. Prick the meat pieces with a fork and add them to the marinade. Mix well. Cover and refrigerate for 4–20 hours.

Preheat the grill. Set a shelf so that, when they cook, the kebabs will be a distance of about 13 cm/5 inches from the source of the heat. Thread the kebabs on to skewers. I like long, flat skewers that can be rested on the edges of a shallow baking tray. The sheet catches the drips and the kebabs themselves remain suspended above it. Brush the kebabs generously with oil and grill for 3–4 minutes on the first side and then for another 3–4 minutes on the other side. Take off the skewers and sprinkle lightly with the *chaat masala*. Garnish with mint sprigs and serve with the lime or lemon wedges.

Royal Lamb Kaati Kebab (Shahi Kaati Kabab)

INDIA

Calcutta is quite famous for its traditional *kaati kebabs*. In the evenings, the better *kaati kebab* restaurants are packed. Even the best ones are rough places, more open street stalls than proper restaurants, and are rarely found in smart neighbourhoods. Yet, the most expensive cars can be seen jostling to line up outside them. These kebabs are superb.

They are not grilled. Instead, the pieces of meat are marinated and then cooked on an enormous griddle set up so it is open to the street. All the better to tempt passersby with enticing aromas.

They are traditionally served rolled up in flatbreads (such as the Indian or Guyanese Flaky Breads, pages 275 and 282) along with finely sliced raw onions (try the Raw Onion Ring Salad, page 314), chopped fresh mint and fresh coriander and some sliced green chillies, if liked. Having said this, let me add that my husband likes them just the way they are, with rice and a salad for accompaniments.

SERVES 4

FOR THE MARINADE

- 450 g/1 lb boneless lamb, preferably from the shoulder, cut into 2–2½-cm/¾–1-inch cubes
- 1 tablespoon peeled and finely grated fresh ginger
- 7 cloves garlic, peeled and crushed to a pulp
- 1 tablespoon ground coriander
- ¾ teaspoon cayenne pepper, or to taste
- 1 teaspoon salt
- 1 tablespoon lemon juice

FOR COOKING THE KEBABS

- 1 tablespoon chickpea flour
- 3 tablespoons corn or peanut oil
- 90 g/3 oz onion cut into very thin half-rings
- 1 tablespoon finely chopped fresh mint or fresh coriander or a combination of the two

Combine the meat with all the marinade ingredients, massaging the spices into the flesh. Cover (I just put the meat in a zip-lock bag) and refrigerate for 4–24 hours.

Put a small, cast-iron pan on a medium-low heat. Spoon in the chickpea flour. Stir it about until it is a very pale golden-brown. It will smell roasted. Remove to a small bowl immediately.

Pour the oil into a heavy, non-stick, lidded pan and set over a medium heat. Put in the onions and fry, stirring, turning the heat down as needed, until the onions are reddish-gold and crisp. Remove with a slotted spoon, leaving behind as much oil as possible, and spread out on kitchen paper to cool and crisp further.

Put the meat, together with its marinade, into the same pan. Turn the heat to medium.

Stir the lamb pieces for a minute, cover, and cook for 15 minutes or so, removing the lid every few minutes to stir. When the meat has browned and there is hardly any liquid in the pan, reduce the heat as low as possible. Keep covered and continue to stir now and then. Cook for a further 15 minutes, but keep an eye on the meat. Do not let it burn. If it looks as if it might, sprinkle in a little water and cover again. (If the meat has marinated for 24 hours, it should be done. Shorter marination periods might require slightly longer cooking times.)

Chop up the fried onions finely, then add them and the roasted chickpea flour to the meat. Stir and cover again. Cook very gently for another 5–10 minutes. Sprinkle the mint over the top and stir.

Masala Lamb Chops, Grilled — INDIA

These chops are generally made in a *tandoor* oven. Here is my grilled version. You may use rib or loin chops, but make sure that they are not more than 1 cm/½ inch thick. If the loin chops are too large, ask the butcher to halve them, crossways.

SERVES 3–4

4 teaspoons fresh ginger, peeled and finely grated
7 cloves garlic, peeled and crushed to a pulp
1 tablespoon ground cumin
½–¾ teaspoon cayenne pepper
½ teaspoon *garam masala* (see page 327)
1 teaspoon salt
4 teaspoons lemon juice
675 g/1½ lb lamb chops (see above)
freshly ground black pepper
about 6 tablespoons double cream
mint sprigs for garnishing

Combine the ginger, garlic, cumin, cayenne pepper, *garam masala*, salt and lemon juice in a bowl. Add the lamb chops. Rub the marinade over them thoroughly, massaging it well in. Put the chops in a zip-lock or other plastic bag and refrigerate for 4–24 hours.

Preheat the grill, setting a shelf about 15 cm/6 inches from the source of the heat. Sprinkle black pepper on all sides of the chops. Lay the chops on any perforated or open-meshed rack set on a solid baking tray. Spread half the cream over the top of the chops and grill for about 7 minutes or until browned. Turn the chops over, spread the remaining cream over the top and grill the second side in exactly the same way.

Garnish with mint sprigs and serve.

With Fatma Zakaria's help

Baked Lamb Kebabs (Lagania Sheek) INDIA

SERVES 4–8

FOR THE LAMB

450 g/1 lb minced lamb (see note opposite)
1 tablespoon finely chopped fresh mint
1 tablespoon finely chopped fresh coriander
1½ tablespoons fresh ginger, peeled and finely grated
3 cloves garlic, peeled and crushed to a pulp
2–3 green bird's eye chillies, finely chopped
½ teaspoon *garam masala* (see page 327)
1 teaspoon salt
freshly ground black pepper
½ teaspoon cayenne pepper
½ teaspoon ground coriander
½ teaspoon ground cumin
¼ teaspoon ground turmeric
4 teaspoons natural yoghurt
5 tablespoons corn or peanut oil
1 medium onion, peeled and sliced into very thin half-rings
4 teaspoons chickpea flour

FOR THE EGG TOPPING

2 eggs, well beaten
⅛ teaspoon salt or less
freshly ground black pepper
a pinch of cayenne pepper
a few coriander leaves, chopped
1 small bird's eye chilli, finely chopped
1 tablespoon chopped tomato (it is best to peel and seed it first)

Put the meat in a bowl. Add the mint, chopped coriander, ginger, garlic, chillies, *garam masala*, salt, black pepper, cayenne pepper, ground coriander, cumin, turmeric and yoghurt. Mix well and put in a plastic bag. Refrigerate for 16–20 hours.

Pour the oil into a medium frying pan and set over a medium-high heat. When the oil is hot, put in the onion and stir and fry until the slices are crisp. This will take 10–12 minutes. Remove the onion with a slotted spoon, saving all the oil left behind in the pan, and spread out on double layer of kitchen paper. The slices will crisp up further as they cool. Change the kitchen paper and spread out the slices again to get rid of most of the oil. Chop up the onions.

Put the chickpea flour into a small, cast-iron pan and set over a medium-high heat. Stir the flour around until it turns a very light golden-brown and emits a faintly roasted smell. Remove the flour from the hot pan. Take the bowl of meat out of the refrigerator and add the browned, chopped onions and roasted chickpea flour. Mix well.

Preheat the oven to 180°C/gas mark 4. Break the eggs into a bowl and beat until light and fluffy. Season with the salt, black pepper, cayenne pepper, coriander, green chilli and tomato. Pour 1 tablespoon of the oil used for frying the onions over the bottom of a non-stick baking tin, about 19 cm/7½ inches square. Put in the meat and, using wet hands, spread it to the edges. Pour the eggs over the top. Dribble another tablespoon of the onion oil over the eggs. Bake for 30 minutes, then place under the grill for about a minute to brown lightly. Cut into 4-cm/1½- inch squares and serve with lime wedges.

IN SEARCH OF PERFECT KEBABS

This is a recipe that I have being trying to perfect for more than fifteen years. When I first ate these kebabs in the Bombay home of a Bohri Muslim family (they are a 1,000-year-old Gujarati community in Western India), I was utterly enchanted. Here was a kind of baked meatloaf, except that it was flat, thin, spicy and topped with beaten egg. It could be cut into squares and eaten as an appetiser. And, what is most important, it just melted in the mouth. Every time I tried to make it, however, it was leaden, nothing like what was served to me by my Bohri hosts. What on earth provided the lightness?

I seem to have the answer now. First of all, the meat needs to be fatty. Twenty to 30 per cent of fat makes the kebabs loosen up. Rather like sausages, lean meat makes for dry, heavy kebabs. As most lamb is fatty anyway, this is seldom a major problem. Then, the meat needs to marinate with all the spices for a generous period. This breaks down its toughness and turns it into a semi pâté.

The name of the dish offers endless fascination. The word *sheek*, rather like *shish* or *seekh*, means 'skewer'. But these kebabs are not made on skewers. They are made in a *lagan* or cooking pan – in this case, a baking tin. So the word *sheek* serves as a stand-in for 'kebab' and the name of the dish, *lagania sheek* or *lagan nu sheek,* means 'kebabs baked in a pan'.

In the olden days, the meat was packed into a flat pan set over very gently burning coals. More coals were placed on the lid. Today, an oven provides the same sort of heat much more easily. Once cooked, the flat 'meatloaf' is cut into squares and served with wedges of lime. It makes for a superb first course and is a Bohri speciality.

Remember that the onion can be fried a day (or more) in advance and kept, unrefrigerated, in a small, tightly closed jar or zip-lock bag. Just strain and reserve the cooking oil. The chickpea flour may also be roasted a day in advance and kept in a jar.

Leftover kebabs are a very popular breakfast food and may be eaten with any flatbreads.

Minced Lamb 'Galavat' Kebabs (Galavat Kabab) INDIA

These tender morsels – *galavat* refers to its melt-in-the-mouth quality – originated in the Muslim courts of Awadh (now Uttar Pradesh) and are served with very thinly sliced onions and fresh mint chutney.

The minced lamb is, traditionally, tenderised with crushed green papaya. I find that this is not necessary with the excellent quality of lamb we get in the West. The same tender result can be achieved with a longer period of marination.

For the delicacy of the kebab, it is important that the meat be fairly fatty.

In this recipe, use my *garam masala* (see page 327). The store-bought variety will not do here as it does not contain enough of the aromatic seasonings.

I sometimes add ½ teaspoon of finely chopped fresh rosemary to these kebabs, along with everything else. They are delicious that way.

Serve with Raw Onion Rings (see page 313) and Fresh Mint Chutney (see page 304).

When forming the kebabs, it is useful to dip one's hands in water since it prevents the meat from sticking to them. Instead of plain water, I often use aromatic *kewra* (screw pine) water. This is sold by all Indian grocers.

MAKES ABOUT 20

- 450 g/1 lb minced, fatty lamb
- 1 tablespoon finely chopped fresh mint leaves
- 1½ tablespoons fresh ginger, peeled and finely grated
- 3 cloves garlic, peeled and crushed to a pulp
- 1½ teaspoons *garam masala* (see note above)
- 1 teaspoon cayenne pepper
- 1 teaspoon salt
- ½ teaspoon fresh rosemary, finely chopped, optional
- corn or peanut oil for shallow frying
- 1 medium onion, sliced into very fine half-rings
- 4 teaspoons chickpea flour
- 4 teaspoons natural yoghurt
- about 2 tablespoons *kewra* (screw pine) water, optional

Put the meat in a bowl. Add the mint, ginger, garlic, *garam masala*, cayenne pepper and salt (and rosemary, if you wish), and mix well. Cover and refrigerate for 3 hours, or up to 24 if desired.

Pour enough oil into a medium pan to come to a depth of 3 mm/⅛ inch and set over a medium-high heat. When the oil is hot, put in the onion and fry, stirring, turning the heat down as needed, until the slices are reddish-brown and crisp. This will take 10–12 minutes. Remove the slices with a slotted spoon, saving all the oil left behind in the pan, and spread out on a double layer of kitchen paper. They will crisp further as they cool. Change the kitchen paper and spread out the onion slices again to get rid of most of the oil. Once the onions look 'dry', put them into a clean coffee grinder or other spice grinder and grind coarsely.

Put the chickpea flour into a small, cast-iron pan and set over a medium-high heat. Stir the flour around until it turns a very light golden-brown and emits a faintly roasted smell. Remove the flour from the hot pan.

Take the bowl of meat out of the refrigerator and add the browned, crushed onions, roasted chickpea flour and yoghurt. Mix well. Wet your hands with *kewra* water (or water) and form about twenty round meatballs, about 3 cm/1¼ inches in diameter. Flatten the balls to make patties that are about 4½ cm/1¾ inches in diameter and about 8 mm/⅖ inch thick. If not eating immediately, lay the patties out in a single layer on two plates, cover with cling film and refrigerate.

Meanwhile, strain the oil left over from frying the onions and reserve.

Just before serving, pour the reserved oil into a non-stick frying pan – it needs to come to a depth of 5 mm/¼ inch, so add extra oil if necessary. Set the pan on a medium-low heat. When the oil is hot, slide in as many kebabs as the pan will hold easily and fry for 2–3 minutes on each side or until reddish-brown. Fry all the kebabs this way. Drain on kitchen paper and serve hot.

Saira Ahmed's

Beef 'Ribbon' Kebab (Pasanda Kabab)

PAKISTAN

When meat is cut into thin strips, it is known as *pasanda* or 'ribbons'. I have made these 'ribbon' kebabs with flank steak (skirt steak or any other steak will do), but you may use chicken breast as Saira does. See page 225 for that recipe.

Serve with Raw Onion Rings (see page 313) and either Fresh Mint Chutney (see page 304) or Coriander Chutney (see page 304). These kebabs may be rolled inside Indian breads and eaten as a snack. (Some Muslim families eat leftovers for breakfast this way.) As a main course, you might also serve them with rice and a salad.

SERVES 4–6 AS A MAIN COURSE, 8–12 AS AN APPETISER

- **120 ml/4 fl oz corn, peanut or olive oil**
- **1 medium onion, peeled and sliced into very fine half-rings, plus 1 medium onion, peeled and coarsely chopped**
- **4 tablespoons natural yoghurt**
- **1 tablespoon lemon juice**
- **3 tablespoons mustard oil or extra virgin olive oil**
- **1 tablespoon blanched, slivered almonds**
- **1 tablespoon fresh ginger, peeled and finely chopped**
- **2 cloves garlic, peeled and chopped**
- **1½–2 teaspoons salt**
- **1 tablespoon cayenne pepper**
- **½ teaspoon ground nutmeg**
- **¼ teaspoon ground mace**
- **2 teaspoons ground coriander**
- **1.15 kg/2½ lb beef flank steak, skirt steak or any other beef steak**

Pour the oil into a medium pan and set over a medium-high heat. When the oil is hot, put in the sliced onions. Stir and fry, turning the heat down as needed, until the slices are medium-brown. Remove with a slotted spoon, saving all the oil left behind in the pan. Put the browned onions into a blender. Add the chopped onion, yoghurt, lemon juice, mustard oil, almonds, ginger, garlic, salt, cayenne pepper, nutmeg, mace and coriander. Blend this marinade mixture to a smooth paste.

Cut the meat, crossways, at a slight diagonal, into 5-mm/¼-inch thick slices. Put in a bowl. Pour the marinade over the top and rub thoroughly into the meat. Cover and refrigerate for 2–6 hours.

Preheat the grill. Using four, flat, sword-like skewers, zigzag the ribbons of meat on as if you were forming Elizabethan ruffles. Push the ruffles tightly against each other so they form a solid band, about 4–5 cm/1½–2 inches wide. Divide the meat between the four skewers this way. Brush all sides with the oil saved after browning the onions. Balance the skewers on the rim of a grill pan and grill 13 cm/5 inches from the source of the heat until all sides are lightly browned. Slide off the skewers and serve.

Beef 'Kaati' Kebab (Kaati Kabab) INDIA

Kaati kebabs are a Calcutta speciality and this is a simplified, Anglo-Indian version. It makes for a quick, easy meal. The kebabs are generally rolled into flatbreads along with thinly sliced raw onions and sliced green chillies, if liked, and eaten just as hamburgers might be. Sometimes the flatbread, say a *paratha*, is spread out on a hot, oiled griddle and an egg broken on it. The egg is spread around to cover the surface and then the *paratha* is flipped over briefly to allow the egg to cook through. This bread-egg combination is then used to wrap the meat. The meat is, of course, put on the egg side.

SERVES 4

450 g/1 lb well marbled, boneless beef steaks, about 2-cm/¾-inch thick, cut into 2½-cm/1-inch pieces
1 tablespoon fresh ginger, peeled and very finely grated
4 cloves garlic, peeled and crushed to a pulp
½–1 teaspoon cayenne pepper
2 teaspoons ground coriander
¼ teaspoon ground turmeric
¾ teaspoon salt
freshly ground black pepper
2 tablespoons corn or peanut oil

Put the steak pieces on a plate. Rub the seasonings, plus 1 tablespoon of the oil, all over the steak pieces, put in a plastic zip-lock bag and refrigerate for 4–6 hours.

Just before serving, set a large, cast-iron pan or griddle on a medium-high heat. Allow it to get very hot. Brush the pan with the remaining oil. Now put in the steak pieces in a single layer, doing two batches if necessary, and let them brown on one side. This will only take a minute or less. Turn and brown the other side. Now toss the pieces around for a minute. Serve immediately.

Vietnamese Beef (or Veal) Kebabs (Cha Bo) VIETNAM

These kebabs (pictured here with Chicken Boti Kebabs, page 221) are served in a very Vietnamese manner. You pick up a small, hamburger-like kebab, wrap it in a soft lettuce leaf, along with some crushed peanuts, fresh herbs, bean sprouts, sliced spring onion, Crisply Fried Shallot Slices (see page 312) and cucumber, then dip the whole bundle in a salty, limey, hot sauce and eat!

These kebabs are normally skewered and grilled over a fire. I pan-grill them instead.

SERVES 4

FOR THE KEBABS

225 g/8 oz minced beef or veal

1½ teaspoons very finely chopped fresh lemon grass or ½ teaspoon ground

½ teaspoon fresh red or green chilli, finely chopped

1 tablespoon fish sauce (*nuoc mam*)

2 tablespoons roasted peanuts, ground to a powder in a clean coffee grinder or other spice grinder

4 teaspoons shallots, peeled and very finely chopped

4 teaspoons thick coconut milk, taken from the top of a can left undisturbed for 3 hours or more

½ teaspoon hot curry powder

½ teaspoon sugar

FOR SERVING ON THE SIDE

3 tablespoons roasted peanuts, lightly crushed

16 small sprigs of mint

16 small sprigs of fresh coriander

a cupful of fresh bean sprouts, their tops and tails removed

2 spring onions, cut, crossways, into very fine slices

about a handful of Crisply Fried Onion or Shallot Slices (see page 312)

16 leaves of any soft lettuce, washed and arranged prettily on a plate

16 thinnish cucumber slices

Seasoned Fish Sauce (see page 305)

Combine all the ingredients for the kebabs and mix well. Divide into sixteen balls and then flatten each ball into a small, hamburger-like patty. (These may be covered and refrigerated for several hours.)

Gather and arrange all the side seasonings on your dining table.

Just before serving, put a cast-iron frying pan or griddle on a medium-high heat. When the oil is hot, brush the bottom of the pan lightly with oil. Place on the pan as many patties as will fit without crowding. Cook until one side is browned. Turn each patty over and brown the other side. You may leave the patty slightly rare, if you wish, or keep turning it until it is done to your liking. Lower the heat, if necessary. Remove. Make all the patties this way. Serve hot, as suggested above.

Minced Beef 'Chappli' Kebabs (Chappli Kabab)

PAKISTAN/AFGHANISTAN

These are the flat, hamburger-like kebabs of the Frontier. That is what we called it, the Frontier. We all knew what we meant. Named so by the British when they ruled us, it was the North West Frontier of India when I was growing up and that was the region's official name as well. (Today, after the partition of India, it is the northwest frontier of Pakistan.)

These kebabs are found all over Pakistan today and there is a fair amount of variation between those found in one city (or indeed, one kebab stand), and another. What all *chappli kebabs* have in common is that they are made with what Pakistanis call 'big' meat, i.e. the minced flesh of either cow or water buffalo. They all contain crushed coriander seeds, onions, cumin seeds and some sort of chillies – fresh green or crushed, dried red. There is always a binding agent, either chickpea flour or cornmeal. And they are always fried in animal fat, usually what is rendered from the tail of a fat-tailed sheep or *dumba*, or failing that, *ghee* (clarified butter).

Beyond this, the sky seems to have become the limit. I have enjoyed *chappli kebabs* with *ajwain* seeds, fresh coriander, dried pomegranate seeds (*anardana*) and even the addition of turmeric.

Traditionally, *chappli kebabs* are eaten with *naans* or other flatbreads but may just as easily be put between two slices of toasted bread or in a hamburger bun or, better still, in a large, crusty roll. A layer of Fresh Tomato-Coriander Chutney (see page 297) or Walnut Mint Chutney (see page 300) and some Raw Onion Rings (see page 313) on top of the kebab would not be at all amiss. Indeed, I have offered all of the above at many of my barbecue parties.

MAKES 6 PATTIES

- 4 teaspoons chickpea flour
- 450 g/1 lb minced beef
- ¾ teaspoon salt, or to taste
- 1 tablespoon whole coriander seeds, coarsely crushed in a mortar or coarsely ground in a clean coffee grinder
- ¾ teaspoon whole cumin seeds
- 4 tablespoons fresh coriander, coarsely chopped
- 6 tablespoons finely chopped, peeled onion
- 12 cherry tomatoes, each cut into quarters
- 2–3 fresh, bird's eye chillies, finely chopped
- corn or peanut oil, *ghee* or suet for shallow frying (roast beef dripping may also be used)

Put the chickpea flour in a small, cast-iron frying pan and set over a medium-high heat. Stir the flour around until it turns a very light golden-brown and emits a faintly roasted smell. Remove the flour from the hot pan. Allow to cool.

Put the beef in a bowl. Add the salt, coriander seeds, cumin, chopped coriander, onion, tomatoes and chillies. Mix well and form six, thin patties (1 cm/½ inch or less thick).

Put the fat, enough to come to a depth of 3 mm/⅛ inch when melted, in a large pan, and set on a medium-high heat. When the fat is hot, put in as many patties as will fit in a single layer and cook for about 2 minutes on each side or until browned. Serve hot.

Silken Chicken 'Tikka' Kebabs (Reshmi Tikka Kebab)

INDIA

These kebabs are very easy to prepare and have a delicate, delicious flavour.

SERVES 4 AS A MAIN COURSE, 8 AS AN APPETISER

- **675 g/1½ lb boned and skinned chicken breasts, cut into 2½-cm/1-inch pieces**
- **1¼ teaspoons salt**
- **3 tablespoons lemon juice**
- **1 tablespoon fresh ginger, peeled and very finely grated**
- **2 cloves garlic, peeled and crushed to a pulp**
- **1 teaspoon ground cumin**
- **1 teaspoon bright red paprika**
- **½–¾ teaspoon cayenne pepper**
- **6 tablespoons whipping cream**
- **½ teaspoon *garam masala* (see page 327)**
- **3 tablespoons corn or peanut oil**

Put the chicken in a bowl. Add the salt and lemon juice and rub them in. Prod the chicken pieces lightly with the tip of a knife and rub the seasonings in again. Set aside for 20 minutes. Then add the ginger, garlic, cumin, paprika, cayenne pepper, cream and *garam masala*. Mix well, cover, and refrigerate for 6–8 hours. (Longer will not hurt.)

Just before serving, preheat the grill. Thread the meat on to two to four skewers (the flat, sword-like ones are best.) Brush with oil and balance the skewers on the rim of a shallow baking tray. Place about 13 cm/5 inches from the source of heat and grill for about 6 minutes on each side or until lightly browned and cooked through.

Moghlai Chicken Kebab (Mughlai Murgh Kabab) INDIA

What gives these kebabs their special flavour is the use of almonds and *berista* (crushed browned onions) in the marinade. You cannot actually taste these seasonings, but their presence adds a haunting richness, typical of Moghlai foods.

Serve with Raw Onion Rings (see page 313), and any chutneys of your choice.

I often serve them with a salad for lunch or dinner.

SERVES 4 AS A MAIN COURSE, 8 AS AN APPETISER

675 g/1½ lb boned and skinned chicken breasts, cut into 2½-cm/1-inch pieces
1 teaspoon salt
2 tablespoons lemon juice
2 tablespoons blanched, slivered almonds
3 tablespoons corn or peanut oil
1 medium onion, about 140 g/5 oz, peeled and sliced into fine half-rings
2 teaspoons fresh ginger, peeled and very finely grated
2 cloves garlic, peeled and crushed to a pulp
½ teaspoon cayenne pepper
120 ml/4 fl oz whipping cream
½ teaspoon *garam masala* (see page 327)

Put the chicken in a bowl. Add the salt and lemon juice and rub them in. Prod the chicken pieces lightly with the tip of a knife and rub the seasonings in again. Set aside for 20 minutes.

Put the almonds into a clean coffee grinder or other spice grinder and grind to a powder. Set aside.

Pour the oil into a medium frying pan and set over a medium-high heat. When the oil is hot, put in the onion. Stir and fry until the onion turns reddish-brown and crisp, turning down the heat as necessary. Remove the onion with a slotted spoon, saving as much of the oil in the pan as possible, and spread out on a layer of kitchen paper. When the onion slices have cooled and are relatively free of oil, put them into the coffee grinder and grind to a paste.

Once the chicken has marinated in the lemon and salt mixture for 20 minutes, add the almonds, onion paste, ginger, garlic, cayenne pepper, cream and *garam masala*. Mix well and cover. Leave in the refrigerator to marinate for 6–8 hours. (Longer will not hurt.)

Just before serving, preheat the grill. Thread the meat on to two to four skewers (the flat, sword-like ones are best.) Brush with the oil saved from browning the onions and balance the skewers on the rim of a shallow baking sheet. Place about 13 cm/5 inches from the source of the heat and grill for about 6 minutes on each side or until lightly browned and cooked through.

From Bar-B-Q Tonight, Karachi

Chicken Boti Kebabs (Murgh Boti) PAKISTAN

Bar-B-Q Tonight is a Karachi landmark that has grown as much in size as it has in popularity. When I was there, the restaurant already served a thousand people daily at its indoor and outdoor tables and was still expanding. It even welcomes guests as late as two in the morning. During Benazir Bhutto's regime, many of her dinner guests ended up coming here to dine.

Afghan refugees fleeing their country in the late 1970s started the restaurant. The food, its owners say, is not their tribal Pakhtoon food but 'modern' Karachi food. Which perhaps explains the interesting use of tomato ketchup in some of the marinating sauces and chutneys that accompany the kebabs. (For a chutney with peanuts and ketchup, see page 298.)

SERVES 4 AS A MAIN COURSE, 8 AS AN APPETISER

675 g/1½ lb boned and skinned chicken breasts, cut into 2½-cm/1-inch pieces
1 teaspoon salt
2 tablespoons lemon juice
1 tablespoon fresh ginger, peeled and very finely grated
2 cloves garlic, peeled and crushed to a pulp
1 teaspoon ground cumin
1 teaspoon bright red paprika
¾ teaspoon cayenne pepper
6 tablespoons tomato ketchup
freshly ground black pepper
¼ teaspoon ground turmeric
3 tablespoons corn or peanut oil

Put the chicken in a bowl. Add the salt and lemon juice and rub them in. Prod the chicken pieces lightly with the tip of a knife and rub the seasonings in again. Set aside for 20 minutes. Then add the ginger, garlic, cumin, paprika, cayenne pepper, ketchup, lots of black pepper and the turmeric. Mix well, cover, and refrigerate for 6–8 hours. (Longer will not hurt.)

Just before serving, preheat the grill. Thread the meat on to two to four skewers (the flat, sword-like ones are best.) Brush with oil and balance the skewers on the rim of a shallow baking tray. Place about 13 cm/5 inches from the source of the heat and grill for about 6 minutes on each side or until lightly browned and cooked through.

Chicken Satay (Satay Ayam)

INDONESIA

Indonesian *satays* probably started out in Java and then spread to all the other islands. Small pieces of meat are marinated, threaded on to small, bamboo skewers and then grilled over charcoal on narrow braziers. They are often served with a peanut-based dipping sauce. The ingredients for the marinade are mostly East Asian, with just the presence of ground coriander to remind us of the *satay's* origins.

I cut my chicken into slightly larger pieces than those on Indonesian market stalls and thread them on to flat, metal skewers. I also generally grill them indoors, though in the summer it is great fun to light up the charcoal and do the grilling outdoors. Just make sure that the charcoals are ashen before you set the skewers on the barbecue.

SERVES 4

- 4 teaspoons Chinese light soy sauce
- 1 tablespoon lime or lemon juice
- 1 clove garlic, peeled and crushed to a pulp
- 2 teaspoons fresh ginger, peeled and finely grated
- 1 tablespoon grated onion
- 1 teaspoon ground coriander
- ½ teaspoon sugar
- ¼ teaspoon cayenne pepper
- 450 g/1 lb boneless and skinless chicken thighs, cut into 2-cm/¾-inch pieces
- a little oil for brushing on the chicken while cooking
- Spicy Peanut Sauce (see page 299)

Combine the soy sauce, lime (or lemon) juice, garlic, ginger, onion, ground coriander, sugar and cayenne pepper in a bowl. Mix well. Add the chicken pieces and mix again. Cover and refrigerate for 3–24 hours.

Preheat the grill. Set a shelf so that, when they cook, the kebabs will be a distance of about 10 cm/4 inches from the source of the heat. Thread the kebabs on to skewers. I like long, flat skewers that can be rested on the edges of a shallow baking tray. The sheet catches the drips and the kebabs themselves remain suspended above it. Brush the kebabs generously with oil and grill for 3–4 minutes on the first side and then another 3–4 minutes on the opposite side. Take the chicken off the skewers. Heat the Spicy Peanut Sauce and beat it lightly. Pour a few tablespoons over each serving and pass the rest on the side.

‘Tangri’ or Chicken Drumstick Kebabs (Tangri Kabab)

INDIA

Chicken drumstick kebabs are very popular throughout India and Pakistan. They can be picked up in the fingers and eaten at picnics and parties. You may also serve them with a salad. These are very easy to make.

MAKES 6

- 6 small or medium-sized chicken drumsticks, about 675 g/1½ lb, skinned
- ¾ teaspoon salt
- 1 tablespoon lemon juice
- 4 tablespoons natural yoghurt
- 1 tablespoon fresh ginger, peeled and finely grated
- 1 clove garlic, peeled and crushed
- 1 teaspoon cayenne pepper
- 1 teaspoon ground cumin
- freshly ground black pepper
- 3–4 tablespoons corn or peanut oil or melted *ghee* or melted butter
- ½ teaspoon bright red paprika

Using a sharp knife, make two deep slits on each of the flatter sides of the drumsticks, making sure that you go all the way down to the bone, then lay them side by side on a plate. Sprinkle both sides with the salt and lemon juice, rubbing them in well. Set aside for 20–30 minutes.

Combine the yoghurt, ginger, garlic, cayenne pepper, cumin and lots of black pepper in a bowl. Add any accumulated juices from the chicken. Rub this marinade over the chicken, making sure to go deep into the slits. Cover and refrigerate for 8–24 hours.

Preheat the oven to its highest temperature. Set a shelf in the top third of the oven.

Brush the chicken legs all over with oil (or *ghee* or butter) and place on a perforated grill pan that allows the juices to fall through. Sprinkle the top with half the paprika. Bake for 12 minutes. Again brush with oil (or *ghee* or butter) and turn over. Sprinkle the remaining paprika over the top. Bake for a further 12 minutes or until cooked through.

Chicken 'Kut-a-Kut' Kebab

PAKISTAN

'Kut-a-kut', also known as 'tuck-a-tuck', is the sound of two sharp-edged spatulas cutting and cooking simultaneously on a large, somewhat concave, hot griddle.

Rather like the *teppan-yaki* of Japan that was once very much in vogue, when diners sat at 'counters' that were actually griddles and food was expertly cooked and chopped right in front of their eyes, the foods produced this way in Pakistan owe as much to showmanship as they do to flavour.

Here is what happens. 'Kut-a-kut' is a street food. You drive your car up to your favourite 'kut-a-kut' guy who has a street stall and place your order. Innards are favoured here, testicles, kidneys, heart, liver . . . you get the picture. These are thrown on the griddle with some garlic water and covered briefly with a domed lid. This is the blanching process. The dome is lifted and the water pushed off with a spatula on to the ground. The meat is cut very fast, using the two spatulas. Chopped onion, ginger, green chillies, tomatoes, salt and chilli powder are thrown on to the meat and moved about with great flourish. More garlic water gets poured on and the dome goes back. Big pats of butter are placed around the outside of the dome. As they melt, they slide in. The dome is lifted again and there is much cutting and stirring. Yoghurt, cumin and shredded ginger are added. More kut, kut, kut. Fresh coriander is sprinkled over the top and the result scraped up on to a plate. I ordered kidneys and they were delicious. I have made my recipe with chicken as I just know that most of you will not touch kidneys or any of those other things.

SERVES 3–4

- 1 clove garlic, peeled and crushed to a pulp
- 4 tablespoons onion, finely chopped
- 1 teaspoon fresh ginger, peeled and finely grated
- ½–1 teaspoon fresh, hot green chillies, finely chopped
- 90 g/3 oz tomatoes, peeled and chopped
- ¾ teaspoon salt
- ¼ teaspoon cayenne pepper
- 1 tablespoon natural yoghurt
- 1 tablespoon ground cumin
- ½ teaspoon ground coriander
- freshly ground black pepper
- 1 tablespoon corn or peanut oil
- 450 g/1 lb boneless and skinless chicken thighs, cut into 2-cm/¾-inch pieces
- 45 g/1½ oz unsalted butter

FOR THE GARNISHING

- fresh lemon or lime juice, to taste
- 3 thin slices of fresh ginger, peeled and cut crossways into fine shreds
- 3 tablespoons fresh coriander, finely chopped

Put the garlic in a small bowl. Add 120 ml/4 fl oz water and set aside near your cooking area. Combine the onion, ginger and green chillies in a small bowl or on a plate and put next to the garlic. In yet another bowl, combine the tomatoes, salt, cayenne and another 120 ml/4 fl oz water. Have the yoghurt measured and ready. Combine the cumin, ground coriander and lots of black pepper.

Pour the oil into a heavy, non-stick, lidded pan and set on a medium-high heat. Put in the chicken pieces and stir them around until they turn opaque on the outside. Pour in the garlic water and cover. Cook for about 5 minutes. Now and then, remove the lid, stir quickly, and cover again. When there is only about 1 tablespoon or so of water left, uncover and add the onion, ginger and green chilli combination. Stir for about 2 minutes. Add the tomato combination. Cover and cook for a further 5 minutes. Again, remove the lid now and then to stir and keep an eye on the meat. Add the butter. Cover and cook for 2 minutes. Remove the lid (you won't need it again) and stir vigorously. Add the yoghurt and toss the meat. When the yoghurt disappears, add the cumin, coriander and pepper mixture. Keep stirring and tossing the chicken for another minute or so. It should appear browned on the outside. Turn off the heat. If serving immediately, add lemon juice to taste, the ginger and chopped coriander. Toss to mix and serve. (You may also hold the chicken for an hour or so and reheat it, adding the garnishes just before serving.)

Saira Ahmed's

Chicken 'Ribbon' Kebabs (Murgh Pasanda Kabab)

SERVES 4–6 AS A MAIN COURSE, 8–12 AS AN APPETISER

Follow the recipe for Beef 'Ribbon' Kebabs (see page 214), almost exactly, substituting the same weight of skinned and boned chicken breasts for the beef, but prepare the chicken as follows.

Lay the breasts in a single layer in a large zip-lock or other plastic bag. Close the bag, removing most of the air. Now lay the bag flat in your freezer. Let it stay there for 1–1¼ hours. The chicken will become partially frozen but you will still be able to slice it easily. Holding your knife at a 45-degree angle, cut each breast piece, crossways, into 5-mm/¼-inch thick slices.

Now proceed with the recipe.

Turkey Kebabs

USA

In this kebab minced dark turkey meat gets transformed into something gorgeously Indian. The 10-cm/4-inch patty in this recipe will shrink a bit and then fit into a hamburger-sized bun for a casual dinner. Add a thin slice of onion and some Fresh Mint Chutney (see page 304) for extra flavour. Smaller, thinner patties can be placed on rounds of bread that have been crisped in the oven. Top the canapés with a mint leaf and a couple of thin slices of red and green chillies.

SERVES 4–8

6 tablespoons rich, thick natural yoghurt
1 tablespoon chickpea flour
4 tablespoons corn, peanut or olive oil
2 spring onions, the white and half the green parts, cut crossways into fine rounds,
450 g/1 lb minced dark turkey meat
3 tablespoons finely chopped fresh coriander leaves
1 tablespoon fresh ginger, peeled and finely grated
4 cloves garlic, peeled and crushed to a pulp
2–3 fresh hot green bird's eye chillies, finely chopped
1 teaspoon whole cumin seeds
¼ teaspoon cayenne pepper
¾ teaspoon salt
freshly ground black pepper

Spoon the yoghurt into a sieve lined with a piece of muslin, set over a bowl and leave for 2 hours to drip.

Put the chickpea flour into a small, cast-iron pan and set over a medium-high heat. Stir the flour around until it turns a very light golden-brown and emits a faintly roasted smell. Remove the flour from the hot pan. Clean the pan.

Pour 1 tablespoon oil into the same pan and set over a medium heat. When the oil is hot, put in the spring onions. Stir and fry them for about 3 minutes or until they turn reddish-brown. Remove the browned onions, together with the oil, to a bowl. Allow to cool. Add the drained yoghurt, the roasted chickpea flour, the turkey, chopped coriander, ginger, garlic, chillies, cumin seeds, cayenne pepper, salt and black pepper. Mix well, cover, and refrigerate for 4–24 hours.

Just before serving, divide the meat into four, and shape into patties about 10 cm/4 inches in diameter.

Pour the remaining oil into a large, non-stick pan and set on a medium-high heat. When the oil is very hot, put in all the patties. Let them cook about for 30 seconds or until browned on one side. Turn them over and reduce the heat to medium-low. Let the second side brown for 30 seconds. Now keep flipping the patties every 30 seconds for about 8 minutes or until they are well browned and no longer feel soft and spongy in the centre. Serve immediately.

Curried Pork Satay (Satay)

THAILAND

Generally, these pork pieces are threaded on to small, well-soaked bamboo skewers and grilled on narrow charcoal braziers. I like to pan-fry them as it is much easier.

SERVES 4

FOR THE MARINADE

4 tablespoons dark Chinese soy sauce
2 tablespoons coconut milk, from a well-shaken can
8–10 roots from fresh coriander stems, well washed and chopped
2 cloves garlic, peeled and chopped
2 teaspoons sugar
½ teaspoon curry powder
1 teaspoon ground white pepper
450 g/1 lb boneless pork loin, cut into ½ x 4–5 x 2½ cm/¼ x 1½–2 x 1 inch pieces

FOR THE DIPPING SAUCE

45 g/1½ oz shallots, peeled and chopped
3 cloves garlic
¼ teaspoon ground cumin
1 teaspoon ground coriander
1 teaspoon cayenne pepper
1 tablespoon bright red paprika
1½ tablespoons corn or peanut oil
175 ml/6 fl oz coconut milk, from a well-shaken can
4 tablespoons roasted peanuts, well chopped
2 teaspoons palm sugar or brown sugar
½ teaspoon salt

FOR BASTING AND FINAL COOKING

250 ml/8 fl oz coconut milk, from a well-shaken can
2 teaspoons curry powder
a pinch of salt
corn or peanut oil

Combine the soy sauce, coconut milk, coriander roots and garlic in a blender and blend until smooth. Empty into a large bowl. Add the sugar, curry powder and white pepper. Mix well. Add the pork and mix with the marinade. Cover and refrigerate for 2–24 hours.

Make the dipping sauce. Put the shallots and garlic into a blender along with 2 tablespoons water. Blend until smooth, then empty into a bowl. Add the cumin, ground coriander, cayenne and paprika. Make a paste, adding a tiny bit more water if needed.

Pour the oil into a small, preferably non-stick, pan and set it over a medium heat. Put in the paste from the blender. Stir and fry it for 3–4 minutes or until it browns lightly. Add the coconut milk, peanuts, sugar and salt. Stir and cook until it is thick, 2–3 minutes.

Combine the coconut milk for basting with the curry powder and salt.

Rub a cast-iron or heavy, non-stick frying pan with a little oil and set on a medium-high heat. When the oil is hot, dip some of the pork pieces in the basting sauce and place them on the pan in a single layer. Do not overcrowd them. Cook for a minute or until browned. Turn the pieces over and cook the second side the same way. Remove to a warm plate. Cook all the meat this way and serve with the dipping sauce.

Grilled Venison 'Hunter's' Kebabs (Shikari Hiran Kay Soolay Kabab)

INDIA

There are many paintings, small and large, of Rajput royalty fighting and hunting in the central Indian Rajasthan Desert. In one of the royal palaces that dot this grand landscape, there is a large oil painting of a maharajah on a horse. The horse has its front legs raised dramatically in the air. The turbaned maharajah, equally dramatically, is thrusting his long spear into what looks like a campfire. The spear, we notice, is doubling as a skewer and is holding a piece of *shikar* (hunt) meat. These warriors, we are told, grilled and ate their hunt meat, frequently on the run.

It is to be assumed that when the warriors were really in a hurry, they used a minimum of spices on their meats. But around the turn of the last century, when the British were firmly in control of India, Indian Maharajahs, with ever-increasing leisure time, went on grand hunts with armies of cooks amongst their other 'help'. There are hundreds of black and white photographs of such events. Often the British came along as guests. We see them lolling about in *solar topees* (sun hats). There was time enough then to cook more elaborate hunt dishes.

The Hindu Rajputs of Rajasthan have always been meat-eaters but, starting around the 16th century, many of the royalty gave their princesses in marriage to Moghul emperors and princes who were Muslim. While the vegetarian dishes in Rajasthan remained traditionally Hindu, many of the meats began to take on a more Moghul culinary cast. These kebabs are a typical example.

SERVES 4

FOR THE FIRST MARINADE

450 g/1 lb boneless venison, cut into 2½-cm/1-inch cubes

1 tablespoon fresh ginger, peeled and finely grated

7 cloves garlic, peeled and crushed to a pulp

1 tablespoon ground coriander

¾ teaspoon cayenne pepper, or to taste

1 teaspoon salt

1 tablespoon lemon juice

FOR THE SECOND MARINADE

3 tablespoons corn or peanut oil

90 g/3 oz onions, cut into very thin half-rings

3 tablespoons natural yoghurt

½ teaspoon *garam masala* (see page 327)

melted butter, *ghee* or oil for basting

Combine the meat with all the ingredients for the first marinade, massaging the spices into the flesh, then cover (I just put the meat in a zip-lock bag) and refrigerate for 4–24 hours.

Pour the oil into a heavy, non-stick pan and set over a medium heat. Put in the onions and and fry them, stirring at the same time, and turning the heat down as needed, until they are reddish-gold and crisp. Remove the onions with a slotted spoon, leaving behind as much oil as possible, and spread out on a layer of kitchen paper to cool and crisp further. When cool, chop finely. (The oil left behind may be added to the basting fat.)

Put the chopped onion in a bowl, add the yoghurt and *garam masala* and mix well. Add the marinated meat and mix it well with its second marinade. Leave for an hour or longer.

Just before serving, slide the meat pieces on to two or more skewers, leaving a little space between the meat cubes. Preheat the grill and set a rimmed baking sheet about 13 cm/5 inches from the source of the heat. Brush the meat with melted butter (or *ghee* or oil) and rest the skewers on the rim of the sheet. Grill for about 4 minutes on each side or until browned and cooked to your liking.

Prawns with Sesame Seeds (Til Mil Jheenga) — INDIA

Most prawn 'kebabs' are either grilled or cooked in a *tandoor* oven. I like to stir-fry mine and stick cocktail sticks into them if I wish to serve them with drinks. If all the ingredients are prepared beforehand, this dish takes less than 5 minutes to prepare. Indeed, it tastes best if cooked just before serving.

SERVES 4 AS AN APPETISER, 3 AS A MAIN COURSE

- 3 tablespoons corn or peanut oil
- ½ teaspoon whole brown mustard seeds
- 2 teaspoons sesame seeds
- 10–15 fresh curry leaves, if available
- 450 g/1 lb raw, headless, shell-on prawns, peeled and deveined (if buying prawns with heads, you will need an additional 225 g/8 oz)
- 1 teaspoon fresh ginger, peeled and finely grated
- 2 cloves garlic, peeled and crushed to a pulp
- ¼ teaspoon cayenne pepper
- 2 teaspoons thick tamarind paste (see page 345) or lemon juice
- ½ teaspoon salt
- ½ teaspoon sugar

Pour the oil into a large, non-stick pan and set over a medium-high heat. When the oil is hot, put in the mustard and sesame seeds. As soon as they start to pop, a matter of seconds, put in the curry leaves, prawns, ginger, garlic and cayenne pepper. Stir once or twice, then reduce the heat to medium. Add the tamarind, salt and sugar. Continue to stir and fry for a further 2–3 minutes or until the prawns are just cooked through. Serve immediately.

Swordfish Kebabs with Ajowan Seeds

PAKISTAN

Sitting in a rooftop restaurant in Peshawar in the dead of winter, surrounded by dozens of braziers and with quilts draped over my legs, I was offered the most scrumptious river fish smelling faintly of oranges.

Most Indian river fish are unavailable in the West, but I have adapted the recipe to make the most delicious swordfish kebabs.

It is important to keep the marination period short as fish can disintegrate.

SERVES 6–8

- 1.35 kg/3 lb swordfish steaks
- 2 tablespoons lemon juice
- 2 tablespoons orange juice
- salt
- 4 cloves garlic, peeled and crushed to a pulp
- 1 tablespoon fresh ginger, peeled and finely grated
- 1 teaspoon cayenne pepper
- ½ teaspoon freshly ground black pepper
- 1 teaspoon ground cumin
- ½ teaspoon *garam masala* (see page 327)
- ½ teaspoon ground turmeric
- ½ teaspoon *ajowan* seeds or 1 teaspoon dried thyme
- 4 tablespoons corn or peanut oil, for dribbling
- *chaat masala* (see page 325), or store-bought, enough for a light dusting
- lemon wedges

Remove the skin along the side of the steaks and then cut them into kebab-like pieces of about 5-cm/2-inches. Place them in a single layer on a large platter. Bathe them with a combination of the two citrus juices, then sprinkle both sides with 1½ teaspoons salt. Set aside for 15–20 minutes, tossing them gently now and then.

Drain off the liquid that will have collected in the platter and spread the garlic, ginger, cayenne pepper, black pepper, cumin, *garam masala*, turmeric and *ajowan* seeds on both sides of the fish.

Preheat the oven to 180°C/gas mark 4.

Line a baking tray with foil.

Set a large, non-stick pan on a medium-high heat and rub the bottom with 1 tablespoon oil. Dust the fish pieces very lightly with salt and then place, salt side down, in the pan in a single layer. Do not crowd them. Dust the top lightly with salt and dribble a little oil over the top. When the bottom is lightly browned, turn the pieces over and brown the second side. As the pieces get done, put them, in a single layer, on the baking sheet. Brown all the fish pieces this way, then put in the oven for 10 minutes to cook through. Sprinkle with *chaat masala* and serve with lemon wedges.

Mrs Kusum Lal's

Spicy Tomato Spinach Soup

INDIA

Tomato soups were introduced into India by the British, who were probably pleasantly surprised by the long, almost never-ending, tomato-growing season. When I was young, most Indians were under the impression that all British meals had to begin with a soup and that tomato soups were the cream of the crop. Even in our family, where at least one evening meal a week was 'English', it started with a soup, made with either tomato or *dal* and served with fried croutons. Tomato soups remain equally popular today and may be had, good, bad and indifferent, in the smallest of hotels. In homes, they are often Indianised now with a variety of spices.

Here is my adaptation of a delicious soup served to me for lunch at the home of an archaeologist and Sanskrit scholar in Delhi. I have taken the liberty of making it a bit spicier, but if you want it mild, just leave out the curry powder. I like to tie the whole spices in a small piece of muslin, but if you do not feel up to that, just drop them into the pan and then fish them out before you blend the soup.

I use fresh seasonal tomatoes for this soup. If the tomatoes are very sour, you can always add a tiny bit of sugar.

SERVES *4*

½ teaspoon black peppercorns
2 whole, black cardamom pods
2 bay leaves
1 medium stick cinnamon
900 g/2 lb tomatoes, chopped
140 g/5 oz onions, peeled and chopped
1¾ teaspoons salt
600 ml/1 pint chicken stock or water
15 g/½ oz unsalted butter
4 oz/115 g trimmed and chopped spinach
2 teaspoons curry powder
4 tablespoons whipping cream

Tie the peppercorns, black cardamom pods, bay leaves and cinnamon in a small piece of muslin and put it in a medium, lidded pan. Add the tomatoes, onions, salt and chicken stock or water. Bring to the boil, cover, reduce the heat to low, and simmer very gently for 30 minutes. Remove the muslin bag, squeezing out all the liquid. Blend the tomato mixture until smooth.

Put the butter in a wide pan and set over a medium-high heat. When it has melted, put in the curry powder. Stir it around for 10 seconds, then add the spinach and stir until it is completely wilted. Now add the blended tomatoes and bring to a simmer. Simmer gently for 5 minutes, then add the cream. Return to a simmer, stirring, and taste for a balance of flavours.

Manjula Gokal's

Gujarati Mango Soup (Fajeto)

INDIA/SOUTH AFRICA

Amongst Gujarati families in India and South Africa, this wondrous, sweet, sour and hot, soupy dish is served in small bowls (*katoris*) as part of the meal, with Fried Puffy Breads (*pooris*) as an accompaniment. What I do at my dinners is something different. I strain it, removing most of the seeds and leaves, and then serve it all by itself as a soup in very small quantities.

Both India and South Africa produce excellent mangoes so this is a really a seasonal dish made when good mangoes are abundant. In the West, mangoes of that calibre are hard to find and I make use of the canned purée of India's very best Alphonso mangoes, sold by all Indian grocers. It takes me about 10 minutes to make the soup, from start to finish!

If you are lucky enough to find fresh, sweet, juicy, fully-ripe mangoes, wash them, then, one at a time, squeeze them with both hands, almost as if you were giving them a good massage. The flesh should turn to pulp. Now peel them. 'Milk' the stone, collecting all the juice in a bowl. Pour a little hot water on the stone and 'milk' it some more. Do the same to the skin, pouring a tablespoon or so of hot water on it to get at all the juice. You should have about 1.25–1.5 litres/2¼–2½ pints. Use this thin juice whenever water is called for, letting it cool first. You may need to add a bit more sugar.

SERVES 6–12

- 2 tablespoons chickpea flour
- ⅛ teaspoon ground turmeric
- ¾ teaspoon ground cumin
- ¾ teaspoon ground coriander
- 120 ml/4 fl oz natural yoghurt
- 700 ml/30 fl oz thick Alphonso mango pulp (sweetened) from a can
- 1¼–1½ teaspoons salt
- ½ teaspoon sugar, or to taste
- 2 bird's eye chillies, with small slits cut in them
- 2 tablespoons corn or peanut oil, or a mixture of 1 tablespoon oil and 1 tablespoon *ghee*
- a generous pinch of ground *asafetida*
- ½ teaspoon whole brown mustard seeds
- ½ teaspoon whole cumin seeds
- 2 whole, dried, hot red chillies
- ⅛ teaspoon whole fenugreek seeds
- 10–15 fresh curry leaves, if available

Put the chickpea flour, turmeric, cumin and coriander in a medium bowl. Very slowly add 120 ml/4 fl oz water, mixing with a wooden spoon as you go. There should be no lumps left. Add the yoghurt, mixing it in with a whisk. Pour in the mango pulp and an additional 475 ml/16 fl oz water. Add the salt, sugar and fresh chillies. Mix well.

Pour the oil (or oil and *ghee*) into a thick, medium, lidded pan and set over a medium-high heat. When the oil is very hot, put in first the *asafetida* and then, in quick succession, the mustard and cumin seeds, the chillies, the fenugreek seeds and, lastly, the curry leaves. Take the pan off the heat. Stir the mango mixture well and quickly pour it into the pan. Stir. Put the pan on a medium heat and bring to a simmer. Simmer on very a low heat for 5 minutes, stirring with a whisk or spoon as you do so. Take the pan off the heat, cover, and leave for at least 30 minutes to allow the spices to release their flavours.

Before serving, stir the soup and reheat it gently. Strain it through a coarse strainer. Spoon out some of the smaller seeds – the mustard and cumin – from the strainer and stir them back into the soup to add some colourful flecks.

Sarnsern Gajaseni's

Thai Beef Curry Soup (Ghway Tiaw Gaeng) THAILAND

This dish is served by the Muslim community in Thailand. Beef brisket is stewed slowly with curry powder, red curry paste, sugar, fish sauce (*nam pla*) and coconut milk to make a thin soup. The brisket is removed and sliced. When the soup is to be served, some cooked, flat rice noodles, called *senlak*, which are rather like linguine, are put into bowls. The thin slices of brisket are then arranged over the noodles and hot soup is poured over the top. There are further garnishings of diced pieces of pressed bean curd, fresh bean sprouts, crisply fried shallots, chopped coriander, sliced spring onions and crushed peanuts. The soup goes to the table this way.

On the table is more fish sauce, sugar, white pepper, Green Chillies in Vinegar (see page 308) and red chilli powder. You add anything you want.

This thin curry is really a meal in itself. I have simplified it somewhat into a soup. I do without the brisket entirely and just use a beef stock that I can buy commercially. I use a small amount of beef skirt to cook in the soup quickly towards the end. You may even leave that rare, or uncooked if you wish. (The boiling soup will cook it.) For the noodles, I use the dried rice noodles, *banh pho*, sold by Asian grocers. (See Rice Noodles, page 271.)

It was not until I was testing this soup that I realised how similar in philosophy it was to the Malaysian Prawn Curry Soup with Noodles (following recipe.) Of course, they come from neighbouring areas. This one has a decided Thai flavour.

SERVES 4

225 g/8 oz dried, flat rice noodles (preferably *banh pho*) or *lo-mein* noodles, cooked according to the directions given on page 271
4 tablespoons corn, peanut or olive oil
5 tablespoons red curry paste (see page 318)
2 teaspoons hot curry powder
1 litre/32 fl oz beef stock
1 teaspoon thick tamarind paste (see page 345) or lemon juice
1 teaspoon palm sugar or brown sugar
400-ml/14-fl oz can of coconut milk, well shaken
fish sauce (*nam pla*) or salt to taste
225 g/8 oz beef skirt or well-marbled steak

FOR THE TOPPING
4 tablespoons pressed bean curd (the yellow-ish type), cut into 5-mm/¼-inch dice
60 g/2 oz very fresh bean sprouts, with their tops and tails pinched off
1 spring onion, cut crossways into very thin slices
4 tablespoons Crisply Fried Shallot Slices (see page 312)
coriander leaves
4 tablespoons crushed, roasted peanuts

FOR SERVING AT THE TABLE
Green Chillies in Vinegar (see page 308)
crushed, dried red chillies or coarse chilli powder
fish sauce (*nam pla)*
sugar
white pepper

If you are using dried rice noodles, soak them in water for 2 hours.

Pour the oil into a wide, non-stick, lidded pan and set on a medium-high heat. When the oil is hot, put in the curry paste and curry powder. Stir and fry until the oil separates and the paste is lightly browned. Add the stock, stir, and bring to a simmer. Cover, reduce the heat to low, and simmer very gently for 15 minutes. Add the tamarind paste, sugar and coconut milk. Stir it in thoroughly. Taste and add as much fish sauce or salt as you need. The basic soup is now ready. You may strain it if you desire smoothness.

Just before serving, bring the soup to a very gentle simmer again and drop in the piece of meat. Simmer for about 5 minutes or less. The meat should turn greyish all over on the outside. It can remain rare inside. Remove the meat. Take the soup off the heat.

Meanwhile, bring a large pot of water to a rolling boil. Drain the rice noodles and throw them in. (For instructions on cooking *lo-mein* noodles, see page 274.) The rice noodles will cook in about a minute or less. Drain them and divide between the soup bowls. (You may not need to use all of them.) Cut the meat, crossways, into thin slices and laythem in a pretty pattern on top of the noodles. Reheat the soup, if needed, and ladle it over the meat. Top the soup with some of the bean curd, bean sprouts, spring onion, Crisply Fried Shallots, fresh coriander and peanuts. Serve with the seasonings at the table, which should be used as desired.

Malaysian Prawn Curry Soup with Noodles (Curry Mee)

MALAYSIA

This curried, coconut-enriched soup is often served as a snack in Malaysia, but a large bowl of it would certainly be a whole meal.

Fresh lemon grass stalks have a knot at the very bottom. Remove that before slicing, finely, crossways and at a slight angle, starting at the bottom end and going up about 15 cm/6 inches. Lemon grass will not blend thoroughly unless it has been sliced first. Galangal is fairly tough as well, and needs first to be to cut crossways into thin slices, and then chopped before being put into the blender.

SERVES 4

225 g/8 oz dried, flat rice noodles (preferably *banh pho*), or lo-*mein* egg noodles, cooked as described on page 274
6 hot, dried red chillies (of the long, cayenne variety)
5 cloves garlic, peeled and chopped
5 oz/140 g shallots, chopped
1 tablespoon fresh lemon grass, thinly sliced
6 thin slices peeled, fresh or frozen galangal, or ginger, finely chopped
½ teaspoon shrimp paste, or 2 anchovies from a can, chopped
½ teaspoon ground cumin
½ teaspoon ground coriander
½ teaspoon ground turmeric
1 tablespoon bright red paprika
4 tablespoons corn, peanut or olive oil
900 ml/32 fl oz chicken stock
400-g/14- fl oz can of coconut milk, well-shaken
salt
freshly ground black pepper
225 g/8 oz raw, headless, shell-on prawns, peeled and deveined (if buying prawns with heads, you will need an additional 115 g/4 oz)

FOR THE TOPPING

60 g/2 oz very fresh bean sprouts, with their tops and tails pinched off
4 tablespoons finely diced tender celery
1 spring onion, cut crossways into very thin slices
4 tablespoons Crisply Fried Shallot Slices (see page 312)
2 fresh, hot bird's eye or other green or red chillies, thinly sliced, crossways
lemon or lime wedges

If you are using dried rice noodles, soak them in water for 2 hours.

Soak the red chillies in 5 tablespoons hot water for 1–2 hours. (You could also put them in a microwave oven for 2–3 minutes and then let them sit for 20–30 minutes.) Put them and their soaking liquid into a blender, together with the garlic, shallots, lemon grass, galangal, shrimp paste, cumin, coriander, turmeric and paprika. Blend, pushing down with a rubber spatula until you have a smooth paste.

Pour the oil into a wide, non-stick, lidded pan and set on a medium-high heat. When the oil is hot, put in the curry paste from the blender. Stir and fry until the oil separates and the paste is lightly browned. Add the stock, stir, and bring to a simmer. Cover, reduce the heat to low, and simmer very gently for 15 minutes. Add the coconut milk and stir it in thoroughly. Taste and add as much salt and pepper as you need. The basic soup is now ready. You may strain it if you desire smoothness.

Just before serving, bring the soup to a gentle simmer again and drop in the prawns. They will turn opaque in minutes. Remove the soup from the heat but keep it warm.

Bring a large pot of water to a rolling boil. Drain the rice noodles and throw them in. (For instructions on cooking *lo-mein* noodles, see page 274.) The rice noodles will cook in about a minute or less. Drain them and divide between the soup bowls. (You may not need to use all of them.) Ladle the hot soup over the noodles, dividing the prawns evenly. Top the noodles with the bean sprouts, celery, spring onion and fried shallots. Pass the sliced chillies and the lemon or lime wedges on the side.

PASTA

While the 'who had pasta first' wars have raged between enthusiasts of Italian and Chinese cuisine, India has quietly been eating all manner of noodles ever since we have had wheat (about 4000 BC), rice (some say as far back as 8000 BC) and chickpeas (about 2500 BC.) Yes, pastas are made from all of them and are eaten by almost every Indian in some form or other.

Look at a map of what was once Greater India at the start of the Christian era when Buddhism was in full swing. Start with what is now Afghanistan. They have the *montu*, a kind of ravioli stuffed with minced meat and served with a topping of garlic-flavoured yoghurt, baked beans and parsley. There is *aash* or *aashak*, a kind of lasagne in which a flat pasta is layered between spicy minced meat and a yoghurt-goat cheese mixture seasoned with garlic, cumin and red chillies. The whole dish is then served with a topping of finely chopped spring onions, green and red chillies, chives, fresh coriander, mint and crisply fried onions.

Further south in Pakistan, near the ancient city of Taxila, a fine-grained pasta rather like couscous is eaten in all the surrounding villages. And throughout Pakistan and India, *seviyan*, a very fine vermicelli, is toasted and made into desserts or pilafs.

In south India, one of my favourite dishes is *idi-appam* or *sevai*, a freshly steamed, rice flour noodle that may be eaten with curries, stir-fried with chillies, mustard seeds and curry leaves, or else devoured at breakfast with cardamom-flavoured coconut milk.

Along India's west coast, Gujaratis not only make hundreds of crisp, chickpea flour noodles, which are eaten as snacks, but also many types of wholemeal noodles. One, in the form of small nests, can be seen drying on cots in village courtyards. Another, and it would be considered an everyday food, is this next dish, *dal dhokli*.

It consists of two parts, a soupy base and the noodles themselves. The base is made with one of India's native split peas, *toovar dal*. I am convinced that once, rather like the south Indian *sambar*, the second major ingredient for the base was tamarind, but that seems to have metamorphosed into tomatoes over time. The pasta is made by rolling out balls of wholemeal flour dough into thin, flat rounds and then cutting them first into wide ribbons and then into diamonds or rectangles. These are then just dropped into the simmering base until cooked.

Gujarati Split Pea Soup with Pasta (Dal Dhokli) INDIA

Dal dhokli is normally ladled into a *katori* (bowl) that is set on the traditional Gujarati *thali* (large serving plate), one dish amongst many, to be eaten with pickles, relishes and other foods.

What I have done here is transform it into a soup that stands by itself. Instead of making fresh noodles, I have chosen to use an Italian dry pasta, *farfalle* (bow ties), as they are just as good, about the same size, and spare me a lot of labour. I cook them according to the packet instructions, about 12 minutes. You may use other dry pastas such as *orecchiette* (ears) or even *macaroni*. I use only a small amount of pasta as this is a soup, but slightly more may be added for a more substantial meal. However, the soup base should not be overwhelmed by the more solid pasta.

SERVES 4

140 g/5 oz *toovar dal* (see page 335), washed and drained
½ teaspoon ground turmeric
salt
3 tablespoons corn, peanut or olive oil
a generous pinch of ground *asafetida*
¾ teaspoon whole cumin seeds
¾ teaspoon whole brown mustard seeds
3 cloves garlic, peeled and coarsely chopped
about 20 fresh curry leaves, if available
675 g/1½ lb chopped fresh tomatoes
¾ teaspoon cayenne pepper
600 ml/1 pint chicken stock or water
60 g/2 oz *farfalle* or other pasta (see above)

Combine the *toovar dal*, turmeric and 1 litre/32 fl oz water in a large, lidded pan and bring to the boil. Reduce the heat to low quickly to avoid a spill, partially cover with the lid and cook for 1 hour or until the split peas are tender. Add ½ teaspoon salt and push through a coarse strainer. Set aside.

While the split peas are cooking, pour the oil into another lidded pan and set over a medium-high heat. When the oil is hot, put in the *asafetida*, followed, a second later, by the cumin and mustard seeds. As soon as the mustard seeds begin to pop, a matter of seconds, put in the garlic. Stir for a few seconds, then add the curry leaves, tomatoes, cayenne pepper, chicken stock and ¾ teaspoon salt. Stir and bring to the boil. Cover, reduce the heat to low, and simmer very gently for 25 minutes. Push the tomatoes through a course strainer and combine with the cooked and strained *toovar dal*. This is your soup base. Taste it for a balance of flavours. Reheat the soup when needed.

Just before serving, cook the *farfalle* according to the packet instructions, drain it and divide it amongst the soup bowls. Ladle hot soup over the top and serve.

Lamb or Chicken Mulligatawny Soup

INDIA

Even though there are some recipes for vegetarian Mulligatawny in old cookbooks, most often they are made with mutton or poultry.

SERVES 4–6

4 tablespoons blanched, slivered almonds
5 tablespoons chickpea flour
1½ litres/48 fl oz chicken stock
1 teaspoon ground cumin
1 teaspoon ground coriander
¼ teaspoon ground turmeric
¼ teaspoon cayenne pepper
1 teaspoon hot curry powder
2 tablespoons corn or peanut oil
340 g/12 oz boneless lamb or boned and skinned chicken thighs, cut into 2-cm/¾-inch cubes
2 teaspoons fresh ginger, peeled and grated to a pulp
4 cloves garlic, peeled and crushed to a pulp
salt
1 tablespoon lemon juice
lemon wedges, served on the side
Plain Basmati Rice (see page 257), served on the side

Soak the almonds for 4 hours in hot water or overnight in tap water. Drain. Put into a blender together with the chickpea flour and 250 ml/8 fl oz chicken stock and blend until smooth. Leave in the blender.

Combine the cumin, coriander, turmeric, cayenne pepper and curry powder in a small bowl.

Pour the oil into a wide pan and set over a high heat. When the oil is hot, put in the meat and cook, stirring, until the pieces are lightly browned. Remove with a slotted spoon and set aside. Reduce the heat to medium. Quickly put in the ginger and garlic. Stir for 30 seconds, then add all the dry spices from the bowl. Stir for another 30 seconds. Add the remaining chicken stock and stir it in. Strain in the paste from the blender and add the reserved meat. If your stock is unsalted, add ½ teaspoon salt. Stir and bring to the boil. Cover, reduce the heat to low, and cook gently for 1 hour for lamb and 35 minutes for chicken thighs. Taste for salt. Stir in the lemon juice.

Serve with the rice and lemon wedges. (If you are serving this as a first course soup, scatter about 1–3 tablespoons of cooked rice in each serving just before you eat. If this is a main course, offer individual bowls of rice on the side. Diners can scoop in as much as they like with each mouthful.)

MULLIGATAWNY

A classic of the mixed race, Anglo-Indian community in India (for more on Anglo-Indians, see page 114), this soup is an essential part of my childhood. I had it in the homes of Anglo-Indian friends and it was served, sometimes well-made and sometimes not, in almost every Indian hotel we travelled to for our holidays. When I wrote my very first cookbook, I included in it my favourite Mulligatawny recipe. That recipe had been modified over the years and simplified. One of the ingredients it called for was white poppy seeds. I find it almost impossible to grind them to a smooth paste without a grinding stone. So I gave up on them long ago. I use blanched almonds instead. Also, after much experimentation, I have now come to the conclusion that some curry powder has to be included for a true East-West flavour.

A true Mulligatawny Soup is really a curry, a meal in itself. Anglo-Indian families often ate it for Sunday lunch, accompanied by rice, relishes and chutneys. Its history can be traced to the early days of the East India Company in Madras.

Traditionally, Indians have not drunk soups, though there have been many soupy dishes in their national repertoire, such as the meat broths (*aab gosht* or *shorva*) of the Muslims, the fruit and vegetable broths of the states Karnataka and Maharashtra (*saar*) and the spice-infused pepper-waters (*millagu-thannir*, hence, mulliga-tawny) of Tamil Nadu, where Madras is the capital city.

The spice-infused pepper-waters come in many flavours and are known, generally, as *rasams*. Before the arrival of red chillies and tomatoes, the main spice in the infusion was lightly roasted peppercorns, with additions of roasted cumin and coriander seeds. The souring agent was usually tamarind water, a coolant in the Madras heat. A thin liquid lifted from the very top of a pot of cooked split peas frequently made a welcome addition, providing a slight thickening as well as some protein. *Rasams*, always sour and hot, were either drunk as a digestive at the start of a meal or eaten with rice as a first course. The British initially followed this custom. Over time, a more official soup evolved. The thickeners used were as varied as versions of the soup. The Singapore Raffles Hotel, for example, in its turn-of-the-century recipe, used oatmeal and still does.

Almost every cookbook from British India or Britain in the days of the Empire has a recipe for Mulligatawny Soup: Mrs Beeton, writing in the late 19th century, uses flour, curry powder and apples in hers;

Richard Terry, *chef-de-cuisine* at London's Oriental Club around 1861, used ham, carrots, turnips, all-spice, mace, thyme, potato flour and curry powder to flavour and thicken his; a charming mid-19th century cookbook I found, *Nabob's Cookery Book*, quotes Shakespeare on its title page, 'And ginger shall be hot i' the mouth too', and then goes on to offer two recipes – one a simple chicken broth seasoned with garlic, onion, curry powder and Madeira, and thickened with butter and flour – and a second which begins, 'Skin and cut up a rabbit . . .'

In 1859, George Francklin Atkinson, a captain with the Bengal Engineers, put out a satirical book, *Curry & Rice*. In words and drawings, it showed the British with dozens of servants waiting on them, enjoying the charms of India. It begins with:

What varied opinions we constantly hear
Of our rich Oriental possessions;
What a jumble of notions, distorted and queer,
Form an Englishman's 'Indian impressions!'

First a sun, fierce and glaring, that scorches and bakes;
Palankeens, perspiration, and worry;
Mosquitoes, thugs, cocoa-nuts, Brahmins and snakes,
With elephants, tigers and Curry . . .

Then jungles, fakeers, dancing girls, prickly heat,
Shawls, idols, durbars, brandy-pawny;
Rupees, clever jugglers, dust storms, slipper'd feet,
Rainy season, and mulligatawny.

Burmese Chicken-Coconut Soup (Ohn-No Khaukswe)

MYANMAR

There was a time in India, in the 1970s and early 80s, when Indian ladies who throw 'luncheon' parties for each other, very proudly offered 'kao swey'. It was foreign, it was different and it was delicious. Instructions were offered for the uninitiated . . . 'take some of the noodles and put them in a bowl . . . ladle the soup on top . . . now take anything from these many bowls . . . fresh coriander, sliced spring onions, sliced hard-boiled eggs, chilli powder, lime halves . . . and season the soup as you like'. All the guests were enchanted and left determined to throw their own 'kao swey' parties for yet another group of impressionable guests.

In Myanmar, the soup is a much loved breakfast dish, also sold by hawkers and informal restaurants in the bazaars. It can, indeed, be had at any time of the day. I noticed that the hard-boiled eggs offered here are the much loved duck eggs. Crisply fried noodles are also scattered over the top, and the chilli powder used in the seasoning is *nga yoke thee hmont*, made from roasted, lightly crushed red chillies.

When I was being shown around Yangon's Kon Sae Dan or 'Indian market' and later the larger Nyaung Pin Lay Sae market, I was struck by the bins of dark, aromatic, roasted chilli powders, some of them with seeds, many made from short, stocky, dried red chillies. It is this powder that gives some Burmese foods their dark, red look.

Chillies are roasted all over the world – it changes their colour and flavour. They are certainly roasted in the lands of their origin, Central and South America, and in India thousands of recipes require that they be fried briefly in hot oil or be roasted on cast-iron griddles before being crushed into curry pastes. In Thailand, in a potters' village, I actually saw a woman take a few chillies and wave them in the direction of a flame emerging from a kiln. They were instantly seared and ready to be pounded for a minced pork noodle sauce. But it was only in Yangon (formerly Rangoon) that I saw dozens of roasted chilli powders being sold openly in the market. (In Myanmar, it is jokingly said that these fumes are fatal to those in the neighbourhood who are already ill, and to babies!) As so little is required, you can also do without the roasting and just use a good quality, coarse, unroasted chilli powder.

Rather like Mulligatawny Soup, to which this soup is second cousin, *ohn-no khaukswe* is a meal in itself. Unlike the Mulligatawny, which is served with rice, this is always served with noodles. If you want to serve this soup as a first course, just put the soup in bowls and drop a few cooked noodles in each to suggest its origins. The traditional *khaukswe*, or noodles, are rounded, wheat noodles, but you may use any that you like. Chinese fresh and dried *lo-mein* noodles are acceptable, as are the rice noodles sold in Chinese and Thai markets as *banh pho* or 'rice sticks'. I frequently use Italian angel hair pasta, *capellini* or *spaghettini*. I cook them as instructed, then rinse them out under cold water and let them drain a bit. I put them in a bowl and toss them with a tablespoon of oil. Just before serving, I drop them into boiling water for a second. They are then ready for the table. The soup, of course, should be very hot and is ladled directly on top of the noodles in individual bowls.

The traditional method for making this soup involves taking a whole bird and cooking it thoroughly so you end up with both soup and meat. I find this most unsatisfactory, as a bird that has given its all to a soup is basically dry and tasteless. I use a rich chicken broth as the base and cut-up, boneless chicken thighs for the meat.

SERVES 4

FOR THE CURRY SOUP

1 medium onion, peeled and chopped, and 1 medium onion peeled and then sliced into very fine half-rings
5-cm/2-inch piece fresh ginger, peeled and chopped
4 cloves garlic, peeled and chopped
340 g/12 oz boneless, skinless chicken thighs, cut into 1-cm/½-inch cubes
salt
freshly ground black pepper
2 tablespoons chickpea flour
900 ml/32 fl oz chicken stock
4 tablespoons corn or peanut oil
½ teaspoon cayenne pepper
2 teaspoons bright red paprika
¼ teaspoon ground turmeric
250 ml/8 fl oz coconut milk, from a well-shaken can

FOR THE NOODLES

350–450 g/12–16 oz *lo-mein*-type Chinese noodles, cooked according to the instructions on page 274, or rice noodles such as *banh pho* or rice-sticks, cooked according to the directions given on page 271, or angel hair, *capellini* or *spaghettini*, cooked as suggested above

FOR THE ACCOMPANIMENTS

a bowl of crisply fried noodles (these are sold by many Chinese grocers – you may also make them yourself by throwing well-separated *lo-mein* noodles into medium-hot oil until they are golden and crisp)
lime or lemon wedges
4 spring onions, cut crossways into thin rounds
2 hard-boiled eggs (duck or chicken), peeled and cut crossways into slices
Crisply Fried Onion Slices (see page 312), optional
very lightly roasted, coarse chilli powder (see page 336)

Put the chopped onion, ginger, garlic and 4 tablespoons water into a blender. Blend until smooth.

Spread out the chicken on a plate. Sprinkle lightly with salt and pepper and toss to mix.

Put the chickpea flour in a bowl. Very slowly, add 250 ml/8 fl oz of the stock, mixing thoroughly as you do so.

Pour the oil into a wide, medium-sized pan and set over a medium-high heat. When the oil is hot, put in the chicken. Stir and fry until the chicken begins to brown. Remove with a slotted spoon. Add the sliced onions to the pan and fry, stirring, until they begin to turn brown at the edges, about 3–4 minutes. Put in the cayenne pepper, paprika and turmeric. Stir once, then add the chicken, together with the juices that have accumulated on the plate, and the remaining chicken stock. Stir. Now pour in, through a strainer, the chickpea and stock mixture, and stir again. Bring to the boil, reduce the heat to low and simmer gently, uncovered, for 15 minutes. Taste for salt. Much will depend on whether your stock is presalted. Add what is needed. Also add the coconut milk. Stir to mix and return to a simmer.

Serve with noodles and accompaniments as suggested above.

Cold Cauliflower-Almond Soup

USA

When I first came to America, more than forty years ago, I had hardly any money in my pockets. So I ate at home, and when I went out, it was to the cheaper coffee shops and Chinese restaurants. One year, an English friend I had gone to drama school with in London came visiting, at the invitation of a rich American aunt. The aunt wanted both of us to meet her at an East-side restaurant in New York for lunch. There are only two things I remember about the lunch. One was the sense of starchy 'poshness' and the other was the first course, a vichyssoise soup.

The soup was cold, smooth and utterly unctuous.

Over the years I have tried to give that soup an Indian twist and here is the version I am serving at my parties today.

I used three medium leeks in the recipe. If yours are very fat, use fewer.

Serves 6

- 1 tablespoon chickpea flour
- 1.2 litres/2 pints chicken stock
- 2 tablespoons corn or peanut oil
- 2 teaspoons peeled and finely grated fresh ginger
- 2 good-sized cloves garlic, peeled and crushed to a pulp
- 1 teaspoon ground coriander
- 1 teaspoon ground cumin
- ¼ teaspoon ground turmeric
- 1½ teaspoons hot curry powder
- 225 g/8 oz small cauliflower florets
- 1 medium potato, about 140 g/5 oz, peeled and chopped
- 115 g/4 oz leeks, sliced
- 1 tablespoon blanched, slivered almonds
- salt
- 2–3 teaspoons lemon juice
- 250 ml/8 fl oz whipping cream
- finely chopped chives for garnish

Put the chickpea flour in a bowl. Slowly add 900 ml/32 fl oz chicken stock – start by making a thick, lumpless paste and then add the rest, stirring as you go.

Pour the oil into a medium pan set over a medium heat. When the oil is hot, put in the ginger and garlic. Stir for a minute. Add the coriander, cumin, turmeric and curry powder. Stir for 30 seconds. Stir the chickpea and stock mixture and add that as well, along with the cauliflower, potato, leeks and almonds. Bring to the boil, cover, reduce the heat to low, and simmer gently for 30 minutes. Taste for salt. Much will depend on whether the stock was salted or not. Add what you need.

Wait for the soup to cool slightly, then blend it in batches until smooth. Add the remaining stock, the lemon juice and cream. Stir and check for a balance of flavours. Chill.

Sprinkle the chives over the top before serving.

Cold Tomato Soup with Cumin

USA

Tasting a bit like the gazpacho of southern Spain and a bit like my mother's home-made tomato juice, this cooling soup is best made when there is an abundance of fresh summer vegetables.

Use the coarse side of a grater or a coarse microplane to grate the tomato. The skin will be left behind in your hand.

It is best also to use young or small cucumbers here. If they are old and seedy, scrape the seeds out with a spoon and just use the peeled shell.

The cucumbers are best added just before you serve.

I like to serve this soup at room temperature, but if you make it in advance you may chill it in the refrigerator, but stir it well before serving.

SERVES 8

- 8 large tomatoes, about 2 kg/4½ lb
- 1 clove garlic
- 2 thin slices white bread, broken up (you may use the crust)
- 3 tablespoons extra virgin olive oil
- 2 tablespoons lemon juice
- about 2¼ teaspoons salt, or to taste
- freshly ground black pepper
- 1½ teaspoons ground, roasted cumin seeds
- ¼ teaspoon cayenne pepper, or to taste
- 225 g/8 oz finely diced, peeled cucumber
- 2 teaspoons finely cut fresh chives for garnishing

Grate the tomatoes into a large bowl. Take 475 ml/16 fl oz of the grated tomatoes and put them in a blender. Add the garlic, bread, oil and lemon juice and blend until smooth. Pour this mixture back into the bowl with the rest of the grated tomatoes and mix. Add the salt (taste as you go), pepper, cumin, cayenne pepper and cucumber. Mix again and taste for a balance of flavours. Ladle into bowls and garnish with a sprinkling of chives.

7

RICE, NOODLES AND BREADS

What do you serve with a curry? Most people think in terms of curry and rice. This is certainly true in much of South-East Asia, Myanmar, Sri Lanka, Bangladesh and south India. But for much of north India and Pakistan – and their emigrants in the United Kingdom, the United States, Trinidad and Guyana – it is breads that are the mainstay.

RICE

Each curry-eating nation serves with it the rice it grows or has developed a taste for over time. The Japanese eat a shorter-grained, slightly glutinous rice that they can pick up easily with chopsticks. The Thais eat jasmine and other similar long-grain rices in the south and glutinous rice in the north. Malays, Singaporeans and Indonesians might use imported basmati for some pilaf-like festive dishes, but prefer their own medium-grain rice for everyday foods. South Africans love parboiled basmati rice, Kenyans use both basmati and other, cheaper, long-grain rices, and in Bangladesh there are many aromatic rices with tiny grains.

In India itself, there are many types of rice. Here, too, preferences change according to regions of origin. Basmati is much loved in the north but most people cannot afford it for everyday meals. Other, cheaper, long-grain rices suffice. Hotels tend to use parboiled basmati as it holds its shape through thick and thin. Along India's west coast, a partially milled, medium-grain red rice is eaten daily; in many parts of south India, it is a parboiled, medium-grain rice.

I suggest you do not worry too much about this. Find a rice you like and can buy easily and cook it to accompany all your curries. For specific rice dishes follow the suggestions given in individual recipes.

Rice may be cooked using many different techniques. Often, it is cooked in its own steam using only as much water as will get fully absorbed. For this, you need to use a pot that will hold the cooked rice comfortably – and leave a little space. Remember that rice expands to about thrice its normal size. A pot that is too large or too small does not provide the best results. Also, for this method of cooking, a tight-fitting lid is required. If you do not have one, cover first with foil, crimping it so it encloses the pot tightly, and then with the lid.

This absorption method of cooking requires that the heat, once the water has boiled, be turned down very, very low. The new, monster, semi-professional gas stoves that some of us have acquired cannot do this. If you have one of them, use an oven-proof pan. Preheat your oven to 150°C/gas mark 2 and, once the combination of rice and water is boiling, cover the pan well and put in the oven for 30 minutes.

Rice may also be cooked like pasta in lots of boiling water. This water is then drained and the rice covered and allowed to rest over a very low heat or in the oven until it has fluffed up and dried out.

I like to measure my rice by volume and that is what I have done in all my recipes. Also, when I use basmati rice, I always wash and soak it first to make sure that the grains stay light and fluffy. Allow time to do this.

One of the more elaborate rice dishes that requires that rice be cooked by the pasta method, is the *biryani*. As it is nearly always served at banquets, I have devoted a special section to it.

RICE BIRYANIS

In what was once India, and is now India, Pakistan and Bangladesh, *biryanis* hold a privileged place in most hearts. As *risottos* are to Italy, *paellas* are to Spain (and the Philippines) and *polos* are to Iran, *biryanis* are the pinnacle of rice cookery for all of South Asia. We reserve them for festive occasions. They do take time to prepare. But as they are often one-dish meals and made only when guests are invited, the time is considered well spent. The most expensive seasonings such as saffron and cardamom are added unflinchingly.

Most *biryanis* are made with rice and meat. Both are generally partially cooked first and then they are layered and cooked together. The method of this final cooking was known as *'dum'* during the Moghul period (16th–19th centuries) and is still called that today. It requires that a pot be sealed shut with dough and then placed on embers. More embers are then placed on the lid so gentle heat flows from two directions and the contents of the pot cook slowly in their own steam. Today an oven can do almost the same thing.

Traditional *biryanis* fall into two categories, those made with cooked meat and those made with raw meat. Those made with cooked meat were always considered easy enough. All you had to do was layer the cooked meat with almost-cooked rice and *'dum'* briefly. The challenge for the great Moghul cooks was using raw meat. They solved this with clever timing. First of all, they marinated the raw meat in seasonings that would tenderise it – yoghurt, garlic and ginger. Then they parboiled the rice for a much shorter period, so it had more time to cook along with the meat. This kind of *biryani* was a triumph of technique and much appreciated by the cognoscenti.

Sealed pots of *biryani*, redolent of saffron, cardamom, nutmeg, cloves and mace, were often opened at the table, to overwhelm the guests with their aromas. Originally, *biryanis*, often combining meat with sweet and sour fruit such as dried plums, were not in the least bit spicy. They were, however, highly aromatic. In the court of the wealthy Nizam of Hyderabad, it was not uncommon to add rose petals and long peppers for additional aroma. Hot and spicy *biryanis* are a much later development. As time went on, the Indian love of hot foods overwhelmed the *biryani* as more and more spices found their way into the dish.

The restaurant *biryani*, especially in Western countries, was another deal altogether. A restaurant could hardly afford to make a proper *biryani* for the few guests who ordered it. In any case, one guest might ask for a chicken *biryani*, another for a lamb and a third for a vegetarian one. If an order for a chicken *biryani* came in, all the restaurant had to do was throw some oil and onions into a pan, perhaps add a few sliced green or red chillies, stir them about, then throw in some cooked chicken curry and then some cooked rice. This has passed for a restaurant *biryani* for decades and continues to do so today.

Biryanis are made in South-East Asia as well. In Thailand's Muslim restaurants, they are known as *khao moag*. Thai jasmine rice is mixed with coconut milk, curry powder, salt, sugar and chicken thighs, or pieces of mutton, and then cooked slowly with the heat coming both from the top and the bottom.

This chapter has just four *biryanis* in it. The first recipe is for a vegetable *biryani*. Such dishes were obviously created by vegetarians who felt that they were being left out. I have created my own, using, among other ingredients, fresh shiitake mushrooms.

The second recipe is from Pakistan. It is made with cooked goat meat (though lamb may be substituted.) It is a modern recipe, using tomatoes and a wealth of seasonings.

The third is a South-African chicken *biryani* created by Indian migrants. It is in the book because I love it. It belongs to the school of 'put-everything-in-and-no-regrets'. It is hot, pungent and addictive, and loved by everyone from Nelson Mandela down. It has become a national favourite.

The last *biryani* is a classic Moghul one from India/Bangladesh made with raw, marinated lamb. How fortune smiled on me with regard to this recipe is a story in itself. See page 269 for more.

NOODLES

Curries are served with both rice and noodles in most of South-East Asia and in parts of south India as well. In south India it is always freshly made rice noodles. These are extruded out of delightfully designed wooden or brass moulds and steamed. Every household has this mould and making the noodles is not considered a big deal. For this book, I have suggested you buy dried rice noodles that are sold as *banh pho* in most South-East Asian shops. For a recipe on how to cook them, see Rice Noodles (page 271).

Lo-mein-style white flour and egg noodles are also used for some of my dishes, such as curried soups from Malaysia and Myanmar. These may be bought fresh, frozen or dried from all Chinese grocers. For directions on cooking them, see Lo-Mein Noodles (page 274).

BREADS

Some Indian breads are made with wholemeal flour, others with white flour, some are leavened and baked in *tandoor* ovens, others are flatbreads cooked on a *tava* or griddle. There are more superb Indian breads that are not known by the rest of the world than those that are. For the purposes of this book, I have chosen only a few that are both common and popular.

Wheat has been around on the Indian subcontinent for over 8,000 years. Ancient ploughed fields have been excavated that show us how the land was tilled and ancient stone mills have revealed wheat grains hidden in their crevices. Wheat storage jars, clay griddles and *tandoor*-like ovens complete a picture that was certainly true for what was once the north-western corner of India and is now north-western India and Pakistan.

Most everyday breads are made with wholemeal flour. The quality of Indian wheat is superb and most Indians are totally spoiled by its texture and taste. Nothing compares to it. In the West, a *chapati* flour is sold in its place. It does have the fine texture that is required but that is all. You may use this flour or else use an equal mixture of sifted wholemeal flour and white plain flour.

I have noticed that emigrants to South-East Asia and the Caribbean use only white flour for breads that in India would have been made with the whole grain. I can only guess that as whole grain flours spoil faster, they were probably more expensive or, initially, just unavailable.

For the leavening in 'raised' breads like the *naan*, Indians and Pakistanis use leftover dough that is allowed to ferment naturally. If you do not make *naans* every day, this is difficult. I have suggested the use of baking powder and bicarbonate of soda instead.

Just the other day, I attended a formal dinner thrown in the New York area by a Kashmiri family. The guests were of all colours and ethnicities. Flatbreads were offered with the meal. I noticed that while all the Europeans began eating with forks, none of the Indians and Pakistanis could resist breaking the bread with their fingers and then folding the meats and vegetables in these bite-sized pieces to form the perfects morsels to deposit in their mouths. This is how we eat. Bread always brings out the fingers.

Indian griddles or *tavas* are very useful when making flatbreads. They are slightly concave, so, if oil is to be used, only a little is needed as it drizzles down quickly. *Tavas* are generally made out of cast-iron and sold by most Indian grocers in all sizes. They need to be heated before the first bread is slapped on. Remember that the thinner the bread the hotter the griddle and the faster the cooking time. Thicker breads must cook more slowly at a slightly lower temperature so the insides do not remain raw. Thinner breads must cook fast or they will turn hard and brittle. If you do not have a *tava*, a cast-iron frying pan makes a good substitute.

Plain Japanese Rice

JAPAN

All Japanese and Korean groceries sell Japanese-style rice. It is short-grained and just sticky enough to be picked up easily with chopsticks. The proportion of rice to water is 1¼:1. The rice is always washed and allowed to sit before it is cooked.

SERVES 4–6

a 500-ml/16-fl oz measure of Japanese rice

Put the rice in a bowl and wash in several changes of water, swishing the rice around gently each time. Pour into a sieve and leave to drain for an hour.

Combine the drained rice and 625 ml/1 pint water in a small, heavy, lidded pan. Bring to the boil, cover, and reduce the heat to very, very low. Cook for 20 minutes. Increase the heat to high for 5 seconds and then turn it off, without uncovering the pan at any stage. Let the pan sit this way for 10 minutes. Japanese rice is best removed with a slightly wet, wooden paddle or wooden spoon.

Plain Jasmine Rice

SOUTH-EAST AND SOUTH ASIA

This is our everyday rice in New York. It goes with curries from around the globe. For me, jasmine rice is multi-purpose and beautifully aromatic to boot. It does not require washing and soaking.

Remember that the proportion of rice to water for jasmine rice, in volume, is 1:1½.

SERVES 4–6

a 500-ml/16-fl oz measure of jasmine rice

Measure the rice into a medium-sized, heavy-bottomed pan. Add 750 ml/25 fl oz water and bring to the boil. Cover with a tight-fitting lid (if you are unsure, put some foil on top of the pan, crimp it, and then the put the lid on), reduce the heat to very, very low, and cook for 25 minutes without removing the lid.

Parveen and Hameed Haroun's

Tomato-Garlic Rice

PAKISTAN

Here is a most wonderful rice dish that I had not only never eaten before my visit to Pakistan, but could not even have dreamt up. The Sindhi family in Karachi who were hosting me, pair it, rather specifically, with Black-Eyed Beans with Spinach and Dill (see page 194), but I have got to love it so much that I serve it with all manner of foods now, including roast chicken.

Its method of preparation is rather unusual. Rice is first cooked the normal way. Then, you add some water to it and mash it up bit, adding tomato purée and garlic. It is then spread out on a *thali,* a metal plate, and baked briefly. I just cannot stop eating it. Instead of a *thali,* I use a non-stick baking tin.

At formal dinners, I cut the baked rice into squares or diamonds.

You may use any rice of your choice, but I just love the texture of jasmine rice for this dish. As soon as the Plain Jasmine Rice is cooked according to the instructions given opposite, proceed with this recipe while it is still hot.

- freshly cooked Plain Jasmine Rice (see opposite)
- 1 tablespoon tomato purée
- 1½ teaspoons peeled and finely crushed garlic
- 1½ teaspoons salt
- a little corn, peanut or olive oil for greasing the baking tin and spreading over the top of the rice

Preheat the oven to 180°C/gas mark 4.

As soon as the Plain Jasmine Rice is cooked, pour 250 ml/8 fl oz water into the pan and stir well with a wooden spoon, mashing the rice a bit as you do so. Mix in the tomato purée, garlic and salt.

Lightly grease an 20–23 cm/8–9 inch square, non-stick baking tin and empty the rice into it. Grease one hand well with oil and pack the rice down, spreading it evenly in the pan. Bake for 15 minutes.

Curried Jasmine Rice

THAILAND

This rice dish is from southern Thailand, near its border with Malaysia. You can almost taste the influence of its southern neighbour. Fresh red chillies, fresh turmeric, garlic, shallots and curry paste or specific spices are all ground together and sautéed. Cooked rice is added and the two blended together. Extra flavouring comes from shredded kaffir lime leaves, which are sprinkled over the top at the end.

I have used red pepper instead of the fresh red chillies, and turmeric powder instead of the fresh turmeric.

SERVES 4

- a 350-ml/12-fl oz measure of jasmine rice
- ½ medium red pepper, about 90 g/3 oz, seeds removed and chopped
- 45 g/1½ oz shallots, peeled and chopped
- 2 cloves garlic, peeled and chopped
- ½ teaspoon ground cumin
- ½ teaspoon ground coriander
- ¼ teaspoon ground turmeric
- ¼ teaspoon cayenne pepper
- 4 tablespoons corn, peanut or olive oil
- 1 teaspoon salt
- 2 fresh kaffir lime leaves or ½ teaspoon grated lemon zest

Combine the rice and 525 ml/18 fl oz water in a small, lidded pan and bring to the boil. Cover tightly and reduce the heat to very low. Cook for 25 minutes.

Meanwhile, put the pepper, shallots, garlic, cumin, coriander, turmeric and cayenne pepper into a blender and blend until smooth.

Pour the oil into a large, non-stick pan or wok and set over a medium-high heat. Pour in the paste from the blender. Stir and fry for 3–4 minutes. Turn off the heat. Add the hot rice and salt. Gently turn the rice around in the paste to mix as well as possible.

Before serving, either tear up the lime leaves or else remove the central vein and cut them into fine strips. Scatter over the top of the rice.

Plain Basmati Rice

INDIA

In order to keep basmati grains well separated, it is best to wash off all milling powders first and then to soak the rice for at least 30 minutes. Longer does not hurt.

The ratio of basmati rice that is to be washed and soaked to the water that is required to cook it is 1: 1⅓. I find it easier to measure in volume.

If a little aroma is desired, you may add two or three cardamom pods and two or three cloves to the boiling water.

SERVES 4–6

a 500-ml/16-fl oz measure of basmati rice

Put the rice in a bowl and wash in several changes of water. Drain, add fresh water to cover generously, and leave to soak for 30 minutes. Drain.

Combine the rice and 650 ml/22 fl oz water in a heavy, lidded pan that will just hold the cooked rice comfortably. Bring to the boil. Cover. Reduce the heat to very, very low and cook for 25 minutes.

Yellow Rice with Peas

INDIA

The yellow in this rice comes from ground turmeric. The peas may be fresh or frozen. Just drop them into lightly salted boiling water and boil until tender. Drain and rinse under cold, running water.

SERVES 4–6

a 500-ml/16-fl oz measure of basmati rice
½ teaspoon ground turmeric
1 teaspoon salt, optional
140 g/5 oz fresh or frozen peas, cooked as suggested above

Put the rice in a bowl and wash in several changes of water. Drain, add fresh water to cover generously, and leave to soak for 30 minutes. Drain.

Combine the rice, 650 ml/22 fl oz water, the turmeric and salt in a heavy, lidded pan that will just hold the cooked rice comfortably. Stir and bring to the boil. Cover. Reduce the heat to very, very low, and cook for 20 minutes. Lift the lid and add the peas. Replace the lid and continue to cook on a low heat for a further 5 minutes. Mix the rice gently when you serve.

Basmati Rice with Cinnamon and Saffron

INDIA

This is a wonderful rice for a formal dinner or party (pictured here with Basmati Pilaf with Dill and Cardamom, page 260). The quantities can easily be increased.

SERVES 4–6

1 teaspoon saffron threads
3 tablespoons hot milk
¼ teaspoon ground cardamom
¼ teaspoon sugar
a 500-ml/16-fl oz measure of basmati rice
2 tablespoons corn, peanut or olive oil or *ghee*
2 medium sticks cinnamon
1 teaspoon salt

Place the saffron on a piece of foil. Fold some of the foil over the saffron and crush it with a rolling pin or a wooden potato masher. Put the crushed saffron in a small cup. Add the hot milk, ground cardamom and sugar. Mix with a cocktail stick or the handle of a small spoon and set aside for 3 hours.

Put the rice in a bowl and wash in several changes of water. Drain, add fresh water to cover generously, and leave to soak for 30 minutes. Drain.

Pour the oil into a heavy, lidded pan that will just hold the cooked rice comfortably and set on a medium heat. When the oil is hot, put in the cinnamon sticks. Stir for 10 seconds, then add the rice. Reduce the heat to medium-low and stir the rice around until all the grains look translucent, about 2 minutes. Add 650 ml/22 fl oz water and the salt. Bring to the boil. Cover. Reduce the heat to very, very low and cook for 25 minutes. Turn off the heat. Lift the lid and quickly dribble in the saffron milk in any haphazard pattern. Quickly cover again and leave for 10 minutes. Mix the rice very delicately with a slotted spoon before serving.

Basmati Pilaf with Dill and Cardamom (Sooay Ka Pulao)

INDIA

A very aromatic rice dish, perfect for serving with meat and chicken.

SERVES 4–6

- a 500-ml/16-fl oz measure of basmati rice
- 3 tablespoons corn, peanut or olive oil
- 1 medium stick cinnamon
- 5 whole cardamom pods
- 2 bay leaves
- 85 g/2½ oz onion, sliced into fine half-rings
- 30 g/1 oz finely chopped fresh dill
- 650 ml/22 fl oz chicken stock
- salt

Put the rice in a bowl and wash in several changes of water. Drain, add fresh water to cover generously, and leave to soak for 30 minutes. Drain.

Pour the oil into a heavy, lidded pan that will just hold the cooked rice comfortably and set on a medium heat. When the oil is hot, put in the cinnamon stick, cardamom and bay leaves. Stir for 5 seconds, then put in the onions. Stir and fry until the onions turn reddish-brown. Add the rice and dill. Reduce the heat to medium-low and stir until the rice grains look translucent, about 2 minutes. Add the stock, plus about 1 teaspoon salt if the stock is unsalted, and bring to the boil. Cover tightly. Reduce the heat to very, very low and cook for 25 minutes.

Plain Parboiled Basmati Rice

In south India, where they eat a shorter-grained rice, the technique of parboiling it briefly before drying and hulling it has been used since ancient times. This preserved the grain better for storage and increased its nutritional content.

These days, 'golden sela', as this parboiled basmati is called, is the rice of choice in South Africa and is also popular in north India.

While parboiled basmati does not have the aroma of traditional basmati, it is reliable and forgiving of small mistakes.

SERVES 4–6

- a 500-ml/16-fl oz measure of parboiled basmati rice

Put the rice in a bowl and wash in several changes of water. Drain.

Combine the rice and 1 litre/32 fl oz water in a heavy, lidded pan that will just hold the cooked rice comfortably. Bring to the boil. Cover. Reduce the heat to very, very low and cook for 20 minutes. Turn off the heat. Let the pan sit, covered and undisturbed, for a further 10 minutes.

Parboiled Basmati with Whole Garam Masalas — INDIA

This is a very aromatic pilaf. If you can buy dried rose petals, you may add a few of those as well. You may remove some of the larger whole spices before serving.

SERVES 4–6

- a 500-ml/16-fl oz measure of parboiled basmati rice
- 2 tablespoons corn, peanut or olive oil
- 1 medium stick cinnamon
- 4 whole cardamom pods
- 2 whole, black cardamom pods
- 4 whole cloves
- 2 bay leaves
- ½ teaspoon whole black peppercorns
- ½ teaspoon whole black cumin seeds
- 85 g/2½ oz onions, peeled and sliced into fine half-rings
- 1 litre/32 fl oz chicken stock or water
- 1 teaspoon salt, if needed

Put the rice in a bowl and wash in several changes of water. Drain.

Pour the oil into a heavy, lidded pan that will just hold the cooked rice comfortably and set over a medium-high heat. When the oil is hot, put in the cinnamon, the two types of cardamom, cloves, bay leaves, peppercorns and black cumin. Stir once or twice and add the onions. Stir and fry until the onions are reddish-brown. Add the rice and reduce the heat to medium-low. Stir the rice for 2 minutes. Add the stock, plus the salt if the stock is unsalted, and bring to the boil. Cover. Reduce the heat to very, very low and cook for 20 minutes. Turn off the heat. Let the pan sit, covered and undisturbed, for a further 10 minutes.

Parboiled Basmati Pilaf with Carrot and Mint

INDIA

A pilaf that may be served with kebabs or curries.

SERVES 4–6

a 500-ml/16-fl oz measure of parboiled basmati rice
2 tablespoons corn, peanut or olive oil
½ teaspoon whole cumin seeds
1 medium carrot, peeled and cut into 5-mm/¼-inch dice
about 10 mint leaves, very finely chopped
1 small, fresh, hot green chilli, finely chopped
1 litre/32 fl oz chicken stock or water
1 teaspoon salt, if needed

Put the rice in a bowl and wash in several changes of water. Drain.

Pour the oil into a heavy, lidded pan that will just hold the cooked rice comfortably and set over a medium-high heat. When the oil is hot, put in the cumin seeds. A second later, add the carrot and stir for a minute. Now put in the drained rice, mint and chilli. Reduce the heat to medium-low and stir the rice for 2 minutes. Add the stock, plus the salt if the stock is unsalted, and bring to the boil. Cover. Reduce the heat to very, very low and cook for 20 minutes. Turn off the heat. Let the pan sit, covered and undisturbed, for a further 10 minutes.

Vegetable Biryani

USA

Here is a *biryani* I have created that uses fresh shiitake mushrooms and sweet red peppers.

I used half of a very large red pepper here. After removing the seeds, I cut it into 5-mm/½-inch wide strips and then halved them, crossways.

SERVES 6–8

1 teaspoon saffron threads
5 tablespoons hot milk
700-ml/1¼ pint measure basmati rice, washed and drained
5 tablespoons corn, peanut or olive oil
a generous pinch of ground *asafetida*
1 teaspoon whole brown mustard seeds
1 teaspoon whole cumin seeds

115 g/4 oz red pepper, cut into 5 mm x 5 cm/¼ x 2 inch strips
225 g/8 oz fresh shiitake mushrooms, stems discarded and caps cut into 3-mm/⅛-inch thick slices
225 g/8 oz button mushrooms, cut lengthways into 3-mm/⅛-inch thick slices
115 g/4 oz French beans, cut crossways into 2½-cm/1-inch pieces
8 tablespoons natural yoghurt
1 teaspoon ground coriander
salt
½ teaspoon cayenne pepper
2 teaspoons lemon juice
2 x 7½-cm/3-inch sticks cinnamon
5 whole cardamom pods
30 g/1 oz butter, cut into small pats

Place the saffron on a piece of foil. Fold some of the foil over the saffron and crush it with a rolling pin or a wooden potato masher. Put the crushed saffron in a cup. Add the warm milk, cover, and set aside.

Meanwhile, wash the rice in several changes of water. Drain. Leave to soak in water that covers it generously for at least 30 minutes but no longer than 3 hours. Drain.

Pour the oil into a large, preferably non-stick pan and set over a medium-high heat. When the oil is hot, put in the *asafetida*, the mustard seeds and the cumin seeds. As soon as the mustard seeds begin to pop, a matter of seconds, put in the red pepper strips. Stir for a minute. Add the two kinds of mushroom and the beans. Stir until the mushrooms have softened. Add the yoghurt, a tablespoon at a time, and stir until it is absorbed. Add the coriander and stir once. Reduce the heat to low, add ½ teaspoon salt, the cayenne pepper, lemon juice and 2 tablespoons water. Toss and turn off the heat.

Preheat the oven to 150°C/gas mark 2.

Pour 5 litres/9 pints water into a large, lidded pan. Add the cinnamon stick and cardamom and bring to the boil. Add 4 teaspoons salt and the drained rice. Stir gently, partially cover with the lid, and bring to the boil. Boil the rice for 5–6 minutes or until it is three-quarters done. Test it by removing a grain and pressing it between the thumb and forefinger. It should have a slim, hard core. Drain.

Work quickly now. Lay the butter at the bottom of a heavy, wide, ovenproof, lidded pan. Spread half the vegetables over the butter. Spoon half the rice over the vegetables, spreading it out so it reaches the edges of the pan. Spread the remaining vegetables over the rice and then spread the remaining rice over the vegetables. Dribble the saffron milk over the top. Cover tightly, first with foil, crimping the edges, and then with the lid. Put the pan over a medium heat for 3 minutes and then put it in the oven for 35 minutes or until the rice is just cooked through. Mix gently with a slotted spoon before serving.

Marina Fareed's

Goat Biryani

PAKISTAN

Rather like a Spanish *paella* or an Italian *osso bucco* combined with rice, this dish is often the star of a festive meal. Its required accompaniments are a yoghurt dish, or a simple *raita*, salads and pickles.

Pakistanis in New York generally buy a whole kid and then use a selection of cuts, with bone, from the leg, shoulder, neck and ribs to make the *biryani*. You may use just the leg or shoulder, with the bone in. If you cannot get goat, use lamb shoulder, with bone.

SERVES 10

- 1 teaspoon saffron threads
- 250 ml/8 fl oz warm milk
- 900-ml/32-fl oz measure basmati rice
- 350 ml/12 fl oz corn or other vegetable oil
- 6 medium onions, peeled and sliced into fine half-rings
- 2½-cm/1-inch piece fresh ginger, peeled but left whole
- 8 cloves garlic, peeled and cut into slices
- 8 cardamom pods, lightly crushed but left whole
- 2 x 7½-cm/3-inch sticks cinnamon
- 3 large whole black cardamom pods
- 2 bay leaves
- 1 teaspoon whole cloves and 1 teaspoon whole peppercorns tied in a small square of muslin
- 1.35 kg/3 lb goat meat with bone, from the leg, shoulder, neck and ribs or just from the leg or shoulder, cut into 2½–4-cm/ 1–1 ½-inch pieces
- salt
- 1 tablespoon cayenne pepper (make sure it has a rich red colour or else use a mixture of cayenne and paprika)
- 2 large plum tomatoes, finely diced
- 3 tablespoons tomato purée

Put the saffron threads in the warm milk. Cover and set aside.

Meanwhile, wash the rice in several changes of water, then drain and leave to soak in water that covers it generously for at least 30 minutes but no longer than 3 hours. Drain.

Pour the oil into a large, wide, ovenproof, lidded pan and set on a medium-high heat. Add half the sliced onions and fry, stirring, turning the heat down as needed, until the onions are both a rich medium reddish-brown colour and crisp. Remove all the onions with a slotted spoon or mesh spatula and spread out on a tray lined with kitchen paper.

Carefully remove about 120 ml/4 fl oz of the hot oil and set aside near the saffron milk.

Add the remaining sliced onions to the remaining oil. Also put in the ginger, garlic, cardamom, cinnamon, black cardamom, bay leaves and the muslin bundle. Stir and fry until the onions turn golden with hints of brown. Add the cubed meat, 5 teaspoons salt and the cayenne pepper and stir and cook for 10 minutes. Add 350 ml/12 fl oz water and continue to stir and cook for a further 10 minutes. Cover and cook for another 30 minutes on a medium-high heat, stirring now and then.

Remove the lid and stir in the diced tomatoes. Add the tomato purée and keep stirring for 5 minutes. Reduce the heat to low, replace the lid, and cook for a further 15 minutes or until the meat is tender, stirring occassionally and adding a little water if needed.

Preheat the oven to 150°C/gas mark 2.

When the meat is tender and the sauce very reduced and thick, remove the spice bundle and the knob of ginger. Put the whole covered pan in the oven to keep it warm.

Pour about 5 litres/9 pints water into a very large, wide, ovenproof, lidded pan that can hold the entire *biryani*. Add 1 tablespoon salt to it and then put in the drained rice. Stir the rice gently and partially cover with the lid. Boil the rice for 5–6 minutes or until it is three-quarters done. Test it by removing a grain and pressing it between the thumb and forefinger. It should have a slim, hard core. Drain the rice. Work quickly now. Put a tablespoon of the reserved oil into the rice pan. Cover with a third of the rice. Cover this with a little less than half of the meat (with some juices). Sprinkle a third of the browned onions over the top and a third of the saffron milk as well. Cover all this with another third of the rice, then a tablespoon of oil, then most of the remaining meat (reserve a generous ladleful), then a third of the onions and then a third of the milk. Cover with the final layer of rice, the last of the oil, meat and juices, the onions and finally the saffron milk. Cover, first with foil and then with a lid. Put the pan briefly over a medium-high heat so the oil at the bottom heats up, and then put the pan in the oven for 25 minutes.

Stir gently before serving.

Mariam Vally's

South-African Chicken Biryani

SOUTH AFRICA

While a Moghlai *biryani* is mild, pale, elegant and delicately savoury, and designed to be eaten with equally delicate yoghurt preparations, a South-African one is vibrant, spicy and piquant: definitely the hot chick at the dance. It comes studded with potatoes and peas and lentils and chicken, requiring little else but the 'sauce' it is served with, a fresh chutney made with coriander leaves, green chillies and garlic, all liquidised in a blender and mixed with South-African 'sour milk'. We would have to use yoghurt or buttermilk instead. This is very much a party dish. You could easily double the recipe for a larger group. All you will need is double the ingredients and a larger pan.

Once the *biryani* is made, it will stay warm for a good hour if left covered. You could also put it into a warm oven for 20 minutes to reheat it.

South Africans use parboiled basmati rice to make their *biryani*. It is tougher and more tolerant of minor miscalculations. Indian grocers sell it but, if it is unavailable in your area, use any parboiled long-grain rice.

SERVES 8

FOR MARINATING THE CHICKEN

1 teaspoon saffron threads
285 g/10 oz onion, thinly sliced into half-rings, fried in 6 tablespoons oil according to the directions given on page 312 for Crisply Fried Onion Slices
1 tablespoon ginger, peeled and finely grated
6 cloves garlic, peeled and mashed to a pulp
2 teaspoons cayenne pepper
2 teaspoons bright red paprika
1 teaspoon ground turmeric
1 tablespoon whole cumin seeds
1 tablespoon ground coriander
1 medium stick cinnamon
8 whole cloves
6 cardamom pods
1 tablespoon salt
4 teaspoons lemon juice
1 tablespoon corn, peanut or olive oil
350 ml/12 fl oz natural yoghurt, whisked
1.4-kg/3¼-lb chicken, skinned and cut into serving pieces

95 g/3¼ oz *sabut masoor* (whole red lentils), or brown or green lentils
125 g/4½ oz peas, fresh or frozen
4 medium boiling potatoes, about 620 g/1 lb 6 oz, peeled and halved
salt
¼ teaspoon ground turmeric
6 tablespoons corn, peanut or olive oil or *ghee*
1 medium stick cinnamon
5 whole cardamom pods
1 teaspoon whole cumin seeds
700-ml/1¼ -pint measure parboiled basmati rice, washed and drained
30 g/1 oz butter, cut into small pats

Place the saffron on a piece of foil. Fold some of the foil over the saffron and crush it with a rolling pin or a wooden potato masher. Put the crushed saffron in a cup, add 250 ml/8 fl oz hot water and set aside for an hour or longer.

Crush the crisply fried onions coarsely. Put them in a large bowl. Add all the other ingredients for the marinade, except the chicken. Mix well, then add half the saffron mixture. Mix again. Cover the remaining saffron mixture and put it away in a safe place. Remove 120 ml/4 fl oz of the spice paste, cover it, and set aside with the saffron. You may refrigerate both, if you like. Add the chicken to the large bowl of spice paste, mixing well. Cover and refrigerate for 4–24 hours. Remove from the refrigerator an hour before baking to allow the meat to come closer to room temperature.

Put the *masoor* in a lidded pan along with 750 ml/1¼ pints water and bring to the boil. Partially cover with the lid, reduce the heat to low, and cook gently for 25 minutes. Drain.

Put the peas in a pan with a little water and cook for a minute. Drain and rinse under cold running water. Drain.

Rub the potato chunks with ¼ teaspoon salt and ¼ teaspoon turmeric.

Pour the oil into a large frying pan and set it over a medium heat. When the oil is hot, put in the potatoes. Stir and fry them until they have browned on all sides. Remove with a slotted spoon and set aside. Reserve the oil.

Pour 5 litres/9 pints water into a large pan. Add the cinnamon stick, cardamom and cumin seeds and bring to the boil. Add 4 teaspoons salt and the drained rice. Stir gently and return to the boil. Boil for 13 minutes, then drain. Take about a 350-ml/12-fl oz measure of the cooked rice and mix it in a bowl with the reserved spice paste.

Preheat the oven to 150°C/gas mark 2.

Take a large pan, about 30–36 cm/12–14 inches wide and 13–15 cm/5–6 inches deep and pour the reserved oil from frying the potatoes over the bottom. Sprinkle over a third of the cooked *masoor* and a third of the cooked peas. Put in all the chicken, together with its marinade, spreading it out evenly. Sprinkle the remaining *masoor* and peas over the top. Tuck in the browned potatoes wherever you find spaces. Spoon in all the rice, both the plain and that mixed with the spice paste. Dot the top with the butter. Pour 120 ml/4 fl oz water around the edges. Dribble the remaining saffron water over the top. Cover tightly, first with foil, crimping the edges, and then with the lid. Set the pan on a medium-high heat. As soon as you see steam escaping from under the foil, put the pan in the oven and bake for 1½ hours.

When serving, carefully lift out the rice-chicken using a slotted spoon and lay on a warmed platter. Do not mix.

A recipe from the collection of the late Hasina Murshed of Calcutta, handed down to her son Syed Mushtaque Murshed

Moghlai 'Raw' Meat Biryani (Kucchey Gosht Ki Biryani)

BANGLADESH

When I was in Dhaka, Bangladesh, I was invited to the home of art-collector and businessman Abul Khair. He had, very generously, thrown a garden party for me where all the food was to be cooked outdoors in my presence. Each dish was more spectacular than the next: there was a whole, deboned fish that had been stuffed; a shad-like fish called *hilsa* had been cooked with pineapple; another *hilsa* had been lightly steamed with oil, lemon, red chillies and sliced onions; the back of a fish had been boned and used to make delicate fish balls; and much, much more.

The one dish that had already been fully cooked was sitting in a gargantuan *degh* (pot) in a side garden. This was the 'raw' meat *biryani*, made by a famous caterer whose speciality it was.

A raw meat *biryani* requires that you combine raw, but marinated, lamb with partially cooked rice and then let them both cook very slowly together. The meat and the delicate basmati rice need to get done at the same moment, a tricky operation where timing and technique are all. It is believed that the best of such *biryanis* are cooked over wood, as this had been.

Well, the *biryani* was glorious. The caterer, however, was hardly about to give me the recipe.

My Bangladeshi hostess, Yasmin Murshed, knew that her aristocratic family did have a treasured family recipe but would they part with it?

I left Bangladesh and continued to pester Yasmin through emails. I remain totally indebted to her brother-in-law, Syed Mushtaque, for his generosity because, when the recipe came, I recognised it immediately for what it is: a true Moghul gem.

These days restaurants have taken to calling every third dish 'Moghlai' in order to bestow it some status, but this recipe was probably used in the 18th century courts of the Moghul emperor and his various governors and noblemen. The recipe could have even earlier origins. There are no chillies in it. It has the very Persian *aloo Bokhara* (the sweet and sour dried plums of Bohhkara used in Persian cookery). It is simple, clean and pure, very Moghul-Persian.

If the South-African *biryani* (see page 266) is the hot chick at the dance, this *biryani* is definitely the true princess at the ball, tall, pale and properly pedigreed, her tastefully chosen diamonds and emeralds glinting in the light of a hundred oil lamps.

The recipe, as it was sent to me, begins, 'With a silent prayer directed heavenwards, commence proceedings'. There is a need for the prayer. Once the pot with all the ingredients is sealed shut, no adjustments are possible. But there is no need to worry. The recipe is also foolproof.

The recipe I received called for meat from 'the hind leg of a castrated he-goat or *khassi ka gosht*'. Not having easy access to a butcher this obliging, I have used loin lamb chops. If they are too large, ask your butcher to cut them in half, crossways, right through the bone.

The *aloo Bokhara* are sold by most Indian grocers. If you cannot get them, substitute dried apricots, whole ones or the pitted halves. *Biryanis* are served with yoghurt relishes, salads and pickles.

SERVES 8

FOR MARINATING THE MEAT
10 whole cardamom pods
5 whole cloves
1 small stick cinnamon, broken up
350 ml/12 fl oz natural yoghurt
2 teaspoons salt
2 tablespoons peeled and finely grated fresh ginger
6 large cloves garlic, peeled and crushed to a pulp
1 kg/2¼ lb loin lamb chops (see note above)

1 teaspoon saffron threads
4 tablespoons rose water
700-ml/25-fl oz measure basmati rice
Crisply Fried Onion Slices, made according to the recipe on page 312, but using smaller onions, each about 90 g/3 oz, and ghee instead of oil
the *ghee* used to fry the onions
8 dried *aloo Bokhara*, also sold as 'golden plums', or dried apricots (see above)
½ teaspoon whole black cumin seeds
1 small stick cinnamon
4 whole cardamom pods, lightly crushed
2–3 whole cloves
4 teaspoons salt
250 ml/8 fl oz milk

Marinate the meat. Put the cardamom pods, cloves and cinnamon into a clean coffee grinder or other spice grinder and grind as finely as possible.

Put the yoghurt in a large bowl. Add the ground spices and salt. Pick up the grated ginger and squeeze all its juice into the yoghurt. Add the garlic and mix well. Trim some (but not all) the fat off the outside of the chops and rub the marinade over them. Cover and set aside in the refrigerator for 4–8 hours.

Place the saffron on a piece of foil. Fold some of the foil over the saffron and crush it with a rolling pin or a wooden potato masher. Put the crushed saffron in a cup. Add the rose water and leave to soak for 4 hours.

Wash the rice in several changes of water, drain, then leave to soak in water that covers it generously for 1–3 hours. Drain just before cooking.

Crumble the fried onions and set aside. Preheat the oven to 160°C/gas mark 3.

Line the bottom of a wide, heavy, ovenproof, lidded pan with about 5 tablespoons of the *ghee* used in frying the onions. Spread the marinated meat and its marinade over the *ghee*. Spread the crumbled fried onions over the meat. Tuck the *aloo Bokhara* into any empty spaces.

Pour 5 litres/9 pints water into a large pan. Add the black cumin seeds, cinnamon, cardamom and cloves. Bring to the boil. Add the salt and the drained rice. Stir gently and return to the boil. Boil for 3 minutes or until a grain of rice breaks into two or three pieces when crushed. Drain. Quickly spread half the rice over the meat. Sprinkle half the saffron water over the rice. Spread the remaining rice over the first batch and dribble the remaining saffron water over the top. Pour over the milk. Cover tightly with foil, crimping the edges, and bring to the boil over a medium-high heat. As soon as steam begins to escape from the edges, crimp the foil again and place the pan lid on top of it. Place in the centre of the oven and bake for 1 hour and 45 minutes or until done. Mix gently with a slotted spoon before serving.

Plain Rice Noodles (Sevai/Senlak) INDIA/EAST ASIA

You could make your own noodles, as they do in south-Indian homes. But they do require special apparatus. I find that dried rice noodles are a wonderful substitute and much more convenient. I buy mine from Thai and other South-East Asian groceries where they are labelled both rice noodles and *banh pho*, their Vietnamese name. They are stiff, translucent, flat and half the packet can usually serve four.

SERVES 4

225 g/8 oz dried rice noodles (*banh pho*)
1 teaspoon corn, peanut or olive oil

Place the noodles in a large bowl, cover well with water, and soak for 2 hours. Drain.

Bring a large pot of water to a rolling boil, just as you would to boil pasta. Drop in the noodles and cook for 1 minute or less, until just done. The water may or may not return to the boil. It does not matter. Drain and rinse in cold running water, washing away as much starch as possible. Drain again and put in a bowl. Pour the oil over the noodles and toss. The noodles are now ready to be stir-fried, put into soups or used in other dishes. If you wish to serve them as they are, they may be reheated in a microwave or dropped again into boiling water for a second. Rub them with a little oil again or they will turn sticky.

Vatsala Narayan's

Lemon Rice Noodles (Lemon Sevai) INDIA

In south India, where rice noodles have been popular since antiquity, they are always made at home when needed. They are variously known as *sevai, idiappam* and string hoppers. Rice flour is lightly roasted and mixed with boiling water, salt and oil to make a soft dough. This dough is then pushed through a mould with tiny holes in it. The noodles land either on an oiled plate or on muslin, forming a small nest, and are then steamed briefly. They may be served immediately with curries, just as rice might be.

They could also be served with sweetened and cardamom-flavoured coconut milk for breakfast, or tossed with roasted and ground sesame seeds, sugar and cardamom powder and eaten as a sweet snack. I love them in all these forms. But my favourite is probably Lemon Rice Noodles, where they are tossed with just a few south-Indian seasonings and lemon juice and then eaten with hot curries or by themselves.

This noodle dish may be served with south-Indian, Sri Lankan or South-East Asian curries instead of rice. You will notice that *urad dal*, a split pea, is used here as a seasoning, a common south-Indian practice.

SERVES 4

- 3 tablespoons corn, peanut or olive oil
- a generous pinch of ground *asafetida*
- 1 teaspoon whole brown mustard seeds
- ½ teaspoon *urad dal*
- 2 whole, dried, hot red chillies
- 8–10 fresh curry leaves, if available
- ⅛ teaspoon ground turmeric
- rice noodles, cooked according to the instructions in the preceding recipe
- 1 teaspoon salt
- 2 teaspoons lemon juice

Pour the oil into a large, non-stick frying pan and set on a medium heat. When the oil is hot, put in the *asafetida*, mustard seeds, *urad dal* and red chillies. As soon as the mustard seeds start to pop and the *urad dal* turns reddish, reduce the heat to very low and put in the curry leaves, turmeric and, a second later, the noodles and salt. Stir gently to mix thoroughly. Add the lemon juice and stir to mix again.

Lo-Mein Noodles

EAST ASIA

Fresh *lo-mein* noodles, made of white flour, eggs and water, are sold by Asian grocers and many supermarkets as well. For four servings, 225 g/8 oz is generally sufficient. It is best to divide the packet of noodles into two by pulling the noodles apart. Use one part, and freeze the rest. Frozen noodles may be dropped directly into boiling water whenever you need them.

These noodles are particularly good in curried soups. You may also serve curries on top of them.

SERVES 4

225 g/8 oz *lo-mein* egg noodles

1 tablespoon corn, peanut or olive oil

Bring a large pot of water to a rolling boil, just as you would to boil pasta. Gently separate the noodle strands and drop them into the boiling water. When the water comes to the boil again, add 250 ml/8 fl oz cold water. Do this twice more. When the water returns to the boil yet again, the noodles should be cooked. Drain and rinse them under cold running water. Drain well again and put in a bowl. Toss with the oil, cover, and set aside until needed.

South-Indian Semolina Pilaf (Uppama)

INDIA

Here is a simple *pilaf* made with semolina. This can also be served with curries. Make sure you get semolina from an Indian grocer as the supermarket variety for puddings is entirely different.

SERVES 4

- 4 tablespoons corn, peanut or olive oil
- 1 teaspoon whole brown mustard seeds
- 1 teaspoon *urad dal*
- 2 dried, hot red chillies
- 7–8 fresh curry leaves, if available
- 180 g/6 oz semolina
- ¾ teaspoon salt

Bring at least 400 ml/14 fl oz water to the boil in a pan. Keep at a bare simmer.

Pour the oil into a large, preferably non-stick frying pan and set on a medium-heat. When the oil is hot, put in the mustard seeds, *urad dal* and red chillies. As soon as the mustard seeds start to pop and the *dal* turns reddish, add the curry leaves. Quickly put in the semolina and salt, and fry, stirring, for 4–5 minutes or until the semolina is golden. Reduce the heat to low. Slowly add the boiling water, a little at a time, stirring and allowing it to become absorbed before adding more. Keep doing this slowly over the next 5 minutes. If all the grains do not look properly moistened, add a few more tablespoons of boiling water. Keep stirring and cooking for a further 10 minutes, breaking up any lumps with the back of a spoon. The *pilaf* should turn fluffy.

Wholemeal Flatbread (Chapati)

INDIA

Chapatis, north India's daily bread, have suddenly become so easy to make. Getting them to puff up properly used to require not just mastering a technique but a fair amount of practice as well. Now, I have discovered that the microwave will do the puffing for you in just 30 seconds or less. I am practically delirious with the discovery.

(If you do not have a microwave oven, make a small wad with a cloth and, after the *chapati* has cooked for 30 seconds, use the last 10 seconds of cooking time to push down on all the different areas of the *chapati* in quick succession. This usually makes it puff up.)

It is best to eat *chapatis* as soon as they are made. As *chapatis* come off the griddle, you may butter them lightly, or leave them dry, and then stack them in a covered container. I often put them on a plate lined with part of a tea towel and then cover them with remaining part of the towel. Finally, I invert a second plate over the top of the towel. They should be eaten shortly thereafter, while still warm, or else frozen, well-wrapped, for future use.

You may treat *chapatis* like *tortillas*. Roll up food in them so they become a kind of 'wrap'. The Indian way is to tear off bits of the *chapati*, one at a time, and then wrap each bit around a piece of meat or vegetable to form individual morsels. For soupy foods, the *chapati* is used like a scoop.

Chapatis are usually made with no added salt. If you want some, use about ¼ teaspoon.

Chapati flour is sold by all Indian grocers. You may also use an equal mixture of sifted wholemeal and plain white flour.

The cast-iron, very slightly concave, *tava*, which Indians use to make their *chapatis*, is also sold by Indian grocers. A cast-iron frying pan works just as well.

MAKES 6

125 g/4½ oz *chapati* flour, plus extra for dusting or an equal mixture of sifted wholemeal flour and unbleached, plain white flour

butter or *ghee* to put on top of *chapatis*, if desired

Make a moderately soft dough using all the flour and about 120 ml/4 fl oz water. Knead well for 10 minutes. Shape the dough into a ball and either put it in a plastic bag or place in a bowl covered with a damp cloth. Leave for at least 15 minutes. You may also refrigerate it for future use.

Set an Indian *tava* or a cast-iron frying pan over a medium-high heat. Allow it time to become hot.

Knead the dough again and then divide it into six balls. Keep five covered as you work with the sixth. Dust your work surface with extra flour when needed and roll out one ball into an even 13½-cm/5¼-inch round. Pick up the *chapati* and slap it around between your two palms to dust off some of the extra flour. Now slap it on to the hot *tava*. Cook for 10 seconds. Flip it over. Cook the second side for 10 seconds. Flip it over a second time and cook for a further 10 seconds. Flip it a third time and cook for another 10 seconds. Now pick up the *chapati* and put it in your microwave. Blast it for about 30 seconds or until puffed. Remove and keep covered.

Using slightly damp kitchen paper, wipe the *tava* or frying pan. You need to get rid of all remains of the dusting flour. Reduce the heat to medium-low while you roll out your second *chapati* and proceed as before, remembering to increase the heat before you slap the next *chapati* on to the *tava*.

Layered Wholemeal Flatbread (Warki Paratha) INDIA

These breads tend only to be made when guests are invited, as they are fairly rich. In India, *ghee* (clarified butter) is the fat commonly used in the cooking process, though many people have taken to using oils as well. The flour is usually a very finely ground wholemeal flour which is sold in the West as *chapati* flour. You may use an equal mixture of sifted wholemeal and plain white flour.

MAKES 4

125 g/4½ oz *chapati* flour, plus extra for dusting
¼ teaspoon salt
about 3–4 tablespoons *ghee*, melted butter or corn, peanut or olive oil, kept in a bowl beside you as you work

Make a moderately soft dough using all the flour, the salt and about 120 ml/4 fl oz water. Knead well for 10 minutes. Shape the dough into a ball and either put it in a plastic bag or place in a bowl covered with a damp cloth. Leave for at least 15 minutes. You may also refrigerate it for future use.

Set an Indian *tava* or a cast-iron frying pan over a medium-high heat until hot.

Knead the dough again and then divide it into four balls. Keep three covered as you work with the fourth.

Lightly dust your work surface with a little flour, then roll out one ball into an even 18-cm/7-inch round. Spoon ½ teaspoon of *ghee* over the top, using the back of the spoon to spread it out. Now roll up the round tightly to form a long snake. Starting at one end, coil the snake in a spiral going from the outside in, so it rises into the shape of a cone. Push down the cone to flatten it into a patty. Clear your work surface of loose flour. Put a dab of *ghee* on both sides of the patty and roll it out again into another 18-cm/7-inch round. Pick up the round in the palm of one hand, spreading out your fingers to make this easier, and slap it on to the hot *tava* or frying pan. Cook for 10 seconds. Flip the *paratha* over. Cook for another 10 seconds. Flip the *paratha* over for a second time. Cook for 10 seconds. Flip the *paratha* over a third time and cook for a further 10 seconds. Reduce the heat to medium-low. Pour ½ teaspoon *ghee* over the *paratha*, spreading it out with the back of the spoon. Flip over immediately and pour oil over the second side, spreading it out as well. Flip every 2 seconds now, pressing down with a spatula, about three or four more times. The *paratha* should have reddish-brown spots all over. Remove to a plate and cover with another upturned plate. Keep the heat under the *tava* at medium-low as you roll out the next *paratha*, making sure to increase the heat again before you make the next one. Make the other *paratha*s the same way.

*Paratha*s may be reheated one at a time, in a microwave oven or flip them on a hot *tava* or frying pan, for a few seconds on each side until heated through.

Layered Wholemeal Flatbread Stuffed with Spicy Potatoes (Aloo Paratha)

INDIA / USA

Right in the neighbourhood where I shop for my Indian groceries in New York is a small cafeteria where I often stop for a stuffed potato *paratha*. I ask for nothing more than a bit of natural yoghurt to eat the *paratha* with and a hot cup of tea to soothe and balance the spiciness. This recipe is for that *paratha*, only I make it much smaller as it is easier to handle.

The ideal flour is a very finely ground wholemeal flour that is sold in the West as *chapati* flour. You may use an equal mixture of sifted wholemeal and plain white flour.

You may serve these breads at all Indian meals, including breakfast.

MAKES 6

FOR THE STUFFING

- **225 g/8 oz boiling potatoes, boiled in their skins, then peeled and mashed slightly coarsely while still hot**
- **½ teaspoon salt**
- **freshly ground black pepper**
- **¼ teaspoon cayenne pepper**
- **½ teaspoon well-crumbled *amchoor* or 1 teaspoon lemon juice**
- **2 bird's eye chillies or other slim, fresh green chillies, finely chopped**
- **½ teaspoon fresh ginger, peeled and finely grated**
- **a few tablespoons of fresh coriander. chopped**

FOR THE DOUGH

- **195 g/6¾ oz *chapati* flour, plus extra for dusting**
- **⅓ teaspoon salt**
- **about 3–4 tablespoons *ghee*, melted butter or corn, peanut or olive oil, kept in a bowl beside you as you work**

Combine the potatoes with all the other ingredients needed in the stuffing. Mix well and taste for a balance of seasonings. Divide into six balls, cover, and set aside.

Make a moderately soft dough using all the flour, the salt and about 175 ml/6 fl oz water. Knead well for 10 minutes. Shape the dough into a ball and either put it in a plastic bag or place in a bowl covered with a damp cloth. Leave for at least 15 minutes. You may also refrigerate it for future use.

Set an Indian *tava* or a cast-iron frying pan over a medium-high heat. Allow it time to become hot.

Knead the dough again and then divide it into six balls. Keep five covered as you work with the sixth.

Lightly dust your work surface with a little flour and roll out one ball into an even 13-cm/5-inch round. Put a ball of the potato stuffing right in the centre of it. Lift the edges of the dough and bring them towards the centre so as to enclose the potato ball and rise above it slightly. Give the section rising above it a slight twist for a good seal. It should look like a round dumpling. Now flatten it into a patty. Clear your work surface of loose flour. Put a dab of *ghee* on both sides of the patty and roll it out, turning it over once or twice, into a 14-cm/5½-inch round. Do not worry about any small spaces where the potato shows through. Pick the round up in the palm of one hand, spreading out your fingers to make this easier, and slap it on to the hot *tava* or frying pan. Cook for 10 seconds. Flip the *paratha* over. Cook for another 10 seconds. Flip the *paratha* over for a second time. Cook for another 10 seconds. Flip the *paratha* over a third time. Cook for 10 seconds. Reduce the heat to medium-low. Pour ½ teaspoon *ghee* over the *paratha*, spreading it out with the back of the spoon. Flip it over immediately and pour oil over the second side, spreading it out as well. Flip every 2–3 seconds now, pressing down with a spatula, for a total of about 2 minutes. The *paratha* should be cooked through and have reddish-brown spots all over. Remove to a plate and cover with another upturned plate. Keep the heat under the *tava* at medium-low as you roll out the next *paratha*, making sure to increase the heat again before you make the next one. Make the other *paratha*s the same way.

*Paratha*s may be reheated, one at a time, in a microwave oven or you may put them back, one at a time, on a hot *tava*, flipping them over for a few seconds on each side until heated through.

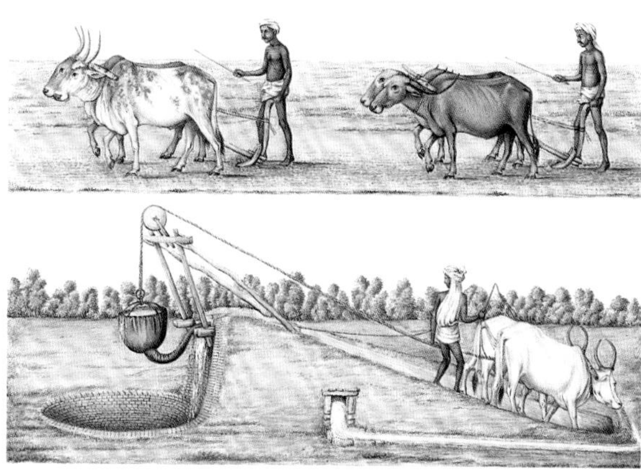

Basic Recipe for Deep-Fried, Puffed Breads (Poori) INDIA

This same bread, if made with all plain flour, is called a *loochi* and eaten throughout West Bengal and Bangladesh. Instead of water for the dough, you may also use milk. This makes for silkier *pooris* that travellers take with them on journeys, as they are meant to last longer.

In my family, we made very small, delicate *pooris*, no more than 10 cm/ 4 inches in diameter, that we loved to eat with potato curries and pickles for breakfast on Sundays.

If you are not used to making *pooris*, it may be easier if you have a companion to help you. One person can roll while the other fries. *Pooris* cook very fast. You can have the whole batch done in less than 10 minutes and then eat them right away, all still puffed up.

If you wish to eat them somewhat later, stack them one on top of the other (they will deflate, but no matter) and keep them well covered. Do not refrigerate them. Serve them at room temperature or else wrap them in a bundle of foil and heat the bundle in a medium oven for 10 minutes.

MAKES 12

125 g/4½ oz sifted wholemeal flour
125 g/4½ oz plain, unbleached flour
½ teaspoon salt
1 tablespoon corn, peanut or olive oil for the dough, plus more for deep-frying and rubbing on the dough
about 250 ml/8 fl oz milk or water

Put the two flours and salt into a bowl. Dribble in the oil and rub it into the flour. Slowly add enough milk or water to enable you to gather all the dough together into a ball. Knead the dough for 10 minutes until smooth. Shape into a ball, rub with a little oil, slip into a zip-lock or other plastic bag and leave for 30 minutes.

Pour the oil for deep-frying into a wok, *karhai* or frying pan and set on a medium heat. In a wok or *karhai*, the oil should extend over a diameter of at least 15 cm/ 6 inches. In a frying pan, the oil will need to come to a depth of at least 2½ cm/1 inch. Give it time to become hot. Keep a large baking sheet lined with kitchen paper next to you.

Meanwhile, knead the dough again and divide it into twelve balls. Keep eleven covered. Take the twelfth ball and rub it lightly with oil. Now flatten it into a patty and roll it out into a 13–14-cm/5–5½-inch round. Lift the round and fearlessly lay it on top of the hot oil without allowing it to fold up. It may well sink but should rise to the surface almost immediately. Now, using the back of a slotted spoon keep pushing the *poori* under the surface of the oil with rapid, light strokes. It will resist and puff up in seconds. Turn it over and count to two. Now lift the *poori* out of the oil and deposit it on top of the kitchen paper. Make all the *pooris* this way.

Plain Guyanese Bread (Saada Roti)

GUYANA/TRINIDAD

The simple, daily bread of the Guyanese and Trinidadian Indians is very much like the *roti* of north India. It is made the same way on a *tava* or cast-iron griddle and carries the same name. The major difference is that it is leavened with baking powder and made with white flour instead of wholemeal flour. In the end, it looks more like a pitta bread than an Indian *roti* and is very simple to make, especially if you have a microwave oven.

MAKES 4 BREADS

360 g/12½ oz equal mixture of unbleached strong and plain flour, plus extra for dusting

2½ teaspoons baking powder

Put the flour and baking powder in a bowl. Slowly add 250 ml/8 fl oz water to make a soft but workable ball of dough, adding a tiny bit more water if necessary. Knead for 8–10 minutes, then let the dough rest for 15 minutes or more. Divide the dough into four balls. Let them rest for 10 minutes.

Set a large *tava*, cast-iron griddle or frying pan on a medium-high heat. (You may need to turn this down to medium if it gets too hot.)

Dust your work surface with a little flour and roll out a 20-cm/8-inch round. Pick it up in the palm of your hand and slap it on to the hot pan. Keep turning it over every 20 seconds for about 2 minutes or until both sides have golden-brown spots. Now slide the bread on to a piece of kitchen paper and place it in the microwave oven for a minute. It will puff up. Remove to a basket lined with a tea towel and cover. Make all the breads this way. If not eating them immediately, the breads should be allowed to cool and then placed in a plastic bag. They can be reheated individually in the microwave for a minute or less.

Sabiroon Eshak's

Guyanese Flaky Bread (Paraata-Roti) GUYANA/TRINIDAD

These breads are like the *paratha*s of India, only they are leavened with baking powder and made with white flour.

Because these breads are very large, you need a 30-cm/12-inch cast-iron frying pan to cook them. If you do not have any such pan, just make eight breads instead of four and make them half the size.

MAKES 4 BREADS

360 g/12½ oz plain, unbleached, flour, or an equal mixture of unbleached strong and plain flour, plus extra for dusting

2 teaspoons baking powder

about 175 ml/6 fl oz corn or peanut oil, in a bowl

Put the flour and baking powder in a bowl. Slowly add 250 ml/8 fl oz water to make a soft but workable ball of dough, adding a tiny bit more if necessary. Knead for 8–10 minutes, then let the dough rest for 15 minutes or more. Divide the dough into four balls. Flatten the balls into patties and let them rest for 10 minutes.

Dust your work surface with a little flour, then roll out a very rough 20-cm/8-inch round. Take about 1 teaspoon of oil and rub it over the surface. Dust very lightly with flour. Fold over a third of the round, leaving a third exposed. Rub a little oil over this fold and then fold the exposed remaining third over this first fold. You will now have a long rectangle. Fold this over itself in thirds and set aside. Do this with all the patties. Let these squares rest for 10 minutes.

Set a large *tava*, cast-iron griddle or frying pan on a medium-high heat. (You may need to turn this down to medium.) Keep the bowl of oil and kitchen paper nearby.

Again, using a little flour to dust your work surface, roll out one square into a 28-cm/11-inch round. Pick it up, allowing it to spread across your palm and forearm, and slap it on to the hot pan. Keep turning it over every 10 seconds for about 2 minutes or until both sides have golden-brown spots. Spread about 1 teaspoon oil over the top using kitchen paper. Turn over and do the same on the second side. Fold the *paraata-roti* in half and press down with a spatula. Turn over, still doubled up, and press down again. The total cooking time should be about 3 minutes. Take the *paraata-roti* out of the pan and lay it on a tea towel, still doubled up. Get your hands under the towel and mash it a few times by bringing the two long ends together and playing the *paraata-roti* like a concertina for a second. Set aside, still doubled, covered in a tea towel. Make all the *paraata-rotis* this way. Keep covered. When cool, put the doubled *paraata-rotis* in a plastic bag. They can be reheated individually in a microwave oven for a minute or less.

THE STORY OF ROTI CANAI

The first time I had this thin flaky bread in the streets of Malaysia, I bought if off a Malaysian vendor of Indian descent. I fell in love with its taste and texture but was left puzzled by its origins. There was nothing quite like it in India.

It was layered, thin and enormous in size, almost 60 cm/2 feet in diameter, but had been folded up. The first part of its name is the Indian word for bread so I understood it. The second part, pronounced chaa-naa-ai, was a mystery. It was served with a thin stew of yellow split peas and vegetables (*dalcha*, see page 192) which acted as a dip.

Since the salesmen were of Tamil origin and the *dalcha* distinctly resembled the *dalchas* and *sambar*s of the south-Indian state of Tamil Nadu, I understood the sauce. But where did the bread come from?

It has been a grand puzzle to solve and has taken me twenty years to put all the parts together. The old name for Madras, the capital city of Tamil Nadu, was Chennai. Indeed, they have gone back to that name now. Many of the labourer-immigrants sailed from the port city of Chennai/Madras. So *roti canai* was the bread of people who were, generally speaking, from Madras or sailed from that port.

The breads themselves were a version of the *paratha* made frequently by Muslim Tamilians. In many parts of Singapore, the bread is sold today as *roti prata*. Close enough. In Guyana, the breads are smaller and called *paraata roti*. Well, fine. Everywhere outside India where Indians were taken as a labour force, all versions of the *paratha* are made with white flour. Wholemeal was probably harder to get. In Trinidad and Guyana, baking powder was added to make the breads a little more recognisably Western. But the basic concept of the bread – and much of the name – remained the same.

In Singapore and Malaysia the bread got larger and larger. As vendors tried to attract the attention of passersby, they began to fling the dough into the air to increase its size, rather like pizza throwers. In Singapore today it is transformed into a giant, square pastry-shell to enclose the meat from a chicken curry. The coconut-enriched sauce of the same curry is served on the side. You can get *roti pratas* stuffed with vegetables, *keema* (curried minced meat) and, would you believe it, *kimchee*, the Korean pickle.

Until now, the very size of the *roti canai* had intimidated me. But then, I met Hajrah Sarwar in Penang, Malaysia. She explained that these breads had, traditionally, been made by women at home. The women did not need to throw them dramatically into the air for effect. No one was watching them. Very often, they pulled the very flexible dough by hand or else they used a rolling pin to get the dough so thin that you could see through it. And who said they had to be enormous?

The basic ingredients for the dough are flour, condensed milk and oil. Very South-East Asian. The dough needs to sit overnight, after which it becomes really elastic. But it is an easy dough and fun to work with. My breads are small, slightly sweet and utterly wonderful. Make a stack of them and keep them covered with a tea towel. They may be reheated, one at a time, in a microwave oven or else on a *tava,* the cast-iron frying pan used to cook them.

Roti Canai

MALAYSIA/SINGAPORE

Roti canai may be served with all curries and is particularly good with those containing coconut milk. In Thailand, Muslim shops also offer this *roti* topped with butter and fine sugar (or condensed milk), as an accompaniment to tea and coffee.

MAKES 12 BREADS

300 g/10½ oz plain flour
4 tablespoons sweetened condensed milk
4 tablespoons corn, peanut or olive oil, plus more for lubricating the dough later
1 egg, lightly beaten

Put the flour in a large bowl. Make a well in the centre and pour in the milk, oil and egg. Slowly mix the flour with the other ingredients, adding about 120 ml/4 fl oz warm water to make a soft dough. Knead the dough for 10 minutes. Divide it into twelve balls and put them in a single layer on a large plate. Pour 2 tablespoons of oil over the top. Turn the balls around in the oil so they are well coated. Now cover the balls and plate with cling film and set aside for 9–10 hours.

Work with one ball at a time. Grease both your hands and the work surface. Roll out the ball into a 21-cm/8½-inch, or bigger, round or stretch it with your hands. You may also do a combination of the two, rolling and stretching. Do not worry if you do not have a perfect round. Starting at one end, roll up the round tightly into a long snake. Coil the snake in a spiral going from the outside in, so it rises into the shape of a cone. The outside will be about 5 cm/2 inches in diameter. Push down the cone to flatten it into a patty. Make all the patties this way. Put them back on the oiled plate and cover again with cling film. Leave for 30 minutes or longer. These patties may also be refrigerated.

Put a *tava* or cast-iron frying pan on a medium-low heat and allow it to become hot.

Take one of the patties and roll it out into a 15-cm/6-inch round. Pick it up and slap it on to the hot *tava* or frying pan. Leave for 10 seconds. Flip it over and cook for another 10 seconds. Flip it over a second time and cook for 10 seconds. Flip it over a third time and cook for 10 seconds. Flip it over a fourth time and press down on it with a spatula, turning it slightly each time you press. Do this for 10 seconds. Flip again and press down. Continue this flipping and pressing for a further 30 seconds or so until the bread no longer has translucent spots and is dotted with reddish patches. Remove to a plate lined with a tea towel. Cover with the rest of the tea towel and then an upturned plate. Make all the breads this way.

My Own Wholemeal 'Roti' USA

Rather like other immigrants before me, especially those coming West, I have created my own, everyday *roti*, or bread. It is not unlike those created by the much more deprived Guyanese and Trinidadian Indians of more than a century ago who came as indentured labourers. They could not get wholemeal flour. I can. I wanted to make a bread that was a bit like a wholemeal *tandoori roti* and a bit like a *chapati*, something nourishing and wholesome that I could make with ingredients from the supermarket, cook easily, and eat every day, even toast, if I needed to.

Here is what I have come up with. It does require the microwave oven. It may be served with all Indian meals.

I use the Indian, cast-iron, very slightly concave, *tava*, to make this, but a cast-iron frying pan works just as well.

MAKES 4 BREADS

125 g/4½ oz wholemeal flour, plus extra for dusting
⅓ teaspoon salt
¼ teaspoon bicarbonate of soda
1 tablespoon rich, natural yoghurt
butter or *ghee* to put on top of the chapatis, if desired

Combine the flour, salt, bicarbonate of soda and yoghurt in a bowl and rub together. Add 120 ml/4 fl oz less 1 tablespoon of warm water. Make a moderately soft dough. Knead well for 10 minutes. Make a ball and either put it in a plastic bag or a bowl covered with a damp cloth. Leave for at least 30 minutes or longer.

Set a *tava* or cast-iron frying pan over a medium heat. Allow it time to become hot.

Knead the dough again and then divide it into four balls. Keep three covered as you work with the fourth. Dust your work surface with the extra flour when needed and roll out one ball into an even 15-cm/6-inch round. Pick up the *roti* and slap it around between your two palms to dust off some of the extra flour. Now slap it on to the hot *tava*. Cook for 5 seconds. Flip it over. Cook the second side for 5 seconds. Continue to flip and cook a further six times. Now pick up the *roti* and put it in your microwave oven. Blast it for about 30 seconds or until puffed, slightly or fully. Remove and keep covered in a tea towel. You may butter it or put *ghee* on it first, if you wish.

Using slightly damp kitchen paper, wipe the *tava*. You need to get rid of all remains of the dusting flour. Reduce the heat to medium-low while you roll out your second *roti* and proceed as before, increasing the heat to medium before you slap the next *roti* on to the *tava*.

My Basic Naan Recipe

USA

Naans are leavened breads baked in a clay oven known as a *tandoor*. Such ovens may well have come down to the Indian subcontinent from western Asia, though ancient excavated sites in both western Pakistan and western India have revealed stones for grinding wheat and ovens for baking breads. Similar breads also exist all over the Middle East.

What I do know for sure is that Delhi and most of India knew little of the *tandoor* or the *naan* until after the partition of India into India and Pakistan in 1947. At that time refugees from western Punjab came bearing portable ovens to make their daily bread. Delhi restaurants picked up on them and today *naan*s are known throughout the world.

*Naan*s need the high temperature of a clay oven where they bake plastered to its inner walls. We, at home, can best approximate this method of cooking by using a large, cast-iron frying pan – I like to use a 35-cm/14-inch pan, but a 30-cm/12-inch one will do – in conjunction with the grill.

MAKES 8

- 620 g/1 lb 6 oz strong white bread flour, plus more for dusting
- 1½ teaspoons baking powder
- 1 teaspoon bicarbonate of soda
- ½ teaspoon salt
- 1½ teaspoon sugar
- 2 tablespoons natural yoghurt
- 250 ml/8 fl oz milk
- 1 egg
- 15 g/½ oz butter, melted, plus 225 g/8 oz butter, melted, or 250 ml/8 fl oz oil, for assorted other uses
- 250 ml/8 fl oz water
- 2 tablespoons oil
- about ½ teaspoons *kalonji* (nigella)
- about 2 teaspoons sesame seeds (the beige kind)

Sift the flour, baking powder, bicarbonate of soda and salt into a bowl.

Put the sugar and yoghurt into a separate, large mixing bowl. Beat with an electric whisk (which is much easier) or with a wooden spoon. Add the milk and 250 ml/8 fl oz water and continue beating. Now beat in about 255 g/9 oz of the flour, a little at a time. Beat thoroughly, to encourage the gluten to go to work (a hundred strokes if you are using a wooden spoon). Your batter should look a little pasty. Add the egg and 15 g/½ oz melted butter and continue beating. Now slowly add another 255 g/9 oz flour, still continuing to beat. By the end of this, your whisk will hardly move and you will have a very elastic dough-batter. Remove the whisk. Using a wooden spoon, add enough of the remaining flour to make a soft, sticky dough. Empty the dough on to a floured board and knead briefly with oiled hands. Still with oiled hands, divide the slightly sticky dough into eight balls. Dust a baking sheet rather generously with flour and place on it the eight balls, spaced well apart. Press on each with a hand dipped in oil to flatten it. Cover with cling film and set aside for 30 minutes or longer. You may even refrigerate the covered sheet for up to 48 hours.

To make the *naan*, put a very large, cast-iron frying pan on a medium-high heat. Preheat the grill, setting a shelf at a distance of 13 cm/5 inches from the source of the heat.

Take one of the *naans*. Dip the bottom in fresh flour. Dip both of your hands in melted butter (or oil) and press down on it, enlarging it with your fingers until it had the traditional tear shape and is about 23 cm/9 inches at its longest and 13 cm/5 inches at its widest. Dab more melted butter on the top with your fingers, and scatter over about ⅛ teaspoon of the *kalonji* and ¼ teaspoon of the sesame seeds. Press down in the centre with your fingers leaving an edge of about 2½cm/1 inch unpressed. Lift up the *naan* with both hands and stretch it a bit so it is 30 cm/12 inches long and about 18 cm/7 inches wide. Now slap it on to the hot pan, seed side up. Cook for 1 minute and 15 seconds on the first side, moving the *naan* around after the first 30 seconds so it browns evenly. Dab with a little butter and put the whole pan under the grill for 1 minute. The *naan* should develop a few reddish spots. Remove the pan from the grill. Dab the *naan* with more melted butter and serve. Make all the *naan*s this way. If not eating immediately, put the *naans* on a towel and fold the towel over them. They will stay warm for a while. To store, wrap the *naan*s in foil and refrigerate. To reheat, the whole foil bundle may be put in a medium oven (190°C/gas mark 5) for 15 minutes. To heat just one *naan*, you can sprinkle it lightly with water and microwave it for a minute or so.

8

RELISHES AND ACCOMPANIMENTS

Just as Indians, like my mother, were once led to believe that it was not possible to have an English meal without a soup, for the British, a curry without rice and a chutney was a non-starter. The chutneys they seem to have focused on were of the sweet, sour and hot, preserve variety – rather like their own mint jellies and jams, only hot. For the British, these were the perfect foils for spicy, savoury curries and rice. Soon, a tradition of serving a vast array of condiments was established. This may be seen even today at old, colonial-style hotels such as the Raffles Hotel in Singapore. Roasted peanuts, sliced bananas, grated coconut, fried onions, pickled chillies, as well as sweet and sour chutneys were all laid out at noon with every curry-and-rice Sunday 'tiffin'.

Is any of this 'authentic'? Well, yes and no. Indians do, indeed, serve chutneys, pickles and relishes with their meals. But they are not in the least bit standardised and the taste of each item is very regional and specific to that home. For example, in our family, we always had my grandmother's black lemon pickle. An almost magical potion, it was black with both age and black pepper. Then, we had my mother's green chilli pickle. It was full of crushed mustard seeds and red chilli powder and quite sour from lime juice. Also, sometimes, we would take out my grandmother's mango and ginger sweet chutney – which was, indeed, of the preserve variety – but this was generally saved for teatime, when we used it to smother a special, savoury biscuit called a *mutthrie*.

These pickles and chutneys were permanently in the larder. What was made fresh everyday was a green chutney (usually with mint, fresh coriander and green chillies) and a salad with onions and tomatoes. According to the season, there were freshly-cut cucumbers, kohlrabi, radishes, carrots and spring onions on the table as well. There was always yoghurt, either natural or made into a *raita* with roasted cumin as its main flavouring.

A Gujarati family in Bombay would have completely different pickles and chutneys and salads, seasoned with a different set of spices. So would a family in Madras or Calcutta. What the British did was just simplify and standardise what seemed like a general Indian trend.

I find it very interesting that, while yoghurt relishes are much loved throughout what was once the Indian subcontinent, they are totally absent in East and South-East Asia. It could be a lactose intolerance that is responsible for this. I have seen Malaysians put a tiny amount of yoghurt into certain meat dishes such as *kormas* in an almost symbolic gesture. They seem much more confident about the coconut milk that they pour into the same curry.

In this chapter you will find a variety of yoghurt relishes, fresh chutneys and salads, preserved chutneys and pickles and also some garnishes, such as crisply fried onions, which add an enormous amount of flavour and excitement to all Indian meals.

What do you drink with Indian meals? Indians usually drink plain water with their meals. Occasionally they may have a yoghurt *lassi*, but not much more. When I serve Indian food at dinner parties in New York, I nearly always accompany all courses with good wine. Be unafraid about this and do not be bullied into serving lager or fruity Alsatian wines. I really think they do fine Indian food an injustice. Try a good Chablis or Pinot Grigio. Amongst the reds, try an Australian Merlot or reasonably priced Bordeaux. Most dry white and red wines complement Indian foods. Non-drinkers may be offered Fresh Limeade (see page 315), *lassi* (see pages 315–316), or seltzer water. After dinner, serve a mildly spiced black tea or, if you like, a glorious Kashmiri saffron tea.

Papadum are the Indian wafers, generally made out of split peas, that are often served with meals. There are many parts of India where a meal without some variety of 'crunchy munchy' is quite unthinkable. It could be green plantain chips, jackfruit chips, potato, sago or rice *papadum*, crisply fried fresh or dried fish, fried vegetable fritters, anything as long as it crunches. Crispness is considered vital to the overall balance of desirable textures at a meal.

Having said that, let me add that I did not grow up with this habit. *Papadums*, we called them *papar*, were either served with drinks in our north Indian home or at wedding banquets. Sometimes when we were on a train journey and passing through the town of Hapar (which conveniently rhymed with *papar*), my mother made a special allowance and let us buy and eat its famous *papar* from hawkers at the railway platform. '*Hapar kay papar*', the hawkers with monster baskets on their heads would cry, 'the *papar* of Hapar'.

My mother used to make one variety at home out of chickpea flour. It was called *papri*, and was served only at two major religious festivals, Divali and Holi. For us, *papadums* had their time and place. It is the Indian restaurants in the West who have perpetuated the myth that all Indians eat *papadum*s at all meals.

Papadums come in all sizes and flavours. Today you can even buy 'cocktail' *papadum* that are sufficient for a mouthful. When you go to your Indian grocer, he will probably have a large selection. Pick any flavour you like. There is plain, garlic flavour, green chilli, red chilli, black pepper, cumin and so on. My favourite is black pepper. The size does not matter. You can always break a *papadum* in half. What does matter is that the *papadums* be slightly flexible. If they are rock hard and brittle, they are old. Bend the packet slightly to test them. If you want to make your own *papadums*, see page 343.

This section also contains some of the basics needed for preparing curries. You will find Thai curry pastes here of all hues, spice mixes from Guyana, India, South Africa and Trinidad, as well as 19th-century British curry powders and curry sauces.

Tahira Mazhar Ali's

Yoghurt with Jaggery (Dahi Aur Gur) PAKISTAN

All over northern India and Pakistan, when the winter crop of sugar cane is harvested, much of it goes to make refined sugar. But not all of it. Perhaps in faithful memory of our culinary history going back to ancient times, every village saves some of the sugar cane juice to boil down and make lumps of sweet, crumbly jaggery, an unrefined sugar.

Jaggery is sold in all Indian and Pakistani markets, though it is more blessed if it comes from your own family village where its purity and freshness is guaranteed. Avoid jaggery that has turned rock hard. The softer and crumblier it is, the better.

The jaggery in Tahira Mazhar Ali's gracious home in Lahore came from her village, Wah, in north-western Pakistan, where the ground not only yields sugar cane but ancient Buddhist statuary as well, much of it to be seen at the excavations at nearby Taxila. Tahira served us lunch on her sun-drenched verandah. This simple yoghurt dish – no recipe is really required – was part of the winter meal.

SERVES 4–6

475 ml/16 fl oz natural yoghurt

3 tablespoons well-crumbled jaggery

Beat the yoghurt lightly with a fork until it is smooth. Put in a bowl. Scatter the jaggery over the top just before serving.

Yoghurt and Apple 'Raita'

USA

I love apple *raitas*, especially if the apples are sweet and crisp. The slight sourness of the yoghurt mingled with the sweetness of the apple is very alluring. I have taken to using an apple that grows locally in New York State – Honey Crisp – but you may choose any that you like.

SERVES 4–6

300 ml/10 fl oz natural yoghurt
about ¼ teaspoon salt
freshly ground black pepper
⅛ teaspoon good quality pure chilli powder or cayenne pepper
about ½ an apple, peeled and cut into small dice

Put the yoghurt in a bowl. Beat lightly with a fork until smooth and creamy. Add all the remaining ingredients and mix well.

Cucumber, Mint and Tomato 'Raita'

INDIA

A simple, refreshing *raita* that may be served with all Indian meals.

SERVES 4–6

250 ml/8 fl oz natural yoghurt
½ teaspoon salt
freshly ground black pepper
¼ teaspoon cayenne pepper
½ teaspoon ground, roasted cumin seeds (see page 339)
1 medium tomato, peeled, seeded and finely chopped
1 medium cucumber, about 13-cm/5-inch in length, peeled and cut into small dice
2 tablespoons finely chopped fresh mint leaves or 1 tablespoon dried leaves, well crumbled

Put the yoghurt in a bowl and beat lightly with a fork until smooth and creamy. Add the salt, black pepper, cayenne pepper and cumin. Mix well. Add the remaining ingredients and mix again.

Parveen Haroun's

Yoghurt with Spinach and Dill (Dahi Palag) PAKISTAN

A speciality of the Afghans who settled in the western Pakistani province of Sindh, this recipe comes from the Pakhtoon matriarch of a Karachi publishing family.

If you can get them, you may add a few tablespoons of finely chopped fresh fenugreek leaves to the spinach as well.

SERVES 4–6

255–285 g/9–10 oz fresh spinach, washed, drained and coarsely chopped
3 tablespoons finely chopped fresh dill
salt
300 ml/10 fl oz natural yoghurt
2 cloves garlic, peeled and crushed to a pulp
freshly ground black pepper
2 teaspoons crumbled dried mint

Put the spinach, dill, ¼ teaspoon salt and 120 ml/4 fl oz water in a medium, lidded pan. Bring to the boil, cover, reduce the heat to low, and cook for 5 minutes. Remove the lid and boil away all but 1 tablespoon or so of the water.

Put the yoghurt in a bowl. Beat lightly with a fork or whisk until smooth and creamy. Mix in ¼ teaspoon salt, the garlic, pepper and dried mint. Now put the contents of the spinach pan into the bowl with the yoghurt. Stir to mix.

Hameed and Parveen Haroon's

Yoghurt 'Kadhi' (Dahi Ki Karhi) PAKISTAN

Kadhis, a beloved food all over the Indian subcontinent, are soupy stews generally made with chickpea flour and thinned yoghurt that are first mixed, and then cooked with a variety of additions from dumplings to vegetables. They are, for most of us, a familiar, heart-warming comfort food or soul food, call it what you may, with many regional variations.

This particular *kadhi* from the Sindh region of Pakistan is a take on the dish, not quite a true *kadhi*, but a faux one. They do without the chickpea flour altogether here.

I got this particular recipe twice, once from the son, Hameed Haroon (publisher of Pakistan's leading newspaper, *Dawn*) and again, with some subtle differences, from his mother, Parveen Haroon. The mother explained that they are Meman Muslims from Hyderabad, in Sindh (south-western Pakistan), and that the family was of Afghan descent – Afghanis who, many generations back, had settled in what was then India. This was her grandmother's recipe and originated in Afghan Manzil, as their house in Hyderabad was called. There is a fair amount of Irani blood in the family also, so those with a detective's heart should be able to ferret out a variety of influences. The Haroons like to eat this yoghurt with breads, such as the Kandahari *naan*, and with *pilafs*.

The green chillies are either left whole (the son's recipe) or cut into big pieces (the mother's way.) If you are making this dish for Westerners, I suggest you finely chop the chillies so as not to run the risk of them causing undue havoc.

SERVES 6

- 3 tablespoons corn or peanut oil
- 2 smallish onions, about 200 g/7 oz, peeled and sliced into thin half-rings
- 2 large cloves garlic, peeled and crushed
- 3–4 fresh curry leaves, if available
- 2 medium tomatoes, coarsely chopped
- 2–3 fresh, hot green chillies, finely chopped
- 30 g/1 oz fresh coriander leaves and tender stems, chopped
- ⅛ teaspoon ground turmeric
- salt
- 475 ml/16 fl oz natural yoghurt

Pour the oil into a medium-large frying pan and set over a medium-high heat. When the oil is hot, add the onions and stir and fry until they are golden. Put in the garlic and stir for a few seconds. Now put in the curry leaves, tomatoes, chillies, coriander, turmeric and ½ teaspoon salt. Stir and cook until the seasonings turn into a thick, dark sauce and you can see the oil at the edges of the pan. Turn off the heat.

Empty the yoghurt into a serving bowl. Beat lightly with a fork or whisk until smooth and creamy. Whisk in ½ teaspoon salt. Pour the cooked seasonings on top of the yoghurt. Stir just once in a single direction to create a swirl.

Carrot-Sultana Raita (Gajar Aur Kishmish Ka Raita) INDIA

A sweet and sour relish that is perfect with all Indian meals.

SERVES 4–6

4 tablespoons sultanas
350 ml/12 fl oz natural yoghurt
½ teaspoon salt
1 tablespoon sugar
½ teaspoon ground roasted cumin seeds (see page 339)
freshly ground black pepper
¼ teaspoon cayenne pepper, or to taste
2 medium carrots, peeled and coarsely grated

Cover the sultanas in a generous amount of boiling water and soak for 3 hours. Drain.

Put the yoghurt in a bowl. Beat lightly with a fork or whisk until creamy. Add the salt, sugar, roasted cumin, black pepper and cayenne pepper. Stir to mix. Add the carrots and the drained sultanas. Mix again. This *raita* may be covered and refrigerated until needed.

Fresh Tomato Chutney SOUTH AFRICA

Here is a delightful, hot, sour and slightly sweet, fresh chutney recipe from a Gujarati South African. She just throws all the necessary ingredients into a blender. It is that simple. While this chutney complements all manner of vegetarian snack foods (Manjula is a strict vegetarian), I find that it is also an ideal dip for most of the kebabs in this book and for all manner of chips and fried foods. It also makes for an unusual salad dressing.

MAKES ABOUT 350 ML/12 FL OZ

2 medium tomatoes, about 285 g/10 oz, chopped
1 clove garlic, peeled and chopped
1-cm/½-inch piece fresh ginger, peeled and chopped
3 fresh, hot bird's eye chillies or any slim, hot fresh green chillies
¾ teaspoon salt
1 tablespoon lemon juice
½ teaspoon ground, roasted cumin seeds (see page 339), or plain ground cumin
2½–3 teaspoons jaggery or brown sugar

Put all the ingredients into a blender and blend until smooth.

Fresh Tomato-Coriander Chutney

PAKISTAN

A simple, fresh chutney that goes particularly well with minced Beef 'Chappli' Kebabs (see page 218), but may be put on the table with all Indian meals.

SERVES 6

285 g/10 oz tomatoes, peeled and finely chopped
30 g/1 oz fresh coriander leaves, chopped
3–5 fresh, hot green bird's eye or other green chillies
½–¾ teaspoon salt

Put the tomatoes, coriander and chillies in a bowl. Toss to mix. Add the salt just before serving and mix again.

Quick Onion and Cherry Tomato Relish

USA

Some version of this Indian relish is made wherever there are Indians. Whereas regular tomatoes are used in most countries, I have taken to using the smaller cherry tomatoes as they are available year round and have a more robust flavour. In the winter, they are amongst the few tomatoes that taste like real tomatoes.

SERVES 4

24 cherry tomatoes, quartered
140 g/5 oz onions, peeled and finely diced
1 teaspoon salt
1 teaspoon ground, roasted cumin seeds (see page 339)
¼ teaspoon cayenne pepper
2–3 tablespoons fresh lemon juice

Put the tomatoes, onions, salt, cumin and cayenne pepper into a bowl and toss. Add the lemon juice slowly, tasting as you go. The amount you need will depend upon the sourness of the tomatoes. Mix again.

Fresh Grape Chutney (Angoor Ki Lonji) INDIA

A sweet, sour and hot chutney that is quick and easy to prepare, it may be served with almost any Indian meal. It is equally wonderful with a roast chicken or any cold poultry.

This chutney is not a preserve. It has a shelf life of just a few days and needs refrigeration.

SERVES 6–8

- ¼ teaspoon whole cumin seeds
- ¼ teaspoon whole *kalonji* (nigella)
- ¼ teaspoon whole fenugreek seeds
- ¼ teaspoon whole fennel seeds
- 1 tablespoons ground *amchoor*
- 1 tablespoon sugar
- ½ teaspoon ground ginger
- ½ teaspoon ground, roasted cumin seeds (see page 339)
- ¾ teaspoon salt
- ½ teaspoon cayenne pepper
- 1½ tablespoons corn, peanut or olive oil
- ¼ teaspoon whole brown mustard seeds
- 340 g/12 oz green, seedless grapes, cut in half, lengthways

Put the cumin, *kalonji*, fenugreek and fennel in a small dish.

Combine the *amchoor*, sugar, ginger, roasted and ground cumin, salt and cayenne pepper in a bowl. Add 250 ml/8 fl oz water and mix.

Pour the oil into a small frying pan and set over a medium heat. When the oil is hot, put in the mustard seeds. As soon as they begin to pop, a matter of seconds, put in the mixture of whole cumin, *kalonji*, fenugreek and fennel. A second later, pour in the liquid mixture from the bowl. Stir and bring to a simmer. Simmer gently on a low heat for 10 minutes. Increase the heat to high. Let the sauce bubble away for a minute. Now put in all the grapes. Continue to cook on a high heat, stirring at the same time, for 5–6 minutes or until the sauce is slightly syrupy.

Once the chutney has cooked, it may be covered and refrigerated.

From Bar-B-Q Tonight, Karachi

Peanut Chutney PAKISTAN

Pakistanis love their kebabs, and Bar-B-Q Tonight is the Karachi landmark that specialises in them. A huge, rambling, informal restaurant on many floors, feeding a thousand people a day, it prides itself on being both traditional and modern. With its kebabs are served a variety of pickles and chutneys, from mint-flavoured gherkins to this, somewhat newfangled chutney, that combines crushed peanuts with tomato ketchup and chillies. It is also very good in a ham and cheese sandwich.

MAKES 5 TABLESPOONS

2 tablespoons natural peanut butter
2 tablespoons tomato ketchup
1 clove garlic, peeled and crushed to a pulp
½ teaspoon cayenne pepper

Combine all the ingredients. Thin the sauce by adding about 4 teaspoons of water.

Spicy Peanut Sauce

INDONESIA

This is the sweet, sour, salty, hot and nutty sauce that is served over Indonesian *satays*. You may also pass it along on the side with other kebabs or dribble it over salads.

MAKES 475 ML/16 FL OZ

125 g/4½ oz roasted peanuts
2 tablespoons corn, peanut or olive oil
3 tablespoons peeled and finely chopped shallots
2 cloves garlic, peeled and crushed to a pulp
¾ teaspoon cayenne pepper
½ teaspoon salt
2 teaspoons sugar
freshly ground black pepper
4 teaspoons lime or lemon juice

Put the peanuts in a coffee grinder or other spice grinder in four batches and grind as finely as possible.

Pour the oil into a small pan and set it over a medium heat. Put in the shallots and garlic. Stir and fry for 2–3 minutes or until they are golden. Add 475 ml/16 fl oz water, the peanuts, cayenne pepper, salt, sugar and black pepper. Stir and bring to a vigorous simmer. Simmer on a medium-low heat, stirring now and then, for 20–30 minutes, or until the sauce has thickened and is creamy. Add the lime or lemon juice, stir well, and taste for a balance of flavours.

Walnut-Mint Chutney

PAKISTAN

A wonderful fresh chutney from north-western Pakistan that may be served with all manner of kebabs and, indeed, with all Indian meals (pictured here with Tomato and Apple Chutney, page 302). The usual souring agent in this chutney is *anardana* – dried, sour, pomegranate seeds, taken from fruit that grow as abundantly in this region as the walnuts that this recipe also demands. I have had little luck with *anardana* in the West. I can buy it all right. But the seeds are dark and unyielding, nothing like the soft brown, melting seeds found in Pakistan or, indeed, in the villages of Indian Punjab. I have just given up on them and have resorted, as here, to lemon juice.

SERVES 8

- 30 g/1 oz fresh mint leaves, well washed and coarsely chopped
- 60 g/2 oz shelled walnuts
- 1 clove garlic, peeled and crushed to a pulp
- 4–5 fresh, hot green chillies (such as bird's eye chillies or any of the cayenne type of chilli), sliced
- 1 tablespoon lemon juice or to taste
- ½ teaspoon salt
- 4 tablespoons natural yoghurt

Put the mint leaves, walnuts, garlic, chillies, lemon juice, salt and 5 tablespoons water into a blender and blend, pushing down with a rubber spatula when needed, until you have a smooth paste.

Put the yoghurt into a bowl. Beat lightly with a fork until smooth and creamy. Add the paste from the blender and mix. Taste for a balance of seasonings, making any adjustments that are needed.

Richard Terry's

Tomato and Apple Chutney

UK

This very British-Indian recipe has been adapted from *Indian Cookery*, a slim volume published in 1861 and written by Richard Terry who was *chef de cuisine* at the very popular Oriental Club in London. He calls it Tomata and Apple Chutnee.

No Indian ever used apples in a chutney, though tomatoes by themselves were quite acceptable. The base for the preserve-type chutney in India has always the pectin-rich, sour green mango. It is interesting to note a parallel change-around: the British sorely missed their apple pies in India. To make them, Calcutta's desperate British housewives very often resorted to substituting the green mango for the firm, slightly tart apple they would have used at home.

You will notice that ginger powder is used instead of the fresh rhizome. This was the common practice at the time. In the original recipe, chopped chillies are added towards the end. As it was not clear to me if these were dried or fresh, I chose the fresh.

For the kind of curry this chutney was served with, see page 56.

Makes about 1 litre/35 fl oz

800 g/1 lb 12 oz can whole plum tomatoes
4 sour Granny Smith-type apples, peeled, cored and cut into 5-mm/¼-inch dice
350 ml/12 fl oz cider vinegar
3 large cloves garlic, peeled and crushed to a pulp
2 teaspoons ground ginger
2 teaspoons salt
340 g/11½ oz dark brown sugar
1 teaspoon cayenne pepper
3–4 fresh, hot green chillies, thinly sliced
5 tablespoons sultanas

Empty the can of tomatoes into a large, heavy, preferably non-stick pan. Break up the tomatoes with your fingers. Add the apples, vinegar, garlic, ginger, salt, sugar and cayenne pepper. Stir to mix, then bring to the boil. Reduce the heat to medium-low and cook, stirring now and then, for about 1 hour. Stir in the chillies and sultanas and cook gently for a further 5 minutes. The chutney should be just thick enough to lightly coat the back of a spoon. It will thicken more as it cools.

Let the chutney cool completely. Then put it into jars, screw on the lids, and refrigerate.

Quince and Lemon Chutney USA

Indians make chutneys out of whatever they can. Once one person in the family starts preparing it, and if the others like it, it quickly settles into a family 'tradition'. Well, here is one such 'tradition' that I started at our country house.

Every autumn, a quince-growing farmer supplies the fruit to our local food store, charmingly called Random Harvest. They sit in a beautiful basket, lending their magical aroma to the premises, but almost no one buys the fruit. I used to buy the quinces now and then to make a Moroccan lamb *tajine* but mostly I used them to decorate my sideboard . . . until I started making this chutney – which is now present at all meals from Thanksgiving to Christmas.

You need to start preparing the lemon two to three days in advance, so allow yourself the extra time.

MAKES 1 LITRE/1 3/4 PINTS

1 organically grown lemon
salt
5-cm/2-inch piece fresh ginger, peeled and chopped
2 cloves garlic, peeled and chopped
350 ml/12 fl oz cider vinegar
4 quinces, each about 285 g/10 oz
1 tablespoon corn or peanut oil
½ teaspoon *kalonji* (nigella seeds)
1 teaspoon cayenne pepper
¼ teaspoon whole fennel seeds
325 g/11 oz sugar

Cut the lemon, including the skin, into 5-mm/¼-inch dice and put in a glass jar. Add 1 teaspoon salt and shake to mix. Cover the jar and put it in a window that gets a lot of sun for two or three days. Shake the jar every day.

Put the ginger, garlic and 120 ml/4 fl oz of the vinegar into a blender. Blend until smooth.

Pour the remaining 250 ml/8 fl oz vinegar into a non-metallic bowl. Peel the quinces and core. Cut each of them into six to eight sections. Now cut these sections, crossways, into 3-mm/⅛-inch thick slices, letting the slices fall into the bowl with the vinegar.

Pour the oil into a stainless steel or porcelain-lined pan and set over a medium-high heat. When the oil is hot, put in the *kalonji* seeds. Let them sizzle for 2–3 seconds, then add the ginger-garlic paste from the blender. Stir a few times, then add all the fruit with their vinegar, the cayenne pepper, fennel and sugar. Bring to the boil, stirring as you do so. Reduce the heat to low and let the chutney simmer gently for 20 minutes.

Allow the chutney to cool. Then bottle and refrigerate it.

Green Sauce or Coriander Chutney

SOUTH AFRICA

In South Africa this is known as the sauce that is served with *biryani*. It is actually a simple, coriander chutney. Instead of the 'sour milk' that South Africans can get in their supermarkets, I have used yoghurt.

This vitamin-rich, fresh chutney may be served with all Indian foods.

SERVES 6–8

30 g/1 oz fresh coriander leaves, well washed
2–3 fresh, hot green chillies, chopped
1 large or 2 medium-sized cloves garlic, peeled and chopped
½ teaspoon salt, or to taste
1 tablespoon lemon juice
250 ml/8 fl oz natural yoghurt

Combine the coriander, chillies, garlic, salt, lemon juice and 3 tablespoons water in a blender. Blend, pushing down with a rubber spatula as needed, until smooth.

Put the yoghurt in a bowl. Beat lightly with a fork until smooth. Add the contents of the blender and mix in. Taste for a balance of seasonings.

Fresh Mint Chutney

INDIA

Try to make this chutney without adding any water to your blender. You will need to push down with a rubber spatula several times.

MAKES ABOUT 5 TABLESPOONS

Bunch fresh mint, enough to yield 50 g/½ oz of just leaves
115 g/4 oz tomato, chopped
4–8 fresh, hot, green chillies, chopped
4 cloves garlic, peeled and chopped
1 teaspoon ground *amchoor* or lemon juice
⅛ teaspoon salt, or to taste

Remove the leaves from the mint stalks and wash well. Leave them with the water that clings to them naturally. Put the tomato into the blender first and blend to a paste. Now add the mint and all the other ingredients. Blend to a paste, pushing down with a rubber spatula whenever necessary. Store, covered, in the refrigerator.

Thai Cucumber Salad

THAILAND

This, sweet, sour, salty and hot salad may be served with Thai and other South-East Asian curries.

SERVES 4

- a young cucumber with undeveloped seeds, about 18 cm/7 inches in length, or 2 smaller cucumbers, sliced, without peeling, into 3-mm/⅛-inch rounds
- 120 ml/4 fl oz white vinegar
- 100 g/3½ oz sugar
- ½ teaspoon salt
- 1 teaspoon coarsely crushed red chilli powder
- 2 fresh, green and red bird's eye chillies, sliced into fine rounds.

Put the cucumber in a bowl.

Combine the vinegar, sugar, salt and chilli powder in a small pan and bring to a simmer. Simmer on a low heat for 10 minutes. Pour this syrup over the cucumbers. Allow them to sit in the syrup for at least an hour, tossing now and then. When wanting to serve, lift the cucumber slices out of their syrup and arrange on a plate. Scatter the cut chillies over the top.

Seasoned Fish Sauce (Nuoc Cham)

VIETNAM

Perfect for serving with Vietnamese grilled and fried foods.

SERVES 4

- 5 tablespoons fish sauce (*nuoc mam*)
- 3 tablespoons white vinegar
- 2 tablespoons lime or lemon juice
- 2 tablespoons sugar
- 1–3 fresh, hot green and red chillies (or just one colour), cut crossways into thin slices

Combine all the ingredients in a bowl and mix well.

Mixed Vegetable Pickle

INDIA

This is the sort of pickle that is put on the table in South Africa with Beans-in-a-Loaf (Bunny Chow, page 185), but you could serve it with all Indian meals. Rather like *cornichons*, it also goes well with roast beef, roast lamb, sausages and baked hams.

When cutting the cauliflower, take care to make small neat pieces. Just chopping it up will only end up in a lot of unusable debris. The best method is to break off large florets and then begin by slicing their stems into rounds, crossways. Keep cutting the florets into ever-smaller florets until the desired size is reached.

MAKES 1 LITRE/1 3/4 PINTS

- 3 medium carrots, about 225 g/8 oz, peeled and cut into 5-mm/¼-inch cubes
- 225 g/8 oz cauliflower florets, cut neatly into 5-mm/¼-inch pieces
- salt
- 3 tablespoons corn, peanut or olive oil
- 3 cloves garlic, peeled and cut into fine slivers
- 2½-cm/1-inch piece fresh ginger, peeled and cut first into thin slices and then into thin slivers
- 10 fresh, hot green bird's eye chillies, cut crossways into rounds
- ¼ teaspoon ground turmeric
- ½–2 teaspoons cayenne pepper (any pure chilli powder with a bright red colour is ideal)
- 2 teaspoons whole brown mustard seeds, lightly ground in a clean coffee grinder or other spice grinder
- 300 ml/10 fl oz cider vinegar

Put the carrots and cauliflower in a bowl. Sprinkle with 1 tablespoon salt and rub it in. Cover with an inverted plate and set aside for 24 hours.

Pour the oil into a frying pan and set over a medium heat. When the oil is hot, put in the garlic, ginger and green chillies. Stir for a minute, then take off the heat. Add the turmeric, cayenne pepper and mustard seeds. Mix.

Pour the vinegar into a 1-litre/1¾-pint jar and add 4½ teaspoons salt. Mix well. Add the contents of the frying pan. Place a non-corrosive lid on the top. This pickle can now be refrigerated and used as needed. It will keep for 3–4 weeks.

Green Chillies in Vinegar

SOUTH AND SOUTH-EAST ASIA

There are many versions of this, using both lime juice and vinegar. My mother used to slice her green chillies into fine rounds, put them in a bowl with finely shredded young ginger and a little salt and then mix this with lime juice that she had brought to the boil once. This made for a quick pickle. It lasted several days. It was only eaten in small quantities but we all loved it.

This simpler version, which is served on tables all over South-East Asia, consists of nothing more than sliced chillies in vinegar. I measure by volume here. You need an equal volume of chillies and vinegar. You may use just fresh green chillies – bird's eye or the slim, long cayenne variety – or a mixture of fresh green and red chillies, which look very pretty together. Remember that in most Asian recipes, seeds are never removed from fresh chillies. The whole point, after all, is to excite the palate with minor, controlled fireworks!

SERVES 6–8

4 tablespoons cider vinegar or any other vinegar of your choice
1 teaspoon salt
4 tablespoons fresh, hot green chillies, thinly sliced

Combine the vinegar and salt in a small jar. Mix. Add the chillies. Cover with a non-corrosive lid and set aside for 24 hours before using. Refrigerate after that.

My sister Kamal's

Instant Punjabi-Style Pickle (Gobi, Shaljum, Gajar Achar)

INDIA

Pickles are an essential element of all Indian meals and have been since ancient times. Two or three jars of them, nearly always homemade, are fixtures at the table. Whether diners want to dip into them or not is their choice. Each region has its own specialities, not one but dozens.

This particular pickle is fairly common in the north-west region of Punjab. Sweet and sour, it is always made in winter with winter vegetables – cauliflower, turnips and carrots. The sweetening comes from the boiled down and solidified form of sugar cane juice known as jaggery, also a winter product, and the souring comes from local vinegars. (When buying jaggery ask for the softest and crumbliest kind available.)

Pickles take time to mature. The most amenable aspect of this pickle is that just a little bit of cooking makes it instantly edible. Once made, it can be stored in the refrigerator for several weeks.

Try this with your Christmas meal. I love to put it out with my turkey or Smithfield ham, just as you might a piccalilli. I am convinced the Western piccalilli is based on the pickles and chutneys of India. Indeed, Mrs Isabella Beeton, the Victorian cookbook author, writing in *The Book of Household Management* in 1861, refers to piccalilli as 'India Pickle'. Piccalilli was seen as a very desirable accompaniment to cold roasts and potted meats in the United Kingdom as early as 1694. Well, here is the real product – or one of them – that piccalilli was trying to imitate.

Mustard oil is the traditional oil used for pickling in most of India. Extra virgin olive oil makes an interesting substitute. Corn oil and peanut oil may also be used.

MAKES 1 LITRE/1 3/4 PINTS

3 tablespoons well-crumbled jaggery or light brown sugar
175 ml/6 fl oz cider vinegar
120 ml/4 fl oz mustard, extra virgin olive, peanut or corn oil
1 teaspoon garlic, peeled and crushed
1 teaspoon fresh ginger, peeled and finely grated
400 g/14 oz delicate cauliflower florets
5 medium carrots, peeled and cut into 5 x 1 cm/2 x ½ inch pieces
255 g/9 oz small turnips, about 3, peeled, quartered and cut into 1-cm/1/2-inch thick slices
2 teaspoons whole brown mustard seeds ground in a clean coffee grinder
2 teaspoons salt
a mixture of ¾ teaspoon cayenne pepper and 1¼ teaspoons bright red paprika
½ teaspoon garam masala (see page 327), or store-bought

Combine the jaggery (or sugar) and vinegar in a small pan and set over a low heat until the jaggery has dissolved. Remove from the heat.

Pour the oil into a large pan and set over a medium heat. When the oil is hot, add the garlic and ginger. Stir for 30 seconds, then put in the cauliflower, carrots and turnips. Stir and cook for about a minute or until the vegetables are coated with oil and still fairly crisp. Reduce the heat to low and add the ground mustard, salt, cayenne and paprika mixture and *garam masala*. Stir to mix. Add the jaggery-vinegar mixture and stir. Take off the heat and allow to cool. Put in a clean jar and refrigerate. This pickle may be eaten immediately but will also keep for 3–4 weeks.

Blood Oranges with Black Pepper (Malta Aur Kali Mirch)

PAKISTAN

In north-western Pakistan, the area around Peshawar, blood oranges are plentiful and often served in slices as a salad, with a sprinkling of black pepper.

SERVES 4–6

4 blood oranges
freshly ground black pepper

Peel the oranges, retaining their round shape, and then cut them crossways into 5–6 slices. Arrange the slices in a single layer and dust generously with freshly ground, slightly coarse black pepper.

Zarrin Zardari's

Fruit 'Chaat' (Phul Ki Chaat)

PAKISTAN

This *chaat* was offered to me by one of Karachi's most elegant hostesses, who also happens to be Benazir Bhutto's stepmother-in-law. It was served from a trolley at teatime, along with an array of pastries, delicate sandwiches and sweetmeats. *Chaat*s, on the entire Indian subcontinent, are a world unto themselves and hard to categorise. They are hot, sour and sometimes slightly sweet snack foods. They could be made out of chickpeas, potatoes, sweet potatoes (the dry, floury kind), cucumbers and all kinds of fruit that are smothered with ground spices and then doused with either fresh chutneys (tamarind, mint, coriander) or just plain lime juice. We buy them from vendors on beaches and eat them off leaves, we make them at home for humble lunches and we are not afraid to serve them at grand teas for presidents. This particular fruit *chaat* may also be considered to be a kind of salad.

I like to cook my chickpeas at home in a pressure cooker with a touch of salt (you will need to soak 90 g/3 oz dried chickpeas and then pressure-cook them with ½ teaspoon salt, but you could just as easily use canned chickpeas. Just rinse them out well first.

Do not be put off by the strong, truffle-like aroma of black salt. It is essential to the flavour of many *chaat*s. The aroma recedes into the background, leaving its undefinable but required essence. (From the Ayurvedic point of view, black salt is a digestive.)

Most of the fruits in this recipe are available year round. Instead of the peach, you could use grape halves, sliced star fruit, sliced kiwis or large strawberries. It is best to cut fruit that discolours, such as bananas and peaches, at the last minute, shortly before serving.

SERVES 6

FOR THE TAMARIND-DATE CHUTNEY

- 180 g/6 oz seedless dates, chopped
- 8 tablespoons thick tamarind paste (see page 345)
- ½ teaspoon salt
- 5–6 generous grinds of fresh black pepper
- ⅛ teaspoon well-crumbled black salt
- 1½ teaspoons lime or lemon juice
- 1½ teaspoons sugar, or to taste

- 2 waxy potatoes, about 90 g/3 oz, boiled, allowed to cool and cut into 7-mm/⅓-inch dice (do not refrigerate)
- 285 g/10 oz cooked, drained chickpeas
- 1 orange, peeled and cut first into 1-cm/½-inch thick rounds and then into quarters
- 1 large ripe peach, peeled and cut into 1-cm/½-inch pieces
- 1 medium banana, peeled and cut into 7-mm/⅓-inch thick rounds
- ½ teaspoon salt
- freshly ground black pepper
- ¼ teaspoon cayenne pepper, or to taste

Combine the dates and 300 ml/10 fl oz water in a small pan and bring to a simmer. Cover and simmer gently for 20 minutes. Push the dates through a coarse strainer to get a thick pulp.

Put the tamarind paste in a bowl. Add the date pulp and all the other ingredients for the chutney. Mix well and taste for a balance of seasonings.

In a large stainless steel or non-metallic bowl, combine the potatoes, chickpeas, orange, peach, banana, salt, black pepper and cayenne pepper. Toss to mix. Add the tamarind chutney and toss again. Serve immediately.

Crisply Fried Onion or Shallot Slices for Garnishing and Sauces

INDIA

Sliced onions, fried until they are reddish-brown and crisp, are an essential flavour in Indian Muslim cookery. They may be used as a garnish over *pullaos*, *biryanis* and *dal*s or they may be ground or crumbled and added to the marinade for kebab meats or to the sauces of stewed meats. In their ground or crumbled form, they are known as *berista*. In South Africa, fried onions meant for crumbling are frozen first as this makes the crushing much easier. Fried shallots are equally important in South-East Asian cookery, where they are sprinkled over soups, snacks and curries.

Do not use very large onions for this. They have very thick rings. Here you need the rings to be as delicate as possible. Onions that weigh 140 g/5 oz or less are ideal, as are all shallots.

The oil used in frying these onions and shallots is never wasted. It has a lovely aroma. I strain it through a sieve lined with a sheet of kitchen paper and then use it for cooking my vegetables and meats. Sometimes, when I have just blanched green beans in salted water and drained them, I toss them with a few tablespoons of this oil.

Fried onions and shallots keep well for several weeks in a tightly closed jar or a zip-lock plastic bag. I generally make more than I need and store what is left over for future use. They do not need refrigeration. They are, as I always say, like money in the bank.

MAKES ABOUT A 500 ML/18-FL OZ MEASURE

3 medium onions, about 425 g/15 oz, or an equal weight of shallots

corn or peanut oil for shallow frying

Cut each onion in half, lengthways, and then slice it evenly, crossways, into thin slices. Shallots should be cut similarly into very fine slivers.

Line two plates with a double layer of kitchen paper and keep nearby.

Set a large sieve over a bowl and keep near the cooking area.

Pour enough oil into a large frying pan to come to a depth of about 3 mm/⅛ inch, and set over a medium heat. When the oil is hot, put in all the sliced onions (or shallots). Stir and fry for about 8 minutes. The onions will have begun to brown. Reduce the heat to medium-low. Stir and fry for another 2 minutes or so. Now reduce the heat to low. Continue to stir and fry until most of the slices are reddish-brown. This will take about 12 minutes in all. Remove the frying pan from the heat and quickly empty its contents into the sieve set over a bowl. Lift up the sieve, shake it over the bowl once or twice to get rid of excess oil, and then empty the onions over one of the plates lined with kitchen paper. Spread out the onions as much as you can. Let the onions sit for 5 minutes on the first plate, then spread them out on the second plate lined with kitchen paper to absorb more oil. Allow them to cool completely. They may now be put in a lidded jar or zip-lock plastic bag, where they will keep, unrefrigerated, for several weeks.

To make *berista*, the onions are crumbled, or, if more of a paste is desired, they may be put into a clean coffee grinder or other spice grinder and ground to a coarse paste. Some people like to freeze the fried onions first as they are then much easier to crush.

Raw Onion Rings (Pyaz Ka Laccha) INDIA

These are a common garnish for kebabs and are easy to prepare. The most important thing to remember here is that, unlike the raw onion slices used in hamburgers (which are, after all, a kind of kebab), these rings are very delicate and can only be made with smaller onions, those that weigh about 140 g/5 oz or less.

When raw onion rings are used as a garnish for kebabs, they are just spread over them without a dressing of any sort. They can also be dressed and eaten as a salad/relish. See the next recipe for that.

1 medium onion, about 140 g/5oz

Cut the onion, crossways, into paper-thin slices. You could also cut the onion in half, lengthways, and then cut the halves, crossways, evenly into paper-thin slices. Separate the slices into rings or half-rings. Put them into a bowl filled with icy water, cover, and refrigerate for 2–3 hours. Drain the onions and pat them dry. They are now ready to be used as a garnish.

Raw Onion Ring Salad (Luccha) — INDIA

This simple salad was always on our family table when I was a child.

SERVES 4

1 medium onion, about 140 g/5oz
½ teaspoon salt
1 tablespoon lemon juice
1 teaspoon dried mint, well crumbled, optional

Cut the onion, then soak and dry the rings or half-rings as in the preceding recipe. Put them in a bowl. Add all the other ingredients. Toss to mix.

Gingery Salad Dressing — USA

This is a dressing I frequently use when dressing green salads to serve with kebabs. You may also pour this over blanched green beans.

MAKES 10 TABLESPOONS

1 tablespoon red wine vinegar
1 tablespoon lemon juice
½ teaspoon salt
¼ teaspoon cayenne pepper
juice squeezed from a tablespoon of very finely grated, peeled fresh ginger
120 ml/4 fl oz olive or salad oil

Combine all the ingredients in a jar, close the lid tightly, and shake until blended.

Fresh Limeade (Nimbu Paani or Nimbu Soda) INDIA

One of India's most popular drinks, this may be made with water or soda water. In Jakarta, Indonesia, I have had it made with cucumber juice. Just peel a cucumber and chop it, then throw it into a blender and strain the juice.

The recipe may be easily doubled or tripled.

SERVES 1

- **5 tablespoons lime or lemon juice**
- **4 tablespoons extra fine sugar**
- **water or soda water**
- **4–5 ice cubes**

Combine the lime juice and sugar and set aside until the sugar has dissolved. Stir well. Add about 175 ml/6 fl oz water or soda water and the ice cubes. Stir and taste for a correct balance of flavours.

Ginger Lassi INDIA

Lassis are drinks made with thinned yoghurt. They may be salty or sweet, flavoured with fruit or with spices and herbs. This one would be called a '*namkeen*' or 'salty' *lassi* and is a digestive. It may be served before or during a meal.

The recipe may easily be doubled or tripled.

SERVES 1

- **120 ml/4 fl oz natural yoghurt**
- **1 teaspoon peeled and very finely grated fresh ginger**
- **¼ teaspoon salt**
- **¼ teaspoon ground, roasted cumin seeds (see page 339)**
- **about 8–10 ice cubes**

Put the yoghurt into a bowl. Beat lightly with a fork or small whisk until light and creamy. Hold the grated ginger over the yoghurt bowl and squeeze out all its liquid. Discard the ginger pulp in your hand. Add the salt and cumin seeds. Mix well. Now slowly pour in about 120 ml/4 fl oz water, mixing as you go. Add the ice cubes and mix again. Taste for a balance of flavours and pour into a serving glass.

Simple, Sweet Lassi

INDIA

Here is a sweet version of the *lassi*. The recipe may easily be doubled or tripled.

SERVES 1

120 ml/4 fl oz natural yoghurt
2 tablespoons sugar
⅛–¼ teaspoon ground cardamom seeds
about 8–10 ice cubes

Put the yoghurt into a bowl. Beat lightly with a fork or small whisk until light and creamy. Add the sugar and ground cardamom. Mix well. Now, slowly pour in about 120 ml/4 fl oz water, mixing as you go. Add the ice cubes and mix again. Taste for a balance of flavours and pour into a serving glass.

Nepalese Cinnamon Tea

MYANMAR

A lovely, light, cinnamony tea, perfect after a rich dinner. The sweetening comes from jaggery, raw Indian sugar. If you cannot find any, use South-East Asian palm sugar. As a last resort, use dark brown sugar. This Nepalese tea, for some reason, is much loved in Myanmar.

SERVES 4

1 litre/32 fl oz water
2 medium sticks cinnamon
2 tablespoons jaggery or 5 teaspoons dark brown sugar
2 teaspoons black tea

Put the water, cinnamon and jaggery in a lidded pan and bring to a simmer. As soon as bubbles appear, put in the tea, cover, and turn off the heat. Let the tea steep for 3–4 minutes. Strain and serve.

Saffron Tea

INDIA

This is a most unusual, sensuous tea from Kashmir. Saffron grows here in the valley near Pampur, a vast sea of blue crocuses, yielding enough stamens to supply not just Kashmir but all of India.

Amongst the first activities for every Kashmiri family is to light the family samovar. This keeps them well provided with tea from morning until nightfall. If honoured guests arrive, a pinch of saffron is thrown into the samovar and a few almonds added to the tea cups.

But this saffron tea is even more special. It is a tea that has no tea in it. It is made just with saffron, sugar and cardamom. We were served it in a Kashmiri home in gold-rimmed porcelain cups. We were enchanted.

SERVES 4

¾ teaspoon loosely-packed saffron threads
900 ml/32 fl oz water
3–4 cardamom pods, lightly crushed
5 teaspoons sugar

Place the saffron on a piece of foil. Fold some of the foil over the saffron and crush it with a rolling pin or a wooden potato masher.

Put the water, cardamom and sugar in a lidded pan and bring to a simmer. As soon as bubbles appear, add the crushed saffron, cover, and turn off the heat. Let the tea steep for about 1 hour. Heat again, strain, and serve.

From Chef Sarnsern Gajaseni at the Oriental Hotel, Bangkok

Red Curry Paste

THAILAND

This paste is enough for two dishes of pork, beef, chicken, prawns, squid, fish, crabs, lobster meat or hard-boiled eggs, each serving about four people. Because our chillies do not seem to give the same red colour that Thai chillies provide, I have added a fair amount of paprika to the recipe. Make sure that it has a lovely, bright red colour.

Fresh lemon grass stalks have a knot at the very bottom. Remove that before finely slicing, crossways, and at a slight angle, starting at the bottom end and going up about 15 cm/6 inches. Lemon grass will not blend thoroughly unless it has been sliced first. Galangal is fairly tough as well and needs first to be to cut, crossways, into thin slices, and then chopped before being put into the blender.

Fresh coriander, if bought from Indian grocers, generally comes with whitish roots which just need washing and coarse chopping before being put in the blender. If you cannot get them, use a small handful of the leaves for the required aroma.

I like to make double this amount and then divide it in four and freeze it, well labelled, in four separate containers. It freezes very well and is like money in the bank. Thai curries then become so easy to prepare.

MAKES ABOUT 10 TABLESPOONS

10–12 dried, hot red chillies (of the long, cayenne variety)
5 cloves garlic, peeled and chopped
140 g/5 oz shallots, chopped
1 tablespoon fresh lemon grass that has been thinly sliced, crossways
3 thin slices peeled fresh or frozen galangal, or ginger
1 thin slice of fresh kaffir lime rind, about 4 x ½ cm/1½ x ¼ inch, or dried rind, soaked in water for 30 minutes
6–8 fresh coriander roots, washed well and coarsely chopped
freshly ground white pepper
¼ teaspoon shrimp paste or 2 anchovies from a can, chopped
½ teaspoon ground cumin
½ teaspoon ground coriander
2 tablespoons bright red paprika

Soak the chillies in 5 tablespoons hot water for 1–2 hours. (You could also put them in a microwave oven for 2–3 minutes and then let them sit for 20–30 minutes.)

Put the chillies, together with their soaking liquid, into a blender, along with all the remaining ingredients in the order listed. Blend, pushing down with a rubber spatula as many times as necessary, until you have a smooth paste.

What you do not use immediately should be refrigerated or frozen.

From the Grand Hyatt Erawan, Bangkok

Thai-Style Penang Chilli Paste

THAILAND

This is the paste for a wonderful Thai-style curry, best enjoyed with plain rice. The chilli paste is enough for two recipes, using 450 g/1 lb of meat or fish each. I grind the paste all in one go and then freeze half of it for another day.

MAKES 10–11 TABLESPOONS

- ½ teaspoon whole white peppercorns
- 1 teaspoon coriander seeds
- ½ teaspoon cumin seeds
- 10 large, cayenne-type, dried red chillies, seeds removed and soaked in 4 tablespoons boiling water for 1–2 hours
- 1 stick fresh lemon grass, the bottom 15 cm/6 inches cut crossways into very fine slices
- 5 cm/2 inches fresh galangal, peeled and chopped, or frozen galangal or ginger
- 3 fresh coriander roots
- 140 g/5 oz shallots, chopped
- 10 cloves garlic, peeled and chopped
- ½ teaspoon shrimp paste, or 2 anchovies from a can, chopped
- 1 tablespoon peanut butter

Put the peppercorns, coriander seeds and cumin seeds into a clean coffee grinder or other spice grinder and grind to a powder. Empty into a blender. Add the chillies and their soaking liquid, the lemon grass, galangal, coriander roots, shallots, garlic, shrimp paste and peanut butter. Blend until smooth, pushing down with a rubber spatula when needed.

Unused paste may be refrigerated or frozen.

From Chef Sarnsern Gajaseni at the Oriental Hotel, Bangkok

Green Curry Paste

THAILAND

This paste is enough for two dishes of pork, beef, chicken, prawns, squid, fish, crabs, lobster meat or hard-boiled eggs, each serving about four people. It is very similar to the Red Curry Paste on page 318 except, instead of dried red chillies, it requires many more fresh, green bird's eye chillies.

Fresh lemon grass stalks have a knot at the very bottom. Remove that before finely slicing, crossways, and at a slight angle, starting at the bottom end and going up about 15 cm/6 inches. Lemon grass will not blend thoroughly unless it has been sliced first. Galangal is fairly tough as well, and needs first to be to cut, crossways, into thin slices, and then chopped before being put into the blender.

Fresh coriander, if bought from Indian grocers, generally comes with whitish roots which just need washing and coarse chopping before being put in the blender. If you cannot get them, use a small handful of the leaves for the required aroma.

I like to make double this amount and then divide it in four and freeze it, well labelled, in four separate containers. It freezes very well and is like money in the bank. Thai curries then become so easy to prepare.

MAKES ABOUT 10 TABLESPOONS

14 fresh, green bird's eye chillies
5 cloves garlic, peeled and chopped
140 g/5 oz shallots, chopped
1 tablespoon fresh lemon grass, thinly sliced
3 thin slices peeled fresh or frozen galangal, or ginger
1 thin slice of fresh kaffir lime rind, about 4 x ½ cm/1½ x ¼ inch, or dried rind, soaked in water for 30 minutes
6–8 fresh coriander roots, washed well and coarsely chopped
freshly ground white pepper
¼ teaspoon shrimp paste or 2 anchovies from a can, chopped
½ teaspoon ground cumin
½ teaspoon ground coriander

Cut off the chilli stems and chop the chillies coarsely. Put in a blender along with all the remaining ingredients in the order listed. Add 4–5 tablespoons water and blend, pushing down with a rubber spatula as many times as necessary, until you have a smooth paste.

What you do not use immediately should be refrigerated or frozen.

From the Grand Hyatt Erawan, Bangkok

Yellow Curry Paste

THAILAND

Yellow curry paste differs from the red one not only in colour but also in ingredients. It has ginger instead of the stronger galangal. It also has cinnamon, more coriander, turmeric and curry powder. When the cooked dish is served, it is not garnished with kaffir lime leaves but with crisply fried shallots.

This paste is enough for two dishes of pork, beef, chicken, prawns, squid, fish, crabs, lobster meat or hard-boiled eggs, each serving about four people. Leftover paste is best labelled and frozen for later use.

MAKES ABOUT 10 TABLESPOONS

- 7 dried hot red chillies (long ones of the cayenne variety)
- 140 g/5 oz shallots, chopped
- 1 tablespoon fresh lemon grass that has been thinly sliced, crossways
- 10 small or 5 large cloves garlic, peeled and chopped
- 2½-cm/1-inch piece fresh ginger, peeled and chopped
- ½ teaspoon white pepper powder
- 1 teaspoon curry powder
- ½ teaspoon ground cumin
- 1 teaspoon ground coriander
- ½ teaspoon ground cinnamon
- ½ teaspoon shrimp paste or 3 anchovies from a can, chopped
- ½ teaspoon ground turmeric

Soak the red chillies in 5 tablespoons hot water for 1–2 hours. (You could also put them in a microwave oven for 2–3 minutes and then let them sit for 20–30 minutes.)

Put the chillies, together with their soaking liquid, into a blender along with all the remaining ingredients in the order listed. Blend, pushing down with a rubber spatula as many times as necessary, until you have a smooth paste.

What you do not use immediately should be refrigerated or frozen.

From the Grand Hyatt Erawan, Bangkok

Mussaman Curry Paste

THAILAND

The name of this curry paste must have come from *Musalman* (the Indian word for Muslim), traders who landed on Thai shores. It is very similar to Yellow Curry Paste, only the spices are roasted before being ground and galangal is added to the paste. When *mussaman* curries are cooked, bay leaves are thrown in for extra aroma.

This paste is enough for two dishes of pork, beef, chicken, prawns, squid, fish, crabs, lobster meat or hard-boiled eggs, each serving about four people. Leftover paste is best labelled and frozen for later use.

MAKES ABOUT 10 TABLESPOONS

- 7 dried hot red chillies (preferably long ones of the cayenne type)
- ½ teaspoon white peppercorns
- ½ teaspoon whole cumin seeds
- 1 teaspoon whole coriander seeds
- 2½-cm/1-inch piece cinnamon
- 140 g/5 oz shallots, chopped
- 1 tablespoon fresh lemon grass that has been thinly sliced, crossways
- 10 small or 5 large cloves garlic, peeled and chopped
- 2½-cm/1-inch piece fresh ginger, peeled and chopped
- 1 teaspoon curry powder
- ½ teaspoon shrimp paste or 3 anchovies from a can, chopped
- ½ teaspoon ground turmeric

Soak the chillies in 5 tablespoons hot water for 1–2 hours. (You could also put them in a microwave oven for 2–3 minutes and then let them sit for 20–30 minutes.)

Put the peppercorns, cumin seeds, coriander seeds and cinnamon in a small, cast-iron frying pan and set over a medium heat. Stir the spices around until they emit a roasted aroma and turn a shade darker. Empty them into a bowl and allow them to cool. Then grind them as finely as possible in a clean coffee grinder or other spice grinder.

Put the chillies, their soaking liquid and the ground spices in a blender together with all the remaining ingredients, in the order listed. Blend, pushing down with a rubber spatula as many times as necessary, until you have a smooth paste.

What you do not use immediately should be refrigerated or frozen.

Sinda Naidoo's

South-African Red Spice Mixture

SOUTH AFRICA

Almost every South African of Indian extraction – especially those whose ancestors arrived as indentured labourers – has this spice mixture in their house. Some make it themselves, others buy it from Indian merchants. The use of roasted *urad dal,* roasted peppercorns and roasted fenugreek seeds suggest it origins lie in south India, but now the mixture has taken on a 'national' South-African cast. It is rarely used by itself. Other dry spices and herbs are invariably added to make what could be described as the varied taste of South-African curries.

Many homes make this mixture in vast quantities, about 10 kg/ 22 lb at a time, so it can last a whole year. The main ingredient is pure chilli powder, which needs to be roasted slightly. I have decided to omit this step. When I tried it at home, the fumes almost felled my husband. He was coughing and spluttering for the next hour. I, too, was coughing, but a bit more gently, to prove that it was not all that bad.

MAKES ABOUT A 250-ML/8-FL OZ MEASURE

- 5 tablespoons whole coriander seeds
- 2½ tablespoons whole cumin seeds
- 2½ tablespoons *urad dal*
- 2 teaspoons whole peppercorns
- 1 teaspoon whole fenugreek seeds
- 4 tablespoons any mild, pure chilli powder of a good red colour
- 2 tablespoons bright red paprika

Set a small or medium-sized cast-iron pan on a medium heat. When the oil is hot, put in the coriander and cumin seeds. Stir them around until they are a shade darker and emit a roasted aroma. Empty them into a bowl. Now put the *urad dal* into the pan and roast it until it is golden-red. Empty it into the bowl as well. Lastly, put in the peppercorns and fenugreek seeds. Roast them briefly. You will be able to smell the roasted peppercorns. Do not let the fenugreek burn. Empty into the bowl. Allow the spices to cool, then, in batches, grind them as finely as possible in a clean coffee grinder or other spice grinder. Put back in the bowl. Add the chilli powder and paprika and toss. Store in a tightly lidded jar, away from light and moisture.

Amchar Masala

TRINIDAD

A Trinidadian mixture with many of the spices used in Indian pickling. Here they are roasted first, acquiring a dark colour and an intense flavour. This mixture is often sprinkled in towards the end of the cooking period.

MAKES ABOUT 8 TABLESPOONS

- 4 tablespoons whole coriander seeds
- 1 tablespoon whole cumin seeds
- 2 teaspoons whole black peppercorns
- 1 teaspoon whole fennel seeds
- 1 teaspoon whole brown mustard seeds
- 1 teaspoon whole fenugreek seeds

Put all the spices in a small, cast-iron frying pan and set over a medium heat. Stir and roast for 1–2 minutes or until the spices turn a shade darker. Remove from the pan, allow to cool, and then grind as finely as possible in a clean coffee grinder or other spice grinder. Empty into an airtight jar and store in a dark cupboard.

My Curry Powder

INDIA/USA

Here is my basic curry powder. Be sure to roast the spices very lightly or they could turn bitter. If you want to make it hotter, add a good quality, pure chilli powder, anywhere from ½–2 teaspoons. If you wish to buy a commercial curry powder, my suggestion would be to get Bolst's Hot Curry Powder. Most Indian grocers sell it.

MAKES ABOUT 5–6 TABLESPOONS

- 2 tablespoons whole coriander seeds
- 1 tablespoon whole cumin seeds
- 2 teaspoons whole peppercorns
- 1½ teaspoons whole brown mustard seeds
- 5–6 whole cloves
- 3 dried, hot red chillies, crumbled
- 1 teaspoon whole fenugreek seeds
- 1 teaspoons ground turmeric

Set a small, cast-iron frying pan on a medium heat. When it is hot, put in the coriander, cumin, peppercorns, mustard seeds, cloves and chillies. Stir around until the spices emit a light, roasted aroma. A few of the spices will turn a shade darker. Put in the fenugreek and turmeric and stir for 10 seconds. Empty the spices out on to a clean plate to cool. Now put the spices in a clean coffee grinder or other spice grinder, in two batches if necessary, and grind as finely as possible. Store in a clean jar, away from heat and sunlight.

Sri Lankan Raw Curry Powder

SRI LANKA

A wonderful curry powder to sprinkle on vegetable curries.

MAKES ABOUT A 100-ML/4-FL OZ MEASURE

2 tablespoons whole coriander seeds
1 tablespoon whole fennel seeds
1½ tablespoons whole cumin seeds
1 tablespoon whole fenugreek seeds
3 whole sprigs (about 60) fresh curry leaves, if available, or a small handful dried ones
1 tablespoon unsweetened, desiccated coconut
1½ teaspoons raw rice
½ teaspoon whole brown mustard seeds

Preheat the oven to 65°C/lowest possible gas.

Spread out the seasonings on a baking sheet and put them into the oven for 1 hour. Cool. Empty them into the container of a clean coffee grinder or other spice grinder and grind as finely as possible. Store in a tightly lidded jar, away from heat and sunlight.

Chaat Masala

INDIA

This hot and sour spice mixture is sprinkled on snack foods and sometimes on roasted and grilled meats.

MAKES ABOUT 5 TABLESPOONS

4 teaspoons lightly roasted and ground cumin seeds
1½ tablespoons ground *amchoor*
3 teaspoons cayenne pepper
1 teaspoon finely ground black pepper
¾ teaspoon black salt
1 teaspoon salt

Mix all the ingredients, breaking up any lumps. Store in a tightly lidded jar, away from heat and sunlight.

My Mustard Spice Mix (Rai Masala)

USA

This is a spice mixture that I have devised myself. Its mustard flavour is excellent with many foods, particularly pork, fish and duck.

MAKES ABOUT 4 TABLESPOONS

- 2 tablespoons whole coriander seeds
- 1 teaspoon whole cumin seeds
- 1 teaspoon whole fenugreek seeds
- 1 teaspoon whole brown mustard seeds
- 1 teaspoon whole black peppercorns
- 2 whole, dried, hot red chillies
- 5 whole cloves

Put all the spices in a medium, cast-iron frying pan and set over a medium heat. Stir and fry until the spices are just a shade darker and emit a roasted aroma. Empty the spices into a bowl or on to kitchen paper and allow to cool. Then put them into a clean coffee grinder or other spice grinder and grind as finely as possible. Store in a tightly lidded jar, away from sunlight and moisture.

Sambar Powder

INDIA

In a typical south-Indian tradition, split beans and peas are used in this mix as spices. Other than for *sambar*, you may use this to flavour soups and meats. Early British curry powders were probably based on a similar mixture of spices and split peas, as is evident from many 19th-century recipes. Stored in a tightly closed jar, it will last for several months.

MAKES ENOUGH TO FILL A 300-ML/10-FL OZ JAR

- 1 teaspoon vegetable oil
- 5 tablespoons coriander seeds
- 1 teaspoon whole mustard seeds
- 1 teaspoon *moong dal*
- ½ tablespoon *chana dal*
- ½ tablespoons *urad dal*
- 1 teaspoon fenugreek seeds
- 1 teaspoon black peppercorns
- ¼ teaspoon ground *asafetida*
- 1 teaspoon cumin seeds
- 20 fresh curry leaves, if available
- 12 whole, dried, hot red chillies

Heat the oil in a large, heavy frying pan or wok over a medium heat. Put in the coriander seeds, mustard seeds, *moong dal, chana dal, urad dal,* fenugreek seeds, black peppercorns, *asafetida* and cumin. Stir and roast for 3–4 minutes. Add the curry leaves. Stir and roast for a further 5 minutes. Add the dried chillies and continue stirring and roasting for 2–3 minutes or until the chillies darken. Empty the spices into a bowl and allow to cool, then, in small batches, put them into a clean coffee grinder or other spice grinder and grind as finely as possible. Store in a tightly closed jar, away from heat and sunlight.

My Garam Masala

INDIA

According to ancient Ayurvedic texts, only those spices that heat the body, namely black cardamom, black pepper, cinnamon, nutmeg, black cumin, mace, cloves and bay leaves, are called '*garam masalas*' or 'hot spices'. A true *garam masala* mix would have only a selection from these spices; black cumin and green cardamom are often added, but not spices such as coriander or turmeric. However, as these spices tend to be expensive, many people, even in India, add fillers such as the cheaper coriander.

There are hundreds of recipes for *garam masala* mixtures. Each north-Indian family probably has its own. As migrants have left India to live in new nations such as Trinidad and Guyana, they have created new ones from their old memories.

There is a great difference between store-bought *garam masala*, which often uses cheaper spices as fillers, and one that is home-made. A true *garam masala* can be quite potent and is generally used in small quantities.

MAKES ABOUT 3 TABLESPOONS

- 1 tablespoon cardamom seeds
- 1 teaspoon black peppercorns
- 1 teaspoon whole cloves
- 1 teaspoon black cumin seeds
- ⅓ of a nutmeg
- a medium stick of cinnamon, about 5–7½ cm/2–3 inches, broken up

Put all the spices in a clean coffee grinder or other spice grinder and grind as finely as possible. Store in a tightly lidded jar, away from heat and sunlight.

Guyanese Garam Masala

GUYANA

In Guyana, the mix seems to have changed considerably and only hints at the original *garam masala*. Allspice, native to the West Indies, does have a vague cinnamon-cardamom aroma, and is often substituted for them. Other spices, the cheaper staples of Bihari cooking (Bihar being the state many indentured labourers came from), such as fennel, fenugreek, cumin, mustard seeds and turmeric, have also been added.

In Guyana, all the spices required in this mix are first washed, then dried thoroughly in the sun and finally roasted lightly before they are ground. Because of this, they may be added at any stage of the cooking to meats, vegetables and beans and will not taste raw.

MAKES ABOUT 5 TABLESPOONS

- 1 tablespoon whole coriander seeds
- 1½ teaspoons whole cumin seeds
- 1½ teaspoons whole fennel seeds
- 1½ teaspoons whole fenugreek seeds
- 1½ teaspoons whole black peppercorns
- ¾ teaspoon whole brown mustard seeds
- ¾ teaspoon *kalonji* (nigella seeds)
- ¾ teaspoon whole cloves
- ½ teaspoon allspice
- ¾ teaspoon ground turmeric

Put all the spices except the turmeric into a small, cast-iron frying pan and set over a medium heat. Stir and toast the spices until the coriander is a shade darker and the mustard seeds just start to pop. Add the turmeric, stir once, then empty everything quickly into a bowl. Allow to cool, then grind in a clean coffee grinder or other spice grinder. Store in a tightly lidded jar, away from light and moisture.

An Indian Salt Mixture

INDIA

This salt mixture may be used over eggs, in salads and as a dip for raw vegetables.

MAKES ABOUT 2 1/2 TABLESPOONS

1 teaspoon whole cumin seeds
1 teaspoon whole black peppercorns
1 tablespoon sea salt

Put the cumin and peppercorns in a small, cast-iron frying pan and set it on a medium-high heat. Stir and roast for 2–3 minutes or until the cumin seeds turn a shade darker. Turn off the heat and allow to cool. Grind finely in a clean coffee grinder or other spice grinder. Add the salt and mix. Store it a tightly lidded jar, away from heat and sunlight.

19th-Century British Curry Powder

UK

Once I had decided to attempt an 'authentic', 19th-century British curry (see page 56), my next step was to make a curry powder and a curry paste of the same period, both of which seemed to be required. Luckily, Richard Terry, in his 1861 book *Indian Cookery*, provided a recipe for the former. (Though not one for the curry paste.) It is heavy on turmeric and calls for caraway seeds, when he must mean some kind of cumin, but here it is.

MAKES 7 TABLESPOONS

2 tablespoons ground turmeric
5 teaspoons ground coriander
2 teaspoons ground ginger
2 teaspoons cayenne powder
1½ teaspoons freshly ground black pepper
½ teaspoon ground cumin
½ teaspoon ground cardamom seeds
½ teaspoon ground cloves

Combine all the spices in a jar, mix, cover with a tight lid and store away from heat and sunlight.

Sir Ranald Martin's

19th-Century British Curry Paste

UK

In mid 19th-century Britain, proper curries were made by using curry powder as well as curry paste. Both were to be had at the Indian Depot in Leicester Square – and were, we are told, of excellent quality. Whether this was the same as the Oriental Depot at 38 Leicester Square, I do not know, but the latter certainly advertised itself as 'Payne & Co's Real Calcutta Prepared Condiments' and sold 'Bengal Club Chutnee, Curry Paste, Curry Powder, Pickled Chillies, Chilli Vinegar, Pickled Limes, Cayenne Pepper', and much more.

While there are many recipes for curry powders in old cookbooks, there are few for curry paste. I could hardly imagine what a curry paste would be. Then, digging around in London's British Library, I came upon a collection of recipes by a Sir James Ranald Martin, a doctor and food-lover who had been in India in the 1840s. He had a curry paste recipe marked, 'A very old recipe from Madras'. I have no reason to doubt that it is from Madras. The roasted coriander, peppercorns, split peas and cumin attest to a southern heritage. But the paste itself is totally alien. A very southern spice mixture is combined with vinegar, sugar, salt and garlic and then fried lightly in oil, perhaps to preserve it. The bottom of the recipe reads, 'For use on biscuits, fried bread and sandwiches'. It was used for curries as well.

MAKES ABOUT A 350-ML/12-FL OZ MEASURE

- 4 tablespoons whole coriander seeds
- 2 tablespoons *chana dal* or yellow split peas
- 1 tablespoon whole black peppercorns
- 1½ teaspoons whole cumin seeds
- 1 tablespoon whole brown mustard seeds
- 1 tablespoon ground turmeric
- 1 tablespoon cayenne pepper
- 1½ teaspoons ground ginger
- 2 teaspoons salt
- 2 teaspoons sugar
- 3 cloves garlic, peeled and crushed to a pulp
- 120 ml/4 fl oz cider vinegar
- 6 tablespoons corn, peanut or olive oil

Put the coriander seeds, *chana dal*, peppercorns and cumin into a medium, cast-iron frying pan and set on a medium heat. Stir and roast until the *chana dal* is reddish, the coriander is a shade darker and all the spices begin to emit a roasted aroma. Empty them into a bowl and allow to cool. Put the roasted spices, as well as the mustard seeds, into a clean coffee grinder or other spice grinder and grind as finely as possible. Put in a bowl. Add the turmeric, cayenne pepper, ginger, salt, sugar, garlic and vinegar. Stir to mix.

Pour the oil into a small, preferably non-stick, frying pan and set over a medium heat. Put in the spice paste. Stir and fry it for about 5 minutes or until it browns lightly. Cool, then empty into a jar. Cover tightly and refrigerate until needed.

Curry Sauce

UK

Here is a British curry sauce that has been loved for more than two centuries. It may be served over eggs, fish and chicken. Many recipes suggest the addition of two thin slices of apple as well. The chicken stock and milk may be heated together.

MAKES 350-ML/12-FL OZ

45 g/1½ oz unsalted butter
60 g/2 oz shallots or onions, finely chopped
1 tablespoon plain flour
1 tablespoon hot curry powder
250 ml/8 fl oz chicken stock, heated
250 ml/8 fl oz milk, heated
50 ml/2 fl oz whipping cream
salt
a few squeezes of lemon juice, to taste

Put the butter in a heavy saucepan and set over a low heat. When the butter has melted, add the shallots or onions. Stir and sauté for about 8 minutes or until they turn golden. Add the flour and curry powder. Stir for about 2 minutes. Add the heated stock and milk, stirring as you do so. Bring to a simmer and simmer gently, on a low heat, for 15 minutes, stirring now and then. Add the cream, and salt to taste if your stock is unsalted and squeeze in a little lemon juice. Stir and heat through.

Mrs Beeton's

Curry Sauce with Tomato

UK

I have adapted this 19th-century recipe for the modern kitchen. It is a very Indo-British sauce, almost a gravy, which is excellent when served over grilled or roasted chicken or turkey. Drippings from the birds may be used instead of some of the butter, if you like.

MAKES 350 ML/12 FL OZ

45 g/1½ oz unsalted butter
60 g/2 oz shallots, finely chopped
1 tablespoon plain flour
1 tablespoon hot curry powder
500 ml/16 fl oz chicken stock, heated
1 medium tomato, peeled and finely chopped
salt

Put the butter in a heavy saucepan and set over a low heat. When the butter has melted, add the shallots. Stir and sauté for about 8 minutes or until they turn golden. Add the flour and curry powder. Stir for about 2 minutes. Add the stock, stirring as you do so, and then the tomato. Bring to a simmer. Turn heat to low and simmer gently for 20 minutes, stirring now and then. Add salt to taste if your stock is unsalted.

SPECIAL INGREDIENTS AND TECHNIQUES

AJWAIN (or AJOWAN) These small seeds look like celery seeds but taste more like a pungent version of thyme. (A student of mine compared them to a mixture of anise and black pepper!) Used sparingly, they are sprinkled, in India, over breads, fish, savoury biscuits and numerous noodle-like snacks made with chickpea flour. Being rich in thymol, as thyme is, they add a thyme-like taste to vegetables such as green beans and potatoes.

ALEPPO PEPPER See Chilli Powders

ALOO BOKHARA Dried sour plums of Persian origin used in Moghul cooking.

AMCHAR MASALA See page 324 for recipe and details

AMCHOOR (GREEN MANGO POWDER) Unripe green mangoes are peeled, sliced and their sour flesh sun-dried and ground to make amchoor powder. (The dried slices are also used in Indian cookery but are not needed for recipes here.) The beige, slightly fibrous powder, rich in vitamin C, is tart but with a hint of sweetness and is used as lemon juice might be. As the powder can get lumpy, crumble it well before use. If you cannot get amchoor, substitute 1/2 teaspoon of lemon juice for every teaspoon of amchoor powder.

ANARDANA (POMEGRANATE SEEDS) These dried, sour seeds of red pomegranates are used in north Indian cookery, especially as stuffing for *parathas* and in some spice mixtures.

ANCHOVIES AND ANCHOVY PASTE The best substitute I can think of for the varying types of shrimp paste used in South-East Asia. Most of the better supermarkets and certainly all specialty food stores sell them.

ASAFETIDA The sap from the roots and stem of a giant fennel-like plant dries into a hard resin. It is sold in both lump and ground form. Only the ground form is used here. It has a strong fetid aroma and is used in very small quantities both for its legendary digestive properties and for the much gentler, garlic-like aroma it leaves behind after cooking. (James Beard compared it to the smell of truffles.) Excellent with dried beans and vegetables. Store in a tightly closed container.

ATA See Chapati Flour.

BAMBOO SHOOTS Unfortunately, we cannot easily get fresh bamboo shoots in the West and must make do with canned ones. A good can should have bamboo shoots that are crisp, creamy white with a clean refreshing taste. Among the better brands is Companion. Their winter bamboo shoots in water are generally of excellent quality. So are those labelled Green Bamboo Shoots. You can buy bamboo shoots in rather large chunks which can then be cut up into cubes of the desired size or you can buy the cone-shaped and very tender bamboo shoot tips which are usually cut into comb-like wedges. All bamboo shoots that come out of a can have a faint tinny taste. They should be washed in fresh water and drained before being used. Any bamboo shoots that are unused may be covered with clean water and stored in a closed jar in the refrigerator. In order to keep the bamboo shoots fresh, the water should be changed every day.

BASIL I have used two types of basil in this book. Regular European basil and holy basil, *ocinum sanctum* (*bai kaprow* in Thailand). Ordinary basil and fresh mint are the best substitutes for the very aromatic South-East Asian basils. Sometimes, I have also suggested basil leaves as a substitute for curry leaves. It must be remembered that their aromas and textures are totally different.

BAY LEAVES These dried leaves are added to scores of Indian rice and meat dishes for their delicate aroma. Sometimes they are lightly browned in oil first to intensify this aroma, using the 'tarka' technique, page 346.

BEAN CURD A curd made with soya bean milk, now available in firm, soft, silken and other textures. Health food stores and many supermarkets sell it.

BEAN SAUCE, BLACK Commercially prepared sauces made out of fermented soya beans are used throughout Malaysia and other parts of East and South-East Asia. They can be very thick, filled with crumbled beans or they can be smooth and somewhat thinner. Use any black bean sauce that is available. Once you have opened a bottle you should keep it tightly closed in the refrigerator.

BEAN SAUCE WITH CHILLI OR BLACK BEAN SAUCE WITH CHILLI, CHINESE Sometimes called Bean Paste with Chilli, this reddish-brown paste is sold bottled at Chinese grocers. It is quite hot and goes into the making of spicy Sichuan and Hunan dishes.

BEAN SAUCE, YELLOW Like the sauce above, this is a commercially prepared sauce of fermented soya beans, only it has a very pale brown, almost yellowish colour. It can be smooth but I like to use the kind that has whole or halved beans in it.

BEAN SPROUTS, MUNG These are crisp sprouts grown from the same mung beans that are sold in Indian stores as whole *moong*. They can now be bought in supermarkets and health food stores as well as all Eastern groceries. They are good when they are crisp and white. As they are usually kept in water, they tend to get soggier and soggier as they get older. When you buy bean sprouts and bring them home you should rinse them off first and then put them into a bowl of fresh water. The bowl should be covered and then refrigerated. If the beans are not used by the next day, you should change the water again.

It is considered proper to 'top' and 'tail' bean sprouts before using them. This means pinching off the remains of the whole bean at the top as well as the thread-like tail at the bottom. This requires a lot of patience. The sprouts do indeed look better when they have been pinched this way but I have to admit that I very rarely do it. Bean sprouts are also sold in cans. I never use them as they do not have the crunch that makes the sprouts worthwhile in the first place.

BEANS AND PEAS, DRIED In India, beans and split peas are cooked daily into soupy or stew-like dishes. Split peas may also be used as spices. Here are some that you may be unfamiliar with:

Chana dal: The Indian version of yellow split peas but with better texture and a very nutty flavour. It is the split version of a very yellow, small chickpea and, in India, it is this that is used to make chickpea flour. In south India, it is also used as a spice.

Masoor dal: Red lentil. Whole or *Sabut Masoor* are just the unhulled, whole lentils.

Mung beans: This is the same bean that, when whole, is sprouted to make bean sprouts. An ancient Indian bean, it can be hulled and split. It is then known as *mung dal*. Used to make everyday soupy stews, pancakes and fritters.

Sugar beans: What are called sugar beans in South Africa are pale and speckled, very similar to American pinto beans.

Toovar dal: Of the pigeon pea family, this split pea has a dark, dusky flavour. In south India it is used to make the soupy-stew known as *sambar*. The north-Indian version of this *dal* is known as *arhar*.

Urad dal: A small, pale yellow split pea with a slightly glutinous texture. An ancient Indian *dal*, it may be just boiled with seasonings. It is also used to make fritters and used as a seasoning. It is south Indians who seem to have discovered that if you throw a few of these dried, split peas into hot oil, using the 'tarka' method, the seeds will turn red and nutty. Anything stir-fried in the oil afterwards will pick up that nutty flavour and aroma.

BLACK PEPPER Native to India, whole peppercorns are added to rice and meat dishes for a mild peppery-lemony flavour. Ground pepper was once used in large amounts, sometimes several tablespoons in a single dish, especially in south India where it grows. The arrival of chillies from the New World around 1498 has changed that usage somewhat, though it still exists. In some south-Indian dishes peppercorns are lightly roasted before use to draw out their lemony taste.

CARDAMOM, BLACK Not a true cardamom but a large blackish pod with seeds and a cardamom aroma. Used in rice and meat dishes in India.

CARDAMOM PODS AND SEEDS Small green pods, the fruit of a ginger-like plant, hold clusters of black, highly aromatic seeds smelling like a combination of camphor, eucalyptus, orange peel and lemon. Whole pods are put into rice dishes and ground seeds are the main flavour in *garam masala*, page 340. This versatile spice is the vanilla of India and used in most desserts and sweetmeats. It is also added to spiced tea and sucked as a mouth freshener. Cardamom seeds that have been taken out of their pods are sold separately by Indian grocers. If you cannot get them, take the seeds out of the pods yourself. The most aromatic pods are green in colour. White ones sold by supermarkets have been bleached and have less flavour.

CARDAMOM SEEDS, GROUND The seeds of the cardamom pods are sold by themselves in both their whole and ground forms. This powder can be put into rice dishes and desserts.

CASHEW NUTS These nuts travelled from the Americas via Africa and India all the way to China. It might be useful for you to know that all so-called 'raw' cashews have been processed to remove the prussic acid in their outer shells, which they contain in their natural state. They are grown commonly on India's west coast and are used in pilafs, desserts and even made into *bhajis* and curries. They are an important part of the Indian vegetarian diet.

CASSIA BARK This is Chinese cinnamon. It is sometimes known as 'false cinnamon'. It is thicker, coarser and generally cheaper than true cinnamon but with a stronger flavour.

CAYENNE PEPPER This hot powder is made today by grinding the dried, red skins of several types of chillies. It should simply be called chilli powder. But since that name can be confused with the Mexican-style chilli powder that also contains cumin, garlic and oregano, the name 'cayenne pepper' hangs on. Even though chillies came from the New World, India today is the largest producer and one of the largest exporters and consumers. When adding the powder to recipes, use your discretion.

CHAPATI FLOUR Very finely ground wholemeal flour used to make *chapatis*, *pooris* and other Indian breads. Sometimes called *ata*, it is sold by all Indian grocers.

CHAROLI NUT A tiny nut that tastes a bit like a hazelnut. Used in rich meat sauces and in sweets and stuffings in India.

CHILLIES, WHOLE, DRIED, HOT, RED When I call for a whole dried chilli, it is the cayenne-type of dried chilli that I want. This is the most commonly used dry chilli around the world. Chillies are often added to Indian food through the 'tarka' method, page 346. A quick contact with very hot oil enhances and intensifies the flavour of their skins. It is that flavour that Indians want. Sichuan stir-fry dishes use chillies in a similar manner. Then, if actual chilli-heat is desired, the chillies are allowed to stew with the food being cooked. To remove seeds from dried chillies, break off the stem end and shake the seeds out. Rotating a chilli between the fingers can help. Sometimes it is necessary to break the chilli in order to get all the seeds out. Some dishes call for a crumbled chilli. You may remove the seeds if you so wish, as suggested above.

CHILLIES, WHOLE, FRESH, GREEN AND RED The fresh green chilli used in much of Asian cooking is of the cayenne type, generally about 7.5 cm/3 inches long and slender. Its heat can vary from mild to fiery. (Stupid bees, it seems, unthinkingly cross-pollinate different varieties that grow in proximity.) The only way to judge the heat is by tasting a tiny piece of skin from the middle section. (Keep some yoghurt handy!) The top part of the chilli with more seeds is always the hottest, the bottom tip, the mildest. The hot seeds of the chilli are rarely removed in Asia but you may do so if you wish. To do this, split the chilli in half, lengthways and then remove the seeds with the tip of a knife. Try not to touch the seeds. If you do, wash your hands very carefully before touching any part of your face. In the Mediterranean, a very mild, paler green chilli is also very popular.

Red chillies are just ripe green chillies. However, their flavour is slightly different, though their intensity can be exactly the same.

Chillies are a very rich source of iron and vitamins A and C. To store fresh red or green chillies wrap them first in newspaper, then in plastic, and store in the refrigerator. They should last several weeks. Any that begin to soften and rot should be removed as they tend to infect the whole batch.

Chillies originated in the Americas and then travelled via Africa and India all the way to China and Korea. The East has adopted them with a passion.

Other fresh chillies:

Bird's eye: Both red and green, (called *prik-khi-nu* in Thailand), these are very hot. They are often thrown in whole or cut into thin rounds over curries partly as a colourful garnish and partly for flavour.

Congo pepper or Scotch bonnet: These small (2.5–4 cm/1–1 /2 inches) chillies seem as wide as they are long and have a squat, lantern-like shape. They come in orange, yellow, green and red and are fiery. Generally, they are dropped into stews and soups whole and then removed so their main firepower stays inside them. Some people dare to poke a tiny hole or two in them with a needle if they want the heat. Small sections of them are chopped and added to curries and stews. These are the darlings of Trinidad. They are also made into hot pepper sauces.

Wiri wiri pepper: A highly aromatic, small, round, cherry-sized chilli used in Guyana. It is hot with an intense, tropical citrus aroma. It may be frozen. Chop up the flesh and add it to onions and garlic as you sauté them for use in stews and soups. Its aroma is addictive.

CHILLIES, DEALING WITH FRESH First of all, which chillies do you buy? This book calls for only four types of chillies. The most commonly used chilli in India is of the cayenne variety. It is slim, thin-skinned, green and can be anywhere from 5–10 cm/2–4 inches long. The small chillies known as bird's eye chillies, which can be green or red, are also good for Indian food. What are not as good are the thicker-skinned chillies such as jalapeños and serranos. Green chillies are often put in whole or sliced towards the end of the cooking time and both jalapeños and serranos are not appropriate for that. They also have fairly coarse seeds. Since Indian food almost never calls for the removal of the seeds, the coarseness of the skin and seeds makes for an indelicate dish. Thai food also requires bird's eye chillies, so if you have a good source for them, use them for all the recipes in this book.

In Guyana, it is the small, highly aromatic, wiri-wiri pepper of medium-heat that is used, giving local curries an almost citrus aroma. You might be able to find this at West-Indian stores. Just freeze it whole and then chop it up when you need it. If not, use bird's-eye chillies as a substitute.

Trinidadian-Indian dishes require the congo pepper. It is lantern-shaped and comes in glowing red, green, orange and yellow colours. Of the scotch bonnet/habanero family, this is also highly aromatic, but hot, hot, hot. It may be one of the hottest peppers on earth. Some people just prick a hole in it with a needle and drop it into a curry, making sure to remove it before eating. Others chop up sections of it, only as much as they think they can handle. Again, use bird's eye chillies as a substitute.

All chillies should be handled with care. Wash your hands carefully after chopping them and refrain from touching your eyes or mouth before you do so.

CHILLI POWDER, ROASTED To make roasted chilli powder, you can take four whole, hot dried red chillies and put them on a cast-iron frying pan set over a medium heat. Stir them around until they turn a shade darker and then pound them in a mortar until coarsely crushed. You could also take a coarse chilli powder (such as the Korean chilli powder used for pickling or Aleppo pepper from Turkey) and stir it around for a few seconds on a hot, cast-iron frying pan until just a shade darker. Take care, as it can burn easily. Also, watch out for the chilli fumes as they can be powerful.

CHILLI PASTE WITH GARLIC A reddish sauce made with sautéed red chillies, soya beans and garlic. Sold in jars by Chinese grocers, this is used mostly in Western Chinese cooking but may be used to heat up soups and salad dressings.

CHILLI PASTE WITH SOY BEAN A reddish-brown, very hot and spicy sauce made of soy beans, red chillies and other seasonings. It is used in the cooking of Western China and is sold by Oriental grocers in bottles.

CHILLI PASTE WITH SOYA BEAN AND GARLIC Similar to the last two pastes, this has more soya beans than the first and more garlic than the second.

CHILLI POWDERS A powder made by grinding hot, dried red chillies, not the Mexican-style chilli powder that is mixed with cumin. Since people prefer different degrees of hotness, you should add as much or as little of the chilli powder as you like. Be warned that chilli powders vary in their heat. Cayenne pepper is a chilli powder.

Coarse, Korean chilli powder is made by pounding dried red chilli skins. It is hot but not excruciatingly so and has an exquisite carmine colour. I tend to stock up on it whenever I visit Korean supermarkets. They are the only ones who seem to sell it. It is this powder that gives many Korean foods their rich red colour. It is a good chilli powder to know about. There is also a very aromatic Aleppo pepper that I love. It is bright red, comes from Turkey and Syria, is very coarsely ground and is sold by Middle Eastern grocers. Both the Aleppo pepper and Korean coarse pepper should be stored in the refrigerator.

CHINESE SHAO HSING WINE See Shao Hsing Wine, Chinese.

CINNAMON Used mainly for desserts in the West, cinnamon, often in its 'stick' form, is added to many Indian rice dishes for its warm, sweet aroma. This inner bark from a laurel-like tree is also an important ingredient in the aromatic mixture, *garam masala*, page 340. Cinnamon is a major ingredient in Moroccan cookery where it can be used in lavish quantities.

CLAMS AND MUSSELS, CLEANING When you buy your clams or mussels, the fishmonger will probably put them in a plastic bag. Open up the bag as soon as you come home, so the molluscs can breathe, and refrigerate if needed.

1 Scrub the shellfish with a stiff brush, one at a time, discarding any that are partially open and full of sand.
2 If the mussels have beards, pull them off.
3 Leave the molluscs to soak in a bowl of cold water for 1 hour. Some people like to add a tablespoon of cornmeal to the water to help the molluscs get rid of the sand in their shells.
4 Drain and use according to the recipe.

CLOVES The West calls for cloves when making desserts. Indians rarely use cloves in desserts but do use them in bean and rice dishes and in the spice mixture, *garam masala*. Small quantities of cloves also go into a few Thai curry mixes and into north African and Middle Eastern foods.

Indians carry the pungently aromatic cloves as well as cardamom pods in tiny silver boxes, to use as mouth-fresheners when needed. For the same reason cloves are always part of the betel leaf paraphernalia that is offered as a digestive at the end of Indian meals. Indonesians use cloves to flavour their cigarettes! The whole nation smells of cloves, which are native to some of the islands.

COCONUT, FRESH When buying a coconut, look for one that shows no signs of mould and is free of cracks. Shake the coconut. If it has a lot of water in it, it has a better chance of being good. People generally weigh a coconut in each hand and pick the heavier of the two. In the West it is always safer to buy an extra coconut just in case one turns out to be bad.

To break open a coconut, use the unsharpened side of a cleaver and hit the coconut hard all around its equator. You can hold the coconut in one hand over a large bowl while you hit with the other or you can rest the coconut on a stone while you hit it and then rush it to a bowl as soon as the first crack appears. The bowl is there to catch the coconut water. Some people like to drink it. I do. This coconut water, by the way, is not used in cooking. But it is a good indication of the sweetness and freshness of the coconut.

You should now have two halves. Before proceeding any further, cut off a small bit of the meat and taste it. The dreaded word here is 'rancid'! Your coconut should taste sweet. If it is lacking in sweetness, it can be endured. But it must never be rancid or mouldy inside. Now remove the tough outer shell by slipping a knife between it and the meat and then prizing the meat out. Sometimes it helps to crack the halves into smaller pieces to do this.

This meat now has a thin brown skin. If your recipe calls for fresh grated coconut, peel the skin off with a vegetable peeler or a knife, cut the meat into small cubes and throw the cubes into the container of a food processor or blender. When you blend you will not get a paste. What you will get is something resembling grated coconut. You can freeze what you don't use. Grated coconut freezes very well and it is a good idea to keep some at hand.

As a substitute for freshly grated coconut, you can use desiccated, unsweetened coconut, which is sold in most health food stores. Here is how you do this: To get the equivalent of 60 g/2 oz of freshly grated coconut, take 30 g/1 oz unsweetened, desiccated coconut and soak it in 60 ml/4 tablespoons water for about an hour. Most of the water will just get absorbed.

COCONUT MILK This is best made from fresh coconuts but is also available canned or can be made using powdered coconut milk, unsweetened desiccated coconut or blocks of creamed coconut. No prepared coconut milk keeps well – this includes canned coconut milk after the can has been opened. Its refrigerated life is no longer than two days.

Using fresh coconut: First you prise off the flesh as suggested above. Whether you peel the brown skin or not depends on the dish. If it needs to look pale and pristine, remove the skin. If not, leave it on and grate the meat in a food processor or blender (see above). To make about 350 ml/12 fl oz coconut milk, fill a glass measuring jug to the 450 ml/3/4 pint mark with grated coconut. Empty it into a blender or food processor. Add 300 ml/1/2 pint very hot water. Blend for a few seconds. Line a sieve with a piece of muslin and place it over a bowl. Empty the contents of the blender into the sieve. Gather the ends of the cloth together and squeeze out all the liquid. For most of my recipes, this is the coconut milk that is needed. It is sometimes referred to as thick coconut milk. If a recipe calls for thin coconut milk, the entire process needs to be repeated using the squeezed out coconut and the same amount of water. If you let the thick coconut milk sit for a while, cream will rise to the top. That is why I suggest that you always stir the coconut milk before using it. If just the cream is required, then spoon it off the top.

Canned coconut milk: This is available at most Asian groceries but the quality varies. There is a brand which I like very much and use frequently. It is Chaokoh and is a product of Thailand. It is white and creamy and quite delicious. As the cream also tends to rise to the top in a can, always stir it well before using it. Sometimes, because of the fat in it, canned coconut milk tends to get very grainy. You can either whir it for a second in a blender or else beat it well. I find that whereas you can cook a fish, for example, in fresh coconut milk for a long time, canned coconut milk, which behaves differently, is best added towards the end. Canned coconut is very thick, partly because it has thickeners in it. As a result, many of my recipes require that canned coconut milk be thinned before use.

Powdered coconut milk: You can now buy packets of powdered coconut milk from Oriental grocers and supermarkets. Their quality varies from good to poor, the poor ones containing hard-to dissolve globules of fat. Emma brand from Malaysia is acceptable. Directions for making the milk are always on the packets. The process usually involves mixing an equal volume of powder and hot water and stirring well. Unwanted lumps should be strained away. This milk is best added to recipes towards the end of the cooking time.

Using unsweetened, desiccated coconut: Put 115 g/4 oz unsweetened, desiccated coconut into a pan. Add 600 ml/1 pint water and bring to a simmer. Now pour the contents into the container of a blender or food processor and blend for a minute. Strain the resulting mixture through a double thickness of muslin, pushing out as much liquid as you can. You should get about 350 ml/12 fl oz of thick coconut milk. If you repeat the process with the same amount of water again, using the leftover coconut, you can get another 450 ml/3/4 pint of thin coconut milk.

Using creamed coconut: Available in block form, this can also be turned into coconut milk. I do not advise that you do this if you need large quantities of milk. However, if just a few tablespoons are required, you can for example, take 2 tablespoons of creamed coconut and mix them with 2 tablespoons of hot water. The thick coconut milk that will result should only be put into dishes at the last moment.

CONDENSED MILK Canned, sweetened milk is commonly used in East Asia for sweetening tea or coffee, in desserts, even in making breads.

CORIANDER LEAVES, ROOTS AND STEM This is the parsley of the eastern and southern half of Asia. Generally, just the delicate, fragrant, green leaves are used. In Thai curries, however, the equally fragrant white root is ground or chopped in as well. It should be very well washed first. Some recipes also call for the stems, which are generally cut, crossways, into minute dice. When you buy fresh coriander, the best way to keep it is to stand it in a glass of water, cover it with a plastic bag and refrigerate the whole thing. Break off the leaves, stems and roots as you need them and keep the rest refrigerated. The water should be changed daily and dead leaves removed.

CORIANDER SEEDS, WHOLE AND GROUND Native to the Middle East and southern Europe, these are the round, beige seeds of the coriander plant. They are sold either whole or ground. You can grind them yourself in a clean coffee grinder or other spice grinder and then put them through a fine sieve. If roasted and ground coriander seeds are called for, put a few tablespoons of seeds in a small cast-iron frying pan over a medium-high heat. Stir and roast for a few minutes or until the seeds are a few shades darker and smell roasted. Then them grind in a coffee grinder or other spice grinder. If they are very coarse, put them through a fine sieve. What is not needed immediately may be stored in a tightly lidded jar and saved.

CRABS, CLEANING AND CUTTING LIVE The crabs used here are the blue variety, no more than 13–15 cm/5–6 inches across. They are sometimes sold live from big wooden tubs. Look for female crabs as they have eggs. Keep them alive until they are ready to be cooked, refrigerating them in an open bag, if necessary.

1 Turn the crab over so it is lying on its back, pull off the front claws and set them aside in a bowl.
2 Pull back the flap on the underbelly side. Tear it right off and discard it.
3 Continue where you broke off the flap and proceed to pull off the whole back. You will need to place the crab on its stomach to do this or else hold it upright. Sometimes this is hard to do. You may need to insert the tip of your kitchen shears or a screwdriver at the point where you broke off the flap. The back will come off in one piece. It may hold some eggs. Set the whole back aside in the bowl.
4 As you look inside the crab, you will notice some feathery gills. Pull them off and discard them.
5 Using a pair of kitchen shears or a knife, cut the main body of the

crab in half, lengthways. Put these halves into a bowl.

CULANTRO The narrow, serrated leaves of this green herb are used in the Caribbean, Central America and parts of South-East Asia. It is called *pak chee farang* or 'foreign green coriander' by the Thais, *recao* in Hispanic shops, *shadow beni* or *chadon bené* by the Trinidadians of mixed Mediterranean descent and *band-hania* or 'green coriander of the woods' by Trinidadians of Indian descent. If you cannot find it, use green coriander which it resembles in taste.

CUMIN SEEDS, WHOLE AND GROUND These look like caraway seeds but are slightly larger, plumper and lighter in colour. Their flavour is similar to caraway, only gentler and sweeter. They are used both whole and ground. When whole, they are often subjected to the 'tarka' technique, page 346, which intensifies their flavour and makes them slightly nutty. This spice of possible northern Egyptian or Middle Eastern ancestry, has now become very central to the cuisines of India (where it must have reached in ancient times) and Morocco. It is used in Spain and Mexico and in much of the Middle East as well. Sometimes used whole, it can also be ground into various spice mixtures. If roasted and ground cumin seeds are called for, put a few tablespoons of seeds in a small cast-iron frying pan over a medium-high heat. Stir and roast for a few minutes or until the seeds are a few shades darker and smell roasted. Then grind in a clean coffee grinder or other spice grinder. What is not needed immediately may be stored in a tightly lidded jar and saved for later use.

CUMIN SEEDS, BLACK A rare and therefore more expensive form of cumin with sweeter, smaller and more delicate seeds. Their mild pungency is perfect for the aromatic mixture of spices known as *garam masala*, page 327. The seeds can also be lightly dry-roasted and sprinkled whole over rice pilafs.

CURRY LEAVES, FRESH AND DRIED These highly aromatic leaves are used fresh in much of Indian and some of South-East Asian cookery. In Indonesia they are known as *daun salaam* and are a slightly larger variety. They are now increasingly available in the West. You could use the dried leaf if the fresh is unavailable, though its aroma is very limited. Indian grocers sell both fresh and dried curry leaves. The fresh ones come attached to stalks in sprays. They can be pulled off their stalks in one swoop. Keep curry leaves in a flat, plastic bag. They last for several days in the refrigerator. They may also be frozen, so when you do see them in the market, buy a lot and store them in your freezer. For some strange reason, fresh ones frozen quickly in a freezer have a bit more aroma than the sun-dried leaves.

CURRY POWDER This is a blend of spices that generally includes cumin, coriander, red chillies, mustard and fenugreek. The mixtures vary in their strength and potency and are generally sold mild and hot. You will find a recipe for My Curry Powder on page 324.

DAIKON See Radish, White.

DAUN SALAAM See Curry Leaves.

DRIED MANDARIN PEEL See Mandarin Peel, Dried.

DRY-ROASTING SPICES Spices are sometimes dry-roasted before use. It is best to do this in a heavy cast-iron frying pan that has first been heated. No oil is used: the spices are just stirred around until they brown lightly. Roasted spices develop a heightened, nutty aroma. They can be stored for several months in an airtight jar though they are best when freshly roasted.

FENNEL SEEDS These seeds look and taste like anise seeds, only they are larger and plumper. To grind fennel seeds, just put 2–3 tablespoons into the container of a clean coffee grinder or other spice grinder and grind as finely as possible. Store in an airtight container.

In north and western India, the whole seeds are used in pickles and chutneys and snack foods. Using the 'tarka' technique, they are also used in the stir-frying of vegetables, particularly in Bengal (eastern India), where they are part of the five-spice mixture called *panchphoran*, page 343. Fennel seeds can be dry-roasted and then eaten after a meal as both a digestive and mouth freshener.

FENUGREEK SEEDS Known for their digestive properties, it is these angular, yellowish seeds that give many commercial curry powders their earthy, musky 'curry'aroma. In most of northern India they are used mainly in pickles, chutneys and vegetarian dishes. They are a part of the Bengali spice mixture, *panchphoran*. In the Arab world, they are soaked and then whipped up into drinks and sauces. They may also be sprouted. They are meant to have cooling properties.

FISH SAUCE Known as *nam pla* in Thailand, *nuoc mam* in Vietnam and *patis* in the Philippines, fish sauce is used in these countries much as soy sauce is used in China and Japan. A thin, salty, brown liquid made from salted prawns or fish, it has a very special flavour of its own. It is sold by Chinese and other East Asian grocers. If you just cannot get it, you may use salt as a substitute. You could also try combining 1 tablespoon water with 1/2 teaspoon salt, 1/4 teaspoon soy sauce and 1/4 teaspoon sugar.

GALANGAL Known as *laos* and *lengkuas* in Indonesia, *langkuas* in Malaysia and *kha* in Thailand, this ginger-like rhizome has a very distinct earthy aroma of its own. It is now sold, both fresh and frozen, by South-East Asian grocers. In the curry-type recipes which require it, you could use the sliced, dried galangal. To make curry paste, you would have to soak it before you grind it.

GARAM MASALA This spice combination varies with each household though the name seems constant. '*Garam*' means 'hot' and '*masala*' means 'spices' so the spices in this mixture were traditionally those which 'heated' the body according to the ancient Ayurvedic system of medicine. They all happened to be highly aromatic as well. Here is how you make a classic ground mixture: combine in a clean coffee grinder or other spice grinder 1 tablespoon cardamom seeds, 1 teaspoon whole cloves, 1 teaspoon whole black peppercorns, 1 teaspoon whole black cumin seeds, a 5-cm/2-inch stick of cinnamon, 1/3 nutmeg and a curl of mace. Grind until you have a fine powder. Store in a tightly closed jar and use as needed. Many people add a bay leaf to the mixture. Generally, though not always, *garam masala* is sprinkled towards the end of the cooking time to retain its aroma. The *garam masala* spices can also be used whole. If two or more of them are used together, they are still loosely referred to as '*garam masala*'.

Many of my recipes call for 'store-bought' *garam masala*. This is where the strong aromas of my cardamom-filled mixture are not required and the milder commercial version, which tends to fill up with the cheaper coriander and cumin, will do.

GARLIC, CRUSHING TO A PULP The easiest way is to peel the garlic and push the cloves through a garlic press, one at a time. That is what I do.

GHEE (CLARIFIED BUTTER) This is butter that has been so thoroughly clarified that it can even be used for deep-frying. As it no longer contains milk solids, refrigeration is not necessary. It has a nutty, buttery taste. All Indian grocers sell it and I find it more convenient to buy it. If, however, you need to make it, take 450 g/1 lb unsalted butter, put it in a pan over a low heat and let it simmer very gently until the milky solids turn brownish and either cling to the sides of the pan or else fall to the bottom. The time that this takes will depend on the amount of water in the butter. Watch carefully towards the end and do not let it burn. Strain the ghee through a triple layer of muslin. Homemade ghee is best stored in the refrigerator.

GINGER, DRIED, GROUND Called *sont* and considered very different from fresh ginger in India, it, nonetheless, always had its very special uses. Outside India, it is frequently used as a substitute for fresh ginger.

GINGER, FRESH You almost cannot cook without ginger in South Asia and the Far East. This rhizome has a sharp, pungent, cleansing taste and is a digestive to boot. It is now said to help with travel sickness as well. Its brown skin is generally peeled, though in Chinese cookery the skin is often left on.

When slices of ginger are called for, just cut a thinnish slice, crossways, from a knob of ginger. If peeled slices are needed, peel a section of the knob before you start slicing.

When slivers or minute dice are called for, first cut the ginger into very thin slices. The slices should then be stacked and cut into very fine strips to get the slivers. To get the dice, cut the slivers, crossways, into very fine dice.

When finely grated ginger is required, it should first be peeled and then grated on the finest part of a grater so it turns into pulp. I now use a microplane for grating ginger as it quick and efficient. When a recipe requires that 2.5 cm/1 inch of ginger be grated, it is best to keep that piece attached to the large knob. The knob acts as a handle and saves you from grating your fingers.

When a little ginger juice is called for (excellent for salad dressings), just pick up a teaspoon or two of finely grated ginger and squeeze out as much liquid as you can.

Ginger should be stored in a dry, cool place. Many people like to bury it in dryish, sandy soil. This way they can break off and retrieve small portions as they need them while the rest of the knob generously keeps growing.

GINGER, GRATING FRESH Many Indian recipes require a paste of ginger and garlic. I had always used a blender for that. Now, I have started skipping the blender step unless it is totally unavoidable. Instead, I grate the ginger on a microplane. It seems made for the job. The process is easy, fast and very efficient. Peel a knob of ginger but leave it attached to the larger rhizome. This will be your handle, something you can hold on to. Now grate, being very careful to not to let your fingers or thumb get too close to the microplane. Having hurt myself once I am now convinced that it is better to forgo some ginger than to keep grinding to the bitter end.

GROUNDNUT OIL See Oils.

HOLY BASIL (BAI KAPROW) See Basil.

JAGGERY A form of raw, lump, cane sugar. It is sold in pieces that are cut off from larger blocks. You should look for the kind that crumbles easily and is not rock-hard. It can be found in Indian groceries.

KAFFIR LIME, LEAVES AND RIND A dark-green knobbly lime. Its peel and leaves are used in South-East Asian cookery. They are all highly aromatic and their flavour has no substitute. If you are lucky enough to get fresh leaves, you should tear them in half and pull off their coarse centre veins before using them in a dish. If a recipe requires that the leaves be cut into fine, hair-thin shreds, first remove the centre vein and then use a pair of kitchen scissors to cut the shreds. Leftover leaves can be made to last by freezing them in a flat plastic packet. Whole limes may be frozen as well. The peel and leaves are sometimes available dried. You should use them in whatever form you can find them. Far Eastern and some Chinese grocers sell the leaves, dried rind and lime. The rind is sometimes labelled as *piwma grood*. The dried rind needs to be soaked in water first. When soft, discard the soaking water (it is bitter) and then scrape off any pith that may be clinging to it.

KALONJI See Nigella.

KOREAN COARSE RED PEPPER See Chilli Powders.

LEMON GRASS, FRESH AND DRIED Known as *seré* in Indonesia, *serai* in Malaysia, *takrai* in Thailand, and *tanglad* in the Philippines, lemon grass is a tall, hard greyish-green grass used for its aroma and flavour in much of South-East Asian cookery. Usually, only the bottom 15 cm/6 inches are used. The very bottom can be bruised (hitting it with a hammer will do that) and then thrown into a pan, or else the lemon grass can be sliced first.

Lemon grass is fairly hard. To slice, first cut off the hard knot at the very end and then slice crossways into paper-thin slices. Even when lemon grass is to be ground to a pulp in a blender, it needs to be sliced thinly first or else it does not grind properly. Lemon grass is best stored with its bottom end in a little water. This prevents it from drying out. You can also freeze stalks of lemon grass. To defrost, just run under hot water briefly.

In South-East Asia, lemon grass is always used fresh. We are beginning to see it more and more in the West. Unfortunately, many of us in the West still have to make do with the dried variety. I buy the dried, sliced lemon grass and then soak it before I use it. It generally needs to be strained as it is very coarse. Lemon grass, as its name suggests, has a citrus flavour and aroma though it is not at all sour. The best (though nowhere as good) equivalent is lemon peel. The peel of a quarter of a lemon may be used instead of a stick of lemon grass.

LIMES, DRIED, PERSIAN Persian dried limes are a world unto themselves. They are sold by Middle Eastern grocers. Very hard when you buy them, they feel quite hollow, and are. You need to hit them with a well-aimed mallet so they break into 3–4 pieces. The black insides are the gold you are after. To get at it you need to pull or scrape the insides out and collect them in a bowl, making sure you discard the bitter seeds. Now grind this black gold that you have collected in a clean coffee grinder or other spice grinder and store it in a jar. Do just 2–3 limes at a time. If all this sounds arduous, it isn't. It took me less that 5 minutes to do 2 limes, which was more than I needed, but you need to do that amount to make the grinder run properly. As a substitute, use fresh lime juice.

LOBSTERS, CUTTING AND CLEANING LIVE There is nothing more delicious than a lobster curry. The lobster needs to be alive. Here is how you go about preparing it.

1 Lay the live lobster in front of you on a chopping board on its stomach. Administer the *coup de grâce* by sticking the point of a knife right where the head meets the tail. Sever the head.
2 Twist off the spindly legs and put them in a bowl.
3 Twist off the front claws. Using a cleaver or a heavy knife, egged on with a hammer, cut the claws, crossways, into three pieces each. Using a nut cracker or heavy knife, crack part of the shell in all the claw pieces. Put these pieces in the bowl.
4 Using a cleaver or a heavy knife, cut the tail, crossways, into three pieces. Put in the bowl.
5 Now the head. Again use the heavy knife or cleaver to cut off a sliver at the very front of the head where the eyes are. If you can do this at a slight angle, going from the top of the head towards the eyes, so much the better. Just inside the head you will find the stomach sac. Reach in and remove it. Now split the head area, lengthways, into two. Put these sections into your bowl as well. You are done.

MACE See Nutmeg.

MUSHROOMS There are hundreds of different mushrooms, going from tiny pinheads to large meaty ones. Here are the Asian ones you may be less familiar with:

Chinese dried mushrooms: These are available in most oriental shops. The Japanese shiitake is the same mushroom. Price is generally an indication of quality. The thicker the caps, the meatier the texture. They need to be soaked in plenty of warm water before they are used. Once they are soft, lift the mushrooms out of their soaking liquid– this leaves the grit behind. The texture of the stalks remains hard, even after soaking, so they need to be cut off. The water in which the mushrooms have soaked should be strained and saved. It can be added to stocks or used to cook vegetables.

Straw mushrooms: Smooth and meaty at the same time, there is nothing quite as delicious as a fresh straw mushroom. I eagerly await the day when they will be as commonly available in the West as they are in the East. We have to make do with the tinned variety. Drain them first, rinse off, and then use as the recipe suggests.

Amongst the fresh oriental mushrooms now increasingly available in specialty shops are oyster mushrooms – delicate, excellent in stir-fries – and shiitake (the Japanese name for the mushroom commonly used, both fresh and dried, in China, Korea and Japan), which have meaty caps but woody stems and can be used in soups, stews and stir-fries.

MUSTARD SEEDS, BROWN AND YELLOW Of the three varieties of mustard seeds, white (actually yellowish), brown (a reddish-brown) and black (slightly larger, brownish-black seeds), it is the brown and yellow that I use in this book.

All mustard seeds have Jekyll and Hyde characteristics. When crushed, they are nose-tinglingly pungent. However, if they are thrown into hot oil and allowed to pop using the 'tarka' method, page 346, they turn quite nutty and sweet. In India, both these techniques are used, sometimes in the same recipe. Whole mustard seeds, popped in oil, are used to season vegetables, legumes, yoghurt relishes, salads and rice dishes. Crushed seeds are used in sauces and in pickles.

Yellow mustard seeds may be substituted for the brown ones.

MUSTARD SEEDS, HULLED AND SKINNED These, as far as I know, are only used in India, mainly for pickling and in pungent sauces. It is the brown seeds that are skinned and hulled, making them look like tiny grains of yellow *dal* (split peas). Sold only by Indian grocers as mustard *dal*.

MUSTARD OIL See Oils.

NIGELLA (KALONJI) Possibly originating in the southern Caucasus region, these black, aromatic seeds are used extensively on flat breads from Turkey all the way east to India. In India, they are also an important spice for pickling and are a part of the Bengali five-spice mixture, *panchphoran*. Their oregano-like taste is quite strong so they should be used with some discretion.

NOODLES Here are some of the noodles that you might be less familiar with:

Fresh Chinese egg noodles: Ask for *lo-mein* noodles in a Chinese grocery store and *ramen* in a Japanese one. They are usually sold in the refrigerated section in plastic bags – 450 g/1 lb usually serves 4–6 people. If you intend using smaller portions, it is a good idea to divide them while they is still fresh, wrap the portions separately and freeze what you are not going to use that day. The rest can be refrigerated until you are ready to cook them. Frozen egg noodles defrost quickly and easily when dropped into boiling water. Just stir them about in the beginning. The best way to cook these noodles is to drop them into a large pan of boiling water. As soon as the water comes to the boil again, throw in a tea-cupful of fresh water. Repeat this about three times or until the noodles are just tender. The noodles can now be drained and used as the recipe suggests.

Dried Chinese egg noodles: When fresh noodles are not available, use the dried. Drop them into a large pot of boiling water and cook them as you would the fresh. Some varieties tend to cook very fast, so test them frequently.

Fresh rice noodles: These are white, slithery and absolutely delicious. In South-East Asia, they are available in all sorts of sizes and shapes. Their freshness generally lasts for just a day. Many do not need to be cooked at all. Others are heated through very briefly. Unfortunately, these noodles are very hard to find in the West, except in areas where there are large concentrations of East Asians.

Dried rice noodles: We have to make do with dried rice noodles in the West. For most of the recipes in this book, buy *banh pho* or any other flat rice noodle, soak them in warm water for about 30 minutes or until they are soft (or in tap water for 2 hours) and then cook very briefly in a large pan of boiling water. Drain and rinse in cold water before using them as the recipe suggests. This gets rid of the extra starch. If you wish to hold the noodles for a while, rub a little oil on them, cover and set aside. The noodles may be reheated by dropping them into boiling water for a second or two. You may also use the microwave for this.

Soba: These are fine Japanese buckwheat noodles and are often eaten cold. They are cooked by dropping into lots of boiling water just like pasta. Once just done they are removed and rinsed thoroughly in cold water.

Somen : These are fine Japanese wheat noodles that generally come in 450-g/1-lb packets with the noodles tied up with ribbons into five portions. Drop them into boiling water and cook for 1–2 minutes or until just done. Drain and rinse under cold water to remove some of the starch. These noodles are often used as a substitute for fresh rice noodles in South-East Asian recipes.

Udon: These are slightly rounded or flat Japanese wheat noodles. They can be bought most easily in the West in their dried form. Cook them as you would Chinese fresh egg noodles, but then rinse them out under cold water to remove some of their starchiness.

NUTMEG AND MACE Nutmegs are the dried seeds of a round pear-like fruit. Mace is the red, lacy covering around the seeds that turns yellowish-orange when dried. Both have similar warm, sweetish and slightly camphorous flavours, though mace has a slightly bitter edge. Both nutmeg and mace are used here in the *garam masala* mixture, page 340. A nutmeg breaks easily. Just hit it lightly with a hammer to get the third needed for the *garam masala* recipe.

OILS For most of the recipes in this book, I would recommend using peanut (groundnut), corn or olive oil. If oil is used for deep-frying, it can be re-used. Skim off all extraneous matter with a skimmer and then drop a chunk of ginger or potato into it and let it fry. This chunk will absorb a lot of the unwanted flavours. Strain the oil when it is cool enough to handle through a triple thickness of muslin or a large handkerchief. Let it cool completely and then store it in a bottle. When re-using, mix half old oil with half fresh oil.

Mustard oil: This oil has the same characteristics as the seeds it comes from. When raw, it smells hot and pungent. When heated, the pungency goes into the air (you can smell it in your kitchen) and the oil turns sweet. It is used in Indian cookery, and in most Indian oil pickles. It is also good for a massage! Because it has more uricic acid than is allowed for in Western diets, I have suggested extra virgin olive oil as a substitute in many of the recipes. Extra virgin olive oil has an equivalent potency and aroma even though of an entirely different nature.

Olive oil: A mild tasting oil with 4 per cent or more oleic acid, this is best when you do not want a pronounced olive flavour. It is generally labelled just 'olive' oil.

OYSTER SAUCE A thick, brown, Cantonese-style sauce made with oysters, this is salty and slightly sweet at the same time. Once opened, the bottle of oyster sauce should be stored in a refrigerator.

PALM SUGAR This is a delicious, raw, honey-coloured sugar used in much of South and South-East Asia. It is sold by South-East Asian grocers both in cans and in plain plastic containers. It comes in lump or fairly flowing forms. The best substitute for it is either Indian jaggery (make sure it is not rock hard) or brown sugar. It keeps well, if tightly covered. Refrigeration is not needed.

PANCHPHORAN (FIVE-SPICE MIXTURE) This very Bengali spice mixture consists of fennel seeds, mustard seeds, fenugreek seeds, cumin seeds and *kalonji* (nigella) mixed in equal proportion.

PAPADUM Also called *papar*. Indian wafers, made out of dried split peas. Sold either plain or studded with black pepper (or garlic or red pepper) by Indian grocers. They should be deep-fried for a few seconds in hot oil or toasted. They are served with most Indian vegetarian meals. They are also good with drinks.

PAPADUM, HOW TO COOK The old-fashioned method was to deep-fry them, and they are really the best that way. They expand to their fullest, each area gets fully cooked, and they turn quite airy. However, they are oily. They look fattening, and you are left with grease on your fingers after you finish one.

If you wish to fry them, put at least 1 cm/1/2 inch oil into a large frying pan and set it on a medium heat. Allow time for the oil to get hot. Meanwhile, line a large baking sheet with kitchen paper. Drop one *papadum* into the oil. It will expand in seconds. Turn it over and cook for just a few seconds more. Remove it with a slotted spatula and put on the sheet. It should be pale yellow in colour. If your *papadum* starts to brown, even in the slightest, the oil is getting too hot. If it lies listlessly in the oil, it is not hot enough. (This cooking oil is quite useless after you are done. Just throw it away.)

Most Indian restaurants now have *tandoor* ovens with very high heat and cook their *papadum* in these. The *papadum* is held with long tongs and inserted down the mouth of the oven. It cooks in seconds.

The method I use, however, is to grill them. It is quite inexact.

Preheat your grill. Set a shelf at a distance of about 13 cm/5 inches from the source of the heat. Put a *papadum* on the shelf. It will start bubbling up, but unevenly. So turn it this way and that until all of it changes to a paler colour. Turn it over once. Never take your eyes off it, as it can burn easily. You might get some light brown patches but the *papadum* should basically stay pale. It cooks fast.

As humidity can get to cooked *papadum* easily, do not make them too far in advance. If you make them an hour before your guests arrive, let them cool completely and then either put them in a biscuit tin or slide them into large zip-lock plastic bags, as many as will fit without breaking.

PAPRIKA It is important that you use good quality paprika that is bright red. It tends to darken as it sits in glass bottles.

POPPY SEEDS, WHITE Only the white seeds are used in India, mainly to thicken sauces.

PRAWNS, PEELING, DEVEINING AND CLEANING Most of the prawns we buy have been frozen at sea. They are either sold to us that way or they are defrosted before being displayed in the shops. In some places, and at certain times of the year, prawns are freshly caught, but this is rare.

Prawns are sometimes sold without their heads as these decay fast and so are thrown away. A pity, as heads have all the prawn fats and flavour.

To clean and prepare prawns for cooking, defrost if frozen, then:

1 Pull off the head (if it has one), peel off the shell and, with it, the small, clinging legs.
2 Pull off the tail shell with a gentle wiggling motion so as to leave the flesh behind.
3 Make a shallow cut down the back.
4 Pull out the fine digestive cord that runs along the length of it.
5 Put the prawns in a bowl. Add 1 tablespoon sea salt or any coarse salt for every 450 g/1 lb of unpeeled prawns and rub it in as if it were soap.
6 Wash the prawns.
7 Repeat steps 5 and 6 one more time and do a second washing.
8 Drain the prawns thoroughly and pat them dry.
9 Cover and refrigerate until ready for use.

RADISH, WHITE (DAIKON/MOOLI) The oriental radish, the one used in this book is large, thick and mild. It can grow up to 7.5 cm/3 inches in diameter. It should be peeled with a knife in thick strips before it is used. Peelers tend to remove only one layer of the skin so I find them inadequate. In Japan, it is called *daikon*. In the UK, it is often called by the Indian name, *mooli*. It is sold by all oriental and South-Asian grocers.

RICE Many varieties of rice are used in Indian cookery. There is the protein-rich, partially milled 'red' rice used along the Konkan coast south of Bombay. Then there is 'boiled' rice. This is the original parboiled rice that predates Uncle Ben and must have been the inspiration for the rice Uncle Ben produced in 1943. Along India's southern coasts, 'boiled' rice has been produced since ancient times. The process of boiling the rice before it is husked and milled not only makes the grains tough and indestructible but it also pushes the B complex vitamins into the inner kernel. This rice is used not only for everyday eating in the south but also to make a variety of pancakes, cakes and snacks.

Then, there is basmati rice, the pearls of the North. It is a very fine, long-grain, highly aromatic rice grown in the foothills of the Himalaya Mountains. The better varieties are generally aged a year before being sold. This rice is now being grown in America as well. With Japanese curries, Japanese, medium-grain rice should be served. This is sold in Japanese markets.

RICE, ROASTED AND GROUND In many parts of South-East Asia, such as Thailand, Laos and Vietnam, rice is roasted in a dry wok and then ground to a powder. This nutty powder is then used both as a flavouring and as a thickener. Generally, glutinous rice is used for this purpose, though you may use plain long-grain rice as well. To roast and grind rice: put a small, cast-iron frying pan on a medium-low heat. Allow it to get very hot. Now put in about 4 tablespoons rice. Stir and roast it until it turns a medium-brown. Some of the grains might even pop. Empty the rice into a plate and allow to cool. Then put it into the container of a clean coffee grinder or other spice grinder and grind to a powder. Store what is not needed immediately in a tightly-lidded jar.

RICE WINE, CHINESE See, Shao Hsing Wine, Chinese.

ROSE PETALS, DRIED Used in many cuisines with a Moorish or Muslim influence (India, Persia, Morocco), these may be bought from Middle Eastern grocers. You could, of course, dry your own roses, provided they are the old-fashioned kind, highly aromatic and unsprayed.

SAFFRON I have only used 'leaf' saffron (whole saffron threads) in this book. Known in ancient Greece and Rome as well as in ancient Persian and India, this valued spice consists of the whole, dried stigma of a special autumn crocus. Look for a reliable source for your saffron as it is very expensive and there can be a great deal of adulteration. Indians often roast the saffron threads lightly before soaking them in a small amount of hot milk to bring out the colour. This milk is then poured over rice, in dishes such as *biryani*, to give it its orange highlights. In Iran, the saffron is pounded with a cube of sugar and allowed to soak in a buttery syrup before it is used. This also brings out its colour. In much of European cookery a very light pinch of saffron is thrown directly into broths to make risottos and soups.

SCREW PINE The leaves of the screw pine (*Pandanus odorus*) are the vanilla of South-East Asia. Known as *daun paandaan* (in Thailand) and *rampe* (in Sri Lanka), these pandanus leaves are used fresh and lend a sweetish, very tropical aroma to all the foods that use them. Many South-East Asian stores sell an essence made from the leaves. In India, it is the spathes of the flowers from a slightly larger tree (*Pandanus odoratissimus*) that are used to make an essence known as *kewra*. This is used in both savoury and sweet dishes and all manner of drinks. It has an almost overpoweringly sensual, flowery aroma. Synthetic essences abound, but if you can get the real thing, it will take your breath away.

SESAME SEEDS Said to be native to India, they certainly can be found in many ancient Indian recipes as well as in recipes from ancient China, ancient Egypt, ancient Persia and the Roman world.

Hulled sesame seeds are almost white and unhulled ones are beige in colour. I much prefer the unhulled beige ones, though you may use either for all the recipes in this book. Black sesame seeds have much more oil in them and are quite delicious. They are used to decorate and flavour breads in the Middle East and for special seasonings in Japan. When one of my recipes calls for sesame seeds, use the beige ones unless I suggest otherwise.

To roast sesame seeds: Put a small, cast-iron frying pan on a medium-low heat. When it is hot, put in 1–3 tablespoons sesame seeds. Stir them around until they turn a shade darker and give out a wonderful roasted aroma. Sesame seeds do tend to fly around as they are roasted. You could reduce the heat slightly when they do this or cover the pan loosely. Remove the seeds from the pan as soon as they are done. You may roast sesame seeds ahead of time. Cool them and store them in a tightly-lidded jar. They can last several weeks this way, though I must add that they are best when freshly roasted.

To roast and lightly crush sesame seeds: Roast the seeds as suggested above. Now put them into a clean coffee grinder or other spice grinder and whir it for just a second or two. The seeds should not turn to a powder. You may also crush them lightly in a mortar.

SHALLOTS For Westerners who tend to use shallots in small quantities, it is always a bit startling to see South-East Asians and South Asians use shallots in massive amounts. The shallot is the onion of South-East Asia, south and south-western India and Sri Lanka. It is ground into curry pastes, sliced into salads and fried into crisp flakes to be used both as a garnish and as a wonderful flavouring. In places such as Goa, shallots hang in kitchens like long ropes, to be plucked at will.

SHAO HSING WINE, CHINESE A Chinese, whisky-coloured rice wine used in cooking and sold by Chinese grocers or in Chinese liquor shops. A reasonable substitute is dry sherry. I find that La Ina comes the closest in flavour. This sherry has a far better taste than anything labelled 'Chinese cooking wine'. Japanese sake may be used in its place as well, though its flavour is quite different.

SHRIMP PASTE This paste, made out of fermented shrimp or small fish, is used as a seasoning throughout South-East Asia. It comes in many forms, ranging from a grey watery paste to crumbly brown blocks. In the West, we generally get the more solid kind, sold as *blachan*, or *terasi*. I often use canned anchovies as a substitute.

SOY SAUCES Many different soy sauces are used in East Asia. Not only do countries have their very own brands of soy sauces but regions, towns and even villages within these countries sometimes proudly boast of producing their very special creations. All soy sauces are made from fermented and salted soya beans. They range from salty to sweet, from light to dark, from thick to thin, and have many different textures. Dark soy sauces tend to be thicker than the light ones and generally add a dark colour to the dish they are put in. Light soy sauce tends to be thinner and saltier. There are several thick, textured, slightly sweet sauces that are used in parts of South-East Asia, many of which are unavailable in most Western markets. Since soy sauces vary so much in their saltiness, it is always advisable to put slightly less than the amount required in the recipe as more can be added later.

Kecap manis is a thick, very sweet – indeed syrupy – soy sauce used in Indonesia. If you cannot find it you can make an approximation of it yourself by combining 15–45 ml/8 fl oz dark soy sauce with 90 ml/6 tablespoons treacle or molasses and 45 ml/3 tablespoons brown sugar, and simmering gently until the sugar has dissolved

Japanese and Chinese soy sauces have very different flavours. Hence, it is best to use Japanese soy sauces for Japanese and Korean dishes and Chinese soy sauces for Chinese dishes. A good brand of Chinese soy sauce is Pearl River, which is sold by Chinese grocers. It is most confusingly labelled: 'Soy Superior Sauce' is dark and 'Superior Soy' is light. The best known Japanese brand is Kikkoman, though Hi-Maru is also good. The Japanese, too, make dark and light soy sauces –all sold by Japanese grocers.

The roots of *tamari*, which means 'that which accumulates', go back to China when the liquid left over from making fermented soya bean pastes was used as a sauce. This concept was brought to Japan in the 7th century. The Japanese called the fermented soya bean paste *miso* and the sauce left over as the *miso* matured, *tamari*. By the 18th century, the making of soy sauces had been turned into a commercial industry. To make the *miso*, half wheat and half soya beans were used and soy sauces reflected the same mixture. Today's *tamari*, sold by most health food shops, is an attempt to go back to its original source. It is naturally brewed using, primarily, soya beans with very little wheat and is the result of an enzymatic reaction rather than an alcoholic fermentation (as is the case when there is a lot of wheat). *Tamari* has a more complex flavour than commercial soy sauces and is blessed with 18 amino acids.

SQUID, CLEANING Squid come in all sizes. I most commonly use those that are about 13 cm/5 inches in length. Sometimes you can buy them already cleaned and frozen, in which case, all you have to do is defrost and cut them. Otherwise:

1 Twist off the head.
2 Cut off the hard eye area in the head and divide the head, with its tentacles, into two.
3 The inner body sac was probably pulled out with the head. If not, pull or squeeze it out.
4 Peel the slightly mottled skin off the tube-like body.
5 Pull out the smoother inner cartilage from inside the tube.
6 Wash the squid well, head and body, and pat it dry. The body can now be cut into rings or any other desired shape, covered and refrigerated.

STAR ANISE A flower-shaped collection of pods. Brownish-black in colour, this spice has a decided anise flavour. It is used in Chinese-style braised dishes and in several dishes from western India (where the China trade was brisk, especially in ancient times). Store in a tightly-lidded jar. If a pod of star anise is called for, think of a pod as a petal of the flower and break off one section.

STEAMING Steaming is used for cooking anything from rice cakes to custards. Steaming cooks gently and preserves flavour.

One of the most satisfactory utensils for steaming is a wok because its width easily accommodates a casserole or a large plate of food. Use a wok with a flat base or set a round-based wok on a wire stand. Put a metal or wooden rack or a perforated tray into the wok. (You could use a small inverted can instead.)

Now pour in some water. Bring it to a gentle boil and lower in the food so it sits on the rack, tray or can. The water should stay about 2 cm/3/4 inch below the level of the food that is being steamed. Extra boiling water should be kept at hand just in case it is needed to top up the level.

Cover the whole wok, including the food, with a domed wok lid or a large sheet of aluminum foil. The domed lids are preferable as condensed steam rolls down the sides instead of dripping on the food itself.

If you like, you can also invest in the many tiered bamboo or aluminum steamers sold in Chinese markets.

STRAW MUSHROOMS See Mushrooms.

TAMARIND The fruit of a tall shade tree, tamarinds look like wide beans. As they ripen, their sour green flesh turns a chocolate colour. It remains sour but picks up a hint of sweetness. For commercial purposes, tamarinds are peeled, seeded, semi-dried and their brown flesh compacted into rectangular blocks. These blocks need to be broken up and soaked in water. Then the pulp can be pushed through a strainer. This is tamarind paste.

To make your own tamarind paste: Break off 225 g/8 oz from a brick of tamarind and tear into small pieces. Put into a small non-metallic pan and cover with

450 ml/15 fl oz very hot water, and set aside for 3 hours or overnight. (You could achieve the same result by simmering the tamarind for 10 minutes or by putting it in a microwave oven for 3–5 minutes.) Set a sieve over a non-metallic bowl and empty the tamarind and its soaking liquid into it. Push down on the tamarind with your fingers or the back of a wooden spoon to extract as much pulp as you can. Put whatever tamarind remains in the sieve back into the soaking bowl. Add 125 ml/4 fl oz hot water to it and mash a bit more. Return it to the sieve and extract as much more pulp as you can. Some of this pulp will be clinging to the underside of the sieve. Do not fail to retrieve it.

This quantity will make about 350 ml/12 fl oz of thick paste. All the calculations for my recipes have been done with this thick, chutney-like paste, so do not water it down too much. Whatever paste is left over may either be put into the refrigerator, where it will keep for 2–3 weeks, or it can be frozen. It freezes well.

'TARKA' – POPPING SPICES IN HOT OIL The 'tarka' technique, known by many other names, such as *baghaar*, *chownk* or 'seasoning in oil' is quite unique to India though simple versions of it are done in Italy, Spain, Cyprus and even China. First, the oil has to be very hot. Then, spices such as mustard seeds or cumin seeds – or just hot, dried red chillies – are dropped into it. They pop and sizzle. Their whole character changes in an instant. They get much more intense. Their flavours change. Then, either this flavoured oil with the seasonings in it is poured over cooked foods or foods are added to the oil and cooked in it. Since four or five spices can go into a 'tarka', they are often added to the hot oil in a certain order so that those that burn easily, such as dried chillies, go in last. The flavour of each is imparted to the oil. In the case of the chillies, the flavour comes only from the browned skin of the chilli. Any food cooked in this oil picks up the heightened flavour of all the spices.

Doing a 'tarka' takes just a few seconds, so it is important to have all spices ready and at hand. A 'tarka' is sometimes done at the beginning of a recipe and sometimes at the end. Legumes, for example, are usually just boiled with a little turmeric. When they are tender, a 'tarka' is prepared in a small frying pan, perhaps with *asafetida*, whole cumin and red chillies, and then the entire contents of the pan, hot oil and spices, are poured over the legumes and the lid shut tight for a few minutes to trap the aromas. These flavourings can be stirred in later. They perk up the boiled legumes and bring them to life. Sometimes 'tarkas' are done twice, both at the beginning and end of a recipe.

TOMATOES, TO PEEL AND CHOP Drop tomatoes in boiling water for 15 seconds. Remove and peel. Cut in half crossways. Gently squeeze out all the seeds. Now chop the skinned shell.

TOMATOES, GRATING FRESH To make a quick purée of tomatoes, hold up one against the coarsest section of a grater and grate. As you proceed, the tomato skin will be left behind in your hand. Gently grate the pulp off it with a flattened hand before you discard the skin. This purée will contain seeds but no Indian objects to them.

TOMATOES, PEELING WHOLE I would not have thought this possible, but, for the last five years, I have been peeling tomatoes just as if they were apples. I do not use a peeler but a sharp paring knife, going round and round the tomato and creating a big snake in my wake. This is possible to do with nearly all tomatoes except those that are very, very soft. No more dropping tomatoes into boiling water for me. A paring knife is all that is needed. Once the tomato is peeled, it can be chopped or cut as needed.

TURMERIC A rhizome like ginger, only with smaller, more delicate 'fingers', fresh turmeric is quite orange inside. When dried, it turns bright yellow. It is this musky yellow powder that gives some Indian dishes a yellowish cast. As it is cheap and is also considered to be an antiseptic, it is used freely in the cooking of legumes and vegetables.

TURMERIC LEAVES, FRESH These long, highly aromatic leaves are often thrown into soups and curries in South-East Asia. They are hard to get in the West. You could plant the turmeric rhizome in a pot, keep it well watered and then use the leaves when they grow.

VINEGARS There are just so many types of vinegar, each with its own flavour and strength. You should experiment and see which you like. Vinegars may be made out of rice, grapes, sugar cane juice and coconut toddy. One of the mildest is Japanese rice vinegar. You can make a version of this yourself by combining 3 parts of distilled white vinegar, 1 part water and 1/4 part sugar.

INDEX

PICTURE ACKNOWLEDGEMENTS

The**art**archive 10b, 12, 13, 17, 27, 31; British Library, London 30; Durban Cultural and Documentation Centre 8; Hulton/Getty 21; Kobal Collection 28; William Lingwood 16; Private Collection 15, 16, 19; Robert Harding Picture Library Ltd 7; Victoria and Albert Museum, London 1, 2, 10t, 11, 35, 43, 77, 111, 117, 119, 135, 151,155, 179, 203, 237, 249, 279, 289, 333.

PUBLISHERS' ACKNOWLEDGEMENTS

The Publishers would like to thank the following for their help with this book: designers Peter Ward and David Fordham, indexer Phyllis van Reenen, proofreader Nicki Lampon, cartographer Tim Vyner and for editorial assistance: Helen Hutton.

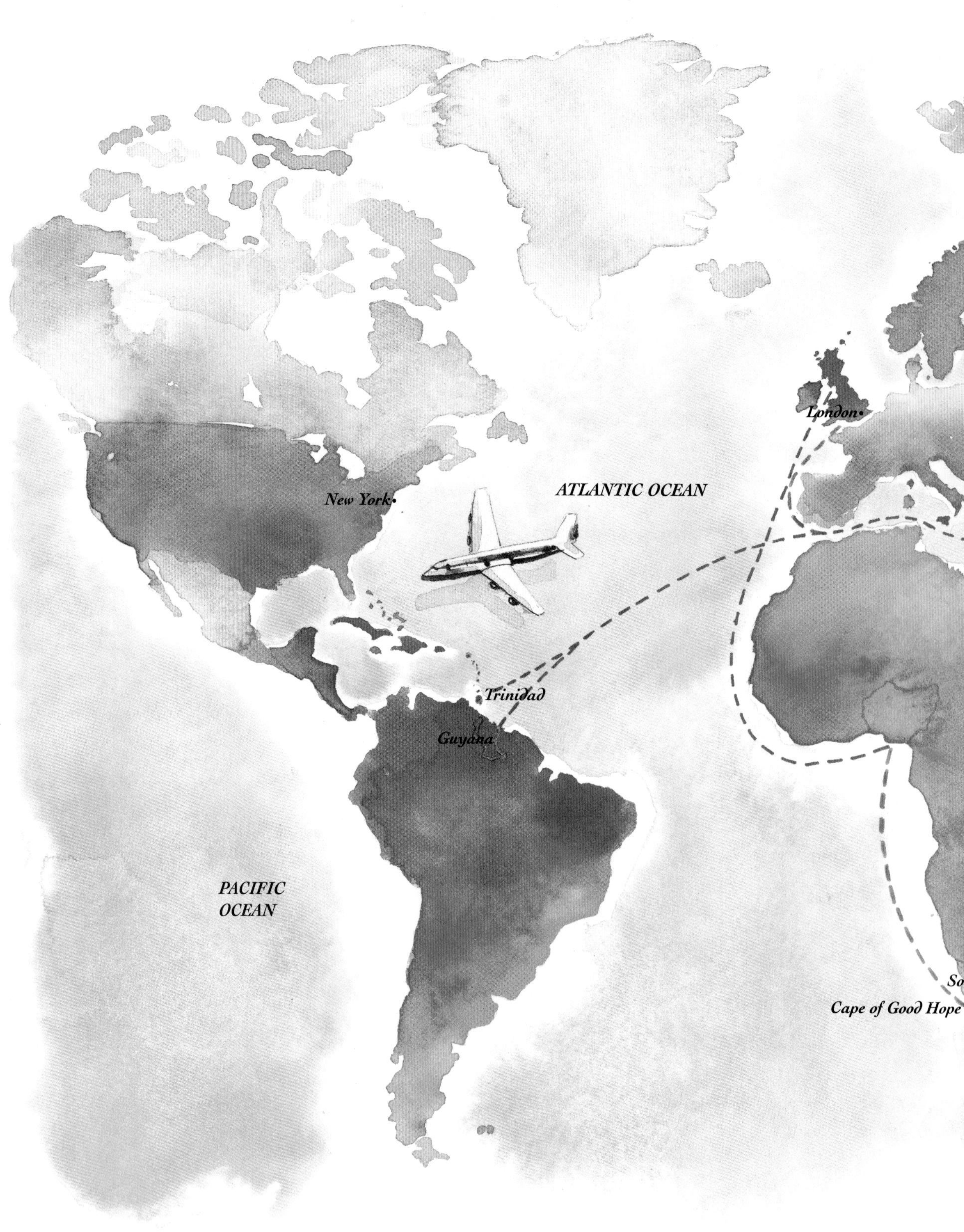
London
ATLANTIC OCEAN
New York
Trinidad
Guyana
PACIFIC
OCEAN
Cape of Good Hope